NOTE

The Report on the "*Policy Conference on Economic Growth and Investment in Education*", which took place at the Brookings Institution, Washington, from 16th to 20th October 1961, was printed in five short volumes. Now a report of the whole proceedings is available under one cover. The separate volumes containing the Conference papers and Summaries of the discussion are as follows :

I. *Summary Report and Conclusions and Keynote Speeches.*
II. *,,Targets for Education in Europe in 1970".* Paper by Professor I. Svennilson in association with Professor F. Edding and Professor L. Elvin.
III. *,,The Challenge of Aid to Newly Developing Countries".* Papers by Professor A. Lewis, Professor F. Harbison, Professor J. Tinbergen in association with Mr. H. C. Bos, and Mr. J. Vaizey.
IV. *,,The Planning of Education in Relation to Economic Growth,,.* Papers by M. R. Poignant, Dr. S. Moberg and Mr. M. Elazar.
V. *,,International Flows of Students".* Paper by Mr. J. R. Gass and Mr. R. F. Lyons of the O.E.C.D. Directorate for Scientific Affairs.

POLICY CONFERENCE ON ECONOMIC GROWTH AND INVESTMENT IN EDUCATION

WASHINGTON 16TH - 20TH OCTOBER 1961

ORGANISATION FOR ECONOMIC CO-OPERATION AND DEVELOPMENT

The Organisation for Economic Co-operation and Development was set up under a Convention signed in Paris on 14th December 1960 by the Member countries of the Organisation for European Economic Co-operation and by Canada and the United States. This Convention provides that the O.E.C.D. shall promote policies designed:

— to achieve the highest sustainable economic growth and employment and a rising standard of living in Member countries, while maintaining financial stability, and thus to contribute to the world economy;
— to contribute to sound economic expansion in Member as well as non-member countries in the process of economic development;
— to contribute to the expansion of world trade on a multilateral, non-discriminatory basis in accordance with international obligations.

The legal personality possessed by the Organisation for European Economic Co-operation continues in the O.E.C.D. which came into being on 30th September 1961.

The members of O.E.C.D. are Austria, Belgium, Canada, Denmark, France, the Federal Republic of Germany, Greece, Iceland, Ireland, Italy, Japan, Luxembourg, the Netherlands, Norway, Portugal, Spain, Sweden, Switzerland, Turkey, the United Kingdom and the United States.

The Directorate for Scientific Affairs, which is responsible for the publication of the present report, has been established within O.E.C.D. to take charge of the activities of the Organisation relating to scientific research and to the expansion and rational utilisation of the scientific and technical personnel available so as to meet the needs arising from economic growth.

1st printing, free of charge (February 1962) out of print
2nd printing, on sale (December 1965)

I. SUMMARY REPORTS AND CONCLUSIONS
   KEYNOTE SPEECHES

PREFACE

This Conference, over which I had the honour to preside, was intended to examine the need for Governments to provide more resources for education. The requirement for sound Government strategies on educational spending stems from two essential factors which dominate our time. The first is that mankind is entering a new and bolder environment where poverty need no longer exist and where education is the vital prerequisite of clear thinking by democratically governed peoples. For this end education must serve to raise man to a new level of culture and human dignity.

The second factor of which Governments should take account in formulating their strategy for education is that science and technology have released forces which are of staggering power and that human beings must benefit from a better education than in the past if they are to harness these forces to the well-being of their countries. This does not mean that science and technology can be separated from the spectrum of human culture. They form a vital part of it, but it does mean that we must succeed in this task of adapting science and technology for human betterment. It is also surely obvious that in the peaceful competition which we hope will characterise the development of this world throughout the coming century the prize of progress will fall to the countries and social systems which succeed in developing their human resources. The Head of the Soviet State has made the issue clear; he is convinced that the way of life he represents can more effectively develop the talents of people through education and translate the power of science into material reality than ours.

This is the challenge which we in the O.E.C.D. countries are facing, and I am confident that we will meet it. New thinking on the necessary volume and structure of spending on education is going on in every O.E.C.D. country. Prevailing educational arrangements throughout the Western world are being subjected to public scrutiny and criticism as a part of an immense effort to re-think the cultural needs of our young people and our growing societies. In virtually every country there is serious criticism of the conventional curriculum, the examination system, the requirements for admission to education, the system of teacher training and other features of the traditional educational system. Educational institutions everywhere are being pressed from all sides to re-adapt themselves to new cultural and technological conditions. On the one hand they must turn out more and better specialists, whether scientists, engineers or technicians, to produce the technology for an opulent peace, and, on the other, writers, artists, sculptors and many others to transform it into the highest form of human experience. By sending their children in ever growing numbers into higher education and by turning them towards the scientific disciplines more than in the past, the common people have demonstrated that they are conscious of the new world towards which we are turning. In a real sense it is the pressure of parents and young people which has created the crisis of education that the policy makers were brought together to discuss in Washington.

There is another reason why the West is responding to the challenge of "putting its educational house in order". It is that economic progress itself is increasingly dependent on the development of education and on scientific research. The expansion of educational effort is everywhere hampered by a shortage of resources which only the national economies can provide. There is in consequence an absolute necessity for the economic and educational spheres of policy to be much more closely in contact than in the past. It is for this reason that investment in education and science will become a central consideration in Western policies for the achievement of economic growth and expansion which have been agreed.

The development of our educational structures is necessary not only for our own social and economic needs, but also so that we may undertake a growing burden of aid to the underdeveloped countries. This is a question of men as well as money. The lessons of the last decade of technical assistance surely indicate that the vital bottleneck is the shortage of trained people. We cannot break the bottleneck unless we take into account the needs of the underdeveloped countries as well as our own when we set our sights on the targets for the educational future.

I am very pleased to record that, in relation to both these problems, the Conference clearly expressed its view that Governments should establish the major targets for education in the next decade along the lines suggested by the distinguished economists and educators who contributed to the Conference proceedings. For let there be no doubt that unless the needs ahead are foreseen, and the effort which will bear its fruit in the years ahead undertaken, the decade may be one of lost opportunity. I like to hope that the contrary will be true and that this Conference gave a clear signal of success.

Philip H. COOMBS
Chairman of the Conference

PROCEEDINGS OF THE CONFERENCE
TABLE OF CONTENTS

I.	PREFACE	5
II.	PURPOSE OF THE CONFERENCE	9
III.	SUMMARY REPORT	9
IV.	KEYNOTE SPEECHES BY:	
	The Honourable Dean RUSK, *U.S. Secretary of State*	17
	Mr. Thorkil KRISTENSEN, *Secretary-General of O.E.C.D.*	21
	The Honourable Philip H. COOMBS, *Assistant Secretary of State for Educational and Cultural Affairs, U.S. Department of State*	24
	Mr. Walter W. HELLER, *Chairman, Council of Economic Advisors to the President of the United States*	30
	LIST OF PARTICIPANTS	37

PURPOSE OF THE CONFERENCE

The O.E.C.D. Conference on Economic Growth and Investment in Education took place at the Brookings Institution, Washington, D.C., from the 16th to 20th October 1961. It brought together those with policy responsibilities for education and national budgets as well as professional economists and experts, to discuss two challenging questions:

I. What is the nature and the magnitude of the task facing education in the next decade to meet the needs of social and economic progress in the O.E.C.D. area?

II. In addition to meeting their own needs, what should the O.E.C.D. countries do to respond effectively to the requests of the underdeveloped countries whose needs for educational expansion are relatively even greater than their own?

SUMMARY REPORT

The Conference recognized that fundamental changes are taking place in the conditions under which social and economic progress is achieved. On the one hand, science and technology are creating power of a new order of magnitude to accumulate national wealth; on the other hand, the political ideas and social policies for employing such wealth are in a state of ferment.

These changes are reflected in new trends in economic thinking. Deeper understanding of the forces affecting long-term economic and social progress is leading to recognition of the fact that investment in education is a prerequisite of economic growth.

On the other hand, there is also a growing realisation of the economic implications of the educational effort which is being advocated. It is universally accepted that a basic education is a human right, justified by its cultural purposes alone and not to be subordinated to economic needs. But the realisation of this right is limited by the total volume of available resources and its distribution as between competing demands. It is only with economic advance, itself dependent on education, that a nation can progressively give more substance to the ultimate ideal of equal opportunity for every individual to develop his latent ability through learning.

During the decade of the 1960's, economic and social needs will lead to a major expansion of education in all countries. Such expansion will become an essential driving force in further social and economic progress. New concepts and policies will need to be formulated and applied to energise and direct this expansion. Discussions between educationalists and economists have now reached a point where the issues can be formulated in policy terms and thereby stimulate action. This was the task of the O.E.C.D. educational, economic and financial representatives gathered at Washington.

The findings of the Conference will provide general policy suggestions for consideration by the advanced countries in developing their own education, and in increasing their assistance to the underdeveloped areas. These suggestions take account of the great magnitude of the task facing the O.E.C.D. countries, both to meet their own needs and to help the less-developed countries to grow economically at a faster rate than the advanced countries.

I. NEEDS OF THE O.E.C.D. MEMBER COUNTRIES

The Relationship between Education and the Economy

The Conference took note of the report on *"Targets for Education in Europe"* by Professor Svennilson and his collaborators, Professors Edding and Elvin. This report was accepted as making a valuable contribution to the assessment of the present situation, the prospects and the objectives for education in Europe. It was, however, recognised that an international survey of this kind cannot reflect, except in a general way, attitudes, facts and policies in individual Member countries; projections of the type presented in the report cannot replace more specific investigations on a national basis.

The Conference had a full discussion of whether expenditure on education should be viewed as consumption or investment. It was accepted that these two aspects of educational spending could not be disassociated and that increased spending on education would be in response to both demands. Education is of importance for daily life in that it equips people for leisure and for the fulfilment of their duties as citizens in a democratic society. Education is also vital from the point of view of productivity and economic growth; it is an investment as important as investment in fixed capital. Indeed, investment in real capital is not as productive as it might be if it is not supported by an appropriate investment in education.

Assessment of Future Needs

In its statistical sections, the report has restricted itself to quantitative measurements in terms of students, teachers and expenditure. It should be emphasized, however, as has been done in the report, that a quantitative development of the educational system may reflect very different patterns of change in organisation, institutions and, above all, in the qualitative characteristics of education. A given sum spent on education may yield quite different results, depending on the efficiency, methods and general direction of teaching. This makes it essential to discuss how to make teaching more efficient. It was pointed out that a mere multiplication of quantities on the basis of present patterns of education might imply conservatism in organisation and methods, and that imaginative reforms of teaching and organisation were just as necessary as quantitative expansion.

Irrespective of these considerations regarding quality and efficiency, the Conference shared the view that the *needs for expansion in the O.E.C.D. area in terms of pupils, teachers, buildings and expenditure over the next decade are very large*. The order of magnitude of the task for the *European O.E.C.D. area* in the next decade, as calculated in the report, is indicated by the following figures:

Increase in the number of students:
Age 5 - 14...... 8 million or 18 per cent;
» 15 - 19...... 4.5 » » 94 » »
» 20 - 24...... 0.8 » » 83 » »

Increase in the number of teachers:[1]
For students aged 5 - 14...... 400,000 or 28 per cent
» » » 15 - 19...... 280,000 » 110 » »
» » » 20 - 24...... 50,000 » 81 » »

This expansion would, according to estimates in the report, mean not less than a doubling of educational expenditure from all sources. The report foresees an expansion of the same relative order of magnitude in *Canada and the United States*.

Such estimates are evidently rough, but they should encourage, and provide a basis for, more detailed and accurate national investigations and estimates. They do, however, indicate the order of magnitude of the task ahead and are reasonable illustrative objectives for a balanced effort.

As the figures indicate, it is now evident that the expansion of education in the next decade will be concentrated on *secondary and higher education*. The next decade should witness a great break-through in these fields in most European countries.

The Conference noted that, if the necessary priority were given to education, the effort indicated by the goals, even though considerable, would not seriously tax the resources of an expanding European economy. If a somewhat higher proportion of the increased income should be diverted to education, it might prove necessary to examine

---

1. These estimates show only the number of new teachers required to teach the increased number of students; they do not take account of existing shortages or of losses in the next decade due to transfer of occupation, retirement or death.

new methods of public finance and accounting so as to facilitate the allocation of the necessary resources to the educational sector.

It was generally recognised that post-school education (other than university), while not included in the estimates of the report, formed an important element in a complete educational system. Adult education and retraining are aids to occupational flexibility, and help to avoid bottlenecks in skilled personnel. These forms of education were valuable also for those who had not sufficiently developed their abilities during their youth. They were an adjunct to civic education in the more leisured societies of today.

THE SUPPLY OF TEACHERS

It was agreed that the primary obstacle to the expansion of education in most O.E.C.D. countries is a serious shortage of teachers, particularly in mathematics and science. Various methods were discussed to overcome this shortage. It was agreed that the only lasting solution was through long-term measures for a larger supply of graduates of which the necessary proportion would pass through teacher-training institutes. Among more immediately effective efforts suggested were improved recruiting methods, upward revision of salaries, scholarships for future teachers, and the attraction of married women back to teaching.

Furthermore, it is necessary to increase the effectiveness of the use of teachers by improving teaching methods. Among methods which might be considered were the use of aids such as television, correspondence courses, learning machines (for the instructional component of education), team teaching and greater use of assistants. None of these should be employed unthinkingly, and none is a real substitute for the personal influence of the teacher, but they could help to husband scarce personnel resources.

THE PLANNING OF EDUCATION

The Conference discussions showed agreement that if the authorities responsible for education are to meet the growing demand, they should give attention to the establishment of medium and long-term objectives for university and school enrolments and for the creation of the necessary resources in teachers and buildings. The decisions regarding financing should, wherever possible, be taken within the framework of educational programmes or plans extending over a number of years.

The methods used for making forecasts and programmes will, it was recognised, vary according to the nature of the administrative or governmental structure and prevailing attitudes towards planning in the country concerned. The establishment of educational objectives should involve local and regional authorities in order to ensure their participation in carrying out the programmes once they are agreed upon.

Educational objectives should be set in the light of demographic trends, changes in the school leaving age and the spontaneous social demand for secondary and higher education. They should take account, particularly for secondary and higher technical and professional education, of economic plans, where plans exist, and perspectives concerning the economy as a whole, as well as the broad consequences of economic trends on the structure and necessary qualifications of the active population. The attention of the Conference was drawn to some of the problems involved in establishing priorities between the different types of specialised professional education. It was pointed out that there was often a considerable time-lag between material investment and the carrying out of the educational programme as a whole. Because of the difficulties and risks involved in making long term forecasts of the structure of the active population, and the frequent changes in techniques and consequently in manpower requirements, programmes for technical education should be as flexible as possible and should be based on a wide general education. This will facilitate the necessary periodical revision of professional and vocational education.

It was agreed that the formulation of forecasts and programmes for the development of education in relation to demographic, social and economic trends was a delicate and complex operation. This task implied the creation or the strengthening of the development and planning function within ministries responsible for education, in co-operation with the governmental and other groups concerned with research and having responsibilities for advising on the most economic allocation of national resources. The Conference took note of the valuable experience already gained by certain O.E.C.D. Member countries in the organisation of this type of research and development.

It was considered of the first importance for sound educational planning and for the development of educational programmes that:

- *a)* excellent statistical data in respect of pupils, teachers, buildings and finance should be available; it would seem desirable that these statistics should be internationally comparable;
- *b)* regular studies should be conducted on all the factors relating to future enrolments in schools and universities, including the manpower structure;
- *c)* in order to reduce building costs, research should be undertaken into methods of school building. Here the example of certain countries, such as the United Kingdom, was mentioned.

II. ASSISTANCE TO THE UNDERDEVELOPED AREAS

THE SIZE AND SCOPE OF THE PROBLEM

The underdeveloped areas are faced with the problem of achieving even faster social and economic progress than the advanced countries. The foregoing observations on the O.E.C.D. area have considerable relevance to the problems of the underdeveloped countries and, indeed, an understanding of these problems will assist the O.E.C.D. countries in finding solutions to their own problems.

No-one doubts the vital rôle which human resources will play in the underdeveloped countries. Many of these have already given priority to educational development. The following basic facts about this strong drive towards education emerged from the expert papers submitted by Messrs. Harbison, Lewis, Tinbergen and Bos and Vaizey.

 a) Education must be developed in these areas more rapidly than has ever been done elsewhere.
 b) Such accelerated educational expansion cannot be achieved by the underdeveloped countries relying solely on their own resources.
 c) It can only be achieved by a strategic approach to educational development which form part of the long term strategy of economic and social advance.

The Conference took note of the substantial assistance by financial and other means already given by the governments and private organisations of the advanced countries as well as by international agencies. They also welcomed the continuing study being given in Government and international circles and by independent experts, including notably those present at the Conference, to the problems involved.

The Conference was, however, convinced—and this seemed to be confirmed by the provisional assessments compiled by Professor Tinbergen and Mr. Bos—that the needs of the underdeveloped countries for education during the decade 1960 to 1970 are so large as to require yet greater support by the O.E.C.D. countries. Further, the task is such an overwhelming one that only bold and imaginative policies are likely to succeed.

FORMS OF HELP

The advanced countries can give help not only in the form of money but by providing teachers, expert advice and capital equipment and by making places available in their universities, colleges and other educational institutions. The Conference believed that in spite of the pressure of domestic demand for the expansion of education during the next two years, the O.E.C.D. countries should be ready to help the underdeveloped countries on a very substantial scale, and should take this help into account in formulating plans for their own development.

The Conference reached general agreement on the importance of the following measures, remembering always that they are proposed as guide-lines for action by the developed countries and that initiative in the formulation of plans for educational development and requests for assistance must lie with the underdeveloped countries themselves.

In the first place, the advanced countries should help the underdeveloped areas to assess their present and long-term needs for education in relation to economic and other development objectives, and to formulate appropriate strategies and priorities for the balanced expansion of education. Such assessments are necessary if the magnitude of the assistance required is to be realistically appraised and priorities for its use properly established. Emphasis on the development of human resources should not, however, lead those concerned to lose sight of the need for equilibrium in the development of physical as well as human capital.

The Conference was agreed that, bearing in mind the extreme shortage of people competent in the preparation and application of strategies for human resource development, the O.E.C.D. countries should urgently seek to multiply the number of such experts. This task presents an unusual opportunity for international co-operation between the various nations and organisations concerned, possibly by building on the experience and skills already developed in the O.E.C.D. programme for the development of human resources, particularly scientific and technical personnel, in the Mediterranean Region.

The advanced countries should also be ready to encourage, support and participate in efforts to re-examine and develop educational structures, curricula, teaching methods, and certificates and degrees, as well as arrangements for financing education, so as to suit them to the special problems and conditions of the underdeveloped areas, and to their need for creative change within the framework of their own traditions and values. To this end, they should make available objective evaluations of their own educational experience, and support endeavours to hasten the process of change by educational research. The need for research and objective evaluation, so as to avoid the adoption of ready-made systems developed for quite different conditions, was an underlying theme throughout the discussion.

MEASURES TO SOLVE THE SHORTAGE OF TEACHERS—ACTION BY THE UNDER-DEVELOPED COUNTRIES

The Conference recognized that the shortage of teachers was likely to be the principal obstacle to the development of education in underdeveloped areas. Emphasis was placed on the provision of qualified teachers for higher education and on supporting teacher training in the underdeveloped countries themselves. Such measures will help to close the teacher gap, but the shortage is so acute that fundamental improvement of the organisation and techniques of teaching, so that teachers can be more effectively deployed and utilized, was recognized as being even more urgent than in the advanced countries.

The underdeveloped countries should be encouraged to develop their own educational systems to progressively higher levels. For some time, however, many of these countries will need to send abroad some or all of their students at higher, and particularly post-graduate, levels. Quite large numbers of such students are now being educated in O.E.C.D. countries, and a substantial increase in student places will be required. The balance of advantage between educating the students in their own countries or abroad will vary from country to country and from one time to another. Closer study of the educational, social and economic problems involved will be valuable. The possibility of founding regional institutions of higher education and research located in an underdeveloped area may in some cases be an appropriate alternative to sending students to the more advanced countries.

The Conference emphasized, however, that the aim of supporting the growth of education in the underdeveloped countries themselves could only be effectively pursued if the donor countries and organisations were ready to contribute finance towards the development and operation of educational institutions and structures, and not merely the exchange components thereof or technical assistance.

RESPONSIBILITY OF THE ADVANCED COUNTRIES

Finally, the Conference recognised that, for some time, there would inevitably be a gap between the needs of underdeveloped countries for qualified personnel and the capacity of their educational systems to produce them. The advanced countries should take this into account and adjust their own targets for educational development so as to be in a position to respond positively to requests for assistance.

The need for economic and educational development in the underdeveloped areas in Africa, Asia, Latin America and in parts of Europe itself was thus recognised as great and urgent. Only if the advanced countries accept the burden of aid in a generous spirit can the underdeveloped countries be assisted to achieve the rapid economic expansion and educational development which are essential to their own and the general welfare.

ADDRESS
by the Honorable Dean RUSK
United States Secretary of State
at the opening session at the Department of State
Washington, D.C.

MONDAY, OCTOBER 16, 1961

It's a very great pleasure for me to take a few moments this morning to welcome you to this O.E.C.D. Conference on Economic Growth and Investment in Education.

The combination of an interest in economic growth and education is something which strikes a particular responsive chord here in the United States. We are delighted that you come here as the first O.E.C.D.-sponsored conference in the United States, one of your newest members. We hope it will not be the last.

We in this country have very great expectations about the possibilities of O.E.C.D. And we pledge that we shall give it our very strongest active support in these crucial years ahead.

It is somewhat encouraging, at a time when there are so many crises, large and small, on the agenda, to be with a group which is settling down to get some of the world's work done, despite these crises of the particular day.

The United States, the American people have had from the beginning what some people have called an inordinate national interest in education. From the very beginning we emphasized on these shores a strong attachment to the educational process. First it was to educate ministers and our other professional manpower. But something very important happened in the middle of the 19th century, which is directly related to our topic today. Because we then were a rapidly developing country, we had great potential of resources, great shortages of trained manpower. We had a continent to open up and develop.

Next year we shall be celebrating the hundreth anniversary of what we call our "land-grant college system". Those land-grant colleges and universities were invented in essence to assist in the process of development. They did not phrase it that way at the time, but that in fact was the purpose which underlay our interest in agricultural, mechanical colleges, and that indeed has been the role played by these great institutions.

Alongside them have been hundreds of private institutions and indeed tax-supported collateral type universities, which have played more traditional roles. But for us in this country, education is not something which is a luxury which can be afforded after development has occurred; it is an integral part, an inescapable and essential part, of the developmental process itself.

Many of you come from countries which reached a degree of economic and social development long before you were born. One thing you might bear in mind, as you think of some of the exuberance, some of the enthusiasm, some of the naivete, if you like, which you might find here in this country about the possibilities of development, is that the more spectacular development of the United States has occurred literally within the generation of people now living; that is, many Americans coming from different parts of the country grew up in a pre-development community or environment, on pre-scientific farms, in communities where there was no medical care, where doctors were relatively unknown, where science and technology had not begun to make their contribution to development.

So that whether you are talking to the Vice-President of the United States or many of our citizens in the ordinary walks of life, you will be in touch with people who remember in their own experience what development can mean, and development under free institutions.

We are not ourselves willing to concede special advantages to totalitarian systems in this field of rapid development because we believe that we have experienced personally and directly the transformation of the lives of people within one generation by the processes of economic growth under free institutions. And in that process, education has played a most vital role. Indeed, I suspect that the Soviet Union today is getting a dividend of a lot of morale out of an aspect which has little to do with Communism as such. For the first time in Russianhis tory, the sons of peasants, the sons of lowly workers, and their daughters, have an opportunity to study medicine, to study law, to turn to science, to teach in universities, to take hold of opportunities which their fathers could never have dreamed about.

We had some of this experience ourselves in the first half of this century, in many parts of the country. And that produces a surge, an interest, a liveliness, a morale which is of very great importance in this process of development, because development depends upon people, their attitudes, their aspirations, their energies, and their willingness to do something about it directly themselves.

One of our problems today in this country is that so many of these things are just now beginning to be taken for granted. In families where the grandfather might have been only one of twelve children who went to college, all of his grandchildren will go to college, because of the change in the educational opportunities that we find here in this country.

I would suggest that the bottleneck in development today right around the world is not exclusively money or capital resources; a crucial bottleneck continues to be people.

During the years when I was working for the Rockefeller Foundation, more often than you will imagine, funds were marking time because there was not the qualified manpower either on the giving side or on the receiving side to make those funds profitable on the other end.

I think if we look at the problems of development in country after country outside the West, we shall find that people are the bottleneck, and this means that education has a crucial role to play. And this I suspect is the great difference between the possibilities of a program like the Marshall Plan and the problems of the developmental programs in the non-Western parts of the world which we see at the present time.

So today in this country we recognize that education has a variety of roles to play. The democratic institutions cannot exist without education, for democracy functions only when the people are informed and are aware, thirsting for knowledge, and are exchanging ideas.

Education makes possible the economic democracy that raises a social mobility. For it is education that insures that classes are not frozen and that an elite of whatever kind does not perpetuate itself.

And in the under-developed economies education itself stimulates development by diplomatically demonstrating that tomorrow need not be the same as yesterday, that change can take place, that the outlook is hopeful.

Even in developed economies, education is a key to more rapid and more meaningful economic growth. The old adage has never been more true than today that there is plenty of room at the top. Advanced education is the base on which research and development rests, and the foundation of technological progress.

But it is through mass education that the discoveries of the laboratory are applied in the production process, insuring more rapid growth than could occur merely through interest in the acres of land or the number of machines and the total number of man-hours worked.

Knowledge can be found by the few, but it must be applied and distributed by the many. This Conference will speak of education as investment rather than as expenditure. For education is an investment, and a good one. It yields a high rate of return.

It is no secret that this Administration believes in education in this country, and in our aid programs we shall devote increasing proportions to educational development, not merely because education is a vitally important social service as it is, but because education is a good investment as it is.

This Administration believes that educational systems and institutions make possible such increases in productivity that they merit support through loans and credits as a form of investment, not only through grants as a form of expenditure. We see clearly that a country's richest assets are not its factories, its roads, its bridges, but its people. We will do our share in aiding the development of this human capital, for this is the richest natural resource of all. And it is indeed fortunate that education, desirable in and of itself, makes sense in economic terms as well.

And so I extend to you my greetings and the welcome of my Government. As you enter your deliberations, you will be discussing that most important of subjects, the people. History indeed shows us that it is people, not things, that ultimately count. And it is only through educational development and the exchange of ideas that man will achieve and fulfil his finest purpose, and that the fundamental of peace will be established.

I do hope that you have an excellent and productive meeting.

ADDRESS
by Mr. Thorkil KRISTENSEN
Secretary-General of O.E.C.D.
at the opening session at the Department of State
Washington, D.C.

MONDAY, OCTOBER 16, 1961

This Conference on Economic Growth and Investment in Education is sponsored by the O.E.C.D., that is the new Organisation for Economic Co-operation and Development, which after a period of preparation was finally established at the end of last month. It comprises the United States, Canada and eighteen European countries, so it is an expression of the Western world in the widest sense. In this Organisation are all the N.A.T.O. countries and also the neutral countries in Europe, and we have a certain liaison with countries like Finland and Yugoslavia.

It is important to have this wide organisation of all the Western industrialised countries: it is not an instrument of the cold war, it is there because of the rapidly growing interdependence of economically highly-developed countries. Because of this interdependence we must work closely together, regarding our own economic policies and regarding our aid to countries in the process of development. Especially in our relations with these countries it is important that this Organisation covers both the European neutral countries and the N.A.T.O. countries, and because Europe and North America are both the largest markets of the less-developed countries and their largest suppliers of capital, it could be said that the O.E.C.D. is a regional organisation with world-wide responsibilities.

Why then are we organising this Conference connecting education closely with economic growth, not only in our own Member countries but also in less-developed countries? This is because we live in the age of science, and experience seems to indicate that a very considerable part of economic growth is due not simply to an increase in the amount of labour and physical capital; indeed, a large and probably increasing part is due to increased knowledge in the widest sense, better techniques, better administration and so on. Therefore education bringing knowledge to ever more poeple is one of the most forceful instruments of economic growth. At the same time education is one of the finest fruits of economic growth, because when we can offer a higher standard of living, I can think of no better use of our resources than giving to everybody more knowledge and more understanding of the world in which we live. So when we develop knowledge as an instrument of economic growth one of the results will be still more knowledge.

This is true of our industrialised countries. There is a great shortage of educated technicians and other experts or skilled people, and there is a great desire on the part of parents to have more education for their children. But it is even much more true for the less-developed countries. In fact it can be questioned whether more knowledge would not be the most efficient means of promoting a more rapid growth in the newly emerging countries. They could certainly have a much higher standard of living if they were able here and now to exploit all the techniques that have been developed by modern science and practical experiment. But they cannot do that because in many cases only a small fraction of their population have higher education and in many cases a large part of their peoples have practically no education at all.

Therefore it is not enough to provide better markets for their products and to supply capital for physical investment in these countries. It may be even more important to share the knowledge we possess with these, for the moment, less-favoured peoples. Indeed, our final goal here is a far-reaching one. There is a very wide gap between the economic standards of the Western world and those of most less-developed countries, and this gap is widening in a dangerous way. The only way of providing for a dignified future of mankind is in fact to reduce this gap and this means that we should help the less-developed countries to grow economically and to grow faster than we are growing ourselves. I wonder whether this has ever in history been the expressed policy of any government, but it surely must be the policy of the industrialised countries to-day. It would be intolerable from a human point of view if we became ever richer while a large part of mankind were left in a state of great poverty and ignorance.

Now there is one thing about education that I would like to stress because it explains the character of this Conference. To provide for education means that we have to look far ahead. If there is to be more education in 1970 or 1980 we must now not only build schools and universities but we must provide for training of teachers of all grades, and it takes many years to educate qualified experts for industry and agriculture, so much so that you must train the teachers who are later on to train the experts. We have for the moment a great shortage of teachers in the Western world. This is because we did not twenty or thirty years ago think enough of the future needs. This is what we have to do now. Therefore one of the purposes of this Conference is to discuss the assessment of the needs of the future, in order to know how much we must invest in school buildings, and in the brains of teachers and so on.

This is an enormous task because it is evident that the amount of teaching will have to rise extremely rapidly in the coming decades, and it is difficult for another reason, too. At the beginning of the nineteenth century there were about 100 scientific journals in the world. Fifty years later there were about 1,000, another fifty years later about 10,000 and to-day there are about 100,000. We may approach 1 million at the turn of this century. Nobody could read more than a mere fraction of these journals and then I have not mentioned the books that we also publish. But this means that the way in which we have to manage an increasing amount of knowledge will have to be rationalised, and this is another aspect of our policy of education. The way in which to manage the results of science is itself becoming a science, so we have every reason to put our resources and experiences together in order to provide sufficient knowledge for the Western world and for the underdeveloped countries. Therefore in opening this Conference may I express the hope that when it finishes we will have gained more knowledge of how to spread and utilise the knowledge we have and the knowledge which we hope to gain by more research in the years to come.

ADDRESS
by the Honorable Philip H. COOMBS
Assistant Secretary of State for Educational and Cultural Affairs
Head of the U.S. Delegation and Chairman of the Conference

at the opening session at the Department of State
Washington, D.C.

MONDAY, OCTOBER 16, 1961

EDUCATION: AN INVESTMENT IN PEOPLE AND FREEDOM

We are joined this week—guided by learned papers instead of crisis headlines—to look beyond today's great unresolved conflicts to a brighter set of goals for mankind a decade or more ahead.

Our business, briefly stated, is to seek ways to pursue these goals rapidly and effectively. Our primary focus is on education, viewed as a potent means available to society for promoting economic growth and social development, in both highly developed and less-developed countries. Our aim is not simply to have stimulating talk but to clarify ideas which can shape policy and action, ideas with the power to make a beneficial difference in the course of human events.

A meeting on this subject would not have been held a generation ago. Only lately have significant numbers of able economists and educators turned their attention to probing the vital links between a nation's educational effort and its economic and social advancement. Such relationships have long been assumed to exist—but often the assumption was insufficiently compelling to override more "practical" considerations, such as money.

It is perhaps not unfair to say that in all our countries we have tended to be schizophrenic about education. We praise education's virtues and count on it to help the new generation solve great problems which the older generation has failed to solve. But when it comes to spending more money for education our deeds often fail to match our words. As a result, our rapidly expanding educational needs—quantitatively and qualitatively—have outstripped our national educational efforts, leaving a serious educational gap which now urgently requires closing.

Educators themselves, though chronically in need of funds and rarely reluctant to admit it, have shied away from stressing the practical contributions of education to economic growth because they feared, perhaps with good reason, that the emphasis on materialistic values in Western society had already become too dominant.

It is an encouraging sign that we can to-day talk candidly and openly about the practical economic contributions of education without seeming to betray, belittle, or ignore its other vital purposes. We can agree without difficulty at the outset of this conference, I feel sure, that the high importance of education lies in the very fact that it serves a variety of major purposes. It is both a means and an end. It satisfies consumer want and national investment needs. It serves both material and non-material values. It profits individuals and at the same time all society. It is simultaneously a conservator and transmitter of past values and a powerful force for social change and improvement.

It is surely an evidence of progress and a cause for rejoicing that educators and economists—long mutually mysterious and at times even hostile to one another—have lately embarked on the joint venture of discovering new insights into the economic aspects of education, external and internal. The progress they have made—though still limited—is sufficient to bring us together to-day.

That progress is symbolized, for example, by the fact that economists, who long treated education simply as a "consumer good"—a very fine one, to be sure, if you could afford it—have now begun to view educational expenditures as an "investment" as well. Not only is this a nobler term in the economists' lexicon, but strategically it is a far more effective term for getting increased budgets. Labelling education an "investment industry" implies that the development of people is as important as the development of things—which the educators have been hinting at all along. It helps place education in its quest for funds on a competitive parity with highways, steel mills and fertilizer factories. We can now assert unblushingly and with good economic sense that the accumulation of intellectual capital is comparable in importance—and in the long run perhaps much more important—than the accumulation of physical capital, so long as we recognize that there is much more to education than this term alone implies. And even now we begin to hear bankers—the more daring, at least—speak of education and the development of human resources as a proper area for productive loans.

The educators have also come a long way. They now readily concede that resources are, after all, limited. Where this is the case as every economics student knows, the relationship of output to available resource input depends on the state of technology and the efficiency of resource use. It follows logically that all of the ills and needs of education cannot be met simply by spending more money to do on a larger scale what our schools and universities are already doing. Along with much greater financial support from the outside, which unquestionably is required, education also needs far-reaching improvements on the inside—improvements in curriculum, in organization and in techniques.

Many educators and economists are today agreed not only that organized education must make more effective use of its available resources but to do so, educational developments must be well planned. Such educational development plans, moreover, must be rationally integrated with plans for general economic and social development. We shall give consideration in this conference, I hope, to the need for action to remedy the serious shortage of persons competent to advise less developed nations on the vital matter of educational development planning. In the absence of well conceived educational development plans, external assistance to underdeveloped countries cannot be as efficiently used.

The foregoing propositions are applicable to any kind of society which accepts progress and change as goals, whatever else may be its ideology. But these propositions are peculiarly applicable and urgent at this point in history for those nations—whether less developed or highly developed—whose concept of progress includes greater social justice and greater freedom, opportunity, and choice for each individual. The threats to human justice and freedom are obvioulsy great, and the hour is late. The economists and educationalists of the free world have joined their endeavors none too soon.

It is important that their findings—incomplete as they yet are—be translated promptly into national policy and action. For what we do in the coming decade about education and the development of human resources, in all our lands and in helping the less developed countries, is sure to have a profound influence upon the future course of history.

In coming to grips with the important policy issues before this conference, we will have to make some assumptions about the economic, political and social forces to which education must respond during the next ten years and beyond. Recognizing the hazards of speculation and the differing application of any general proposition to the peculiar circumstances of each country, I venture to suggest a few "plausible assumptions" as a starting point for our discussions. Braver and wiser ones among us, I feel sure, can improve upon these initial propositions. With respect to the more developed countries of Europe and the Western Hemisphere, I suggest the following:

First, we may assume that national output—both in the aggregate and per capita—will continue to grow, though not necessarily at a steady pace. Likewise there will be continued and even accelerated advancement of scientific knowledge and applied technology in virtually all fields, which will spur economic growth. Given this assumption, it will be well within the financial means of Western European nations, Canada and the United States to expand greatly their expenditures on education without serious pain. If the combined national product of the O.E.C.D. countries of Europe rises to something like $450 billion by 1970, as suggested in one of the expert papers before this conference, educational expenditures could be doubled in a decade with no greater sacrifice than diverting less than six percent of the *increment* in GNP into education. This is indeed a modest goal.

Second, the requirements for educated and trained manpower will rise more rapidly than total manpower requirements. In other words, the "mix" of manpower requirements will shift steadily toward greater emphasis upon higher skills and specialized knowledge in virtually all fields and levels, with unskilled labor shrinking in proportion. Accordingly members of the younger generation must, on the average, have considerably more education than any previous generation. Each nation's investment in education must therefore rise, per person and as a proportion of the Gross National Product, if it is to keep pace with its changing manpower requirements.

Third, the demand for highly specialized manpower, especially in the sciences and engineering but elsewhere as well, will rise with the greatest speed, and shortages of high talent will spread from one field to another rather unpredictably. Increasingly the market for high talent will become internationalized. Concerted efforts will be made to break these bottlenecks of specialized manpower as they appear, but basically they will be the product of an overall shortage of highly developed manpower which can only be relieved in the long run by a total expansion of the educational systems aimed at developing more fully the human potential of the whole population, much of which now is wasted.

Fourth, the economic necessity to develop each nation's human resources will in most countries be reinforced by strong political pressures in the same direction. Educational opportunity is the hallmark of a democratic society and people will insist upon it quite apart from its contributions to national growth. There will be mounting insistence that educational avenues of advancement be opened wide to all young people, regardless of their social and economic origins. Popular governments will ignore these demands at their peril, and at the peril of free societies.

Fifth, despite the fact that the formal educational system, as we now know it, will have to provide each individual with more years of education, it will provide him with a smaller proportion of his total lifetime learning. This is because the rapid development of new knowledge and technology will quickly render obsolete and inadequate the education and training which many persons receive in their youth. Increasing provision will have to be made for people in a wide range of professions and occupations, not least of all teachers, to continue learning new knowledge and skills long after they have "completed" their formal education. Moreover, as personal incomes rise and working hours decrease, there will be more leisure time, and if our schools and universities have succeeded in their work, much of this leisure will be used for learning as a means of individual self-fulfilment and pleasure. In short, education, to borrow a well known British phrase, is fast becoming a cradle-to-grave proposition. This will require an even greater investment in education than our conference papers have forecast, along with radically new techniques of teaching and learning. If we are to become nations of teachers and learners, as seems essential, the old forms and rituals of education will not suffice. Nor will old concepts of educational finance.

Sixth, there will be no serious danger of "over-educating" the population; the greatest risks will lie in the opposite direction. To-day's projections of future requirements for well-educated manpower are likely to prove low ten years from now. If national economies maintain a relatively high level of employment and stability, the increased availability of well-educated manpower will stimulate the rate of economic growth and technological advance, thus enlarging more rapidly the capacity of these economies to absorb well qualified manpower.

Seventh, the role of women, in education and in the whole economy, will increase in importance (and at the same time, no doubt, their political importance!). The under-education and under-utilization of women in the professions, in industry, and in government, constitutes the greatest untapped potential of human brain power and energy in most of our nations. Educational institutions, if they will, can play a major role in breaking down the traditional barriers to a fuller and more productive life for women.

The final premise in this list—and one of the most important—concerns the stake which developed countries have in the advancement of less developed nations. In addition to their heavy domestic obligations, the educational institutions of the more developed nations must assist the less developed ones in their crucial efforts to build their own educational systems and to develop their human resources as an essential ingredient of overall economic, social and political development. Large and imaginative efforts in this direction can bring great benefits to education not only in the nations of Asia, Africa and Latin America, but in the more developed countries as well, for educational assistance is a two-way street. To a considerable extent, and with important local variations, the fundamental problems of education in underdeveloped countries are the same as those confronting the more developed ones, but presented in bold relief. Cases in point are the problems of teacher shortage, the need for curriculum reform, the problem of finance, and the need for technological innovation.

Educational assistance to less developed countries, as the expert conference papers emphasize, is no mere matter of exporting a carbon copy of one's own curriculum, methods and organization to nations with very different needs and cultures. Nor is it a simple matter of expanding by a factor of *X* the educational *status quo* which the underdeveloped country already happens to have inherited, usually from some other land. It is clear that such a strategy of educational expansion would fit neither their needs nor their pocketbooks.

The same daring and ingenuity—the same research and development approach—which our educational institutions have helped to create and apply so fruitfully to such other fields as agriculture, industry and communications, must now be applied to education itself, at home and abroad. The need for such an approach is perhaps most obvious in less developed countries, but it is perhaps equally needed in the more developed ones. If this need for imaginative change in education is viewed not with alarm but as an exciting challenge, it can be a rewarding decade for all concerned.

Within this framework of propositions—some perhaps generally agreeable and others no doubt open to vigorous debate—and, more importantly, with a series of brilliant papers before us, we are ready to engage in a serious and enjoyable discussion.

In one final prognostication, I offer with confidence the view that we will all take home from this conference new insights, new ideas for action, and new conviction which can profit our respective nations in future years and which can, beyond this, provide all mankind with a larger measure of freedom and a greater opportunity to profit from such freedom.

REMARKS
by **Mr. Walter W. HELLER**
Chairman, Council of Economic Advisers
at the Sheraton Park Hotel, Washington, D.C.
WEDNESDAY, OCTOBER 18, 1961

EDUCATION AS AN INSTRUMENT OF ECONOMIC POLICY[1]

Thank you for inviting me to be with you this evening. I welcome this opportunity to speak not only as a government official but also as a university professor-on-leave who has concerned himself with the subject of your conference in other contexts. So I find myself in the pleasurable position of indulging in that stimulating activity, shop-talk.

The title of this conference is a sign of our times: "Economic Growth and Investment in Education". The recognition now accorded education and the development of human resources for the promotion of economic growth has made necessary this title. A decade ago the period would have come after the word "investment"; the title would have been: "Economic Growth and Investment", and the representatives here gathered would have met in separate conferences. It is only in the last few years that there has been a revival of interest among economists in the subject of human capital and its productivity, as distinguished from labor and its utilization.

I. *The Concept of Human Capital*

You will note that I used the phrase, "revival of interest". I do so, not because I believe that there is nothing new under the sun, but rather because this really is a revival. There *was* an earlier time when economists were quite concerned with the value of human capital. They not only wrote about the subject, but made valiant attemtps to measure and to quantify.

Interestingly, the examination of the value of human capital was largely undertaken by those, even as you and I, concerned with practical policy questions. This most abstract idea was examined by persons who had to guide decisions in specific problem areas. It may be that

---

1. I wish to acknowledge the collaboration of Rashi Fein of the Council staff in the preparation of these remarks.

this is one of the reasons that no general theory on this subject was developed. Nevertheless there were persons who addressed themselves to the relevant questions: what is the economic value of an education (to the individual and to society)? what is the value or contribution of a skilled labor force? what do immigrants contribute to a nation's growth and what does emigration take away? how much is better health worth?

One of the earliest references—perhaps even the first—to the money value of a human being to society is found in the writings, almost three hundred years ago, of the renowned British political-arithmetician Sir William Petty. At various times Petty calculated the value of a resident of England as ranging between 69 and 90 pounds. Not given to mere exercices, Petty used his estimates to advocate specific policy measures. For example, in discussing the London plagues, Petty estimated the probability of death if one remained in London, the cost of transporting individuals from the city and caring for them outside it, and thus calculated the "return on investment" if people were removed from the city at the time of a plague. By the way, you will be encouraged to know that the investment was, indeed, a good one: an expenditure of one pound would yield a return of 84 pounds. Here was an early example, which your discussions about education can multiply many-fold, where a social policy quite desirable in its own right was found to yield equally desirable long-run economic benefits.

Petty, as did others who followed him, emphasized the importance of better health and its impact on the value of human capital. Yet he was broad enough to cast an argument that we still cite today in relation to mobility of labor. In 1687 he argued that in England a person is worth 90 pounds while in Ireland only 70 pounds. Transplantation, Petty suggested, would be economically desirable. This has the familiar ring of arguments still used today in discussions about migration, depressed areas, technological unemployment.

The seventeenth century is still too early for men to appreciate fully the value of an education. It was not until the nineteenth century that men were to include education in the framework that Petty had outlined earlier. Then a British economist could say "Our transatlantic brethren have determined to turn life to account as early as possible, and to give it the utmost attainable value: hence public provision is made that every free citizen may receive, nearly gratuitously, the highest kind of instruction the times can afford. Would that the example were followed in this country". May I, a century late, thank *my* transatlantic brethren for these kind words.

The problem of human capital continued to be analyzed and discussed. There were those who argued that, "The economist for the advancement of his science may well treat the human being simply as an investment of capital, in productive force," and that it is "unphilosophical to ignore capital in the person of a laborer and to recognize it in a machine".

It is true that the methods of analysis were not always the best and the data used far less than perfect. Nor were these contributions always recognized. Let me interject that, as an American, I am not unhappy that at least some of the recommendations based on this type of analysis were ignored. For the course of American history and the development of its economy would have been materially altered had Englishmen listened to that compatriot who told them to go to New Zealand rather than the United States because in New Zealand immigrants were worth 200 pounds while in America "it has been established" that they were worth 166 pounds 13 shillings 4 pence each. That economic-statistician should be working on national income accounts—with such exactness, all statistical discrepancies would be eleminated! Fortunately for the United States, he suffered the lot of many economists of an earlier day: he wasn't listened to.

Yes, the efforts were primitive and the concept did not take its rightful place in economic thought, but the antecedents of our present concern are there, referred to and examined over the last centuries.

Indeed, noting the uses to which the recent analysis of investment in education is being put, I am reminded of the statement by Edwin Chadwick one hundred years ago when in his presidential address before Section F of the British Association for the Advancement of Science he said "When the sentimentalist and the moralist fails, he will have as a last resource to call in the aid of the economist, who has in some instances proved the power of his art to draw iron tears from the cheeks of a city Plutus." I believe, therefore, that I am fully justified in using the phrase "revival of interest."

II. *Education and Economic Growth and Development*

What has brought about this new birth of interest in an old idea? Why has human capital moved out of the chorus and to the front of the stage? Why do we emphasize education and its role in economic as well as social development? I believe that there are a number of reasons that help explain this phenomenon. Let me focus on two.

First, economists have become increasingly concerned with problems of growth in the developed economies and have sought to analyse and understand the process that underlies it. If we desire, and we do, more rapid growth and development, surely it is necessary that we search and understand the record of the past. We must know not only where we are but how we got here. For we have learned that the rate of economic growth is not a given, not something to which man must adjust; but, rather, is a variable, something which man can, within limits, adjust. It is affected both by our economic policies and by what were once believed to be purely social policies.

So we examine the process of growth and the contributions that increases in quantities of various inputs have made to increases in total output. You know the history of this pioneering work and the remarkable findings. In the United States less than half of the increase in output can be explained by increases in the stock of tangible capital and man-hours worked. This surprising result has caused economists to re-examine their classification of inputs. Several of you in this room tonight have shared in this endeavor. Your findings indicate that for the United States a significant portion, possibly as much as one-half, of the residual—i.e., of the growth not accounted for by increased inputs of capital, land, and labor—can be explained by increased productivity brought about by higher levels of education for greater proportions of our population.

A second reason for our increased interest stems from our concern with the less developed economies. Indeed, much of the postwar reawakening of American interest in education as investment arose out of the analysis of development problems and experience of these economies, which threw into bold relief the high rates of return realized on investments in training and education. Of what avail are engines without engineers or machinery without machinists? Technology can be imported but technicians must be trained. Nor is this a question of only training relatively few skilled workers. That is important, but also of importance is an educational system that reduces illiteracy and diffuses knowledge.

These factors, among others, have redirected our thinking on the subject of education and human capital and have led to the convening of this conference. It is not, after all, caprice which has led to the substitution of the term "investment in education" for the term of earlier decades, "expenditures on education".

Yet there are those who would say that we cannot afford this investment. Surely, no one really believes that we would be richer nations if we were to reduce educational expenditures, use these funds for consumption, and free teachers for other work. So the implication must be that education is a less productive form of investment than alternative uses of funds. What does your research say on this point?

Measuring the direct benefits of education in the form of increased productivity of the labor force—i.e., not allowing for either the consumption aspects or third-party benefits of higher education—research on this frontier indicates that the rate of return on investment in college education in the United States is roughly comparable to the rate of return on business investment. Other studies show the rate of return for elementary and high school education combined as being substantially higher than that for college education. Thus, even using this type of measurement, private research to date suggests that the average rate of return on investment in formal education as a whole is higher than the rate of return for business investment. As just noted, this measurement understates the "payoff" on education since it assumes that *all* educational expenditures are investment expenditures with no consumption aspects and that all returns to education are direct, involving, as it were, the transmission of existing knowledge rather than the extension of knowledge. Yet we know that some part of education is consumption and that the indirect—third-party, or neighborhood, or external, or extra-buyer—benefits of education, while difficult to measure (though obviously not difficult to coin phrases about), are significant. Let us consider these two points for a moment.

It is, of course, difficult to separate the consumption and investment parts of education. This should, however, not serve as an excuse to say that since we cannot divide them conveniently we will lump all education under the heading "investment", or conversely, under the heading "consumption". Education has a significant and an important consumption component, one that may, indeed, be assigned a rising priority in highly developed economies which seek to devote a fair share of their affluence to improvement in the quality of life.

Returns on education are similarly understated by excluding its indirect benefits. We now live in a technological age characterized by large expenditures for research and development and increasing utilization of capital. Technological progress is the result of research and development which in turn is made possible by education. This was recognized explicitly by Alfred Marshall when he wrote: "We may then conclude that the wisdom of expending public and private funds on education is not to be measured by its direct fruits alone. It will be profitable as a mere investment, to give the masses of the people much greater opportunities than they can generally avail themselves of. For by this means many, who would have died unknown, are enabled to get the start needed for bringing out their latent abilities. And the economic value of one great industrial genius is sufficient to cover the educational expenses of a whole town; for one new idea, such as Bessemer's chief invention, adds as much to England's productive power as the labour of a hundred thousand men. Less direct, but not less in importance, is the aid given to production by medical discoveries such as those of Jenner or Pasteur, which increase our health and working power."

We have yet to explore as fully as is desirable—and indeed necessary—the relationship and interaction between education, research and development, technological change, and investment in plant and equipment. It is, nevertheless, abundantly clear that research and development is an education-intensive activity creating technological change that is itself education-using. First attempts at measurement of the ratio of income to cost of education over time in the United States suggest that this ratio is not falling. If true, it is interlinked with a technology which makes possible new capital requiring men with training rather than muscle, with new research activities that increasingly call for scientists in laboratories instead of gadgeteers in garages, and so on.

Beyond the external economic benefits, we are all aware of education's social benefits, which far exceed the personal advantages gained by the individual being educated—indeed, this is the traditional rationale for government entry into the field of education. Society alone can pay for education in the measure of its total yield rather than its direct private gain.

Let me conclude, therefore, that especially when indirect benefits are included and the consumption portion of education is excluded (and not ignoring differences in natural ability), your research findings seem to provide a persuasive answer to the critic who suggests that we cannot afford a good educational system. The question is not, "what can we afford to spend", but rather, "what can we afford not to spend on a strong educational system"?

If it is true—and the findings to date say it *is* true—that education is an important contributor to economic growth, the economic policy adviser must—and I am sure he will—stand shoulder to shoulder with the minister of education in the battle for an expanded educational system. May I say that, in this context, the fight for education is too important to be left solely to the educators.

In President Kennedy's words:"Another fundamental ingredient of a program to accelerate long-run economic growth is vigorous improvement in the quality of the Nation's human resources. Modern machines and advanced technology are not enough, unless they are used by a labor that is educated, skilled, and in good health. This is one important reason why, in the legislative programs that I will submit in the days to come, I will emphasize so strongly programs to raise the productivity of our growing population, by strengthening education, health, research, and training activities." Let me remind you that these words are found, not in a special message on education, but in the President's economic message, "A Program to Restore Momentum to the American Economy".

In the spirit of confession being good for the soul, may I ask this international audience to indulge me in a few purely domestic observations. In spite of President Kennedy's emphasis on the role of education as a generator of growth; in spite of his specific proposals for for Federal aid to strengthen education in *all* school districts for *all* children in the United States; in spite of the growing awareness that the benefits of education know no State and local boundaries—in spite of these compelling considerations, the President's proposals were not accepted and we in the United States still rely on local and State governments to finance 95 per cent of the cost of public education. In testimony before the Congress some three and one-half years ago and even more recently I asserted my beliefs on this matter. The passage of time has not caused me to modify the statement I then made.

"First and foremost, education is an essential instrument for carrying out functions which are a direct federal responsibility. Education is an investment in human resources from which we expect to reap positive gains in the form of higher productivity, more rapid advancement in technology, a better informed and better implemented foreign policy, and a stronger military establishment and greater military potential. Here the benefits of education transcend all state and local lines. They involve our national economic strength, prestige, and security, even our national survival. For the federal government to assume part of the costs of public education to serve these ends is no act of largesse or charity to state and local governments. It is simply the best available method of discharging certain national obligations.

"It is worth noting that this point is quite independent of the adequacy or inadequacy of state-local fiscal capacity and taxing efforts to support education. This point says simply that there is a strong national interest in better schooling to serve objectives that the federal government has been charged with both by the Constitution and by legislation, such as the Employment Act of 1946."

In the Employment Act the Congress stated that "it is the continuing responsibility of the Federal Government... to promote maximum employment, production, and purchasing power". We dare not view this responsibility in narrow terms. Maximum employment and production do not only depend upon capital equipment, agricultural and natural resources, and man-hours—the traditional interests of economists—but also on the education of the total population and the skills of its labor force. Programs and policies that maximize the human resources in our nation are a major concern of national economic policy.

III. Conclusion

The task before all of us is an important one: to educate about education. We must explain that the costs of ignorance and illiteracy are not only the direct costs of teaching the ignorant and illiterate, but also the indirect costs of loss of production caused by ignorance and illiteracy. The latter costs are real ones. They exist, though difficult to measure. Society, all of us, must bear these costs. Reducing the direct costs may, of course, look better for the budget. But this may mean that we are using the wrong kind of measuring rod, the wrong budget. We will take a long step forward when the public understands that the choice lies between paying for schools or paying for ignorance.

None of us can tell society what it *should* spend. This depends upon the values that our individual nations hold. But all of us have the responsibility within the expanding limits of our combined disciplines, to provide the information needed to guide this decision. Assessing and explaining the implications of additional expenditures, the economic benefits obtained, the gains, the costs—this is our task. I am happy to join with you in undertaking it.

LIST OF PARTICIPANTS

Chairman :

    Mr. Philip H. COOMBS
    Assistant Secretary of State for Educational and Cultural Affairs
    Department of State
    Washington 25, D.C.

Rapporteur-General :

    Dr. Alexander KING, C.B.E.
    Director for Scientific Affairs
    O.E.C.D.

Speakers :

    Mr. Moric ELAZAR
    Head of Department for Education Investment Planning
    Federal Secretariat for Education
    New Belgrade

    Professor Frederick HARBISON
    Professor of Economics
    Princeton University
    P.O. Box 248
    Princeton, New Jersey

    Professor W. Arthur LEWIS
    Principal
    University College of the West Indies, Mona
    Kingston 9, Jamaica

    Mr. Sven T. MOBERG
    Head of Department
    Ministry of Education and Ecclesiastical Affairs
    Kanslihuset, Stockholm

    M. Raymond POIGNANT
    Rapporteur
    Maître des Requêtes, Conseil d'État;
    Rapporteur-Général de la Commission de l'Équipement scolaire et universitaire
    Commissariat Général du Plan
    18, rue Martignac, Paris 7e

    Professor Ingvar SVENNILSON
    Rapporteur
    Professor of Economics, University of Stockholm
    Odengatan 61, Stockholm

Professor J. TINBERGEN
Rapporteur
Director, Netherlands Economic Institute
Pieter de Hoochweg 118, Rotterdam 6

Mr. John VAIZEY
Rapporteur
Director of the Research Unit in the Economics and Administration of Education
Institute of Education
University of London
Malet Street, London W.C. 1

Other Invited Experts :

Professor Friedrich EDDING
Department of Economics
Institute for International Education Research
Schloss-strasse 29, Frankfurt/Main

Mr. Lionel ELVIN
Rapporteur
Director, Institute of Education, University of London
Malet Street, London W.C. 1

Mr. Pitambar PANT
Director, Perspective Planning Division
Planning Commission
New Delhi

Country Delegates :

AUSTRIA

Dr. Ludwig WOHLGEMUTH
Director General
Ministry of Education
Minoritenplatz, Vienna 1

BELGIUM

M. F.R. DARIMONT
Directeur général de l'Enseignement Supérieur et de la Recherche Scientifique
Ministère de l'Education Nationale et Culture
155, rue de la Loi, Brussels
(Member of the O.E.C.D. Committee for Scientific and Technical Personnel)

M. Fernand ROGIERS
Membre du Bureau de Programmation Économique
Ministère des Affaires Économiques
23, square de Meeus, Brussels

CANADA

Mr. W.R. DYMOND
Assistant Deputy Minister, Federal Department of Labour
No. 5 Building, Ottawa

Mr. A.S. Rubinoff
Finance Officer, Economic and International Affairs Division
Federal Department of Finance
Room 337 Confederation Building
Wellington Street, Ottawa

DENMARK

Mr. Henning Friis
Director, Danish National Institute of Social Research
38 Nyhavn, Copenhagen
(Chairman, O.E.C.D. Committee for Scientific and Technical Personnel)

Mr. Erik Ib Schmidt
Permanent Under-Secretary, Treasury
Head of the Danish Government's Economic Secretariat
Slotsholmsgade 10, Copenhagen K

Mrs. Agnete Vøhtz
Permanent Under-Secretary
Ministry of Education
Frederiks Holms Kanal 21, Copenhagen

FRANCE

M. Laurent L. Capdecomme
Directeur général de l'Enseignement Supérieur
Ministère de l'Éducation Nationale
rue de Grenelle, Paris 7e

M. Jean Fourastie
Professeur d'Économie Politique
Président de la Commission de la Main-d'Œuvre
Commissariat Général du Plan
18, rue Martignac, Paris 7e

GERMANY

Dr. Kurt A.G. Frey
Secretary General
Ständige Konferenz der Kultesminister der Länder in der Bundesrepublik Deutschland
Nassestrasse 11, Bonn

Dr. H. von Heppe
Senatssyndicus der Freien und Hansestadt Hamburg
Senat Hamburg, Hamburg 7

GREECE

Mr. C. Doussis
Director of Economic Planning
Ministry of Co-ordination
3 Amerikis Street, Athens
(Director of the Greek National Team for the Mediterranean Regional Project)

IRELAND

Mr. Sean MacGearailt
Assistant Secretary, Department of Education
Dublin

Mr. J.F. McInerney
Deputy Assistant Secretary, Department of Finance
Upper Merrion Street, Dublin

ITALY

Dr. N. Novacco
Executive Secretary
Svimez
Via di Porta Pinciana 6
Rome
(Director of the Italian National Team for the Mediterranean Regional Project)

Mr. Emilio Prisinzano
Director General
Ministry of Education
Rome

Professor
Francesco Vito
Member of the Council of the International Association of Universities
President, Catholic University of Milan
Piazza S. Ambrogio 9, Milan

THE NETHERLANDS

Dr. Johan H.E. Ferrier
Counsellor, Science Department
Ministry of Education, Arts and Sciences
Koningin Emmakade 153, The Hague
(Member of the O.E.C.D. Committee for Scientific and Technical Personnel)

Mr. Alexander B. Hermsen
Chief Inspector of Finance
Division of Estimates of the Bureau of the Budget
Ministry of Finance
Kneuterdijk 22, The Hague

NORWAY

Mr. Per Kleppe
Under-Secretary of State
Ministry of Finance
Akersgt 42, Oslo

Mr. Robert Major
Director, Royal Norwegian Council for Scientific and Industrial Research
Gaustadalleen 30, Blindern
(Member of the Secretary-General's ad hoc Advisory Group on Science Policy, O.E.C.D.)

Mr. Enevald SKADSEM
Under-Secretary
Ministry of Education
Bygdøy allé 1, Oslo

PORTUGAL

Professor C. ALVES MARTINS
Director, Centre for Statistical and Economical Studies
Av. Infante Santo, Lote 3, 1ºC, Lisbon 3
(Director of the Portuguese National Team for the Mediterranean Regional Project)

SPAIN

Mr. Antonio ESPINOSA
Cultural Affairs Attaché, Embassy of Spain
Washington D.C.

Don Angel MADRONERO PALAEZ
Chief, Section of Economic Affairs and International Organizations
Ministry of Finance
Madrid

Dr. Joaquin TENA ARTIGAS
Director General
Ministry of Education
Madrid
(Director of the Spanish National Team for the Mediterranean Regional Project)

SWEDEN

Mr. Hans LÖWBEER
Rapporteur
Under-Secretary of State, Ministry of Education and Ecclesiastical Affairs
Kanslihuset, Stockholm 2
(Member of the O.E.C.D. Committee for Scientific and Technical Personnel)

Mr. Gösta REHN
Chief, Economic Department
Ministry of Finance
Kanslihuset, Stockholm 2

SWITZERLAND

Mr. Lukas BURCKHARDT
Labor Counsellor, Embassy of Switzerland
2900 Cathedral Ave. N.W., Washington D.C.

H.E. Mr. August LINDT
Ambassador to Washington, Embassy of Switzerland
2900 Cathedral Ave. N.W., Washington D.C.

Dom Ludwig RAEBER O.S.B.
President, Swiss Association of Gymnasium Teachers
Director, Stiftschüle Einsiedeln
Einsiedeln

TURKEY

Mr. Necat ERDER
Head of Social Planning Division, State Planning Organization
Prime Minister's Office, Ankara
(Director of the Turkish National Team for the Mediterranean Regional Project)

Mr. Nihat SAYDAM
Under-Secretary of State for Professional and Technical Education
Ministry of Education
Ankara

UNITED KINGDOM

Mr. W.A.B. HOPKIN
Deputy to the Economic Adviser H.M., Treasury
Great George Street, London S.W. 1

Mr. Antony A. PART, C.B., M.B.E.
Deputy Secretary
Ministry of Education
Curzon Street, London W. 1

UNITED STATES

Mr. Manuel ABRAMS
Office of European Regional Affairs, Department of State
Washington 25 D.C.

Dr. David E. BELL
Director, Bureau of the Budget
Washington 25 D.C.

Mr. Philip H. COOMBS
Chairman of the Conference
Assistant Secretary of State for Educational and Cultural Affairs, Department of State
Washington 25 D.C.
(Head of Delegation)

Mr. Kermit GORDON
Council of Economic Advisers, Executive Office Building
The White House, Washington 25 D.C.

Mr. James P. GRANT
Deputy Director
Office of Program and Planning, International Cooperation Administration
Washington 25 D.C.

Mr. Sterling M. McMurrin
Commissioner of Education, Department of Health, Education and Welfare
Washington 25 D.C.

Dr. Alan T. Waterman
Director, National Science Foundation
1951 Constitution Ave. N.W., Washington 25 D.C.

Expert Adviser :
Professor Theodore Schultz
Professor of Economics
University of Chicago
Chicago 37 Illinois

YUGOSLAVIA

Mrs. Herta Haas
Head of the Division for Personnel
Federal Economic Planning Bureau
Kneza Milosa Br. 20
Belgrade
(Director of the Yugoslav National Team
for the Mediterranean Regional Project)

Dr. Ivan Marinic
Deputy President
Federal Council for Scientific Research
Boz. Adzije 11
Belgrade

Observers :

INTER-AMERICAN DEVELOPMENT BANK, Washington 25 D.C.

Mr. Felipe Herrera
President

Mr. Milic Kybal
Coordination Officer

Mr. Manuel Noriega-Morales
Director, Technical Assistance Division

Mr. Clarence Pierce
Member, Technical Assistance Division

Mr. Guillermo Rossel
Division of Social Development

INTERNATIONAL ASSOCIATION OF UNIVERSITIES,
6 rue Franklin, Paris 16[e]

Mr. H.M.R. Keyes
Secretary-General

ORGANIZATION OF AMERICAN STATES,
Pan American Union, Washington 6 D.C.

Dr. Juan M. CAMPOS-CATELIN
Deputy Director
Department of Technical Cooperation

Dr. Carlos CUETO FERNANDINI
Chief, Division of Education
Department of Cultural Affairs

Mr. Maximo HALTY CARRERE
Chief, Division of Technology and Productivity
Department of Economic Affairs

UNITED NATIONS ORGANIZATION

Secretariat :
Mr. Hans SINGER
Special Adviser, Office of the Under-Secretary
for Economic and Social Affairs
U.N.O.
New York, N.Y.

INTERNATIONAL BANK FOR RECONSTRUCTION
AND DEVELOPMENT, 1818 H. Street N.W. Washington 25 D.C.

Mr. Richard H. DEMUTH
Director
Technical Assistance Department

Mr. Michael HOFFMAN
Director
Economic Development Institute

Mr. Kenneth IVERSON
Assistant Director
Technical Assistance Department

U.N. ECONOMIC COMMISSION FOR LATIN AMERICA

Mr. David H. POLLOCK
Chief, Washington Office

INTERNATIONAL LABOUR OFFICE,
Washington Branch Office, 197 15th Street, N.W. Washington 5, D.C.

Mr. Ralph WRIGHT
Director, Washington Office

Mr. David S. BLANCHARD
Deputy Director, Washington Office

SPECIAL FUND, U.N.O. New York, N.Y.

Mr. Clinton REHLING
Assistant to Managing Director

UNITED NATIONS EDUCATIONAL, SCIENTIFIC AND CULTURAL ORGANIZATION, Place de Fontenoy, Paris 7ᵉ

Mr. Shannon McCUNE
Director, Department of Education

ORGANISATION FOR ECONOMIC CO-OPERATION AND DEVELOPMENT

Mr. Thorkil KRISTENSEN
Secretary-General

Dr. Alexander KING
Rapporteur-General
Director for Scientific Affairs

Mr. J.R. GASS
Secretary of the Conference
Head of Programming and Development Division
Directorate for Scientific Affairs

Mr. M. BENJENK
Head of Technical Co-operation Division
Development Directorate

Mr. O. CARACCIOLO DI FORINO
Head of Washington Office

Mr. D. MALLETT
Head of Information and Press Division

Mr. R.F. LYONS
Principal Administrator
Directorate for Scientific Affairs

Mr. Kjell EIDE
Principal Administrator
Directorate for Scientific Affairs

Mr. H.D. DE VROOM
Executive Assistant
Washington Office

II. TARGETS FOR EDUCATION IN EUROPE IN 1970

Paper by Ingvar Svennilson in association with
Friedrich Edding and Lionel Elvin

PREFACE
by
THORKIL KRISTENSEN
Secretary-General of O.E.C.D.

Now that economic expansion has become the watchword of governments and peoples all over the world, it is difficult to realize that only a generation ago the main preoccupation of economists and statesmen was how to rescue the world from economic depression or stagnation. Today every government is striving for rapid economic growth, and the more advanced countries have made it a matter of policy to aid the less advanced countries in this endeavour. Indeed, if the gap between the highly-developed nations and those emerging from a primitive economy is to be reduced, we must hope that the latter will have a faster rate of economic growth than the former.

If we ask what are the factors behind economic growth, the classical economist will generally enumerate three factors of production: labour, capital, and land. But the modern economist will add a fourth factor which is not very clearly defined and which is often seen as "organization", the art—or science—of bringing the three other factors to bear on production in the best possible way. Technological progress is undoubtedly an important part of it, but I think that there is much more to it than that. This fourth factor also comprises such things as good administration, stable political systems, enlightened attitudes towards change and innovation, and all those elements which together make up what we would call the cultural pattern of society. In fact, economic growth means radical change of the whole intellectual quality of our community.

Now the cultural pattern is a mixture of many different things, but I think that its most dynamic element is knowledge. If the twentieth century has seen a tremendous and unprecedented economic growth, it is because we have vastly more knowledge, not only technological in the narrow sense, but knowledge in the wider sense of the word. And this is due mainly to the scientific revolution of our time.

If science produces knowledge, it is education which diffuses it and makes possible its application to the practical tasks of production and economic growth. I think that many of the problems confronting us in this context, particularly with regard to the scarcity of qualified manpower, are due to a large extent to the fact that, in this century, science has been advancing much faster than education: in other words, the mass of knowledge has grown much faster than the means of diffusing it. In fact, the problem of how the mass of knowledge produced by science can be more widely disseminated and made available to those who are capable of assimilating it is becoming almost a science in itself. It is certainly one of the important political issues of today.

The rapid recovery of countries such as Germany and Holland from the tremendous devastation of the Second World War would not have been possible without the vast mass of knowledge which these countries had at their disposal. This shows that the destruction of physical capital need not be fatal if knowledge remains. And this lesson holds out great hopes for the newly developing countries lacking in physical capital. The difference between their standard of production in their present state of knowledge, and the standard of production they could have if the world's vast store of knowledge could be brought to them is tremendous. We have an enormous reserve of knowledge in store for them, and I believe that this intellectual capital would be as important for them as the physical capital provided by international institutions and firms. Knowledge has a peculiar quality: you can give it away and still keep it. In fact, you gain more knowledge by spreading it than by keeping it to yourself—as every scientist knows.

Education does not consist solely of imparting knowledge; it also means implanting an attitude towards life, towards social change and innovation. All those who have worked in the underdeveloped countries feel that the great obstacle to economic progress has been the traditionally hostile attitude of the people towards change and innovation, and that the most important task is to bring about a change in that attitude.

In this respect, the highly-developed countries may need some education themselves. They may be willing to accept the idea that the rate of growth of underdeveloped countries should be faster than their own—so long as the gap is wide enough to exclude serious competition. But when the gap has narrowed significantly and the newly developing countries have become more competitive in such fields as textiles or transistors, the richer countries may find it increasingly unpalatable to go on helping the poorer countries to have further economic growth and thus become even more competitive. I think they should begin to teach themselves to accept this change when it comes—as it inevitably will.

However, the need to diffuse knowledge is not confined exlusively to the newly developing countries; education can hardly be said to have received the attention it merits even in the more highly developed countries of Europe. This is shown convincingly in the study undertaken at my request by Professor Svennilson in association with Professors Edding and Elvin. It will be seen from this study that the European area of O.E.C.D. lags far behind the Soviet Union and even further behind the United States in educational opportunities and facilities. The call of the authors for a greatly intensified educational effort by the O.E.C.D. countries is, therefore, most timely; and the factual basis of their argument is most apposite.

Any educational effort, if it is to be fruitful, obviously involves planning; and the great difficulty in planning an educational policy is that it must look so far ahead. It may take twenty years or more to transform a boy of seven into a scientist or a university professor, and it is therefore important to know what the demand for scientists or university professors will be twenty years hence. But making such long-term projections is a very difficult science indeed, particularly in a world of rapid social, economic and technological change. My personal experience has convinced me that advance thinking, even if it contains some mistakes, has the great advantage that mistakes are made at an early stage and can therefore be corrected in good time.

Professor Svennilson and his colleagues have set out the broad dimensions of the effort which must be made by the O.E.C.D. countries if they are to expand education in the 1960's sufficiently to meet demographic, social and economic needs. Their general message is, if I read it correctly, that something like a doubling of expenditure, with a great expansion of enrolments in advanced secondary and higher education, will be required, but that our economic growth should make it possible for us to achieve this target.

TABLE OF CONTENTS

PREFACE, by Thorkil Kristensen, Secretary-General of O.E.C.D.............. 5
EDITOR'S NOTE.. 13
INTRODUCTION 15

Chapter I
EDUCATION AND SOCIAL WELFARE

THE SOCIAL FRAMEWORK OF EDUCATIONAL POLICY 19
Freedom of Choice and Policy... 19
Education and Economic Policy.. 21
CONSUMPTION ASPECTS OF EDUCATION.................................. 22
Education as Current Consumption..................................... 22
Education as a Durable Consumption Asset............................. 23
The Influence of Education on Other Types of Consumption.............. 23
PRODUCTION ASPECTS OF EDUCATION................................... 23
Education as a Factor of Production.................................. 23
Education and Training... 24
The Importance of Flexibility.. 24
Specialization and Leadership.. 24
Personal and Social Returns on Investment in Education................ 25
Education and Research... 25

Chapter II
PROBLEMS OF POLICY MAKING

AIMS OF POLICY AND LEVELS OF DECISION.............................. 27
The Dual Aim.. 27
The Two Levels of Investment Policy.................................. 28
The Need for Rolling Adjustment...................................... 29
PROBLEMS OF BALANCED EXPANSION 29
Quality versus Quantity.. 29
The Generalization of Secondary Education............................ 31
The Problem of Structure in Secondary Education 32
The Pool of Ability... 34
General versus Specialized Education................................. 34
The Logistics of Balanced Expansion.................................. 35
Educational Policy and Population Trends............................. 37
Marginal Returns.. 38
Bottle-necks and Flow of Student Generations........................ 39
THE GROWTH OF EXPENDITURE ON EDUCATION 40
Current Expenditure and Economic Growth............................. 40
Trends in Capital Expenditure....................................... 44
THE ALLOCATION OF RESOURCES TO EDUCATION.......................... 45
The Policy Problem.. 45
Investment in Education or in Real Capital.......................... 45

Education and Saving... 46
Investment in Education and Technical Progress........................ 47
INSTITUTIONAL ARRANGEMENTS FOR EDUCATIONAL PLANNING............... 48
Planning and Forecasting... 48
The Role of Social Decisions... 49
The Need for an Overall View and Central Decisions................... 49
The Diversity of Administrative Traditions........................... 49

Chapter III
PERSPECTIVES FOR EDUCATION IN THE NEXT DECADE

CURRENT NATIONAL PLANNING... 53
Dynamic and Integrated Planning of Education......................... 53
Machinery for Planning... 53
Measures Planned or under Consideration.............................. 56
    Compulsory Education.. 56
    Secondary Education... 57
    Higher Education.. 58
PRESENT DIMENSIONS OF EDUCATION....................................... 60
The Problematic Statistical Basis.................................... 60
    Obsolescence of Education Statistics............................ 60
    Problems in Measuring Educational Effort........................ 60
    The Fallacy of Enrolment Figures................................ 61
    Enrolment Ratios as a Yardstick................................. 61
    Number of Teachers and Real Teaching Input...................... 62
    Student/Teacher Ratio as Quality Index.......................... 63
    Expenditure on Education—an Uncharted Territory................. 64
    Gross National Product, Population and Base Year................ 66
    Presentation of Statistics...................................... 66
Magnitude of Present Educational Effort.............................. 67
    Population and Student Numbers.................................. 67
    Population of School Age and Enrolment Ratios................... 70
    Teachers and Student/Teacher Ratios............................. 76
    Expenditure on Education.. 79
TARGETS FOR THE SIXTIES... 81
Approach to the Problem.. 81
Methods and Assumptions.. 83
Targets for the O.E.E.C. Area.. 84
    Population Trends... 84
    Enrolment Ratios and Student Numbers............................ 84
    Teachers and Student/Teacher Ratios............................. 86
    Expenditure... 91
Aims for Tomorrow and Past Achievements.............................. 96

APPENDICES

I. NOTES ON SOURCES, STATISTICS AND METHODS......................... 101
   1. Sources... 101
   2. Notes on Statistics and Methods............................... 101
      a) *Enrolment and Teachers*.................................. 101
      b) *Expenditure*... 102

II. STATISTICAL DATA FOR INDIVIDUAL COUNTRIES (TABLES) :
   1. Population of School Age and Students by Age Groups. Base Year. 107
   2. Enrolment Ratios by Age Groups. Base Year and Projections for 1970 (high alternative)... 108

3. Population of School Age and Students by Age Groups. Projections for 1970...... 109
4. Teachers by Age Groups of Students. Base Year and Projections for 1970...... 110
5. Current, Capital and Total Expenditure on Education. Base Year.. 111
6. Current Expenditure on Education from all Sources by Age Groups of Students. Base Year and Projections for 1970...... 112

DISCUSSION...... 115

LIST OF DIAGRAMS

1. Historical Development of Enrolment Ratios in England and Wales by Age Groups 1900-1958. Public Primary and Secondary Schools...... 41
2. Development of Teachers Salaries and Gross National Product Per Capita in the United States, 1870-1955...... 43
3. Population and Number of Full-Time Students in Base Year...... 69
4. Distribution of Students by Age Groups in Base Year...... 69
5. Gross National Product Per Capita and Enrolment Ratios in Base Year for each of the Three Age Groups...... 72
6. Population of Age Groups and Student Numbers by Major Area (Base Year and Projections for 1970)...... 85
7. Increase in Population of School Age and in Student Population—1970 (High Alternative) over Base Year...... 88,89
8. Number of Teachers by Age Groups of Students. Base Year and Projections for 1970...... 90
9. Current Expenditure on Education from all Sources as a Percentage of Gross National Product. Base Year and Projections for 1970...... 92
10. Current Expenditure from all Sources on Education by Age Groups. Base Year and Projections for 1970...... 92

LIST OF TABLES

1. Enrolment Ratios according to French Plans 1954-1976...... 58
2. Duration of Compulsory Full-Time Education by Countries. Base Year. 68
3. Population of School Age. Number of Full-Time Students and Enrolment Ratios by Groups of Countries. Base Year...... 71
4. Enrolment Ratios in Selected Countries taking account of Migrant Students for the Age Group 20-24. Base Year...... 74
5. Enrolment Ratios of Age Group 15-24 in Full-Time Education by Single Year of Age and by Sex in Selected Countries. Base Year...... 75
6. Number of Teachers in relation to Total Population and Population of School Age by Groups of Countries. Base Year...... 76
7. Student/Teacher Ratios by Groups of Countries. Base Year...... 77
8. Student/Teacher Ratios in Selected Countries, 1900-1957...... 78
9. Expenditure on Education in relation to Gross National Product by Groups of Countries. Base Year...... 80
10. Public Current and Total Expenditure on Education in relation to Current Revenue of General Government by Groups of Countries. Base Year.. 81
11. Enrolment Ratios by Groups of Countries. Base Year and Projections for 1970...... 87
12. Current Expenditure on Education from all Sources by Groups of Countries. Base Year and Projections for 1970...... 91
13. Current and Total Expenditure on Education in relation to Gross National Product by country. Base Year and Projections for 1970 (High Alternative)...... 93
14. Population, Students, Teachers, Current Expenditure on Education from all Sources by Age Groups of Students and Gross National Product Per Capita—by countries—Projected Increase by 1970 (High Alternative) over Base Year...... 94

EDITOR'S NOTE

The assignment to carry out a study of the economics of education had originally been accepted by Professor Thorkil Kristensen. When he became the Secretary-General of O.E.E.C., Professor Ingvar Svennilson was asked to take over the responsibility for the Project. At his suggestion, the programme was enlarged to include a study of the comparative position of European education and of the plans and perspectives for its development in the next decade. In order to carry out this wider assignment Professor Svennilson associated himself with Professor Friedrich Edding of the Higher Institute for International Educational Research of Frankfurt, and Professor Lionel Elvin, Director of the Institute of Education of London University. The report is the result of the team-work of these three experts; Professor Edding has also been responsible for the statistics and estimates contained in the last chapter. The report has been produced in consultation with the staff of the O.E.E.C. Directorate for Scientific Affairs. The Economics and Statistics Directorate of O.E.E.C. has provided estimates of the growth of the gross national product.

INTRODUCTION

1.   The importance of education as part of national policy has never attracted as much attention and been as widely discussed as it is to-day —in Europe as well as in North America. Present trends—political, economic, social and technical—are all focussing attention on the role education should and could play in a modern community.

2.   Access to education is increasingly regarded as a "human right". That the implementation of this right must be contingent upon a country's resources may be temporarily accepted; that, at higher levels, this right is contingent upon ability to profit by such education may also be accepted as long as access to it is given in terms of ability rather than of social privilege. But the conviction is now widespread that in a democratic society the right to education must be recognized and given practical effect at a rhythm that keeps pace with economic development. In the past, education has not been made available to everyone who was especially gifted and talented; there have been social barriers which have meant personal handicaps and unjust discrimination. Apart from this loss to the individual, there has been a loss to society which, in modern conditions, cannot afford to leave unused so large a part of its human resources and skills.

3.   At the same time, the revival and rapid upsurge of the European economy after the last war has increased the demand for education as well as the resources for its satisfaction. As personal incomes rise, young people and their parents want and can afford more education; and as national incomes and government revenues rise, increasing resources can more easily be allotted to education.

4.   It is also now generally acknowledged that the progress of society depends on its capacity to utilize the results of scientific research and technical innovation. More people are needed to master the problems of modern technology, not only at the top but all the way down the line. At the same time, the rapid changes in technical processes and in the technological basis of our civilization have placed a premium on flexibility of mind—and also on good human relations to facilitate the social readjustment entailed by these changes. The task of educating everybody for effective living in a complicated and shifting environment has thus become increasingly important.

5. Education is also more and more widely recognized as a means to economic growth which, since the end of the war, has everywhere become a paramount aim of national policy. In the under-developed countries, economic growth is necessary to alleviate widespread poverty. In the more advanced countries, economic growth has become a matter of competition, a yardstick for appraising the ability of different political systems to solve their economic and social problems. This competition has been sharpened by the fact that the Soviet Union has challenged the West in precisely these terms. Those who are quite unimpressed by Marxist doctrine as such might be much more impressed if the Soviet Union were to outstrip the West in material production, even though the volume of production only partly reflects the level of welfare. The marked emphasis on education in the production effort of the Soviet Union has certainly contributed to a re-appraisal by the Western countries of the role of education in their social and economic development.

6. It is now generally accepted that we have the knowledge and the techniques to avoid stagnation and to promote economic growth—and that an appropriate education of all citizens forms one of the main instruments of such a policy. A policy for education cannot be based on present conditions, because its social results will be felt over a long period in the future. It has to take into account scientific and technical progress, as well as social and economic trends, that lie several decades ahead. These long-term perspectives have greatly widened the horizons for educational policy, but have also made its formulation and implementation one of the most difficult, as well as one of the most fascinating, tasks of our time.

7. There is now a widespread conviction that present-day European education is inadequate in relation to the avowed targets of public policy. There is also a strong but so far imprecisely formulated feeling that more education and better education ought to be provided, and that expenditure on it should be increased. Education has, however, already become an expensive sector of the economy, and a large-scale expansion of this sector would absorb considerable national resources. The time has therefore come to investigate more closely the relation between ends and means. Vague ideas and slogans have to be replaced by a precise formulation of targets based on factual research and scientific analysis. Only in this way will it be possible to lay the foundation for a rational educational policy.

8. In the society of to-day it is recognized that education is the concern not only of the individual who benefits from it directly, but of the community at large. All citizens, therefore, have to contribute to the education that is provided through the budgets of local or central government. Irrespective of the extent to which education is organized in private or public forms, governments have accepted a responsibility for its general evolution. The fact that education is a field for public policy must be the starting point for the following discussion.

9. Its purpose is to consider the order of magnitude and the main directions of the educational task with which European countries will be confronted in the next decade. Much of the material used here has been collected from various countries; this applies in particular to the section summarizing prospects for expansion in terms of students, teachers and expenditure in the coming decade. A mere presentation of plans and perspectives would, however, be of limited interest; it has therefore been accompanied by some analysis of the main policy problems involved. While some of these problems are familiar enough in educational circles, the emphasis here is on their relationship with broader social and economic policy. Indeed, educational development is now so closely integrated with the general development of society that its problems can only be satisfactorily defined within that general framework.

I

EDUCATION AND SOCIAL WELFARE

THE SOCIAL FRAMEWORK OF EDUCATIONAL POLICY

FREEDOM OF CHOICE AND POLICY

10. Educational policy, within general national policy, has two main objects: to meet the demands of individuals for their own development, and to meet the needs of society for its general development. In a democracy that respects individual freedoms the first object is served by making education available to all citizens, irrespective of class and income, according to their individual gifts and desires. The second object, for which governments have assumed responsibility, is served by seeing to it that industry, as well as cultural and public institutions, are provided with persons having the requisite general education and skills.

11. At first sight, there may appear to be a conflict in this dualism of aim: a country may need more engineers than artists, but more of its young people may wish to specialize in art than in engineering. However, this conflict between consumer choice and national policy-making may be more apparent than real.

12. In the first place, in the field of endeavour fostered by education supply has a definite influence on demand. The reason is simply that, at all levels of education, people make innovations which change the conditions governing the growth of industries, and consequently change the market for different kinds of education. A striking example is provided by the emergence of the German organic chemical industry towards the end of last century. The German universities had produced a large number of doctors in chemistry. Their research led up to the innovations that for some decades gave the German chemical industry a remarkable lead—and the German chemists a wide market for their services. Another example is provided by the French and Scandinavian experience in the field of "couture" and furniture respectively. It shows how a development of artistic professions may promote the growth of industries based on them, and thus provide a wider market

for artists and designers. Although it is difficult to forecast such effects of supply on demand, innovations being by definition unexpected, a national policy of education must take them into account and assume that an individual is most likely to become useful to society if he is free fully to develop his own particular skills and qualities. Free choice may have its advantages even if it leads to a situation where the number of students in a particular field exceeds the forecast of minimum demand, a forecast which can be made with a fair degree of accuracy.

13. Again, the choice of the individual is largely guided by considerations similar to those which govern public policy. Man is a social being, and a student is likely to be attracted to that kind of study and career in which he feels he will be most useful to society and most wanted by it. This tendency is strengthened by the economic motives provided by the market system. Though this system may have its imperfections and distortions, there is, on the whole, a correlation between private and social returns on investment in various types of education. The unsatisfied demand will be reflected in high incomes which will attract students to the neglected sector of education.

14. Lastly, vocational guidance comes into the picture. Individuals in general cannot be expected to be perfectly informed even about the *present* market situation for various types of trained personnel. In any case, this information might be misleading, as their choice of education should be guided by future and not present demand. As will be seen later, these future trends can only be assessed by a complex analysis which can only be carried out on a national level. It is the result of this analysis which must form the basis for the formulation of a national education policy which, in its turn, will influence market trends. Market forecasting and policy thus form an integrated whole and the national institutions which carry out market investigations and formulate policy are best placed to advise the student on future prospects in various fields. Vocational guidance thus forms an important link between the choice of individuals and national policy.

15. Thus the conflict between individual preferences and public policy is not nearly as great as it might appear at first sight, and what conflict does exist may, up to a point, be accepted by a liberal educational policy. At least, this should be the case as we approach a situation where the total demand for education is balanced by the total capacity of educational institutions. It may, then, be possible to increase the capacity of various types of schools and universities beyond the calculated minimum needs.

16. To-day, however, this stage is still far off. To an increasing extent, the expansion of the educational system depends on support from public funds. The provision of educational facilities by national or local government may take various forms: public schools, where education is supplied free or against a fee that only partly covers total

costs; municipal and private schools subsidized by central government; scholarships that either partly or wholly cover students' expenses. This may be regarded as a system of incentives which stimulates students to take up various lines of studies. And as available public funds are limited, this system must necessarily be selective. In this way, national policies have an influence on the rate of expansion of the educational system.

17.   As public authorities also largely finance the building of schools and are responsible for the training of teachers, the actual physical capacity of various types of schools is largely determined by central or local government. Because this physical capacity is far from adequate, the system of closed entry is still widespread. In the case of the more expensive sectors of education, e.g. medicine and technology, closed entry is almost universal, and students have to be selected according to certain tests.

18.   Such restrictions have to be accepted so long as public funds for education are inadequate in relation to demand. For the time being, student preferences cannot be gratified to more than a limited extent, and certainly not at the expense of national educational policy. It is quite evident that these conditions will persist in all European countries for at least the next decade, i.e. the period for which some definite planning can be made now.

EDUCATION AND ECONOMIC POLICY

19.   Education has always been regarded as a vital factor in achieving the general aims of society, an instrument to make the democratic system more perfect. One important aspect of this concept has been that all citizens should have the same opportunities to take an active part in political, social and economic life. What is more recent—and has so far received less consideration—is the emergence of a concept of education as an important factor of economic policy.

20.   Whatever the economic system, it is now universally accepted that Governments must direct their economic activities towards the welfare of society as a whole. The aims may be expressed in somewhat different ways in different countries, or by different political parties within any one country; but that does not affect the validity of the general statement. The aims are likely to be formulated in terms of distribution of income, of the level of employment, or of general economic progress. What is now being increasingly realized is that educational policy can make a major contribution to the general well-being of society; that it is, in fact, one of the most important instruments of economic policy. It may be used as a complement or as an alternative to other instruments of policy; but in both cases its role is a major one.

21.   Behind this generalization lies a distinction which calls for some consideration. In terms of economic policy, we may distinguish between

two main aspects of education. First, the scale and levels of education have a direct effect on the standard of living. This may be called the *consumption* aspect of education. Second, education has an impact on the efficiency of production. This is the *production* aspect of education.

22. What is characteristic of both these effects is that they are durable, lasting at least for the life-span of the student. Education may thus from a policy point of view be regarded as a type of *investment*, normally a long-term investment. The size and content of this investment cannot be determined solely by the needs of to-day; account must be taken of what the situation will be when the results of education mature. From the nature of the case, educational policy must be long-term policy, and research related to it must concern itself with long-term economic and social trends.

23. This is a most important point. Little enough is spent in most countries on educational research in general, and of this, only a minute proportion is spent on research related to economic and social trends. Yet without such research, what sound basis can there be for long-term educational planning? A much more massive and co-ordinated effort is needed. Planning of education should be an integral part of national economic policy.

CONSUMPTION ASPECTS OF EDUCATION

Education as Current Consumption

24. Education can be regarded as consumption *per se*; like other types of consumption, it satisfies the needs of the consumer. Within a restricted budget, either personal or national, it is an alternative to other types of current consumption, chosen according to the preferences of individuals or governments. In societies where education is wholly or partly paid for from private funds, families have to look at it in this way; if a little extra is spent on the children's education there will be less left over for other things. In societies where education is paid for from public funds. the citizens as tax-payers have to weigh this type of consumption against other kinds of private and public consumption. In the same way, governments who operate within a limited budget have to weigh expenditure on public education against other social services.

25. In education, it is difficult to separate the interest of the individual as a consumer from his interest as a future producer and income earner. We may assume, however, that as total consumption rises society, individually or collectively, will want to spend a larger share of it in the form of education. In other words, from the consumer point of view, the income elasticity of demand for education is probably growing. The attitude of American parents to a prolonged period of formal education for their children may be taken as an illustration of this point.

Education as a Durable Consumption Asset

26. Education, however, cannot be considered solely as current consumption; it also represents what may be called investment in a durable consumption asset. It is not "consumed" once and for all. It has the continuing effect of enriching adult life, and it is on the basis of his education that the individual cultivates his personal interests. Studies open the road to further studies. The importance of education increases as the technical and social environment of personal life becomes more complicated, and as leisure time is extended.

27. Again the steady growth of an economy produces changes in the kind of productive tasks people have to perform. The heavier and dirtier jobs tend to disappear, and the intellectual side of work becomes more emphasized as machines take over manual operation. In other words, as society gets richer, the nature of the tasks becomes pleasanter. But the ability to take full advantage of this situation is related to the level of education, and these effects too should therefore be included as an element in the concept of education as a durable asset.

The Influence of Education on Other Types of Consumption

28. Another important effect of education is that it influences the individual in his choice of other kinds of consumption. A combination of affluence with ignorance too often produces only vulgarity, a failure to use wealth so as to give enduring satisfaction. The value that we attribute to any future growth of consumption in general will be higher if our children are better educated. On both the individual and national level, a sudden affluence of consumer goods, flooding in before knowledge of how to choose and use them has been developed, has raised serious social problems. An American Indian on whose land oil is discovered is a classic example of the man who should have been the beneficiary but, ironically, has too often become merely the victim of good fortune. Affluence without education is likely to result only in wasteful consumption.

29. In short, there will be much greater advantage in economic growth if it is accompanied by appropriate educational growth. Even from the point of view of consumption, we have to educate for a higher standard of living.

PRODUCTION ASPECTS OF EDUCATION

Education as a Factor of Production

30. Economic growth is generated not only by real capital in the form of tools and machinery, but also by men. And just as technological improvements increase the efficiency of machinery, so education increases the efficiency of manpower. Indeed, recent statistical investigations

tend to show that the improvement in the "human factor" accounts for a major part of economic growth. In practice, of course, improvements in the quality of manpower and of machinery go hand in hand; they both reflect the greater effectiveness of the human factor—which is, or should be, an aim as well as a result of education.

EDUCATION AND TRAINING

31. It is difficult to draw the line between formal education, given in institutions like schools, universities, etc., and on-the-job training and learning received when the young man or woman enters the production process. One may perhaps still use the two terms "education" and "training", but this distinction has more reality for the educationist than for the economist. It is clear, however, that schools and universities do not deliver a finished product. In every occupation more knowledge and skill has to be acquired by actual experience of work in a specific job. One important aim of formal education should be to prepare the student for this learning process. And the value of a good previous education is seen in the speed with which the individual absorbs this further learning and is able to adjust to flexible and unforeseen conditions of work. The educationist is thus faced with difficulties in deciding to what extent education in schools and colleges should be general or specialized, and to what extent the knowledge and skills taught should be basic or applied. These are decisions that he would be wise to make in consultation with the economist and the employer.

THE IMPORTANCE OF FLEXIBILITY

32. One of the signs of a progressive economy is its ability to transfer a technical innovation, first from the laboratory to actual production, and then from one unit of production to another. The progress of under-developed or semi-developed countries is highly dependent on an acceleration of this transfer process. It is here that the role of education and the choice of the right kind of education can be so important. There are obvious dangers in an education that is too traditional and that seems only to confirm people in their mental rigidities. But there are equal dangers in an education that is too close to specific processes which may be outmoded in a very short time. The aim must be to make minds more receptive to impulses from the outside and in this way to increase cross-fertilization between different parts of the economy and, one might add, between different countries.

SPECIALIZATION AND LEADERSHIP

33. While flexibility of mind is an asset, it is still true that economic progress is accompanied and promoted by an increasing division of labour. Education, and especially higher education, should aim at facilitating this division of labour: it should prepare people to meet

the demand for new specializations of function. But specialization also means that people increasingly work in teams which contain complementary types of knowledge and skill; we may even regard all members of a national labour force as a highly differentiated team. It is basic for such team-work that the improved productivity of one member should increase the productivity of other members of the team. This complementarity is especially evident in the case of leading members of the group. A skilled leader may organize even unskilled labour into an efficient unit. As a result, education at the leader level yields extra dividends all the way down the line.

PERSONAL AND SOCIAL RETURNS ON INVESTMENT IN EDUCATION

34. The role of educated leadership in production has consequences for the theory of education as investment. If we accept the traditional economic doctrine that each member of a team will be paid according to his marginal productivity, it follows that an appropriate high-level education of one member of a team will increase not only his own remuneration but also that of the other members. Thus the social profitability of investment in education cannot be measured by the increased income of the highly-educated man alone; it must be measured in terms of the group or the community.

35. All the indications are that private returns on investment in prolonged education are high. But they represent only a part of the additional social return. This is an important reason why society as a whole should contribute to investment in education.

EDUCATION AND RESEARCH

36. There is one field in which investment in higher education is especially desirable; the highly profitable field of research. In this context education may be regarded as an "enrichment process" for selecting and developing the best talents. As relevant studies have shown, certain types of talent for advanced research are very rare within any generation of students. This is a strong reason for making education available to all according to their special talents. Otherwise there will be a loss of potential research ability which, had it been fostered through education, would have made important contributions to scientific and economic progress.

II

PROBLEMS OF POLICY MAKING

AIMS OF POLICY AND LEVELS OF DECISION

THE DUAL AIM

37.   The preceding analysis indicates the considerations that have to be taken into account in formulating targets for education as part of an integrated social and economic policy. The aims of this policy may in broad terms be stated as follows:
  a)   A maximum of present welfare within the limits of available resources;
  b)   A growth of production as a basis for the future improvement of the standard of living.

38.   The two aims are partly conflicting. It is usually assumed that economic growth can only be accelerated by saving for the future at the expense of present consumption. This view is derived from the conventional concept of national accounts, where a sharp distinction is made between production for consumption and production for investment. Actually, this distinction does not conform to the real mechanisms of economic growth. In a country where the population is under-nourished, a rise in food consumption may increase production. It has already been shown that education can be regarded as an investment that accelerates economic growth, as well as raising standards of living both in the present and in the future, quite apart from its roundabout effects on production (as defined by national accounts).

39.   This dual role of education has important effects in deciding the amount of investment to be allocated to education and in making the choice between investment in education and investment in material capital equipment. If we want to compare the profitability of education with that of real capital, we must deduct its consumption value from the investment cost. If $10 million invested in education yields the same return as the same amount spent on real capital, investment in education pays better according to the value we attribute to its direct consumption effects. If we prefer education to the corresponding value

of other types of consumption, it actually represents an investment in production that we get gratis. Up to a point, increased expenditure on education is probably regarded in this way, according to prevalent social valuations. To that extent, we can gain in economic growth without any sacrifice of the current standard of living. The emphasis that in recent years has been placed on education as an investment may thus be misleading, because it makes too absolute an antithesis between consumption and investment, and may lead to less expenditure on education than would be the case if we took into account its dual function.

THE TWO LEVELS OF INVESTMENT POLICY

40. Any national investment policy must be conceived in two stages. First, within a given amount of total investment, we have to select those types of investment that yield the highest return. In the case of material capital equipment, this selection is assumed to be the result of a testing of profitability, calculated on the basis of market prices. If technical changes increase the profitability of certain sectors additional investment will be allocated to them. Second, we have to consider to what extent the aggregate amount of investment should be provided at the expense of consumption, i.e. how far to increase total saving. In a market economy, this allocation of resources to investment may also be determined on the basis of various market mechanisms. These two stages represent respectively the micro- and macro-levels of investment, and are assumed to follow a rational path determined by the market forces. This ideal adjustment of investment to current technical and economic trends may, however, be impeded by inertia in the economic system, by private restrictive practices, by Government regulations or by a lack of foresight or of confidence in the future.

41. In a similar way, the process of arriving at an optimal investment in education may be divided into two stages:

a) What should be the *internal structure* of education —the institutional structure of the system and the pattern of the education itself? How should a given total investment be divided between primary, secondary and higher education? What should be the relative amount of general and specialized education? What specialities should be given priority? What educational methods should be chosen on each of these levels? What standards should be chosen in terms of teachers, buildings and other facilities?

b) How large a part of available national resources should be allocated to education in relation to other types of consumption and investment?

42. These two levels of decision correspond to the micro- and macro-levels of investment decision in the field of real capital. In the case of education, the decisions on the micro-level will to a large extent

depend on educational considerations. However, the structure of the educational systems and the pattern of education itself must also be related to the effects of education on consumption and production. A given total expenditure on education may yield quite different results in terms of consumption and economic growth, according to its internal pattern. If this problem of an optimal internal pattern is solved, a basis will have been laid for solving the *macro-problem*, i.e. deciding on the size of total spending on education in relation to aggregate national resources.

43. It is clear however that in the case of education we cannot entirely fall back on a more or less automatic market system. The role of individual choice, the initiative of private groups, and the importance of incentives should not be overlooked. However, if schools were run by private enterprise without subsidies, the adjustment of the system to technical, social and economic changes would in the nature of the case not necessarily coincide with national interest. We have therefore to accept the fact that the development of education must be guided by public educational policy.

THE NEED FOR ROLLING ADJUSTMENT

44. It is evident that action in the field of education may lag behind what is regarded as an optimum for similar reasons as in the case of private real capital investment; inertia of the institutional system, monopolistic tendencies, lack of foresight. Plans for education must be subject to continual adjustment, corresponding to new perspectives and changing standards of value. Otherwise we risk having an educational system which is suboptimal both in structure and scope. This is probably the present position in many European countries. The primary task then is to move closer to the optimum. But it must always be borne in mind that even the best school system must be kept open to change, because the optimum position is constantly shifting.

45. We are thus facing a problem of rolling adjustment, whether it be in the internal structure of the school system or in its general expansion as expressed in total expenditure. The problem is not only in what direction and how far we should go. Equally important is the question how fast we should go in various directions. The following section deals with these problems as far as the internal structure of the educational system is concerned. The broad problems of allocation of national resources to education will be discussed in a later section.

PROBLEMS OF BALANCED EXPANSION

QUALITY VERSUS QUANTITY

46. When an educational system expands rapidly there is always a risk that quality may be sacrificed to quantity. This risk is particularly

marked when secondary education is made general, and when higher —especially university—education is made available to a larger percentage of the population. The question of whether quality will be sacrificed by a given kind of expansion, and the degree to which this may conceivably be justified by wider social considerations, must ultimately be a matter for policy judgment. But the problem is capable of a measure of analysis, and some aspects of it (e.g. the need for education of a given quality for a given proportion of the labour force) may be susceptible to statistical forecast.

47. Two points may be made at the outset. The first is that the possible effect of a rapid quantitative expansion on educational quality should be considered in advance. Indian observers of the recent rapid expansion of the university population in India seem to be of the opinion that quality has been endangered. Teachers are so over-worked that they have little time for study and research; their classes are so large that they cannot teach properly; buildings and physical facilities are so over-crowded that university atmosphere and amenities have been largely lost. It need not be concluded, however, that a fast university expansion necessarily lowers quality. It might equally well be argued that it need not do so if the expansion of student numbers is matched by a corresponding expansion of staff and facilities. The point remains that a country would be ill-advised to embark on a programme of rapid quantitative expansion without regard to its possible effects on quality.

48. Secondly, the problem of timing is all-important. If the successive phases of expansion have been well planned, then the effects on quality are less likely to be damaging. Again the clearest examples of this are to be drawn from the experience of educationally under-developed countries. From the investment point of view it would be foolish to step up sharply the provisions of schools without having first allocated sufficient funds for the provision and training of teachers. There may of course be other and compelling pressures, such as popular enthusiasm for immediate universal primary schooling. But there is no doubt that some countries on making primary education general have found themselves in great difficulty, much more because of the lack of qualified teachers than because of the lack of buildings.

49. These arguments of course apply also to countries where the educational system is already well-developed. The whole theme of the "Crowther Report" in the United Kingdom (1959) was that there should be a timed and phased plan of development. If the period of compulsory attendance at school was to be raised by a year at some time during the coming decade, it ought to take place at a point where the school population was smallest and the supply of teachers largest, or rather at the point where these two factors taken together were least unfavourable. In this way the risks to quality from quantitative expansion could be minimized.

The Generalization of Secondary Education

50. There is probably no country in Europe that could not plan to have universal primary education (the great majority have it, of course) without any threat to quality in its secondary or higher education. The real problem for most European countries arises from the universalization of secondary education. Hitherto secondary education had been available for what is called an "élite". But this term needs some defining. What kind of an "élite"? To some extent, no doubt, an intellectual "élite", and to some extent a social one. What is the "quality" that is said to be endangered by opening secondary education to all? To answer this question account would have to be taken of different factors, or of factors differently weighed, in different countries; and considerations of social policy would be bound to intertwine with considerations of a more strictly educational or economic kind.

51. It might be useful to have in mind a "model"—though it should be said at once that if this, like other models, assists comprehensibility of a problem and its solution, it distorts more than most models do through excessive simplifications. Let us suppose however—quite apart from wider considerations of human rights and living standards—that in a European economy primary education and little more is needed for unskilled workers; secondary education with a vocational bias for the semi-skilled; secondary education with further vocational education and training for the skilled; a longer and more academic secondary education for professional and administrative people of moderate status; and university or higher technological education for the higler echelons in the professions, industry and administration. We must then ask what relative changes in the size of these respective groups of the population are to be expected in the coming ten or fifteen years. The answer (as the SVIMEZ Report from Italy[1] has recently shown) will lead to the conclusion that a serious quantitative extension of all these kinds of education other than primary is necessary. The question that is worrying many people in Europe is whether this necessary extension of lower secondary and vocational education must endanger the quality of higher secondary education, and, to a lesser extent, whether the extension of higher technological education must endanger the cultural traditions of university education.

52. What are the grounds for this fear? First, the danger already mentioned that expansion may come too fast, with the provision of school places outrunning the supply of teachers not only in the secondary but also in the primary schools. Second, that the trend towards the study of science and technology is gaining such impetus that, with limited resources for expenditure on education, the great heritage of

---

1. SVIMEZ, Trained Manpower Requirements for the Economic Development of Italy - Targets for 1975 - Rome 1961. Published by Giuffré.

Europe's literary tradition may to some extent be neglected. These fears are not groundless. But they overlook the constant rise in the gross national product. If this rise continues, as it reasonably should, and if it is borne in mind that the rate of expenditure on education normally increases faster than the rate of economic growth, then the problem largely reduces itselt to one of a wise assignment of priorities within the educational budget, taking full account of the need for teachers as well as the cultural and economic factors.

53. Then it is contended that generalisation of secondary education inevitably broadens the curriculum to include subjects not hitherto considered academic but which ought to be made available to those who want them and are gifted for them. Is this really lowering standards for the gifted? It should be remembered, too, that there is always a temptation to think that less gifted pupils cannot study even a traditional academic subject, such as algebra. This is almost certainly true below a certain point in the scale of ability. But it may be the case that the problem raises two different questions which put separately would give different answers; what proportion of young people cannot study a given academic subject with reasonable profit; and, what proportion of young people can only study a given academic subject with profit if it is taught by methods more suited to them than the traditional academic methods?

The Problem of Structure in Secondary Education

54. The degree to which quantitative expansion of secondary education may adversely affect quality depends also upon the structure of the school system, and here there are questions which cannot confidently be answered without much more research than has yet been undertaken. There are people who think that if, in a universalised secondary education system, the schools for the academically abler young people are not kept separate from the rest, there will inevitably be a lowering of quality in the education of the abler pupils. This is an assumption, and those who hold it take it to be obvious. But it has by no means been proven. In Sweden, where there is research into this question as part of the current school reform, some findings tend to show that the effect on the less able pupils is one of stimulus rather than discouragement, and that the adverse effect on the abler is either nil or so small as (in Swedish opinion) to be more than outweighed by the social gain in educating these young people together. On the other hand, although the contribution of the common high school to American democracy and sense of unity is everywhere acknowledged, there are American critics who feel that the effect on the abler young people has not been good; they have had too little intellectual challenge, and the standards of the less able have tended to dominate the school.

55. What is needed, in fact, is much more research before an evaluation of this situation can be made. Is any such situation as is said to

exist in the United States causally and necessarily connected with the system of the common school as such, or is it perhaps more closely related to other factors in the school system or in society which (in the opinion of Dr. Conant, for instance) could be dealt with without abandoning the common school basis?

56. However, if one assumes for the sake of argument that quality will suffer unless there are secondary schools for selected abler students separate from the general secondary schools, a very awkward problem remains: that of selection. In England and Wales selection has been made at the age of eleven by methods that are probably about as good as could at present be devised, yet there is widespread dissatisfaction with the results. At best, there will be a not negligible number of young people above and below the selection line who might just as easily have been on the other side of it. This is established beyond reasonable doubt by the subsequent careers of these children. Yet in the mind of probably the majority of educationists, the "comprehensive" secondary school which takes under one roof all ranges of ability, and has been tried in some areas as an answer to the problem of selection, is still an experiment which has not yet proved itself decisively.

57. This problem is one that each country has to work out for itself, however enlightening international comparisons may be. Partly it is a matter of social philosophy. But heavy investment in the existing structure of a school system will already have been made. If the local education authorities of England and Wales were to be convinced tomorrow that the comprehensive school was the right answer, they could not in any case transform the system overnight; any modification would have to be extremely gradual.

58. Perhaps the most difficult question to decide is whether secondary education for the majority should be terminated at about the age of fifteen, and how far further education, taken in conjunction with industrial or agricultural training, should be "school-based or works-based". Traditional systems of apprenticeship have often broken down as educational and training devices. They have been used only too often as devices for regulating the inflow of labour to certain industries and crafts. More broadly, if schemes of combined general education and vocational training are left to the good-will of employers, the small employer will find it difficult to release his one or two young employees for part of the week. Is the answer to this problem a lengthening of the period of compulsory schooling (with a strong vocational bias in the last year for the majority), or a more serious system of part-time education (with a vocational education element but with vocational training in industry itself)? And if the latter, should it be controlled by the school or the firm, by the Ministry of Education or the Ministry of Labour?

The Pool of Ability

59. One thing that can be said with some confidence to chose who fear the effect of quantitative expansion on quality is that there is certainly a much larger "reservoir of ability" than has yet been tapped. Even in the United States qualified observers would hesitate very much to say that the large section of each age-group that goes to college is approximately co-extensive with those that ought to go in terms of ability. In almost all European countries the reservoir of untapped talent is much larger than in the United States. Even where, as in the United Kingdom, access to the university is now reasonably "democratic" for those who have stayed at secondary school till the age of eighteen, there is a serious loss for the simple reason that large numbers of potentially suitable entrants to the university leave school well before they are eighteen. (The evidence of the "Crowther Report" on this is definitive). In other words, there is little reason to fear expansion in the name of quality because of lack of ability in the increased number of students in higher secondary schools and universities. The chief reason for circumspection lies in the difficulties of expanding staff and facilities to match expanding student numbers. It is only unbalanced educational investment that is to be feared.

60. As the proportion of the national income invested in education increases, the proportion of that investment in higher quality education will increase. Because of the steady shift of manpower from the unskilled to the more skilled, from the primary producer to the distributor and administrator, the need is increasingly for the higher quality and more expensive kinds of education, both technical and general. Such kinds of education are more expensive not only in the "plant" they necessitate (laboratories, libraries, etc.) but also in the kind of teachers they postulate. They call for greater numbers of high quality teachers with longer, more specialized, and therefore more expensive training. Furthermore, the inducements to attract them into teaching in preference to highly paid alternative employment will inevitably entail higher salaries. At the very least there will be a higher total salary bill since the number of these high quality teachers will have increased in relation to the total teaching force.

General versus Specialized Education

61. One of the most important needs of a modern economy, with its constantly evolving technology, is flexibility of skills and attitudes from the manager right down to the lower ranks of skilled labour. This need has an important bearing on the degree to which investment should be allocated to general as distinct from specialized education.

62. By and large it is the technologist who has spent longest on his general education who goes furthest, mainly because he has a wider basis of knowledge and can apply it to a wider range of problems than can the specialist with little general education. More and more employers

in Europe are complaining, not that their young recruits are technically inadequate, but that they lack general education. The importance of a sound general education can hardly be over-emphasized at the present time.

63. In this respect there are wide differences between one country and another. In the United Kingdom, for example, there has been growing criticism of what is held to be excessive and premature specialization in the higher secondary school. At the opposite end, it has been noted that in the United States studies remain largely general right to the end of the college career, specialization only beginning with the post-graduate professional school or the higher degrees. Some critics think that more specialization in American colleges would be a good thing. Evidence has recently been collected in England, Germany and France of how students felt about the degree of specialization required of them for the "A" level Certificate of Education, the Abitur and the Baccalaureat respectively. It was not surprising that the English students wanted less specialization and that the German and French students would have liked to present fewer subjects for their examinations. All three however showed a majority who wanted a broad education up to the end of the secondary school, including some subjects from the sciences and some from the humanities. So many careers nowadays call for familiarity with both these modes of thinking that it would be folly not to provide such an education for an increasing number of young people, leaving as late as possible commitment to either the sciences or the humanities. Some thorough specialized study is essential to a good education, but just as the more advanced species give their young longest to mature, so the most advanced societies will tend to postpone specialization for their young people until their minds have had time to mature.

64. Lastly, we must not forget that investment and productivity are after all not ends in themselves, but means to a better and fuller life. If education has not been too narrowly "economic", the generations educated and trained to meet the needs of a growing economy will have developed tastes and interests which will in due course be reflected in a further demand for education both for themselves and for their children. If our society is to offer a full and satisfying life, it is of the greatest importance that tastes and interests should be cultured and not solely concerned with "productivity". Ultimately, quality in education means quality in individual and social life. In the long run and from a broad viewpoint, there is no inherent reason why there should be a conflict between the concept of education as a means to a better and fuller life, and the concept that tests the value of education by its economic returns.

THE LOGISTICS OF BALANCED EXPANSION

65. Having considered the various directions in which education can be expanded and some of the main factors which influence the choice of structure within a given total expenditure, the policy maker is faced

with a problem of strategy: how to develop the army of students of various age-groups and of teachers with various levels of training in such a way that, within a given framework of expenditure, a maximum of benefit is attained. Apart from strategy, the aims of which are by necessity long-term, there is also the problem of tactics, i.e. how to proceed step by step towards ultimate aims.

66. By analogy, the problem of how to let the development proceed in various directions in an optimal way may be regarded as one of logistics. There is need for more systematic operational research in this field. But let us outline the general framework of these problems in a more precise way.

67. The quantitative aspect of educational expansion is expressed by the number of students enrolled in each age-group. This number, S_i, is the product of the size of the population in the age-group concerned, P_i, and its specific enrolment ratio, e_i. Thus

$$S_i = P_i . e_i \qquad (1)$$

The total number of students equals the sum of all the S_i.

68. But the social effects of education also depend on the quality standards. These can be improved to a certain extent without increasing the cost per student—by changing the curriculum and introducing new methods of teaching. But by and large, the qualitative development of education demands a rise of the cost per pupil. New methods and new curricula may entail the use of more expensive equipment. Costs per pupil will also rise if the size of classes is reduced, if the training of teachers is lengthened, if space per pupil and standards of school buildings are improved, and if amenities such as medical care, school meals, libraries and sports grounds are extended. An improved internal organization of the school system may reduce the rise in costs per pupil; that is why internal rationalization represents an important aspect of educational policy. But even if all such possibilities of increasing efficiency are taken into account, we still have to accept that costs per pupil will rise with the quality of the education.

69. A characteristic feature of the cost structure is that, as a rule, the costs per student rise with the stage of education, and are thus correlated with the age of the student. In the higher stages, teachers are more qualified, classes smaller and equipment more expensive. Costs per pupil may be twice as high in secondary as in primary education, and again considerably higher in advanced university education. In other words, for the same additional cost we may have two more students in secondary education or one more in an expensive type of university training. The marginal cost of prolonging studies by one year thus rises with the age of the student. If a prolongation of studies is to be profitable, therefore, the social return on another year's studies should rise with the level of education. The cost relations between the different levels of education should not, however, be assumed to be fixed once

and for all. To find a proper balance that takes into account the social return is one of the tasks of educational policy.

70.   The cost of education can be regarded as a product of the quantity and quality factors. If we designate by C_i the cost per student in age group i, the total expenditure on that age-group, U_i, will, according to (1), be

$$U_i = S_i \times C_i = P_i \times e_i \times C_i \qquad (2)$$

71.   The cost factor, C_i, is dominated by teacher salaries; normally they amount to about 3/4 of total current costs. The size of classes and the number of hours per teacher determine the ratio of teachers to students, t_i. Let us assume that the average annual salary per teacher for age-group i is W_i. *The teacher cost per pupil* is, then, $t_i \times W_i$. Let us further assume that the relation of total cost per pupil to teacher cost per pupil is $(1 + k_i)$:[1]

$$\frac{C_i}{W_i \cdot t_i} = (1 + k_i) \qquad (3)$$

72.   *The cost per student* may then be expressed as a product of three factors:

$$C_i = t_i \times W_i \times (1 + k_i) \qquad (4)$$

By combining (2) and (4) we get the total cost for one age-group of students:

$$U_i = P_i \times e_i \times t_i \times W_i \times (1 + k_i) \qquad (5)$$

73.   We then arrive at total national current expenditure on education, U, by aggregating expenditure for all age-groups, U_i. Alternatively, we may define the cost factors—enrolment ratio, teacher/pupil ratio, teacher salaries and the "other costs" factor—as averages weighted by the school population in each age-group. We may then write:

$$U = P_s \times e \times t \times W \times (1 + k), \qquad (6)$$

where P_s indicates the population in the age-group on all levels of education.

74.   This expression indicates the economics of education as determined by its internal structure. A given expenditure may be distributed in different ways according to various combinations of e_i, t_i, W_i, and k_i. Any educational policy may, from an economic point of view, be expressed in these terms. The considerations relating to expenditure on education in the next decade which are projected in Chapter III are in principle based on this type of cost analysis.

EDUCATIONAL POLICY AND POPULATION TRENDS

75.   One of the cost factors, the population factor, P_i, is determined by earlier trends in the birth-rate and is thus outside the control of

---

1. k_i is then the relation of other-than-teacher costs to teacher cost per pupil.

current policy. It is well known that high birth rates during and after the war produced a wave of large age-groups that is now passing through the school system. In some countries, the number of pupils in the primary and even the secondary schools will decline in the 1960's, while that in the higher age-groups will increase. In other countries, the pattern of change will be different. Changes in the age distribution of the student population affect the total cost of education, as costs per pupil rise with the age of the student. Within a given framework of total costs, they therefore affect the possibilities of expansion in respect of both quantity and quality. A rising population tide will limit the possibilities of raising enrolment and teacher/pupil ratios as well as the qualifications of teachers and the general standards of educational institutions. When the tide is receding, the opposite will be the case.

MARGINAL RETURNS

76. Another aspect of policy decision is how to balance quantity as expressed by enrolment ratios against quality as expressed by the various cost factors. We may further choose between various age-groups when raising enrolment ratios. In all these respects a long-term strategy must aim at a maximum benefit for society within a given framework of total costs. In principle, the optimum solution will have been found when the marginal social return, in terms of consumption values and production growth, equals the marginal expenditure corresponding to variations in any of the cost factors.

77. In economic analysis, it is usually assumed that the marginal return on a given increase of costs declines as we extend the operation. But this assumption does not necessarily apply to education in its present state of development. In many respects, the system is far below the optimum, and for some cost factors the marginal return may actually be increasing, or at least remaining constant, within a fairly wide range.

78. As has been pointed out earlier, the present low enrolment in secondary and higher education does not consist entirely of students who are more able than those who have been excluded. A rise in enrolment ratios combined with a more rational selection of students may therefore take place to a certain extent without a falling marginal return.

79. Similar effects may follow from variations in other cost factors. Classes may be so large and teachers so overloaded that a rise in the teacher/pupil ratio yields a rising or constant return. The same applies to teacher qualifications as reflected by their salaries; a prolonged and more expensive training of teachers may reduce waste of student time in the classroom and thus increase the return. School buildings and other amenities may be so defective that they impede well-organized and efficient studies. Large sectors of the European educational system are so imperfect that increased spending on expansion in several directions may well yield a return that exceeds the marginal

cost. But as long as financial restrictions keep total expenditure below an optimum, we have to strike a balance between the advances that can be made in various directions.

BOTTLE-NECKS AND FLOW OF STUDENT GENERATIONS

80. The attainment of a balanced expansion may in the short term be hindered by:
   a) the existence of bottle-necks;
   b) the time-consuming nature of building a new organization;
   c) the flow of student generations through the school-system.

81. As a result, development in the shorter run may have to be balanced in a way that deviates from desirable long-term objectives.

82. As has been emphasized earlier, the supply of teachers may form a very serious bottle-neck to expansion, particularly so if the drop-out of trained teachers brings about a high ratio of replacement. To train teachers on various levels is a time-consuming process. We may, for example, find it profitable, in relation to the present needs of the economy, to expand secondary education faster than higher education. But this cannot be done for lack of suitably trained teachers. The short-term profitability of expanding higher education then resides in the fact that in due course it will make possible an expansion of secondary education. The effect of a teacher bottle-neck may also be that the expansion of secondary education has to make do with inadequately trained teachers; the long-term benefit of a fast expansion of teacher training may then be high. In a transitional period, a teacher bottle-neck may also force us to keep the teacher/pupil ratio low in order to absorb a growing school population and allow for a rise in the enrolment ratio. Such situations are typical of many European countries and may lead to the acceptance of a suboptimal structure of the school system for a considerable time ahead.

83. Teacher training provides the most important example of the general fact that it takes considerable time to expand a school system without loss of efficiency. It also takes time to plan and organize new educational institutions and to erect the necessary buildings. We might find it profitable to treble the number of university students within the next decade, but the facts of the situation may be such that even a doubling would expose the organization to strains which would lead to a loss of efficiency.

84. Lastly, a basic fact that governs balanced expansion is that students on higher levels of education have to be recruited from the lower levels. A disproportionate development at one level may lead either to a deterioration in the quality of recruits or to an overflow of students at the higher level. It is important therefore to consider how large a part of a student generation can with advantage follow up

their studies on a higher level. This means research into the distribution of student ability. In striking a balance it must be remembered that the market will need a mixture of people with various levels of education. Whether studies should be prolonged for a larger or smaller proportion of students must be decided in the light of the productive effects of marginal changes in this mixture. In striking the balance, we must not forget that we are aiming at a future market, and that these productive effects will depend on the structural changes in the labour market brought about by economic growth.

THE GROWTH OF EXPENDITURE ON EDUCATION

CURRENT EXPENDITURE AND ECONOMIC GROWTH

85. Historical studies indicate that in most countries expenditure on education has in the long run been growing faster than the gross national product.[1] This may partly be explained by the increased demand for educated manpower, partly by the growing propensity to spend on education that follows with growing incomes. Both interpretations may contain an element of truth. The social growth process contains so many complicated inter-relations between technical, social, economic and political factors that any simple causal interpretation would be misleading. All that we can say is that in the general growth process education tends to attract an increasing share of total national resources.

86. The basis for this historical trend is easily seen, if we take into account the behaviour of the various cost factors that make up the total current cost of education.

87. According to expression (6) in para. 73, total current expenditure on education may be regarded as the product of five factors:

$$U = P_s \times e \times t \times W(1 + k) \qquad (7)$$

88. The gross national product, O, may be regarded as the product of two factors, total population, P, and the gross national product per head, o.

$$O = P \times o \qquad (8)$$

89. The relation, R, between total current costs of education, U, and the gross national product, O, may, thus, be written:

$$R = \frac{U}{O} = \frac{P_s}{P} \times e \times t \times \frac{W}{o} \times (1 + k) \qquad (9)$$

90. The five factors which determine the trend in the relation R may

---

1. Cf. Friedrich Edding, Internationale Tendenzen in der Entwicklung der Ausgaben für Schulen und Hochschulen (International Trends in Educational Expenditure). Kieler Studien 47. Kiel 1958.

be studied separately. We shall restrict ourselves here to the following comments.

91. *The relation of population of school age to total population* P_s/P. This relation may change as a result of trends in birth and death rates, trends which may be related to the process of economic growth. The population explosion that follows the transition from a primitive to a more developed society must, for some decades, lead to a rise in the proportion of the population of school age to the total population. The bulge of children that survive pre-school age forms one of the main factors in the rapid rise of expenditure on education in a large number of underdeveloped countries. In more developed countries, there may be temporary shifts in the proportion of population of school age to total population, thus raising or reducing the factor P_s/P. These shifts may be correlated with past economic trends but are in the main independent of current economic growth.

92. *Enrolment ratio* e. As illustrated in Diagram 1, this factor has been growing in most countries. There should, however, be a tendency towards a slackening as a country approaches a high level of development. In underdeveloped countries there may be scope for a rise in enrolment ratios in all age-groups, even though higher education may be slow to develop. In Western Europe, where enrolment in primary schools is almost complete, the rise can take place mainly in secondary and higher education. In the United States, where enrolment in secondary education is probably approaching a ceiling, the rise can take place mainly in higher education.

Diagram 1. HISTORICAL DEVELOPMENT OF ENROLMENT RATIOS IN ENGLAND AND WALES BY AGE GROUPS 1900-1958 PUBLIC PRIMARY AND SECONDARY SCHOOLS

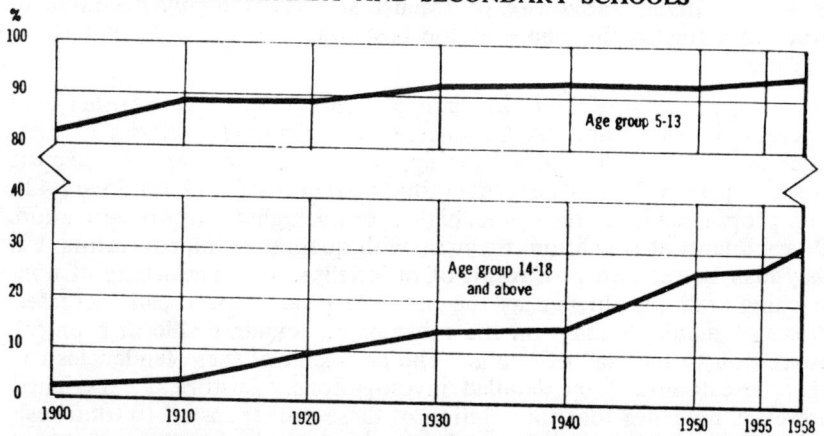

Source: F. Edding, Internationale Tendenzen in der Entwicklung der Ausgaben für Schulen und Hochschulen. (International Trends in Educational Expenditure). Kieler Studien 47. Kiel 1958.—Education in 1950, 1955, 1958, Reports of the Ministry of Education and Statistics for England and Wales. London 1951, 1956, 1959.

93. The rise of enrolment ratios may be related to economic growth and the result expressed in terms of a high income elasticity.

94. *Teacher/pupil ratio* t. In the long term, the number of teachers tends to rise proportionately more than the number of students. This may be explained by three trends:
    a) the number of working hours per teacher is reduced;
    b) the size of classes in various school-stages is reduced;
    c) the shift towards higher levels of education tends on the whole to make for smaller classes.

These trends may explain why income elasticity for the *t* factor is positive.

95. *The relation of teacher salaries to the national product* or income per head $\frac{W}{O}$. It may be expected that in the course of economic growth, salaries of teachers in real terms will in general rise, as do other types of real incomes. The range of salaries for teachers with different qualifications may at the same time change; some evidence indicates that it tends to be narrowed down. An index for salaries with fixed weights for teachers of different qualifications may for reasons of supply and demand rise faster or slower than the general level of income, which may be assumed to follow fairly closely the GNP per head. The weight of teachers with higher salaries will, however, increase, as secondary and higher education is extended. In projecting expenditure on education over a decade, it seems, therefore, to be a reasonable assumption that average teacher salaries do not rise more slowly than GNP per head. Some evidence that seems to support this conclusion is presented in Diagram 2. Turning for a moment to the policy point of view, a relatively rapid rise of teacher salaries is highly desirable in order to attract a fair share of the best brains to the difficult task of teaching.

96. *The relation of total costs to teacher cost* $(1 + k)$. Costs other than teacher salaries include maintenance, school materials, salaries of non-teaching staff, rent of school building, medical services, etc. These costs mostly represent 20 to 30 per cent of total current cost $(1 + k = 1.25 \text{ to } 1.43)$. This proportion is, on the whole, higher for the higher stages of education. On each level of education, they rise with qualitative improvements, but they may be reduced as a result of rationalisation. The wages of non-teaching staff should rise as the national product per head increases. Prices of materials may, on the other hand, remain stable or even fall in relation to the cost of living. The net result of these tendencies can only be established by detailed investigations. Historical experience, however, indicates that the relation of these "other costs" to total costs does not diminish in a process of general economic growth.

97. If we sum up the tendencies of the various cost factors we arrive at a conclusion that may be labelled the "iron law of educational expendi-

Diagram 2. DEVELOPMENT OF TEACHERS' SALARIES[1]
AND GROSS NATIONAL PRODUCT PER CAPITA
IN THE UNITED STATES, 1870-1955

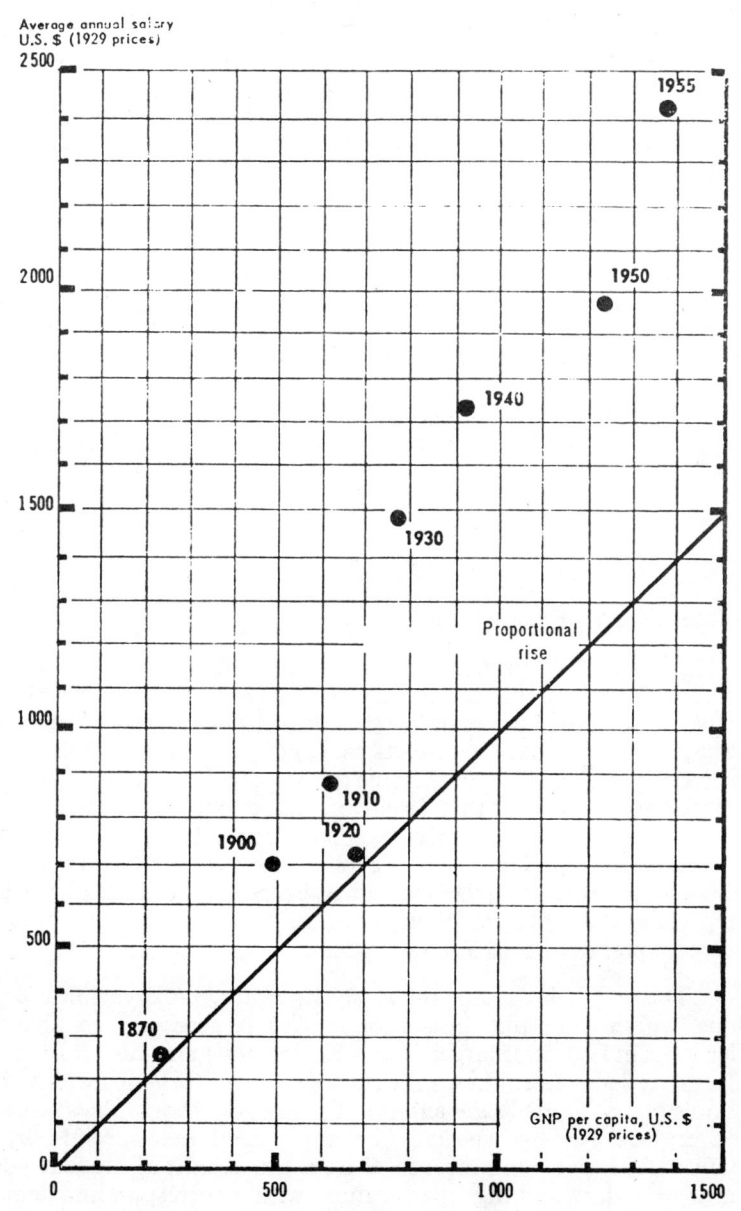

1. Public Elementary and Secondary Day Schools, Instructional Staff.
   Source: Historical Statistics of the United States. Colonial Times to 1957. Washington D.C. 1960, p. 139, 208.

ture" and expressed in the following terms. It is reasonable to assume that, in the long run, teacher salaries will not lag behind the growth of national output per head; it is also reasonable to assume that costs other than teacher salaries will not diminish in relation to the teacher wage bill. If these two assumptions are granted, expenditure on education will rise faster than national output, as enrolment and teacher/pupil ratios have positive income elasticity. The "law" is modified by changes in the age-distribution of the population. It is valid *a fortiori* if the student age-groups rise faster than the total population.

98. It is quite evident that there is no fixed relation between the rise in educational expenditure and the growth of output; there may be periods of acceleration and retardation, depending on the behaviour of the various factors which determine aggregate expenditure. In the end, what happens in a given period depends on the policy decisions that are taken. The argument developed here leads to the conclusion that in the coming decade the share of educational expenditure in European countries should be considerably increased. The implications of such a development may be illustrated by the following example: let us assume that the gross national product of a country in the sixties rises by 50 per cent, and that the share of education in national spending increases from 3 to 4 per cent. Expenditure on education would, then, be twice as high ($1.5 \times 1.33 = 2.0$) in 1970 as it was in 1960.

TRENDS IN CAPITAL EXPENDITURE

99. Investment in buildings and durable equipment for educational institutions should be related to the rate of expansion in the number of students. A study of European investment plans in the field of education indicates, however, that the trends in capital expenditure are largely accounted for by factors other than the growth of the student population. Even in countries where, as a result of falling population figures, the number of students does not increase, plans are made for extensive construction of new buildings. This is explained by the replacement of old buildings by new ones of higher standards, by the migration of population and especially the move to urban areas, and by changes in the internal structure of national educational systems.

100. The last point is not the least important. A diversification of teaching within the same institution makes it necessary to abandon smaller units in favour of larger ones. Larger units may also result from an effort to reduce costs. In some countries, the location of various types of schools has been made the subject of systematic geographical studies. Moreover, new types of specialised schools need new special-purpose buildings. As expansion proceeds, there is also a shift of student population to secondary and higher education, with a corresponding demand for new buildings.

101. These conditions vary from country to country, and it is not

possible to forecast the trend in capital expenditure without a detailed knowledge of local conditions and policies. Any assessment of the trends in the next decade must therefore be based on current expenditure. A rough estimate would, however, be that capital expenditure will continue to amount to some 20 per cent of total expenditure.

THE ALLOCATION OF RESOURCES TO EDUCATION

The Policy Problem

102. The attitude to educational policy may differ between individuals, social groups and political parties. They may have different expectations, as to the social effects of education. We shall, however, assume that educational policy is guided by a certain set of expectations and preferences.

103. Let us suppose that we want to determine the share of educational expenditure in the national product during, say, the next five or ten years. We shall assume that manpower and other factors of production are fully utilized. An increase of expenditure on education can, then, only be obtained at the expense of other types of consumption or investment.

104. A transfer of ressources to education may, however, affect the size of the national product during the period under consideration. If students prolong their studies, the labour force will temporarily be reduced. Over a limited period this reduction cannot, however, be more than fractional in relation to the total supply of labour. A more important effect of an expansion of education may be that some highly trained people will be deflected from industry into the teaching profession; the corresponding loss of production may more than outweigh the increased "output of the educational industry" (as measured in national accounts). In underdeveloped countries, where the number of highly trained people employed in industry is small, such a deflection from industry to education may create serious bottle-necks, with a consequent heavy loss in aggregate current national product. This may be a reason for not letting education expand too fast, though in the more advanced countries where the numbers of highly educated people are already large the risk of creating bottle-necks is far less serious. In the latter case, we may therefore neglect the effects of an expansion of education on the current national product, and concentrate on the longer-term effects on production of allocating more or less resources to education.

Investment in Education or in Real Capital

105. Let us for a moment limit the policy alternatives to a choice between expenditure on education and expenditure on other types of investment. Let us further assume that a policy target is a maximum rate

of growth. The decisive question then arises: would a marginal transfer of, say, $10 million from real capital investment to current expenditure on education accelerate economic growth? On the answer to this question depends how far we want to go in transferring resources to education from other types of investment. If an expansion of both these types of investment is subject to declining marginal return, an optimum point of allocation can evidently be found where the marginal returns are the same. In the case of real capital, the law of declining marginal return has traditionally been taken for granted. But, as has already been pointed out, it may not apply to an "underdeveloped" educational system. If an expansion of education implies that a "reserve" of highly gifted students gets a prolonged education, the marginal return may actually be rising or constant. It is only if we go beyond a certain enrolment ratio that we may expect a declining return. In a situation of "underdevelopment" of the school system, it may therefore pay to raise the level of education far beyond the present point at the expense of real capital investment.

106. We should, however, expect a complementarity, from a productivity point of view, between real capital and investment in education. The marginal return on investment in capital equipment will increase with the supply of educated labour. As accumulation of real capital proceeds, each man has to handle more and more of it. He will handle it with more responsibility and greater efficiency the better he is educated. An historical example of low productivity of real capital as a result of lack of education may be found in the Soviet Union under its first five-year plans; and it was this experience which formed the background for the later emphasis on education in the Soviet Union.

107. However, the consumption aspect of education must also be brought into the picture. If this is done, the allocation of resources to education will rise for two reasons:

a) the value of education as consumption may be deducted from the cost of investment in education, while investment in real capital has no consumption value;

b) we may regard education as complementary, from a welfare point of view, to economic growth. Even if we can reach the same additional growth by $10 million spent on real capital we may prefer education, because growth becomes more meaningful for welfare if the future consumer has a better education.

EDUCATION AND SAVING

108. Since the end of the war, most European countries have raised the share of their gross national product allocated to investment in real capital—which partly explains the acceleration in the growth of their production. How far they want to go in this direction is mainly a question of choosing between consumption now or a more affluent con-

sumption in the future. Will the realization that education is an alternative to investment in real capital induce countries to save more for the future by investing in education now?

109. The arguments developed in this study should provide at least a partial answer to this question. But the problem of saving versus investment may be stated more precisely on the basis of figures drawn from national accounts.

110. Most of the more developed countries in Western Europe have a gross saving that amounts to about 20 per cent of their gross national product. This saving corresponds to investment in real capital. In addition, they are spending about 3 per cent of the gross national product on education. If we add these two figures we get an overall savings and investment ratio of 23 per cent. Countries may hesitate to reduce their current consumption by one per cent and thus raise the overall investment ratio to 24 per cent, if this one per cent is to go into real capital. They may, however, take another view if this one per cent is transferred to investment in education. They have then to weigh the effects on growth of an increase in real capital investment by 1/20 or 5 per cent, against the effects of an increase in expenditure on education by 1/3 or 33 per cent. They also have to take into account the value of this additional education as both current and future consumption. We cannot be certain that countries are willing to increase their savings quota if this additional investment is allocated to education. But it seems very likely that such a policy would be accepted in view of the returns expected from it.

INVESTMENT IN EDUCATION AND TECHNICAL PROGRESS

111. An acceleration of technical progress may partly be a result of an expansion of education, and may therefore be included in the returns on education. However, if we consider nations individually, it becomes evident that technical progress is in part an exogenous factor, most technical innovations being imported. This inflow of technical innovations can be more fully exploited if the educational level is raised. Again, we come back to a complementarity between technical progress and education as factors of production. This complementarity is especially evident in the case of re-education of labour for adjustment to a new technology. This feature should be especially marked in a period when technical progress favours more "intelligence-intensive" industries, as probably is the case at present.

112. But investment in real capital is also complementary to technical progress; it pays to replace old equipment more rapidly if the flow of technical innovations increases. An acceleration of technical progress does not therefore necessarily favour investment in education at the expense of real capital. It pays better, in terms of future growth, to increase investment in both. But this fact must be balanced against the

prevailing time preferences. In a very rich society, the standard of living may already be so high that a possible acceleration of economic growth as a result of technical trends does not induce people to save more and consume less. The growth of production will accelerate anyway, and there will thus be more available for consumption in the future. In a less rich society, on the other hand, the desire for an improvement in the standard of living may be so strong that an acceleration of technical progress, and consequently of economic growth, will induce people to save and invest more in, among other things, education.

INSTITUTIONAL ARRANGEMENTS FOR EDUCATIONAL PLANNING

PLANNING AND FORECASTING

113. The word "planning" has been used as convenient shorthand in this study. What is meant by it, of course, is simply the most careful forecasting of factors in a future situation and intelligently co-ordinated series of actions to secure, within the limits of the possible, the kinds of results that are desired. The preceding sections have emphasized how important it is that, for this purpose, educational development be considered in relation to economic growth and to the general social purposes of democratic society.

114. A pre-requisite for such educational planning is good statistical information. There is always risk in extrapolating from a present situation; one cannot be certain, for instance, whether the trend towards larger or smaller families will continue. But it is even worse to be without up-to-date knowledge of present trends and, in particular, to be unaware of new trends that may be developing. If the age of entry into school is six, one can at least know how many children will have to be provided for in the first class six years from now, though one cannot tell what this figure may be sixteen years hence. One may even try to isolate the factors that have changed the average size of families or the average age of marriage, and hazard a not totally uninformed judgment as to whether these are likely to go on operating for some time ahead.

115. For the purposes of planning education in relation to economic development, information has to be collated from a good many different sources. Obviously, there must be demographic information; information about the tendency to geographic and social mobility of the population; information about the present rate of growth of the economy as a whole, and of different sectors of it, and an analysis of the factors that may make for the continuance or for modification of these rates of growth in the near future; information as to the apparent supply and demand trends for manpower and skills in broad sectors of the economy, and also in certain special professions, not least the teaching profession. All this forms the research basis for educational planning.

The Role of Social Decisions

116.   The future, however, will be built not only on the basis of certain trends, but as the result of deliberate decisions taken by governments or other public or private bodies. These decisions are sometimes a matter of clearly stated aims. For instance, a country that feels itself to be too dependent on a single product, may adopt a deliberate policy of diversifying its economy in clearly defined directions. This will make demands upon the educational system that need to be foreseen and prepared for. Or, to take an example from the social field, a deliberate government policy for generous family allowances, or alternatively of State support for family planning clinics, would be bound to affect the demographic position in so far as the policy was successful. Over a period of, say, a decade, there will certainly be a number of policy decisions taken by governments or by influential organizations of employers that will have repercussions on education.

The Need for an Overall View and Central Decisions

117.   Both these sets of considerations, those relating to research and those relating to policy decisions, indicate the need for an overall view. On the research side, a mass of statistical evidence has to be collated from many different sources: on the policy side, many different decisions have to be brought into the picture and their resultants determined. The conclusion would seem to be inescapable that the machinery for doing this must be central machinery. And the most obvious kind of central machinery would be governmental. Much of the basic evidence can only be collected through government action (e.g. the census). And the most important policy decisions can only be made in the light of knowledge of overall governmental aims and intentions.

The Diversity of Administrative Traditions

118.   It does not follow, however, that educational development can only be properly related to economic growth if there is a single central statistical office, a single central plan, and a single central machine for implementing this plan. There is great variety in the administrative traditions of the different countries of Europe, and no arrangements are likely to be successful if they do serious violence to historic traditions and existing practice.

119.   The aim is one thing, the machinery for attaining it is another. It should be stressed here that the problem of appropriate machinery for relating educational and economic growth is one to which serious attention should be given in every country; for at present it is often done in a haphazard way, and at best governed by *ad hoc* consideration of particular needs without reference to general trends which set limits and entail balancing some factors against others.

120. In countries where there is a tradition of centralized administration, it will seem natural to bring education within the orbit of any central planning office. This is indeed the case in France, where the Commissariat du Plan, though not usurping the administrative functions of the Ministry of National Education, is very much concerned with education as an element of economic growth. Indeed, within the framework of political democracy, such a planning office might be assigned tasks coming close to the point of political decisions. This is the case, for instance, in Jamaica, where in recent years educational developments have been coherently related to the projected economic expansion of the island and the resultant increase in government revenue through the agency of the planning staff in the Chief Minister's office.

121. There are, however, countries where the tradition of devolution of powers is strong, and perhaps especially so in education. Here it will probably be useful to distinguish fairly sharply between the research side and the decision side of planning. The research responsibility may rest on institutions affiliated to universities or Government agencies, which will of course be in the closest touch with the Ministry of Education and the economics Ministries. But in such countries (the United Kingdom is a good example) there is usually an intermediate stage between the accumulation of relevant data, research and governmental decisions on policy. This is the stage of the advisory committee. Ministers may or may not accept the advice of such committees. If they do, their position with the public is strengthened. If they do not, they have had at least the opportunity to test reactions on representative people before taking their own line. Now such advisory committees are usually set up by single departments of government and, although officials from other departments may be present on occasion as observers, the experience of several relevant departments is rarely pooled on an equal basis unless the matter for discussion and decision reaches what in the United Kingdom would be called "Cabinet level".

122. Once the realization grows that there is real need fot relating educational planning more effectively with economic growth, it should not be too difficult to make empirical adjustments to existing machinery. The main difficulty may be psychological; in this work, departmentalism must give way to a broader national view—something which is not always easy to bring about. But without it, education will fail the economy and the economy will fail education.

In this Survey, the O.E.E.C. area represents the 18 Member Countries mentioned on the introductory page to this document plus Yugoslavia, which participates in certain of the activities of the Organization. The O.E.C.D. area includes, in addition, Canada and the United States of America.

For the purposes of this Survey countries have been grouped in the following way:

Northern Countries:

Denmark, Iceland, Republic of Ireland, Norway, Sweden, United Kingdom.[1]

France-Benelux:

France, Belgium, Netherlands and Luxembourg.

Austria, Germany (F.R.), Switzerland:

Unless otherwise stated, Germany F.R. excludes West Berlin and the Saar.

Mediterranean Countries (plus Portugal):

Greece, Italy, Portugal, Spain, Turkey, Yugoslavia.

North America:

Canada and the United States.

---

1. The United Kingdom comprises England, Wales, Scotland and Northern Ireland; Great Britain does not include Northern Ireland.

III

PERSPECTIVES FOR EDUCATION IN THE NEXT DECADE

CURRENT NATIONAL PLANNING

Dynamic and Integrated Planning of Education

123.   All European countries are planning to expand their education, but the methods and scope of their planning vary within a wide range. The regular forecasting of possible developments, taking into account the dynamic factors of demographic evolution, economic growth and changes in demand, is a relatively recent practice, and it will take at least a decade for it to be generally adopted.

124.   Only a few countries have so far worked out integrated national plans for the whole educational system. Others have plans for the development of certain sectors only. In some cases, public or private bodies have made studies or prepared plans which are now receiving public or official attention. In many cases study is limited to the basic conditions for educational development, such as the age limits for compulsory education, subsidies to schools, scholarships for the training of teachers, etc.

125.   It should be remembered, however, that selective secondary and higher education being voluntary, the growth of the educational system cannot be decided solely by the government and depends to a large extent on decisions of parents and students. These decisions must therefore be forecast and taken into account in any planning. It is government action that largely determines educational possibilities by providing the physical amenities and the teaching staff.

126.   National plans thus give only a vague idea of the prospective development of education in Europe during the next decade. The situation in individual countries in this respect is summarized below.

Machinery for Planning

127.   The degree to which the various countries appreciate the need for planning in education varies widely, and the type of planning machi-

nery they favour varies correspondingly. An advanced pattern is characterized by close co-operation between government, institutional research, experts from various fields, and representatives of social groups. Besides consultative bodies mainly concerned with *ad hoc* matters, there are "built-in" planning units covering all relevant fields of education and preparing on a continuing basis the necessary information for policy makers. Such planning agencies can exist in principle irrespective of the degree of government centralization. They can be, and are, organized according to a country's political tradition, and should only be judged by their technical efficiency.

128.   *France* offers an outstanding example of advanced educational planning. Forecasting and planning activities are entrusted mostly to the Commission de l'Equipement Scolaire, Universitaire et Sportif, an integral part of the French Commissariat Général du Plan. The Commission incorporates heads of departments of the Ministries of Education, Finance, Interior, Construction, as well as representatives of higher education, municipal administration, trade-unions, employers' associations and family associations. A great deal of work is done by sub-committees concerned with forecasting the development of student numbers, calculating the demand for teachers and buildings, tackling the problems of timing and financing, and also the economic and technical aspects of school construction. The sub-committes co-operate with other national organizations, such as the Institut National d'Etudes Démographiques, the Bureau Universitaire Statistique, and the Institut National de la S atistique et des Etudes Economiques. Experts and private agencies are called in as the need arises.

129.   Whereas France can traditionally rely on forms of centralized administration of public education, the tradition in *Great Britain* is one of devolution to local educational authorities, and indeed to schools themselves. But the Ministry of Education[1] has a clear responsibility for general direction—especially since the Education Act of 1944—and it fulfils a very real function in forecasting and planning. Considered advice on planned developments is given by permanent or *ad hoc* advisory committees, which can avail themselves of information and services provided by officials in the relevant Ministries, particularly the Statistical Branch of the Ministry of Education. Studies pertaining to educational development are also undertaken within the universities (e.g. by the Research Unit in the Economics and Administration of Edu.ation at the University of London Institute of Education) and by interested bodies such as local authorities and teachers' organizations. Decisions may be said to be the resultant of various components; studies of the kind indicated, advice of committees, administrative, financial and political considerations.

---

1. As far as England and Wales are concerned, and the Department of Education in the case of Scotland.

130. Sweden and the Netherlands offer further examples of "built-in" educational forecasting and planning agencies. In *Sweden* a forecasting unit with a large research staff has been established within the Labour Market Board. It investigates long-term trends in the demand for various types of education and training. Special planning problems, such as the extension to 9 years of compulsory schooling to include occupational education and training, are delegated to Royal Commissions. A special unit in the Department of Education co-ordinates all planning activities.

131. In the *Netherlands* the Research Department of the Ministry of Education, Arts and Sciences is concerned with the regular forecasting of the number of pupils in primary education and the corresponding demand for teachers. Other planning work, e.g. on higher education, is carried out by advisory bodies such as the Commission for the Development of Higher Education. Planning activities in the Netherlands find an excellent base in the elaborate education statistics provided by the Central Statistical Office.

132. In the *United States* there is no institutional machinery for planning and forecasting, but the many methods and means used amount, in fact, to planning. Thus, several States initiate and support work on educational planning which is carried out by special commissions or private bodies. Federal bodies, or institutions working on a federal level (e.g. the Office of Education, or the National Science Foundation), concern themselves to a certain extent with problems related to future needs and demands in the field of education. In the U.S.A., as in some other countries, central teachers' unions have done remarkable work in the field of forecasting. The fact that the control of education lies with the States and the local school districts makes it difficult effectively to deal with some of the fundamental issues in education on a national basis. Planning activities on the federal level are, therefore, usually of a guiding nature only.

133. In certain countries the backbone of permanent planning units is still missing, and planning is mostly done by *ad hoc* commissions. The *Federal Republic of Germany* can be taken as an example. Here education at all levels is controlled almost entirely by the States. Only two or three of the eleven States' Ministries, however, employ a statistician or see to it that probable changes in the number of pupils and teachers are regularly forecast. A certain harmonization of developments is assured by the Permanent Conference of Ministers of Education (Ständige Konferenz der Kultusminister) and its large secretariat. Since 1954 a central committee on education has been working out recommendations for expansion and reform of educational institutions. These proposals, predominantly concerned with changes in structure and content, and lacking statistical background information, have been widely discussed; but, so far, the proposed reforms have only been partially adopted. A more realistic kind of planning is done by the

Council for the Development of Higher Education and Research (Wissenschaftsrat). In 1960 representatives of the States, the Federal Government and the universities, together with some leading personalities, assisted by an efficient planning unit and numerous working groups, completed the first part of their task. Their recommendations contain a flexible overall plan for university development giving a quantitative framework for personnel, buildings and costs for the period 1960 to 1965.

134. A similar situation can be found in *Switzerland*, where no systematic forecasting has been done so far. But this attitude seems to be changing. In 1957 the Federal authorities established an *ad hoc* commission to promote the expansion of scientific and technical personnel. This commission submitted in 1959 a final report on the demand and supply, present and future, of scientists, engineers and technicians. Furthermore, it recommended that systematic forecasting should in future be carried out by the universities, institutes of technology and technical schools on the supply side, and by the Federal Bureau for Industry, Arts and Crafts and Labour, working in conjunction with economic associations and industriel organizations, on the demand side.

135. The Mediterranean countries, together with Portugal, have agreed to collaborate with the O.E.E.C. in the establishment of national planning teams to relate their educational expansion to the requirements of future economic growth. The major endeavours by the six countries concerned—*Greece, Italy, Spain, Portugal, Turkey* and *Yugoslavia*— to work out their educational needs for the next fifteen years and to provide Ministers of Education and Finance with detailed programmes is undoubtedly one of the most advanced projects of its kind within the O.E.E.C. and beyond. Both the work and the costs are shared by the Office for Scientific and Technical Personn 1 of O.E.E.C. A good deal of research work has already been carried out and the governments concerned have shown themselves to be encouragingly open-minded towards the idea of long-term planning in education.

MEASURES PLANNED OR UNDER CONSIDERATION

136. If one surveys the decisions taken and the targets set, it becomes apparent that most countries aim at both the expansion and the reform of the educational system at all levels.

Compulsory Education

137. One obvious trend is the general drive for longer compulsory education. In some of the Mediterranean countries prolongation from 4, 5 and 6 years to 6, 7 and 8 years is officially envisaged. These are big strides. In most other countries one year more, i.e. a ninth compulsory year, is actually planned. For some of the highly-industrialized countries the prolongation of compulsory education will be no

more than the statutory confirmation of a spontaneous development. The constant rise in the standard of living and the changing demands of employers in these countries have induced more and more parents to give their children a better education. This is particularly true of the urban population. In *Sweden*, for instance, where compulsory education is to be extended from 7 to 9 years, 80 per cent already attend the eighth school year and 30 per cent the ninth year. In *France* the extension of compulsory education to 10 years has already been decided by the Ordonnance of 9th December, 1959, on educational reform, and the same target is under serious consideration in other countries. In *England* and *Wales*, the "Crowther Report" has recommended the introduction of an eleventh year of compulsory education from 1968 onwards, but so far the Government has not given priority to this reform. Nevertheless, the United Kingdom is at the head of the list as regards the length of compulsory education, but will soon be sharing this position with France. In the *Federal Republic of Germany* the Permanent Conference of Ministers of Education has agreed gradually to introduce a ninth compulsory school year. A tenth year has been discussed but does not seem likely to be introduced in the near future. The Mediterranean countries are all aware of the desirability of raising educational standards on both economic and social grounds. The need for improvement in this area is illustrated by the example of *Italy*. While in Northern Italy enrolment ratios in primary schools are comparable with those of North European countries, in Southern Italy a certain proportion of pupils do not even complete five years' compulsory education.

138. It is obvious that the extension of compulsory education will raise considerably the enrolment ratios of the age groups concerned. In *Norway*, for example, the enrolment ratio for the 15-year old is expected to rise from 66 per cent in 1960 to 100 per cent in 1970, and that for the 16-year old from 62 per cent to 100 per cent. In France the enrolment ratio for the 15-year old will go up from 56 per cent to 100 per cent in 1970. These rises will doubtless aggravate the serious problems of the supply of teachers, buildings and equipment, and careful planning will clearly be of great help in mastering these difficulties.

Secondary Education

139. Another obvious trend is the expansion and democratization of secondary education. In *Sweden*, for example, education in the age group 17-19 is being rapidly expanded; more than 30 per cent of this age group is now enrolled in various types of schools and, according to the estimates of the Swedish Department of Education, the proportion will approach 50 per cent at the end of the 1960's. In *Norway* the proportion of the 19-year age group having completed the "gymnasium" is expected to rise from 13 per cent in 1961 to 25 per cent in 1970. In *Denmark*, too, the expansion of secondary education facilities is well

under way. Among the Mediterranean countries, *Yugoslavia* is planning to expand secondary education and to step up the enrolment of the relevant age group from 17 per cent in 1957 to 29 per cent in 1965.

140. In *England* and *Wales* the proposals of the Crowther Committee are now being followed up by the work of the Newsom Committee[1] which is considering the content of full-time education between the ages of 13 and 16 of pupils of average or less than average ability. In *France* the 1959 law stipulates the progressive institution of a two-year period of "observation" (cycle d'observation) for all children between the ages of 12 and 14, i.e. at the beginning of secondary education, in order to evaluate their aptitudes and intellectual ability and to guide them into short or long, technical or general education. In *Germany (F.R.)* similar recommendations (Förderstufe) have been worked out by a central committee on education. They are being widely discussed but are unlikely to be generally implemented in this decade.

TABLE 1. ENROLMENT RATIOS ACCORDING TO FRENCH PLANS
(1954-1976)

Percentages.

AGE	1954	1957	1960	1963	1966	1969	1972	1976
15	45.0	50.0	56.0	64.0	71.0	100.0	100.0	100.0
16	37.0	40.5	45.5	51.0	57.5	62.0	63.5	65.0
17	23.5	26.2	29.5	33.5	38.0	41.5	42.8	44.0
18	13.2	15.2	17.5	20.5	24.0	27.0	28.7	29.5
19	8.3	9.8	10.4	11.9	13.4	14.6	15.6	16.2
20	5.7	6.1	6.6	7.3	8.1	9.1	9.8	10.4
21	4.0	4.3	4.5	5.1	5.6	6.3	6.7	7.1
22	2.8	3.1	3.4	3.8	4.2	4.6	4.9	5.3
23	2.3	2.5	2.8	3.1	3.4	3.7	3.9	4.2
24	1.8	2.0	2.2	2.4	2.6	2.8	3.0	3.3

Source: Unpublished calculations and estimates made by the Institut National de la Statistique et des Études Économiques. Paris - 12283 60.

Higher Education

141. For obvious reasons, economic and political, educational policies are focussed on higher education, particularly on science and technology. In the *United States*, for example, the number of college students is expected to be almost doubled by 1970, rising from 3.58 million in 1959 to 6.44 million in 1970, 2.2 million of the latter being in private institutions. In particular, mathematics, natural sciences and engineering are to be given a larger place within the educational framework.

142. In *Great Britain* it would seem that on the basis of preliminary agreements the number of university students in 1970 can be

---

1. The former Amory Committee.

estimated at 154,000 (as against some 100,000 in 1959). This target is to be reached by expanding existing universities and by creating seven new ones. But many influential voices have been raised in favour of a much higher target and seem agreed upon a figure of 170,000 to 175,000 student places by 1970. Sir Geoffrey Crowther, in a personal capacity, has suggested that the aim should be between 250,000 and 350,000 places as soon as possible. In the field of technical education the number of students is expected to double in a decade.

143. In *France* a great effort is being made by the Government with the broad aim of increasing the capacity of the universities and equivalent institutions from the present 220,000 places to 500,000 places in 1970. The expansion of science education is receiving special attention.

144. The *Swedish* Parliament, too, has adopted a plan for rapid university expansion. The student number is expected to rise by 50 per cent to 100 per cent in the various faculties, which would mean an enrolment of about 11 per cent of the relevant age groups. The most rapid expansion is to take place in scientific and technical education. Parliament has adopted a law by which financial assistance to universities is automatically adjusted to the student number. Similar developments can be seen in Norway and in the Netherlands. In *Norway*, the capacity of higher institutions is to be increased from 10,000 students in 1960 to at least 18,500 in 1970. In *the Netherlands* the total number of students is expected to double in the period 1959-1973. Again stress is laid on science and technology.

145. In comparison, the position in *Germany (F.R.)*, as far as expansion is concerned, seems to be less favourable. There is a loose overall plan for university development, but the basic problems of university reform have not yet been brought nearer to solutions. *Switzerland* is concentrating its efforts on the expansion of technical education. *Austria* is planning a re-organization of university studies, but no major changes are to be expected.

146. The Mediterranean countries are also stepping up their higher and technical education. *Yugoslavia* believes that the number of university students can be raised from 3.5 par cent of the age group 20-24 in 1957 to 11 per cent in 1965. In *Spain* and *Portugal* interest is centred on expanding scientific and technical education. *Italy* is improving higher education within the general framework of the Government's ten-year education development plan, which provides for a 50 per cent increase (in constant prices) of public expenditure on all levels of education between 1959 and 1969. This plan has not yet received Parliamentary assent.

147. A survey of all these plans gives the impression that expansion is more stressed than reform. There is, however, a certain awareness that expansion will of itself bring about a change of content.

PRESENT DIMENSIONS OF EDUCATION

The Problematic Statistical Basis[1]

Obsolescence of Education Statistics

148. Almost all the reports on education published in the last ten years point out the inadequacy of statistical information. It is generally felt that statistics of education are inadequate in coverage, precision and analytical value in comparison with most other social and economic statistics. If this has been a handicap at the national level, even in the most highly-developed countries, it has proved a veritable obstacle in any attempt to assess and analyze educational developments at the international level. Experts in comparative education are therefore resigned to restricting their efforts mostly to comparisons of ideas, systems and tendencies.

149. The situation is even worse when it is a question of investigating inter-dependencies of economic and educational developments and making forecasts for a decade ahead. Education statistics are not as yet designed to answer questions raised by the more dynamic thinking of modern economics and social sciences. It cannot be emphasized too strongly that they should be conceived in terms of demographic change and of inter-dependencies between economic growth and education, in short, in terms of inter-dependencies between education and the dynamics of social and economic change. Nor can the importance of an international standardization of education statistics be stressed too much.

150. In attempting to overcome the statistical obstacles and to trace at least an outline of the magnitudes and relationships involved, in terms of students, teachers and expenditure for this study, gaps of information had in many cases to be closed by personal estimates. The figures given here may therefore be subject to many criticisms in respect of both the information they provide and the information they do not provide. It is obvious that this lack of proper statistics is undermining the positions of education in society and that it is a problem no less serious than any other in the field of education.

Problems in Measuring Educational Effort

151. Any assessment of the dimensions of education must be based mainly on measurable quantities, such as numbers of students and teachers and amounts of expenditure as regularly reported to authorities and organizations. This means leaving out of account education in the family, in religious communities, in the army, in industry, in youth organizations, in political parties, etc. and, last but not least, education by mass media. These forms of education do not lend themselves to

---

1. See also Manual of Educational Statistics, first edition, Unesco, 1961. The manual was prepared under the supervision of Dr B. A. Liu.

measurement and they vary considerably in strength and formative power from country to country. To grow up in an industrial and highly-developed civilization, or in a predominantly agricultural society, may mean two very different kinds of "functional" education. On the other hand, it can be argued that formal education in the countries covered in this study reflects to a large extent the level of social and economic development and the strength of the other forms of education.

152. In assessing the dimensions of formal education, the deficiency of our statistical basis becomes apparent. It lies not so much in the incomplete coverage of formal education as a whole as in the lack of data relating to certain essential factors of formal education.

The Fallacy of Enrolment Figures

153. Double counting may lead to errors, and it is not known how far they have been avoided here. In many cases, a choice had to be made between two or three different enrolment figures—all provided by official sources! But even graver inaccuracies result from the very wide variations in the number of hours students spend in formal education. We tried to get over this difficulty by counting, for example, four part-time pupils each attending 8 hours a week as the equivalent of one full-time pupil; but this attempt had to be abandoned because most countries do not give the average number of hours spent in part-time education. By using almost exclusively figures of full-time education, we have thus understated the educational effort of countries in which part-time education is of more than average importance.[1] The figures are restricted in general to the age groups 5 to 24. Since education before and after these age limits is of considerable and increasing importance in many countries, we have here another possible source of understatement and distortion.

154. These pitfalls only serve to stress the need for more and better educational statistics. The counting of students as well as teachers by the number of hours they work in school would be more realistic than counting enrolments and teaching staff in the conventional way. After all, we are quite accustomed now to measuring the input of work in industry by the number of hours. Since the differences in the length of time students spend in various types of formal education tend to increase, the mere counting of students is becoming more and more meaningless.

Enrolment Ratios as a Yardstick

155. The percentage of single year age groups of the population receiving formal education can be a good index of educational effort. To

---

1. For the Soviet Union, evening courses and correspondence courses have been included as, more than in other countries, they form an essential part of the educational system; their content is the same and they lead to the same examinations as full-time courses.

compare the numbers of students in different countries by types of educational institutions is rather confusing; there are too many variations of terminology and content. Classification by "level" in the Unesco definition may partly help to overcome this difficulty, but it can never give completely clear-cut results. The surest way of measuring educational efforts is—possibly in combination with the "level" concept—to count students in terms of percentage of their age group. It may be interesting to know that 100,000 young people are in education at the second level, but from the point of view of the economist and the forecaster it is more essential to know what percentages of the 17-year old and of the 18-year old are in formal education, and thus withheld from gainful employment.

156. Enrolment ratios are certainly one of the most important elements of forecasting. A growing number of countries, therefore, are now regularly compiling statistics of students by single year of age. On this basis we have been able to establish enrolment ratios for standard age groups. But for about half the countries covered here this had to be done more or less by estimates, and in some cases these estimates are not all that could be desired. Furthermore, it was soon found that the enrolment ratios provided by national agencies sometimes included part-time education of unspecified size and proportion. An effort was made to eliminate such distortions, but there is no way of knowing how far it has been successful. The necessity of conforming to a standard method in calculating these ratios cannot be stressed too strongly.

Number of Teachers and Real Teaching Input

157. Teachers are the key factor in formal education—results depend essentially on their number and quality. Teachers' salaries are the predominant item in education expenditure. One might expect, therefore, that records of the number of teachers would always be established with great care. Unfortunately, this is not the case, and to assess the numbers of teachers in the base year was one of our most difficult tasks. For one highly-developed country no official figures for the number of teachers could be obtained at all. The difficulties are due partly to the inadequacy of reports from private institutions, partly to the fact that many principals do administrative work as well as teaching, and partly to the fact that instructors in subjects like needlework, cooking, craft, etc. are traditionally counted as teachers in certain countries but not in others. Confusion also results from the fact that teachers often work in two or more types of school; the same person may teach in the morning in a grammar school, in the afternoon in a vocational school, and lecture at night at a university. In some countries such double counting seems to be quite extensive.

158. In order to avoid overstatement, only full-time teachers were taken into account. But since part-time teaching is gaining more and more in importance, we may in fact have relatively understated the real

teaching capacity in some countries. Here the solution seems to be to count by the number of hours "at the desk".

159. There is also need for a much better classification of non-teaching personnel in educational institutions. This should be done on the basis of some kind of "job analysis" which is now the basis of work organization in other spheres. The division of labour in education is already leading to the employment of more and more non-teaching staff (secteraries, supervisors, administrators, librarians) which enables teachers to concentrate on their essential task. This should be taken into account when measuring educational effort. Unfortunately the inadequacy or complete absence of information on non-teaching personnel tends to distort international comparisons considerably.

160. But it is the quality of teachers which is really the decisive factor. It is not easy to measure this quality. To some extent it may be expressed in length of training; some countries have begun to give a break-down of teacher numbers by length of training. The extent to which division of labour permits the teacher to give his optimum can be regarded as another indicator. The relative position of teachers' salaries in the salary structure would also be an excellent indicator; unfortunately, the relevant statistics are as yet very rare and certainly not adequate as a basis for international comparisons. Last but not least, the student/teacher ratio can greatly influence the quality of education. Here, fortunately, we have a great deal of statistical data at our disposal.

Student/Teacher Ratio as Quality Index

161. The average number of students per teacher in different parts of the educational system is an important index. A low ratio may mean that a teacher in forty years of work will have guided through school life only a few hundred students; a high ratio that he has guided a thousand or more students. The results, both for the students and for society in general, are supposed to be better in the first case; in other words, the productivity concept as related to industry cannot be applied to the student/teacher ratio. Contrary to what happens in industrial production, it is not to be expected that the same or better results can be obtained by an ever-diminishing number of teachers per 100 students. Rationalization can be introduced into education in many ways, but we cannot escape the fact that the very essence of education resides in the close contact between teacher and student.

162. This does not mean that good results can only be expected in small classes, and that the smaller the class the better; there is no proof for such a theory in empirical research; excellent teachers may get excellent results in very big classes. On the other hand, there seems to be convincing evidence that the average teacher does not get optimal results if the classes have more than 25 to 30 students; otherwise it would be difficult to understand why the average class in general education has been reduced to this size in most of the higlhy-developed countries.

Classes of 80 to 100 were common in primary education in Europe around 1900, and there must have been good reason to go to all the expense of providing the large additional number of teachers needed to reduce the class size.

163. But the number of hours of weekly work in the classroom scheduled for each student and for each teacher is at least as important as the average size of classes. The perfomance of the average teacher depends largely on the number of hours he has to work in and outside school. Diminishing his work load will in general improve his performance, and a low student/teacher ratio would tend in this direction. This is not to say that better use could not be made of the skilled teacher. Many teachers spend much time and energy on minor non-teaching duties; this is a waste of manpower, at least in reasonably large schools. It may also be that in teaching (especially in that part of it that is merely instructional) there could be a more rational distribution of work between the highly-trained and experienced teacher on the one hand, and the less trained or experienced teacher and teaching machines on the other.

164. The immediate question is whether the student/teacher ratio can be considered as an index of quality for international comparisons. It is our opinion that it could be—provided it were supplemented by other information. For this, adequate statistics would have to be available. Unfortunately, this is not the case at present. The different factors, such as the hours of weekly work, etc. which have been mentioned above, are seldom sufficiently analyzed. Furthermore, the relative part played by small schools such as rural one-teacher schools is usually not clearly shown. Strangely enough, it is about the most important factor in education—the teacher—that we know the least.

165. Statistics of teachers (as well as of other personnel in education) should be established on the basis of length of training, function and hours of work. To get something more realistic than the present student/teacher ratio, the teaching input calculated on this basis should be related to the number of hours students are in class. In making this calculation, education in small communities should also be treated separately.

Expenditure on Education—an Uncharted Territory

166. Education in most countries is controlled and financed not only at different levels of government, but even at the same level by different authorities; and it is also partly controlled and financed by private institutions. The attempt to base our survey on the accounts from all these sources has not been altogether successful, in particular, because the accounts of private education seem often to be shrouded in mystery. In the latter case, rough estimates of expenditure have been made on the basis of student numbers in private schools and of current expenditure per student in public institutions. Subsidies from public funds for private formal education had then to be deducted. Capital expenditure of

private schools had often to be omitted as there was no valid way of estimating it.

167. International comparisons of educational effort in terms of money would be very much distorted if countries having no private schools were compared with countries having a large sector of private education but showing only public expenditure in their statistics. The example of the United States, which has a large sector of private education, proves that no harm is done by revealing expenditure on private education. Effort should be made to introduce similar reporting procedures everywhere. In particular, public subsidies should be given only to institutions regularly and fully reporting on their finances.

168. By tradition education expenditure is often aggregated in the budget with expenditure on general cultural activities and research. We have tried to exclude expenditure not having a direct bearing on formal education (e.g. for youth activities, libraries, museums, research outside educational institutions, and mass media like radio and television), but this could only be done where a break down of total expenditure was available. In order to ascertain that part of current expenditure which is serving purely educational purposes, Unesco has introduced in its questionnaires the concept of instructional expenditure. This concept has been very useful for our survey. It is useful for instance, to separate fringe expenditure (meals, board, grants, etc.) from salaries.

169. It has not been possible to ascertain how far pensions or payments into pension funds are considered part of salaries and therefore of instructional expenditure. We assumed that some allowance for pensions or payments into pension funds is included almost everywhere, this item being relatively large in some countries and relatively small in others. It seems probable that salaries are higher in the latter case, in order to permit teachers to contribute to private pension funds. On this hypothesis, international comparability would not be too much affected by the different methods of providing for retirement.

170. On the whole, an international survey of education expenditure still resembles the exploration of an uncharted territory. To work out an international system of standard definitions for educational finance as has been done for national accounts in general, but also as far as the detailed costing of educational enterprise is concerned, must indeed be considered a very urgent task. It would serve not only for macroeconomic purposes and for international comparisons, but also provide a better basis for the much neglected field of internal cost accounting.

171. Expenditure figures given here are expressed in U.S. dollars at the 1959 rates of exchange.[1] No doubt these rates do not always express the particular purchasing power of education expenditure, and thus do not provide a perfect basis for international comparability; but there

---

1. The exchange rate of March 1960 was taken for Iceland.

appeared to be no alternative. Figures for 1970 are given in base year prices.

172. For all these reasons, the international tables on expenditure given here should not be regarded as exact indicators of comparative educational effort; they give only a very rough outline of the magnitudes involved and their main value is as a means of demonstrating the need to increase the share of educational expenditure in the gross national product of each country.

Gross National Product, Population and Base Year

173. We have used national statistics and data from O.E.E.C. publications. The gross national products have been converted into U.S. dollars at the official exchange rates of 1959. Figures of GNP as well as of population do not always refer to exactly the same period or date as the figures from expenditure accounts and school statistics. In relating those different sets of figures, therefore, certain discrepancies could not be avoided.

174. Nor was it possible to get the basic educational figures for all countries for the same year. As can be seen from tables on individual countries (see Appendix II) the base year in most cases is 1957-1958, but for some countries the appropriate figures were only available for 1956 or for 1959-1960. In grouping together certain countries, there was no choice but to add together figures for different years.

Presentation of Statistics

175. In presenting the statistics, the aim could not be to give a collection of case studies employing different terms and figures according to the usage in different countries; there would have been hardly any international comparability in such a collection of data or in forecasts based on them. The data have therefore been transformed so as to have a standard model of presentation which makes it possible to show clearly the effects of changes in population, enrolment ratios, student/teacher ratios and GNP *per capita* on the educational systems of some twenty countries.

176. Much could be said for the use of "levels" of education as recommended by Unesco, but this definition does not yet seem to be generally or uniformly used. Furthermore, in the present state of statistics, it seemed impossible to express population and enrolment changes adequately by "level". It was therefore decided to use standard age groups of population (5 to 14, 15 to 19, 20 to 24) as an overall framework for presenting figures of students and teachers as well as of expenditure. Nearly all figures had thus to be transformed accordingly, either by calculation or by estimate. Such standardization has certain drawbacks; significant features and even certain sectors of national systems of education are altogether ignored. As already mentioned,

nurseries, infant schools and similar institutions, in as far as they enrol children under five, are not included in our figures; rather large numbers of students over 24 had also to be excluded.

177. Because of a later entrance age, it may appear as though some countries had a rather low enrolment ratio in the age group 5-14. In many cases, however, a later entrance age will also result in relatively higher enrolment ratios in the next age group, as children starting school at the age of seven are more likely to stay on until the age of sixteen than children starting school at the age of five or six. For similar reasons, and also the length of courses, the average age limits of higher education will differ.

178. The classification by standard age groups may seem inadequate to those seeking information about groups in certain specific types of education in their own country. They find, for example, some students in higher education in the age group 15-19 and some in the group 20-24, mingled in both cases with students in many other types of education. Higher education proper does not appear at all. This may seem odd but, on the other hand, in an international survey there are definite advantages in classifying full-time students by standard age groups, irrespective of the type of educational institution they attend. This procedure gives unprecedented possibilities of outlining orders of magnitude, of assessing proportions and of forecasting possible developments.

179. Instead of presenting the statistical details for each of the 22 countries, ranging small countries like Iceland or Luxembourg alongside big nations like the U.S.A. or the U.S.S.R., it was decided to aggregate countries in groups more or less equal as regards population and gross national product. In forming these groups, the authors were guided by certain historical and geographical affinities.

MAGNITUDE OF PRESENT EDUCATIONAL EFFORT

Population and Student Numbers

180. In the base year there were some 50 million full-time students in the O.E.E.C. area (including Yugoslavia). This represents about one in seven of the population, and does not take account of full-time students over 24 nor of part-time students. The distribution of these 50 million students by the three age groups is shown in Diagram 4. While it is true that the first is a ten-year group and the other two are only five-year groups, the disproportion in their sizes also reflects the comparatively low enrolment ratios in the higher stages of education in Europe.

181. How does the European educational system compare numerically with those of North America (U.S.A. and Canada) and of the Soviet Union?

182. In North America student numbers account for 23 per cent (almost one in four) of the total population, as against 15 per cent in the O.E.E.C. area. The most striking difference appears in the second age

TABLE 2. DURATION OF COMPULSORY FULL-TIME EDUCATION BY COUNTRIES IN BASE YEAR[1]

AREAS AND COUNTRIES	AGE LIMITS[2] SCHOOL ENTRANCE	END OF COMPULSORY EDUCATION	NUMBER OF YEARS IN COMPULSORY EDUCATION[3]
Northern countries:			
Denmark	7	14	7
Iceland	7	15	8
Ireland	6	14	8
Norway	7	14/15	7-8
Sweden	6/7	14/15	7-8
United Kingdom	5	15	10
France—Benelux:			
France	6	14	8
Belgium	6	14	8
Netherlands	6/7	14/15	8
Luxembourg	6	14	8
Austria, Germany, Switzerland:			
Austria	6/7	14/15	8
Germany, F.R.	6	14/15	8-9
Switzerland	6/7	14/16	7-9
Mediterranean countries: [3]			
Greece	6	12/14	6-8
Italy[4]	6	11	5
Portugal	7	13	6
Spain	6	12	6
Turkey	6	12	6
Yugoslavia	7	15	8
Canada—United States:			
Canada	6/7	13/16	7-10
United States	5/7	14/18	9-12
Soviet Union	7	14/17	7-10

1. 1958 or nearest year.
2. The fact that in some cases there are several age limits and/or a range of years of compulsory education is due to:
   a) the existence of a transition period during which old regulations are still in force while new regulations are gradually being introduced; and/or
   b) the autonomy of authorities other than central government with respect to the determination of compulsory education.
3. The number of years of compulsory education indicated is, in many cases, not attained in practice because of lack of educational facilities.
4. An extension of compulsory education to 14 years of age is to te introduced in Italy.
Source: International Yearbook of Education. Published jointly by Unesco, Paris and the International Bureau of Education, Geneva. Vols 19 (1957), 20 (1958), 21 (1959).

group (15-19); in North America it represents a percentage of total population more than three times as high as in the O.E.E.C. area —4.72 per cent as against 1.4 per cent. In the third age group (20-24) North America had almost 1½ million students against slightly less than one million in the O.E.E.C. area.

Diagram 4. DISTRIBUTION OF STUDENTS BY AGE GROUPS IN BASE YEAR[1]
NUMBER OF STUDENT AGED 5-24 = 100

O.E.E.C. area — Age group 20-24: 2%, Age group 15-19: 9.5%, Age group 5-14: 88.5%

Canada - U.S.A. — Age group 20-24: 3.2%, Age group 15-19: 20.2%, Age group 5-14: 76.6%

U.S.S.R. — Age group 20-24: 4.5%, Age group 15-19: 22.5%, Age group 5-14: 73%

1. 1958 or nearest year.
Source: See Appendix I.

Diagram 3. POPULATION AND NUMBER OF FULL-TIME STUDENTS IN BASE YEAR[1]
IN MILLIONS

O.E.E.C. area — Total population 339 millions = 130%; Students 5-24: 50 millions 14.7%; Population 5-24: 110 millions = 32.4%

Canada - U.S.A. — Total population 188 millions = 100%; Students 5-24: 44 millions 23.4%; Population 5-24: 63 millions = 33.5%

U.S.S.R. — Total population 208 millions = 100%; Students 5-24: 37 millions 17.8%; Population 5-24: 75 millions = 36.0%

1. 1958 or nearest year.
Source: See Appendix I.

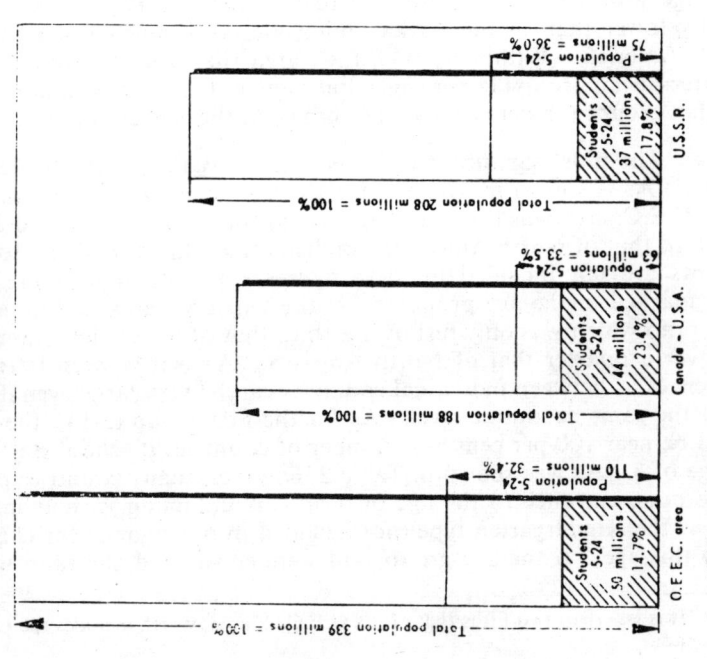

183. In terms of educational effort, the Soviet Union held an intermediate place between North America and the O.E.E.C. area. Student numbers represented almost one in five of the population; but the absolute total was only a little over two-thirds that of the O.E.E.C. area.[1] What is remarkable is the relatively high enrolment in the second and third age groups. This is partly explained by the fact that compulsory education in the Soviet Union begins at the age of 7, while in North America it usually starts earlier.

184. About 15 per cent of all full-time students in the O.E.E.C. area were in private education; the proportion was about one-third in the France-Benelux group and about one-eighth in the Mediterranean group (excluding Yugoslavia). In North America the percentage of students in private education was about the same as in the O.E.E.C. area.

Population of School Age and Enrolment Ratios

185. As can be seen in Diagram 3, the three areas have approximately the same percentage of population of school age. Within the O.E.E.C. area, this percentage is higher in the Mediterranean group (36 per cent) than in the France-Benelux (30 per cent) and the Northern group (29 per cent).

186. The differences are more marked when enrolment ratios are considered. As can be seen from Table 3, the ratio for the whole 5-24 age group was comparatively low in the O.E.E.C. area; it was slightly lower than in the Soviet Union and very much lower than in North America. Within the O.E.E.C. area the ratio was low for the Mediterranean group (36 per cent), but high in the Northern and France-Benelux groups (58 per cent) which surpassed the Soviet figure.

187. The most significant differences are revealed in the higher age groups. As is shown in Table 3, for the age group 20-24 the ratio for the O.E.E.C. area was less than half that of the Soviet Union and about one-third that of North America. Students studying abroad and foreign students are not included in these figures. The differences are even more marked in the age group 15-19; the O.E.E.C. area had an enrolment ratio which was only just over a third that of the Soviet Union and just over a quarter that of North America. As will be seen later, the differences as between individual countries can be very large even if they are at the same economic level. As for the first group (5-14), the ratio would be near 100 per cent in a number of countries if school started at the age of 5. As was shown in Table 2, however, many countries prefer to postpone entrance to the age of 6 or 7, maintaining various institutions of the Kindergarten type (not included in our figures) for children below this age. If the age group 7-14 were considered, the ratio would

---

1. It is less than two-fifths that of the O.E.C.D. area, which includes the U.S.A. and Canada.

be nearly 100 per cent for all the highly-developed countries; even so, the Mediterranean countries would have lower ratios because, for economic reasons, students there tend to drop out in large numbers at an early age.

TABLE 3. POPULATION OF SCHOOL AGE, NUMBER OF FULL-TIME STUDENTS AND ENROLMENT RATIOS BY GROUPS OF COUNTRIES
BASE YEAR[1]

p = population in thousands,
s = students in thousands,
r = enrolment ratio, i.e. students as a percentage of population.

AREA		5—14	15—19	20—24	5—24
Northern countries[2]	p	11,225	4,639	4,322	20,186
	s	10,547	954	217	11,718
	r	94.0	20.6	5.0	58.1
France-Benelux	p	11,214	4,120	4,382	19,716
	s	10,063	1,288	183	11,534
	r	89.7	31.3	4.2	58.5
Austria	p	8,783	5,216	4,967	18,966
Germany, F.R.	s	7,079	910	221	8,210
Switzerland	r	80.6	17.4	4.4	43.3
Mediterranean countries[3]	p	25,382	13,138	12,898	51,418
	s	16,754	1,615	401	18,770
	r	66.0	12.3	3.1	36.5
OEEC-area	p	56,604	27,113	26,569	110,286
	s	44,443	4,767	1,022	50,232
	r	78.5	17.6	3.8	45.6
Canada United States	p	37,414	13,755	12,106	63,275
	s	33,543	8,848	1,417	43,808
	r	89.7	64.3	11.7	69.2
OECD-area	p	94,018	40,868	38,675	173,561
	s	77,986	13,615	2,439	94,040
	r	83,0	33.3	6.3	54.2
Soviet Union[4]	p	37,454	16,967	20,343	74,764
	s	26,769	8,245	1,661	36,675
	r	71.5	48.6	8.2	49.1

1. 1958 or nearest year.
2. Denmark, Iceland, Ireland, Norway, Sweden, United Kingdom.
3. Greece, Italy, Portugal, Spain, Turkey, Yugoslavia.
4. See footnote 1 on page 61.
Source: See Appendices I and II.

188. Diagram 5 shows the enrolment ratios of 22 countries together with their economic level as expressed by the gross national product (GNP) *per capita*. A certain correlation between the educational and the economic level is clearly apparent—as might have been expected.

It is obvious that a country with a low GNP *per capita* cannot afford to have most of its young people between 15 and 19 in full-time education and thus withheld from gainful employment. On the other hand, a highly-industrialized country with a high GNP *per capita* can hardly afford to break off the education of most of its young people at the age of 14. Moreover, in a rich country there is a high demand for education as current consumption and the margin of income available to satisfy demand is large.

189. As can be seen in Diagram 5, the three countries with the highest GNP *per capita* all have very high enrolment ratios (the relatively low ratio for the first group in Sweden is explained by a later entrance age); the countries with the lowest GNP *per capita* all have low enrolment ratios. The dispersion of enrolment ratios in the middle group reflects the fact that, at a certain income level, tradition and belief in the value of education have more influence than the income level itself.

190. The diagram indicates the correlation as well as the dispersion. The regression line indicates a high income elasticity of enrolment ratios for the age groups 15-19 and 20-24. For the 20-24 group, elasticity approaches unity, i.e. if income doubles enrolment doubles. The wide dispersion around this regression line, however, excludes the possibility of extrapolating. In particular, the ratio for the Soviet Union shows the power of political decisions to promote educational expansion far beyond the level which might be expected from the average income figure. Generally speaking, the income level as expressed by GNP *per capita* seems to set the lower limit of educational effort. But above that limit there is a wide margin for choice, whether it be determined by private consumer preferences or by political decision to invest heavily in education in order to accelerate economic development.

191. As already mentioned, students studying abroad were not included in the preceding estimates. But for some countries the number of foreign students received or of national students sent abroad is considerable and affects the size of educational institutions. This is shown in Table 4 for certain selected countries. Austria and Switzerland had by far the highest percentage of foreign students. The percentages for the United States and the Soviet Union are low despite the large absolute numbers of foreign students in these two countries.[1]

192. It should also be borne in mind that the enrolment figures for the second and third age groups do not include part-time students. For three countries where separate figures for part-time students were available, it seemed that four students enrolled in part-time vocational schools could be counted as the equivalent of one full-time student.

---

1. Ref. "International Flows of Students", Vol. V of the present report - Study made by the O.E.C.D. Directorate for Scientific Affairs.

Taking this as a basis, the enrolment ratios in the age group 15-19 in the three countries would be raised as follows:

Austria.......... from 13.1 to 20.4
Germany F.R..... from 17.6 to 26.7
Netherlands...... from 32.8 to 35.1

TABLE 4. ENROLMENT RATIOS IN SELECTED COUNTRIES TAKING ACCOUNT OF MIGRANT STUDENTS FOR THE AGE GROUP 20-24
BASE YEAR[1]

COUNTRY	NATIONAL STUDENTS AT HOME	NATIONAL STUDENTS AT HOME AND NATIONAL STUDENTS ABROAD[2]	NATIONAL STUDENTS AT HOME AND FOREIGN STUDENTS[2]	SHARE OF FOREIGN STUDENTS IN THE TOTAL NUMBER OF STUDENTS[2]
	In the age group 20—24 as a percentage of population			As a percentage
Austria...............	3.7	3.9	5.1	27.4
France	3.8	3.8	4.3	13.4
Germany, F.R.........	4.6	4.8	4.9	7.3
Greece	3.3	4.0	3.3	1.6
Ireland	4.2	4.2	5.1	18.5
Norway	9.5	10.3	9.6	0.9
Switzerland...........	3.4	3.6	4.7	27.7
United Kingdom[3]	3.9	4.0	4.2	8.2
Canada..............	9.3	9.8	9.7	4.7
United States.........	12.0	12.0	12.3	3.5
Soviet Union	8.2	8.2	8.2	0.8

1. 1958 or nearest year.
2. It has been assumed that all foreign students and all national students studying abroad fall within the age group 20 to 24. National students at home are those attending all institutions of full-time formal education. National students abroad and foreign students are those in third level education only.
3. The number of foreign students refers to universities only.
Source: See Appendices I and II.

193. Table 5 shows the enrolment ratios by single years for the age group 15-24 in certain selected countries. In evaluating these ratios, it should be borne in mind, however, that whereas some countries have full-time education with a predominantly vocational content for the 15 to 18-year old, other countries (e.g. the Federal Republic of Germany) traditionally combine apprenticeship with part-time education (which is not included in our figures). However, the differences in ratios cannot be explained simply in terms of historical traditions, regarding the part of formal education and of training by firms in the educational process; a large part of European youth begins active working life as unskilled labour at an early age and never has any apprenticeship. Also, in all these countries the enrolment ratios for the 15-24 group have risen considerably in the last thirty years.

194. This is particularly true of higher education. At the beginning of this century, there were 6 to 8 students in higher education per 10,000 population in the highly-developed European countries, as against

30 to 40 in recent years. National traditions did not prevent this rise and are not likely to prevent it in the future.

TABLE 5. ENROLMENT RATIOS OF AGE GROUP 15-24 IN FULL-TIME EDUCATION BY SINGLE YEAR OF AGE AND BY SEX IN SELECTED COUNTRIES[1]
BASE YEAR[2]

m = male.
f = female.

AGE		BELGIUM	FRANCE	GERMANY (F.R.)	NETHERLANDS	NORWAY	UNITED STATES
15	m	62	51	36	65	58	96
	f	52	57	38	49	59	
16	m	50	42	23	53	54	88
	f	40	46	23	31	46	
17	m	37	28	16	40	41	74
	f	26	28	14	18	26	
18	m	26	18	11	29	32	43
	f	16	16	9	11	22	
19	m	20	12	9	19	19	29
	f	11	8	6	7	16	
20	m	15	8	6	12	15	23
	f	7	5	4	5	10	
21	m	13	6	6	9	14	17
	f	7	3	3	3	8	
22	m	7	4	7	7	10	11
	f	1	3	3	2	5	
23	m	5	3	7	6	10	8
	f	1	2	2	1	5	
24	m	3	3	6	5	10	8
	f	0.4	1	1	1	5	

1. Figures refer only to nationals studying in their home country. In the case of Norway, for instance, many university students enrol at foreign universities. The ratios would be changed if national students abroad were included (cf. Table 4 above).
2. 1958 or nearest year.
Source: Appendices I and II.

195. The sex differential in enrolment ratios indicates the trend towards more education for women. There is little sex differential in the age group 5-14, except in some of the Mediterranean countries. It is above the age of 14 that the differential in the enrolment ratio for women begins to affect the overall ratio significantly, and this is especially true above the age of 20. In the last few decades more and more girls have been receiving prolonged full-time education; there were practically no girls in higher education before 1900, whereas now they account for about a third of all students at this level. Here again, the

new belief in the value of education as opposed to the rigidities of traditional social structures explain the differences in enrolment ratios for women from one country to another, even when these countries (as in Table 5) are, with the exception of the U.S.A., at approximately the same economic level.

Teachers and Student/Teacher Ratios

196. From what has already been said about the supply of teachers, it is obvious that the student/teacher ratio is as crucial a factor in education as the enrolment ratio.

TABLE 6. NUMBER OF TEACHERS IN RELATION TO TOTAL POPULATION AND POPULATION OF SCHOOL AGE BY GROUPS OF COUNTRIES
BASE YEAR[1]

AREA	TEACHERS Thousands	TEACHERS PER THOUSAND OF TOTAL POPULATION	TEACHERS PER THOUSAND OF THE POPULATION AGED 5—24
Northern countries[2]	502.0	7.2	24.9
France-Benelux	439.0	6.8	22.3
Austria, Germany (F.R.) Switzerland	277.0	4.4	14.6
Mediterranean countries[3]	668.0	4.8	13.0
O.E.E.C.-area	1,886.0	5.6	17.1
Canada United States	1,832.0	9.8	28.9
O.E.C.D. area	3,718.0	7.1	21.4
Soviet Union	1.944.0	9.3	26.0

1. 1958 or nearest year.
2. Denmark, Iceland, Ireland, Norway, Sweden, United Kingdom.
3. Greece, Italy, Portugal, Spain, Turkey, Yugoslavia.
Source: See Appendices I and II.

197. As can be seen from Table 6, the three main areas—O.E.E.C., North America, and the Soviet Union—had very nearly the same absolute number of teachers. But the teacher density was much higher in North America and in the Soviet Union than in the O.E.E.C. area. If part-time teachers were added, the absolute number of teachers in the three areas might be estimated at 2 million each. There are, however, big differences in numbers when teachers are allocated approximately to the three standard age groups. It then becomes apparent (see also Diagram 8 and Appendix II, Table 4) that North America had less teachers than the O.E.E.C. area for the first age group, but twice as many for the second age group; the Soviet Union had more than twice as many teachers for the second age group as the O.E.E.C. area, and almost the same number of teachers for the third group as North America.

TABLE 7. STUDENT/TEACHER RATIOS[1] BY GROUPS OF COUNTRIES
BASE YEAR[2]

AREA	AGE GROUP		
	5—14	15—19	20—24
Northern countries[3]	27	14	9
France-Benelux	27	22	14
Austria, Germany (F.R.), Switzerland	32	21	14
Mediterranean countries[4]	31	16	16
O.E.E.C.-area	29	18	13
Canada-United States	28	17	12
O.E.C.D. area	29	17	13
Soviet Union	21	15	14

1. Teachers have been allocated to age groups of students according to estimates.
2. 1958 or nearest year.
3. Denmark, Iceland, Ireland, Norway, Sweden, United Kingdom.
4. Greece, Italy, Portugal, Spain, Turkey, Yugoslavia.
Source: See Appendices I and II.

198. Table 7 shows that student/teacher ratios in the O.E.E.C. area are, on the whole, higher than in the two other areas. It can also be seen that, in all areas, the ratio goes down as the age goes up. For the first age group the prevailing ratio oscillates around 30, except in the Soviet Union where it is close to 20 (in Europe, only Sweden has a similarly low ratio for this group). For the second the ratio oscillates around 18, with the Soviet Union again at the lower limit. For the third group, 13 may be regarded as the median ratio for all the areas.

199. Why are there such differences from age group to age group? The question could be approached from an economic angle which would coincide with the point of view of pedagogics; what is the optimum ratio, i.e. the ratio which assures the best relation of cost and result, for each age group? There seems to have been very little empirical research into this question. Is there sufficient proof that pupils of 5-14 need less intensive teaching than those of 15-19?

200. The differences in the student/teacher ratios seem to be due much more to tradition and narrow financial considerations than to any sound concept of pedagogics. While it is true that cost per teacher increases with the level of education, the bulk of the teaching force is still to be found in the first age group and this situation is likely to continue throughout the next decade. So keeping the student/teacher ratio high for this first group means keeping low the cost of the whole educational enterprise.

201. As is shown in Table 8, in highly-developed countries ratios in primary education have been considerably lowered since the beginning of

the century, but in secondary education there has lately been a tendency towards raising the ratios, and this same tendency also applies to the third age group. The differences in student/teacher ratios as between the various age levels seem to be diminishing.

TABLE 8. STUDENT/TEACHER RATIOS IN SELECTED COUNTRIES (1900-1957)

YEAR	PRIMARY SCHOOLS			SECONDARY SCHOOLS		
	ENGLAND AND WALES	WESTERN GERMANY[1]	SWEDEN	ENGLAND AND WALES	WESTERN GERMANY[1]	SWEDEN
1900	48	60	50			
1910	37	55	40	16	19	18
1930	32	40	24	19	17	18
1950	29[2]	48	21	19[3]	22	22
1957	28[2]	36	24	19[3]	20	21

1. Area of Federal Republic of Germany.
2. Including secondary modern schools.
3. Excluding secondary modern schools.

Source: F. Edding, Internationale Tendenzen in der Entwicklung der Ausgaben für Schulen und Hochschulen (International Trends in Educational Expenditure). Kieler Studien 47. Kiel 1958.

202. It should be stressed that one point more or less in the student/teacher ratio may mean a big difference in the number of teachers, and consequently in expenditure. For instance, to lower the ratio for the first group in the O.E.E.C. area from 29.4 to 28.4 would demand 50,000 more teachers; if the current cost per teacher is taken as $3,000, the additional expenditure involved would be $150 million per year. This explains the reluctance of finance ministries to agree to a lowering of the ratios. Also, the difficulty of finding and training enough teachers should not be underestimated, particularly if a proposed lowering of ratios coincides with a growth of population and a policy for the expansion of the educational system.

203. However, the example of the Soviet Union in this context is highly instructive. As a consequence of the war, the number of students in general schools fell by 15 per cent between 1940 and 1958. Instead of reducing the number of teachers, as many countries would have done, the Soviet Union increased it year by year, so that by 1958 it was nearly 50 per cent higher than in 1940, giving a student/teacher ratio of 16.3 as against 28.6 in 1940. The addition of nearly 600,000 teachers thus necessitated[1] was certainly remarkable in a country where highly-educated manpower was still scarce and other urgent reconstruction tasks

1. This figure refers to the period 1940-1958; but as the "low" in teacher numbers was actually reached immediately after the war, the addition in the 12 years since 1946 was in fact 770,000 teachers.

were competing strongly with education. Obviously, education was considered an investment on which particularly high returns, in the widest sense, could be obtained.

204. The main explanation for the low student/teacher ratio in the general schools in the Soviet Union lies neither in large numbers of small-size rural schools, nor in a particularly small size of classes (classes with more than 35 students seem, however, to be rare), but in the fact that secondary teachers have to work in class only 18 hours per week and teachers in the first level only 24 hours per week. They may often work extra hours, including work in youth clubs, etc., but on the whole their teaching load is much less than in most other countries.

Expenditure on Education

205. In the base year, total expenditure on education of the O.E.E.C. area amounted in round figures to $9,000 million, of which $1,600 million on capital account and $7,400 million on current account. This last figure represents $22 *per capita* of total population. Total expenditure represented 3.2 per cent and current expenditure 2.6 per cent of the gross national product. These percentages may seem low having regard to the part of the population involved but they exclude, of course, subsistence costs of pupils. Current expenditure, in fact, reflects not very much more than the cost of teachers.

206. It should be noted that the figures in Table 9 relate to formal education only and are subject to the reservations made in the section concerning expenditure on education (paras 166-172) of this chapter. No account has been taken of the indirect cost of withholding young people from the labour market,[1] nor of the cost of education within industry. Nevertheless, even with these limitations, the figures can serve as a useful index.

207. Expenditure on education in the O.E.E.C. area was low in comparison with the two other areas. North America spent over four times as much per head of population, partly because of the higher salaries of teachers who are professionals in a richer society. But even if expenditure on education is measured against national output, North America spent a third more than the O.E.E.C. area. This reflects mainly the greater weight of secondary and higher education in North America.

208. Figures of GNP and education expenditure in the Soviet Union are difficult to estimate, but as far as can be seen, the Soviet Union in this respect also holds an intermediate position between the O.E.E.C. area and North America.

---

1. Cf. Theodore W. Schultz, "Investment in Human Capital", the American Economic Review, March 1961; and by the same author, "Capital Formation by Education", Journal of Political Economy, December 1960.

TABLE 9. EXPENDITURE ON EDUCATION IN RELATION
TO GROSS NATIONAL PRODUCT BY GROUPS OF COUNTRIES
BASE YEAR[1]

AREA	GROSS NATIONAL PRODUCT Millions of U.S. dollars	EXPENDITURE ON EDUCATION[2] Millions of U.S. dollars			EXPENDITURE ON EDUCATION AS A PERCENTAGE OF GROSS NATIONAL PRODUCT		
		CURRENT	CAPITAL	TOTAL	CURRENT	CAPITAL	TOTAL
Northern countries[3]	87,784	2,603	570	3,173	2.96	0.65	3.61
France-Belenux	73,366	2,056	494	2,550	2.80	0.67	3.47
Austria, Germany, (F.R.) Switzerland	65,946	1,448	403	1,851	2.20	0.61	2.81
Mediterranean countries[4]	53,053	1,265	141	1,406	2.38	0.27	2.65
O.E.E.C. area	280,149	7,372	1,608	8,980	2.63	0.57	3.21
Canada United States	493,633	17,750	4,316	22,066	3.60	0.87	4.47
O.E.C.D. area	773,782	25,122	5,924	31,046	3.25	0.76	4.01
Soviet Union	263,400	8,350	1,494	9,844	3.17	0.57	3.74

1. 1958 or nearest year.
2. In current expenditure public subsidies to privately operated institutions as well as estimated expenditure of those institutions from other sources of income are included. To estimate private expenditure on capital account was, in general, not possible, but some of the public subsidies may have been used for financing buildings and equipment of private schools. For France and the United States official accounts of capital expenditure of private schools were used.
3. Denmark, Iceland, Ireland, Norway, Sweden, United Kingdom.
4. Greece, Italy, Portugal, Spain, Turkey, Yugoslavia.
Source: See Appendices I and II.

209. Formal education in all the countries under consideration is financed mainly from public funds. The figures for private expenditure are usually less reliable and estimates have been made only for current expenditure of private institutions. According to these estimates, 90 per cent of current expenditure in the O.E.E.C. area, is covered from public funds and the remainder from private sources. The burden of education on public finance may be seen in columns 4 and 5 of Table 10.

210. The figures in Table 9 show that in most advanced economies about one-fifth of total expenditure is used on capital account and four-fifths on current account. Of this current expenditure, salaries generally take 70 to 80 per cent, though in some countries this proportion is reduced to 60 to 65 per cent by a relatively higher welfare expenditure (meals, board, health, etc.). All non-salary expenditures (including capital expenditure) represent in general between 35 and 45 per cent of total expenditure.

TABLE 10. PUBLIC CURRENT AND TOTAL EXPENDITURE ON
EDUCATION IN RELATION TO CURRENT REVENUE
OF GENERAL GOVERNMENT[1] BY GROUPS OF COUNTRIES
BASE YEAR[2]

AREA	EXPENDITURE ON EDUCATION Millions of U.S. dollars — TOTAL (CURRENT AND CAPITAL)	CURRENT	TOTAL CURRENT REVENUE OF GENERAL GOVERNMENT Millions of U.S. dollars	1 AS A PERCENTAGE OF 3	2 AS A PERCENTAGE OF 3
	1	2	3	4	5
Northern countries[3]	2,447	3,017	25,775	9.5	11.7
France-Benelux	1,721	2,215	23,139	7.4	9.6
Austria, Germany, (F.R.) Switzerland	1,439	1,842	21,706	6.6	8.5
Mediterranean countries[4]	1,142	1,283	10,181	11.2	12.6
O.E.E.C. area	6,749	8,357	80,800	8.4	10.3
Canada-United States	14,340	18,656	124,078	11.6	15.0
O.E.C.D. area	21,088	27,013	204,878	10.3	13.2

1. All levels of government, i.e. state, local, municipal, etc.
2. 1958 or nearest year.
3. Denmark, Iceland, Ireland, Norway, Sweden, United Kingdom.
4. Greece, Italy, Portugal, Spain, Turkey, Yugoslavia.
Source: See Appendices I and II.

211. At the lowest levels of education, salaries account for about 90 per cent of current expenditure in most countries, but this proportion diminishes as the level becomes higher and other expenditure gains weight. The proportion of transfer expenditure such as pensions, grants to students, interest on debts, etc. varies very widely from country to country according to tradition and policy, and it would be misleading to give an average.

212. The schools for the 5-14 age group take the highest share of current expenditure: 65 to 70 per cent in most European countries and 57 per cent in North America. The second age group takes between 15 to 25 per cent, and the third between 10 to 15 per cent. In the course of the last 50 years, there has been a clear trend towards higher percentages for the second and third groups. For example, in the United States the share of expenditure for elementary schools which fall within the first age group went down from almost 70 per cent in 1910 to 50 per cent in recent years while the share of the other age groups beyond the elementary level went up correspondingly.

TARGETS FOR THE SIXTIES

APPROACH TO THE PROBLEM

213. National plans and policies provide only a partial indication of the development of education over the next decade. Even when policies

are defined in quantitative terms they often represent only first steps covering a period of three to five years. Long-term plans and projections—where they do exist—will probably be revised according to changes in expectations and policy; "rolling" adjustments will no doubt have to be made. To a large extent, however, national plans are incomplete or non-existent. Our projections had, therefore, to be based mostly on other considerations.

214. The projection of education development in Europe presented here is thus a hybrid of forecasting and policy recommendations. It is in the nature of a model which comes as close to reality as our limited knowledge of educational systems in such a large number of countries allows.

215. In working out these projections we have been guided by the line of thought running throughout this study. It is founded on the basic belief and assumption that more and better education for more people is desirable in itself and is at the same time one of the most important factors in economic growth. It is assumed that this belief will have an increasing influence on national policies in the decade ahead.

216. No immutable relationship between the development of education and the economic level is assumed. Diagram 5 clearly shows that such a relationship does not exist. To the extent that countries recognize that their spending on education is suboptimal, they may expand education at a pace that is not geared to their economic growth. One would expect education to expand fastest in those countries lagging in this field behind countries on the same economic level. The experience of the Soviet Union, however, may suggest that *all* European countries should make an extraordinary effort to go ahead at a faster pace than in the past.

217. In fixing tentative targets for the expansion of education in the 1960's, a "low" alternative as well as a "high" alternative has been devised.

218. The *low alternative* assumes no extraordinary effort, in fact, not much more effort than in the recent past. It assumes that current expenditure will on the whole increase *pari passu* with average real income, and that enrolment ratios in countries lagging behind other countries which are on a similar economic level will rise relatively more, while student/teacher ratios will remain the same as in the base year.

219. The *high alternative* reflects what is regarded as a reasonable maximum effort. In this projection all countries, whether lagging behind or being in advance of others, will make an extraordinary effort, bearing in mind that there is an upper limit to what can be achieved in such a short period as a decade. It takes time to expand the number of teachers, to organize teaching institutions and to plan and to erect new buildings; the supply of teachers is often the most difficult bottle-neck

impeding the expansion of education. A deterioration in the quality of teachers may be too high a price to pay for a rapid increase in the number of students. The more ambitious national plans fall within the range of this high alternative.

220. The criteria on which these two alternative targets are based are to some extent a matter of conjecture. Their realism could only be judged by a detailed study of each country—a task which is beyond the scope of an international survey. It has been quite clear to the authors that only national experts and institutions can fully master all the intricate problems involved; the main purpose of the authors has been to indicate broad potentialities and targets for the O.E.E.C. area as a whole and to demonstrate the interplay of the main factors in educational development.

METHODS AND ASSUMPTIONS

221. *a)* *Population forecasts* provided by the Manpower Division of O.E.E.C. and by national agencies indicate the growth of the relevant age groups.

b) Starting with the *enrolment ratios* in the base year, a high and a low alternative for 1970 has been established, according to assumptions which vary with special conditions in each country and to comparisons with countries on the same economic level. Table 11 shows that, even in the high alternative, European enrolment ratios in the age group 15-24 would still in 1970 be much lower than were those of North America and the Soviet Union in the base year.

c) A combination of *a)* and *b)* gives the high and the low alternative for *student numbers* in 1970.

d) For student/teacher ratios, the low alternative is the same figure as in 1957; the high alternative represents a reduction by a few units. The changes applied were not uniform; the ratio in Spain, for instance, is supposed to fall in the first group from 40 to 34, i.e. by 15 per cent, whereas in Sweden it is scheduled to fall from 22 to 20, i.e. by 9 per cent only.

e) The *number of teachers* in 1970 has been projected by combining *c)* and *d)* to give a "low" teacher number (low enrolment—high student/teacher ratios) and a "high" teacher number (high enrolment—low student/teacher ratios).

f) *Current expenditure* has been estimated by assuming that in real terms salaries per teacher and other instructional expenditure will increase *pari passu* with GNP *per capita*, and that other current expenditure will increase with the number of students. "Low" current expenditure corresponds to a small increase in enrolment ratios and the same student/teacher ratio as in the base year; "high" current expenditure corresponds to a large increase in enrolment ratios and a reduction in the student/teacher ratio.

g) Total expenditure in 1970 has been arrived at by adding in all cases 20 per cent to current expenditure as a provision for capital expenditure.

h) The increase *in gross national product* has been based on forecasts by the National Accounts Division of O.E.E.C.

i) It has been assumed throughout that education in private institutions will develop at the same pace as public education.

TARGETS FOR THE O.E.E.C. AREA

Population Trends

222. According to forecasts, European population trends in the coming decade are, on the whole, favourable for a rapid improvement in standards of education. As shown in Diagram 6, the population of school age (5-24) will rise by less than 1 per cent per year, or by about 10 per cent during the decade. Only the age group 20-24 will rise at a somewhat faster rate—by 14 per cent—as a result of the wave of high birth rates that started in the 1940's. Europe will in fact be in a much better position to raise its standards of education than North America, where the population of school age will increase by about 40 per cent, and in a better position than the Soviet Union, where the increase will be about 20 per cent.

223. There are, however, big differences in population trends from age group to age group and from country to country (see Table 14). France, for instance, will have an overall increase in the 5-24 group of 22 per cent, but the population wave in the first age group has already come to a standstill, whereas in the second and third groups increases of 50 and 40 per cent are to be expected. In Norway and Turkey the population of school age will also grow rapidly —by 20 per cent and 28 per cent respectively— while in Sweden, Germany (F.R.), Austria, Ireland, Greece and Portugal it is expected to remain in total almost unchanged. But these countries also will have considerable increases in some age groups.

Enrolment Ratios and Student Numbers

224. Except for some of the Mediterranean countries, compulsory education up to the age of 14 is effective throughout the O.E.E.C. area. Reforms to extend it below the present entrance age do not seem to be envisaged, not even in countries where school starts at as late an age as seven. The enrolment ratio for the first age group in the O.E.E.C. area as a whole will, therefore, according to our projections, be only moderately increased (see Table 11). The number of students in this age group will rise from 44 million to a "high" of 52 million, an increase of 18 per cent (see Table 14). This age group accounted in the base year for almost 90 per cent of the total student population and absorbed

Diagram 6. POPULATION OF AGE GROUPS
AND STUDENT NUMBERS BY MAJOR AREA
BASE YEAR[1] AND PROJECTIONS FOR 1970 — IN MILLIONS

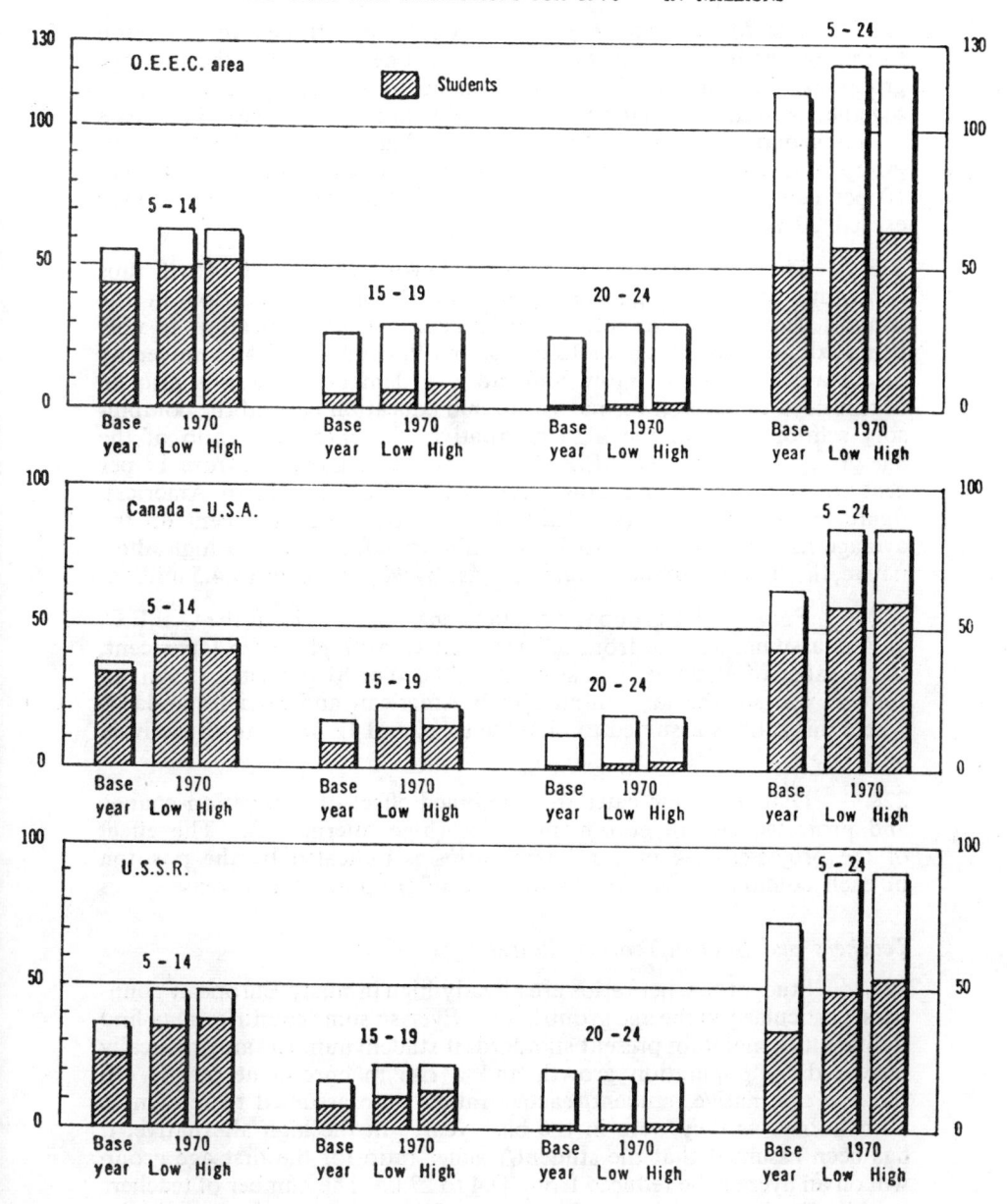

1. 1958 or nearest year.
Source: See Appendix I.

some 70 per cent of total current expenditure. In this predominant part of the education system expansion will thus of necessity be relatively slow in the O.E.E.C. area.

225. The Mediterranean group, however, constitutes an exception to this trend; in this area the average enrolment ratio for the first age group has been assumed to rise from 66 to a "high" of 75. This, together with the population increase, will cause the number of students in this group to rise from 17 million to 22 million. In the Northern group and the France-Benelux group the increase will be less than 10 per cent, while in the Germany-Austria-Switzerland group it may exceed 20 per cent.

226. The prolongation of education beyond the age of 14 will thus constitute the most significant effort in European education in the coming decade. In several countries compulsory education is now being extended to the age of 15 or 16, and "gymnasium" and university places are likely to be more and more in demand. There is also an urgent need to develop formal vocational education beyond the compulsory school age. In the high alternative, the enrolment ratio of the age group 15-19 for the O.E.E.C. area would be increased from 17 per cent to 31 per cent and thus approach half of the North American figure in the base year (see Table 11). A rise to 25 per cent on the average has been assumed to be a minimum effort. In this high alternative, the student number would increase by 94 per cent or by 4,5 million.

227. For the third group the average enrolment ratio in the O.E.E.C. area is assumed to rise from 3.8 per cent to a "high" of 6.1 per cent, the number of students increasing by 830,000 or 81 per cent. Even so, Europe will still be far behind North American and Soviet standards where this ratio is assumed to increase to 16 and 12 per cent respectively (see Table 11).

228. Diagram 7 indicates the combined effect of population change and projected rise in enrolment ratios (high alternative). The effect of the projected rise in enrolment ratios is indicated by the position of each country in relation to the line of proportional increase.

Teachers and Student/Teacher Ratios

229. Student/teacher ratios are already high in many European countries, particularly in the age group 5-14. Even so some countries may find it difficult to maintain present standards if student numbers are drastically increased by population growth and a rise in enrolment ratios. In the low alternative, student/teacher ratios were assumed to remain in all countries as they were in the base year. In the high alternative, it has been assumed that the student/teacher ratio for the first age group will on an average be reduced from 29.4 to 27.0. The number of teachers in this, the largest, sector of the education system would then rise by 28 per cent, or by 415,000 (see Diagram 8 and Appendix II, Table 4).

TABLE 11. ENROLMENT RATIOS BY GROUPS OF COUNTRIES
BASE YEAR[1] AND PROJECTIONS FOR 1970

AREA	AGE GROUP											
	5—14			15—19			20—24			5—24		
	BASE YEAR	1970 LOW	1970 HIGH	BASE YEAR	1970 LOW	1970 HIGH	BASE YEAR	1970 LOW	1970 HIGH	BASE YEAR	1970 LOW	1970 HIGH
Northern countries[2]	94.0	94.6	95.0	20.6	30.0	34.6	5.0	6.7	7.5	58.1	56.5	58.0
France-Benelux	89.7	90.6	91.7	31.3	39.0	46.3	4.2	5.1	7.1	58.5	55.5	58.4
Austria, Germany, (F.R.), Switzerland	80.6	82.9	84.9	17.4	24.3	30.0	4.4	6.1	7.2	43.3	51.5	54.2
Mediterranean countries[3]	66.0	67.6	75.0	12.3	18.6	24.1	3.1	3.4	4.8	36.5	39.9	45.3
O.E.E.C. area	78.5	79.2	83.3	17.6	25.5	31.2	3.8	4.8	6.1	45.5	47.7	51.5
Canada United States	89.7	89.8	89.8	64.3	68.1	73.1	11.7	12.7	15.6	69.2	67.0	68.9
O.E.C.D. area	83.0	83.7	86.0	33.3	43.3	48.7	6.3	7.9	9.8	54.2	55.7	58.7
Soviet Union[4]	71.5	75.0	80.0	48.6	50.0	60.0	8.2	10.0	12.0	49.1	54.5	60.1

1. 1958 or nearest year.
2. Denmark, Iceland, Ireland, Norway, Sweden, United Kingdom.
3. Greece, Italy, Portugal, Spain, Turkey, Yugoslavia.
4. See footnote 1 on page 61.
Source: See Appendices I and II.

For the second group, a reduction of the O.E.E.C. average from 18.4 to 17.1 in the high alternative would, together with the increase in student numbers, more than double the number of teachers. For the third group no marked reduction in the student/teacher ratio is envisaged; in the high alternative it would hardly be changed from 13.9 in the base year to 14.0 in 1970. The number of teachers required for this age group in 1970 would nevertheless increase by 56,600 or 81 per cent.

230. Taking all age groups together, the demand for teachers, in the low alternative, will increase by about 344,000 or 18 per cent. This compares with an increase of 37 per cent for North America and 34 per cent for the Soviet Union, also in the low alternative. In the high alternative, the expansion of student numbers, combined with a reasonable reduction in the student/teacher ratio, would bring the number of teachers in the O.E.E.C. area to about 753,000 or 41 per cent more than in the base year, against an increase of 57 per cent in North America and 59 per cent in the Soviet Union. In the O.E.E.C. area the increase would be highest in the Mediterranean Group (54 per cent) and in the Austria-Germany-Switzerland group (49 per cent).

231. The difficulty of increasing the number of teachers appears to be one of the greatest obstacles to the expansion of education in Europe in future years. To the figures mentioned above, which take account of future needs due to the improvement of quality and the expansion of education, must be added replacement needs arising from the drop

Diagram 7. INCREASE IN POPULATION OF SCHOOL AGE AN

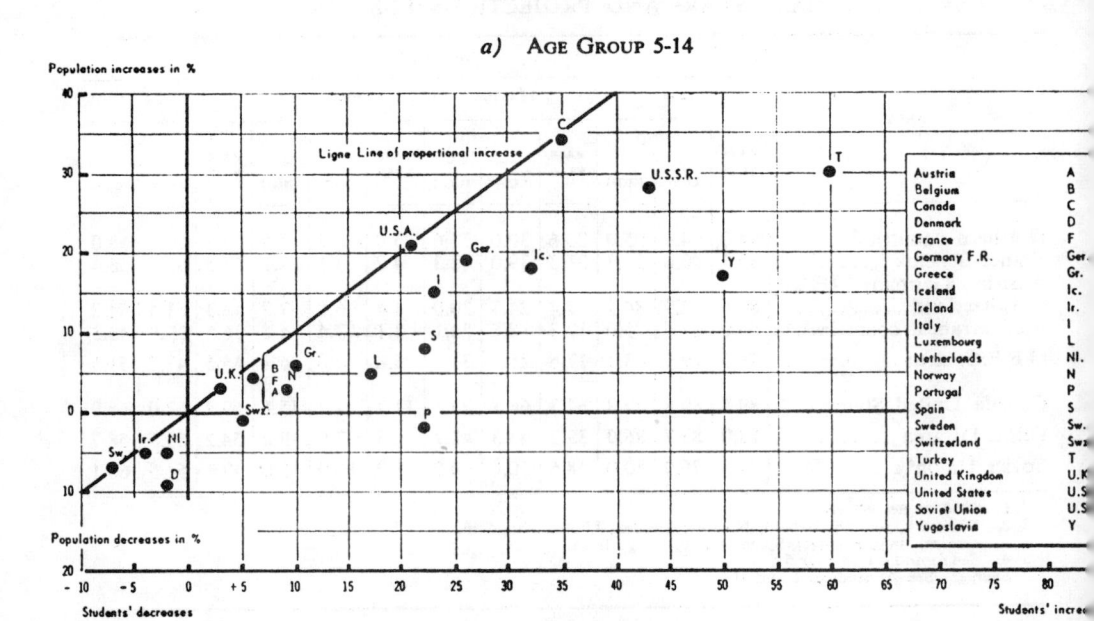

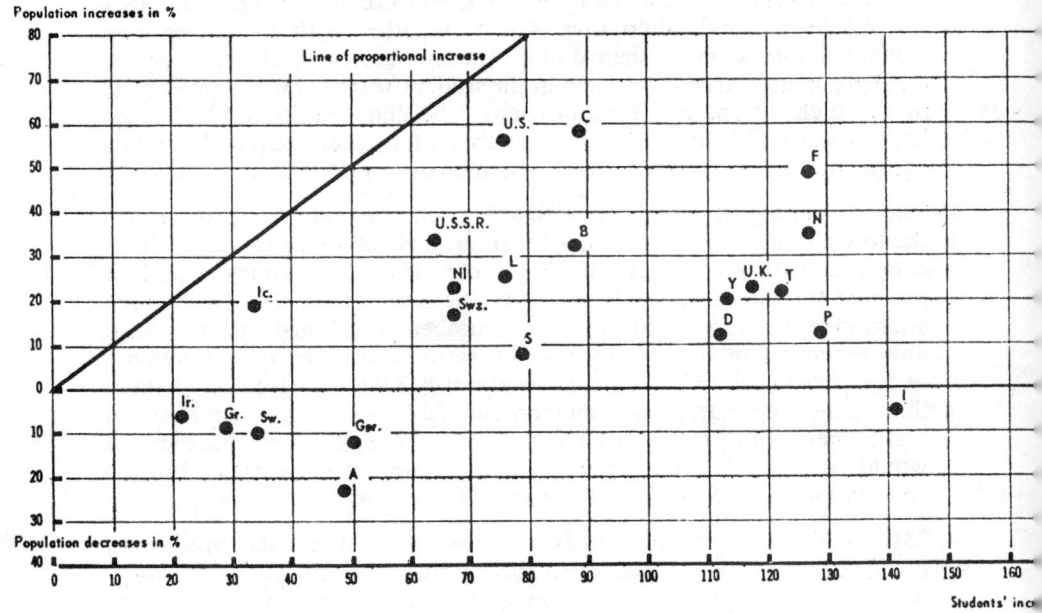

a) AGE GROUP 5-14

b) AGE GROUP 15-19

1. 1958 or nearest year.
Source: See Table 14.

STUDENT POPULATION BASE YEAR[1], 1970 (High alternative)

c) AGE GROUP 20-24

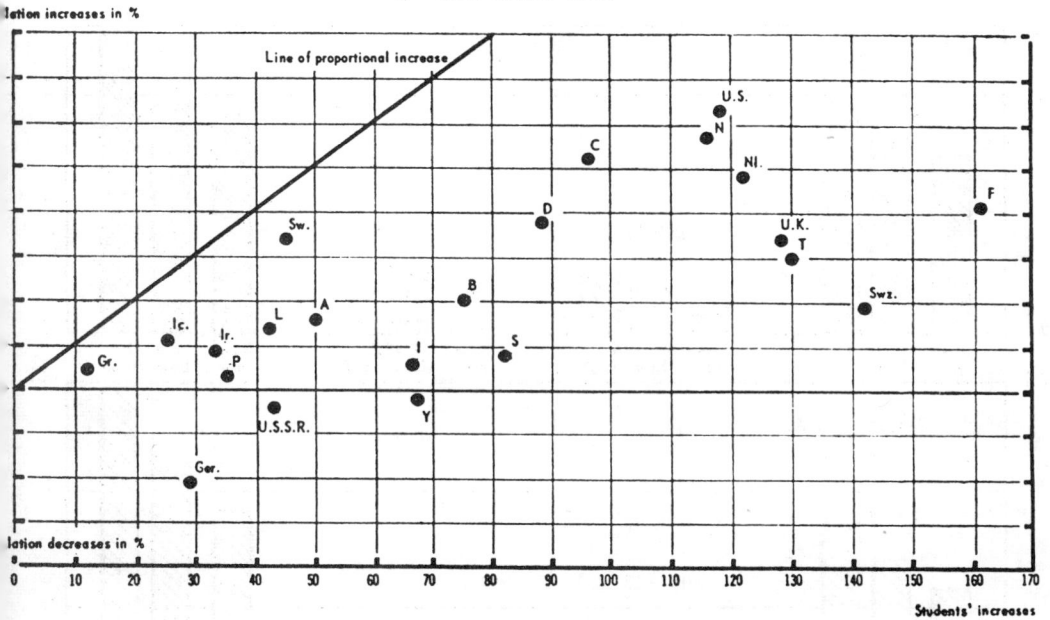

Diagram 8. NUMBER OF TEACHERS BY AGE GROUPS OF STUDENTS BASE YEAR[1] AND PROJECTIONS FOR 1970
MILLIONS

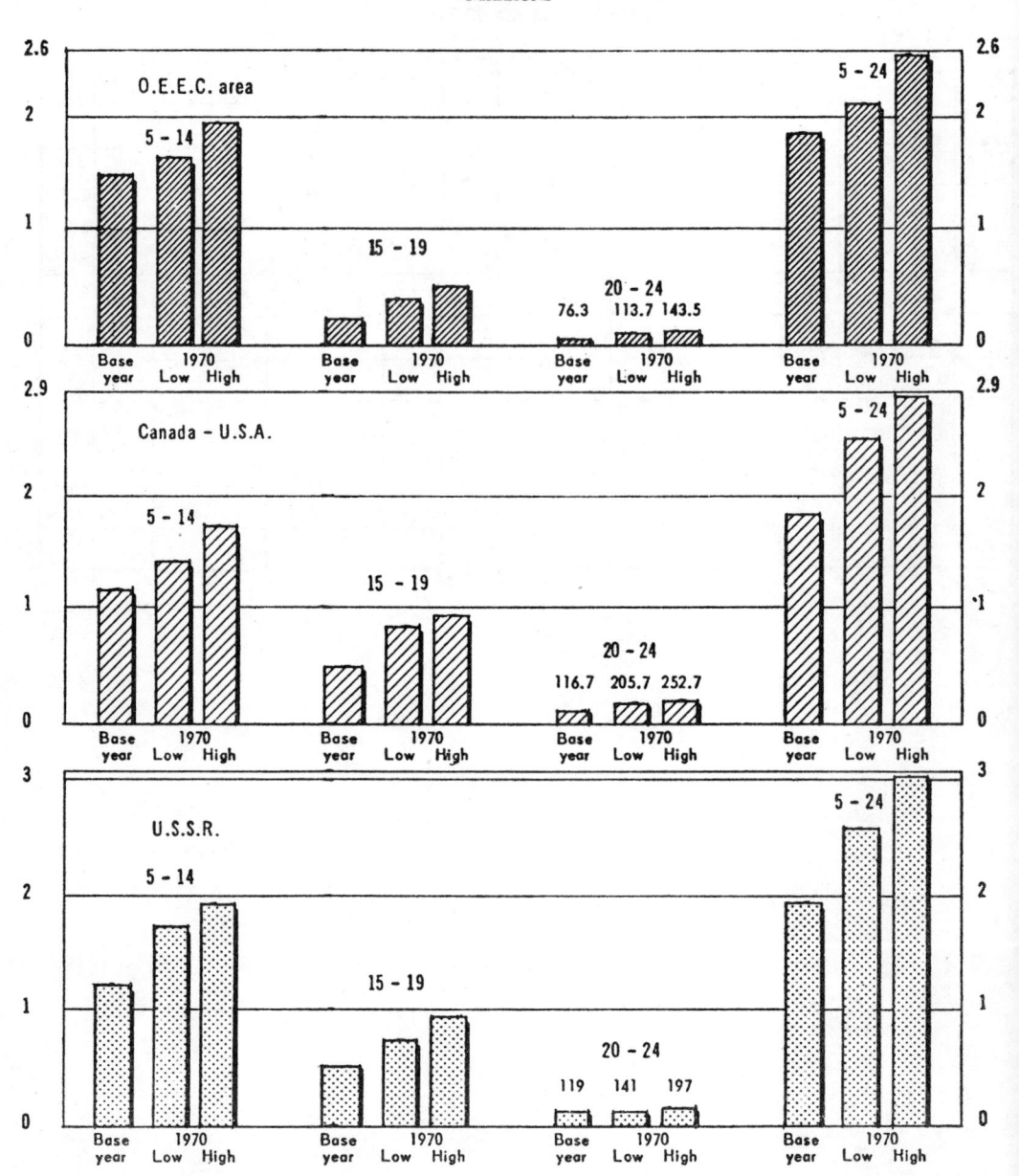

1. 1958 or nearest year.
Source: See Appendix I.

out of teachers from the profession with old age, marriage, alternative employment or other reasons. In many countries replacement needs have grown at a disturbing rate in recent years, and it is important that Governments should take account of them in formulating their longer-term policies to solve the shortage of teachers.

Expenditure

232. The projections in the low and high alternatives of current expenditure on public and private education, in absolute figures and as a percentage of GNP, are given in Table 12. Since we assume that, in real terms, teachers' salaries and other instructional expenditure will rise *pari passu* with GNP *per capita*, and since the number of students and teachers in the low alternative increases by 16 per cent and 19 per cent respectively, it was to be expected that the share of current expenditure in GNP would be raised, even if only minimum assumptions were taken.

TABLE 12. CURRENT EXPENDITURE ON EDUCATION FROM ALL SOURCES BY GROUPS OF COUNTRIES
BASE YEAR[1] AND PROJECTIONS FOR 1970

AREA	GROSS NATIONAL PRODUCT Billions of U.S. dollars BASE YEAR	1970	CURRENT EXPENDITURE Billions of U.S. dollars BASE YEAR	1970 LOW	1970 HIGH	AS A PERCENTAGE OF GROSS NATIONAL PRODUCT BASE YEAR	1970 LOW	1970 HIGH
Northern countries[2]	87.8	118.1	2.6	4.0	4.5	3.0	3.4	3.8
France-Benelux	73.4	112.5	2.1	3.5	4.2	2.8	3.1	3.7
Austria Germany, (F.R.), Switzerland	65.9	111.5	1.4	2.5	3.1	2.2	2.2	2.8
Mediterranean countries[3]	53.1	105.1	1.3	2.7	3.3	2.4	2.6	3.2
O.E.E.C. area	280.2	447.2	7.4	12.7	15.1	2.6	2.8	3.4
Canada-United States	493.6	789.3	17.8	30.3	34.4	3.6	3.8	4.4
O.E.C.D. area	773.8	1,236.5	25.1	43.0	49.5	3.2	3.5	4.0
Soviet Union	263.4	538.0	8.4	22.4	26.8	3.2	4.2	5.0

1. 1958 or nearest year.
2. Denmark, Iceland, Ireland, Norway, Sweden, United Kingdom.
3. Greece, Italy, Portugal, Spain, Turkey, Yugoslavia.
Source : See Appendices I and II.

233. If capital expenditure—as far as it can be ascertained—is added to current expenditure, we get for the O.E.E.C. area a total of some $9,000 million in the base year (see Appendix II, Table 5). As stated earlier, it has been assumed that capital expenditure in 1970

Diagram 9. CURRENT EXPENDITURE FROM ALL SOURCES ON EDUCATION AS A PERCENTAGE OF GROSS NATIONAL PRODUCT BASE YEAR[1] AND PROJECTIONS FOR 1970

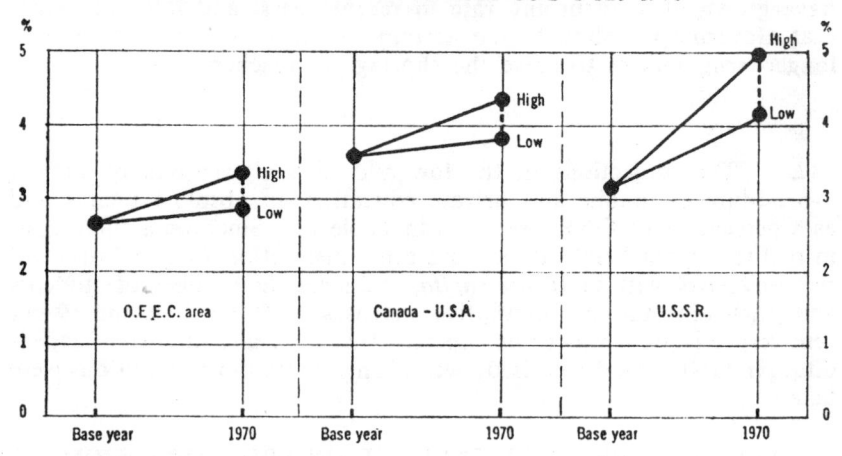

1. 1958 or nearest year.
Source: See Table 12.

Diagram 10. CURRENT EXPENDITURE FROM ALL SOURCES ON EDUCATION BY AGE GROUPS BASE YEAR[1] AND PROJECTIONS FOR 1970
TOTAL CURRENT EXPENDITURE = 100

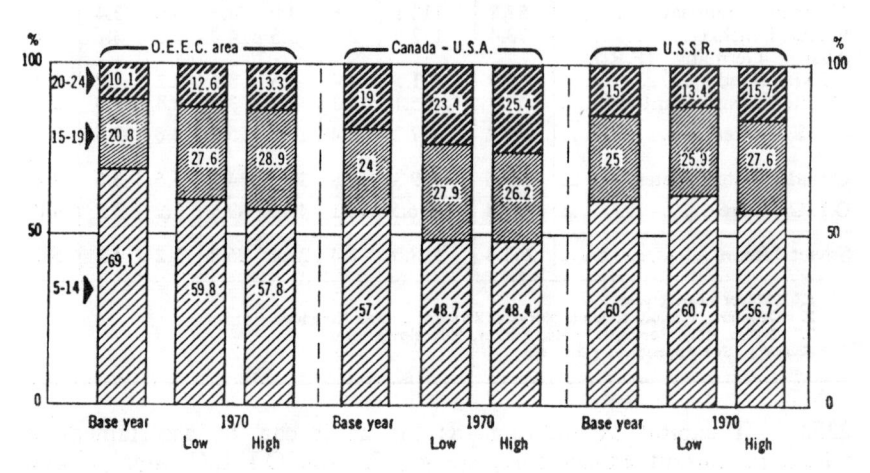

1. 1958 or nearest year.
Source: See Appendix I.

will amount to 20 per cent of current expenditure in all countries. This figure is not valid for certain individual countries, but it gives at least a rough idea of total expenditure. By adding this 20 per cent to forecast current expenditure we obtain for the O.E.E.C. area a total of over $15,000 million in the low alternative, and over $18,000 million in the high alternative, i.e. 3.4 per cent and 4.0 per cent respectively of GNP as against 3.2 per cent of GNP in the base year.

234. The distribution of current expenditure as between age groups is expected to change considerably; expenditure on the two upper groups will take a larger share of the total, while that on the first group will fall from 69 per cent to 58 per cent in the O.E.E.C. area. This reflects past and present trends towards focussing effort on the expansion of secondary and higher education in the highly-developed countries.

TABLE 13. CURRENT AND TOTAL EXPENDITURE ON EDUCATION IN RELATION TO GROSS NATIONAL PRODUCT BY COUNTRY
BASE YEAR[1] AND PROJECTIONS FOR 1970 (HIGH ALTERNATIVE)

Percentages.

COUNTRY	BASE YEAR CURRENT EXPENDITURE	BASE YEAR TOTAL EXPENDITURE	FORECAST 1970 HIGH CURRENT EXPENDITURE	FORECAST 1970 HIGH TOTAL EXPENDITURE
Sweden	3.35	4.14	3.91	4.69
Switzerland	2.46	2.88	3.44	4.13
Luxembourg	1.32	1.37	2.08	2.49
Belgium	2.63	2.79	3.67	4.40
United Kingdom	3.02	3.67	3.95	4.74
France	2.72	3.50	3.69	4.42
Denmark	2.46	3.01	3.22	3.87
Norway	2.79	3.67	3.70	4.44
Germany, F.R.	2.11	2.79	2.68	3.21
Netherlands	3.48	4.23	4.07	4.89
Iceland	1.97	2.53	2.71	3.24
Austria	2.74	2.85	3.32	3.99
Ireland	2.46	2.72	2.97	3.56
Italy	3 21	3 42	4.45	5.35
Yugoslavia	2.00	2.60	2.59	3.11
Spain	1.40	1.57	2.08	2.50
Greece	1.27	1.41	1.41	1.69
Portugal	1.62	2.07	2.22	2.67
Turkey	1.73	2.05	2.38	2.85
O.E.E.C. area	2.63	3.21	3.37	4.04
Canada	3.39	3.72	4.06	4.87
United States	3.61	4.53	4.38	5.26
O.E.C.D. area	3.25	4.01	4.00	4.80
Soviet Union	3.17	3.74	4.98	5.97

1. 1958 or nearest year.
Source: See Appendices I and II.

TABLE 14. POPULATION, STUDENTS, TEACHERS, CURRENT EXPENDITURE ON EDUCATION FROM ALL SOURCES BY AGE GROUPS OF STUDENTS, AND GROSS NATIONAL PRODUCT PER CAPITA — BY COUNTRIES PROJECTED INCREASE BY 1970 (HIGH ALTERNATIVE) OVER BASE YEAR[1]

Percentages.

COUNTRY	5–14 POPULATION	5–14 STUDENTS	5–14 TEACHERS	5–14 EXPENDITURE	15–19 POPULATION	15–19 STUDENTS	15–19 TEACHERS	15–19 EXPENDITURE	20–24 POPULATION	20–24 STUDENTS	20–24 TEACHERS	20–24 EXPENDITURE	5–24 POPULATION	5–24 STUDENTS	5–24 TEACHERS	5–24 EXPENDITURE	BASE YEAR	1970	INCREASE 1970 BASE YEAR	GROSS NATIONAL PRODUCT PER CAPITA INCREASE 1970, BASE YEAR
Sweden	−7	−7	2	30	−10	34	67	99	34	45	117	157	1	1	19	60	3.35	3.91	16.7	27
Switzerland	−1	5	23	64	17	68	106	173	19	142	100	167	8	14	36	102	2.46	3.44	39.8	33
Luxembourg	5	17	41	87	25	76	127	200	14	42	80	100	13	26	59	114	1.32	2.08	57.6	33
Belgium	5	6	18	45	32	88	115	179	20	75	115	157	15	17	35	90	2.63	3.67	39.5	28
United Kingdom	3	3	11	32	18	118	125	171	34	128	117	164	14	13	30	73	3.02	3.95	30.2	25
France	4	6	19	65	49	127	127	202	41	161	162	244	22	22	35	110	2.72	3.68	35.3	40
Denmark	−9	−2	17	60	12	112	113	190	38	88	88	158	6	10	40	96	2.46	3.22	30.9	37
Norway	3	9	19	55	35	127	128	195	57	116	79	131	20	29	43	94	2.79	3.70	32.6	30
Germany, F.R.	19	26	53	118	−12	50	72	148	−21	29	30	87	−1	29	55	121	2.11	2.68	27.0	54
Netherlands	−5	−2	15	62	19	68	87	163	48	84	84	158	−12	9	32	92	3.48	4.07	17.0	41
Iceland	18	32	68	106	19	34	50	100	11	25	25	67	16	33	60	100	1.97	2.71	37.6	27
Austria	4	6	22	69	−23	48	50	114	9	50	57	86	−1	10	28	80	2.74	3.32	21.2	43
Ireland	−5	−4	10	38	−6	21	18	53	6	33	29	60	−2	−2	12	43	2.46	2.97	20.7	28
Italy	15	23	29	106	−5	141	150	298	9	66	65	166	7	36	50	150	3.21	4.45	38.6	60
Yugoslavia	17	50	60	235	17	113	113	350	−2	67	67	262	13	57	69	262	2.00	2.59	29.5	141
Spain	8	22	44	117	8	79	78	170	8	82	106	212	8	29	52	142	1.40	2.08	48.6	51
Greece	6	10	28	96	−9	29	33	164	5	12	40	117	2	12	29	100	1.27	1.41	11.0	62
Portugal	−2	22	26	69	12	129	128	206	3	35	41	86	8	29	40	99	1.62	2.22	37.0	35
Turkey	30	60	71	126	22	122	122	197	30	130	126	211	28	63	76	154	1.73	2.38	37.6	42
O.E.E.C. area	10	18	28	71	11	96	110	185	14	81	88	169	11	26	42	104	2.63	3.37	28.1	40[a]
Canada	34	35	57	104	58	89	84	146	52	96	97	155	42	45	66	122	3.39	4.06	19.8	30
United States	21	21	41	61	56	76	77	109	63	118	118	159	36	36	56	92	2.61	4.38	21.3	29
O.E.C.D. area	15	19	34	66	26	84	88	131	29	102	105	161	21	31	50	97	3.25	4.00	23.1	36[a]
Soviet Union	28	43	51	203	33	64	75	254	−3	43	66	235	21	48	59	221	3.17	4.98	57.1	102

1. 1958 or nearest year.
2. Increase 1970 over 1957. Excluding Yugoslavia, but including the Saar.
Source: See Appendices I and II.

235. Here it should be stressed once more that, in view of the inadequacy of the statistical data available, the projections for 1970 necessarily contain an element of conjecture. The data presented, country by country, in Table 14 show the basis on which the projections have been founded and thus make possible an informed discussion of their usefulness.

236. Table 14 indicates how various factors contribute to the projected rise in expenditure on education in each country. It shows only the high alternative, which is regarded as a reasonable maximum effort. It also shows (in the 5-24 column) that the increase in expenditure for most countries would be roughly around 100 per cent, which is also approximately the average for the O.E.E.C. area and for North America, and therefore also the average for O.E.C.D. area. This result may seem surprising in view of the wide differences in the rate of population growth for the 5-24 group. It is, however, largely explained by the fact that the probable shortage of teachers has forced us to assume a more modest rise in enrolment ratios and a more modest reduction in the student/teacher ratio in cases where population growth is expected to be fast.

237. Enrolment ratios in the 5-14 group, however, had in most countries already reached almost a ceiling in the base year. As the bulk of expenditure goes to this age group, the growth of total expenditure tends to correlate with the growth of this age group. This partly explains the comparatively slow growth of projected total expenditure in countries such as Sweden, the United Kingdom, and Ireland, and the comparatively rapid rise of this expenditure in countries such as Canada, Germany, Yugoslavia, and Turkey.

238. The increase of education for the higher age groups also influences overall expenditure. When population increase in this group is also high, the number of teachers has to be increased at an extraordinarily fast pace to allow for at least some rise in enrolment ratios. This is why an exceptionally fast rise in the number of teachers in the two higher age groups has been assumed in such countries as Canada and France, and also in countries where enrolment ratios were relatively low in the base year, as was for example the case for the 15-19 age group in the United Kingdom and Italy.

239. The differences in the rate of growth of expenditure are also explained by the differences in the projected rates of growth of GNP per head, as average teachers' salaries are assumed to rise in the same proportion, as for instance in the Soviet Union.

240. All these three factors combine with others to make for a rapid rise in expenditure in some of the Mediterranean countries. Here the projections have been based on the expressed intentions of these countries to introduce drastic educational reforms and on the expectation that they will be assisted in this effort by other countries.

Aims for Tomorrow and Past Achievements

241. Can Europe afford the expansion of education that has been sketched out here? Undoubtedly the answer is yes. At present, total expenditure on education in the O.E.E.C. area only accounts for slightly over 3 per cent of the gross national product. In an expanding economy, this low proportion could certainly be greatly increased in the course of a decade without seriously encroaching on other needs. But much hinges on the rate of economic expansion.

242. In the last decade Europe has experienced a rapid and steady economic growth, and it seemed reasonable to assume that this expansion will continue, though at a somewhat reduced rate. For the O.E.E.C. area as a whole, the increase in GNP between 1957 and 1970 has been estimated at 60 per cent, which corresponds to an increase per head of approximately 40 per cent. This may seem a big step forward, but it should be remembered that it would still leave Europe far behind the level which the United States had already reached in the base year.

243. In the high alternative, total expenditure on education in the O.E.E.C. area would reach 4.0 per cent of GNP, as against 3.2 per cent in the base year. The burden which this increase in expenditure would place on national economies can perhaps best be illustrated by remembering that the share in GNP of all other goods and services would fall from 96.8 per cent to 96.0 per cent, i.e. by less than 1 per cent! Expenditure on these other goods and services would increase by 58.7 per cent instead of 60 per cent as it would do if the share of education were not increased. The abstinence represented by the difference between 60 per cent and 58.7 per cent is no doubt a small price to pay for the gain to be expected.

244. Nor does the target appear too ambitious when viewed against the background of earlier achievements. In fact, it may appear modest when compared with the results achieved in some earlier periods. The high alternative assumes a rise in the share in GNP of educational expenditure of 28 per cent in 12 to 13 years. Even in the periods that included the world wars and the crisis of the 1930's, it was possible in some countries to increase the share in GNP of educational expenditure by substantially more than the rates assumed by our high alter-

	GERMANY	NETHER-LANDS	UNITED KINGDOM	U.S.A.
1913/25	24	63	39	69
1925/37	90	13	17	18
1937/49	1[1]	82	25	72
1949/55	14[1]	42	20	43

1. Territory of the Federal Republic.

native, which is shown by the figures given above which indicate the rate of increase in the share of expenditure on education in GNP over historical 12 year periods. The expansion of education will involve an increased budgetary burden. But judging by past achievements, financial difficulties would not appear to be insurmountable.

245. As for the supply of teachers, which in many countries has been the real bottle-neck, here again the high alternative remains within the limits of the possible. The number of teachers for the first age group is assumed to rise by an average of 28 per cent, except in the Mediterranean countries where the rise is assumed to be 40 per cent. If we calculate the increases of teacher numbers for this group in the period 1950-1958 and take into account that the period of the forecast is some 12 years, we get in O.E.E.C. countries rates of between 10 per cent and 90 per cent, the average being near 30 per cent. Countries which are assumed to achieve an increase of 50 per cent or more—like Germany, Yugolavia and Turkey—will have therefore to make a great effort, but it should be remembered that countries like France, the United States and the Soviet Union have in the past achieved rates of this magnitude.

246. For the second age group, the high alternative assumes an average increase in teacher numbers in the O.E.E.C. area of 110 per cent (the low alternative being 63 per cent), with increases up to 150 per cent in some countries. Applying the same method as for the first age group, it is found that the typical rates of increase in the 1950-58 period ranged between 40 and 120 per cent, the average being near 70 per cent. Thus a rate of 110 per cent on an average does not appear to be too difficult to achieve assuming the necessary long term planning and effort are made.

247. For the third age group the high alternative implies an increase in teacher numbers of 88 per cent (the low alternative being 45 per cent). Here, too, the achievements of the past are rather reassuring; rates ranged between 30 per cent and 150 per cent, with an average of about 90 per cent. Thus even the 162 per cent increase foreseen for France does not appear unattainable.

248. It can thus be seen clearly that, viewed against the background of achievements in the recent past, the targets for 1970 do not appear unreasonable. Given the precondition of steady economic growth, the O.E.E.C. countries can undertake with confidence the expansion and improvement of their education systems in the coming decade.

APPENDICES

Appendix I

NOTES ON SOURCES, STATISTICS AND METHODS

I. SOURCES

1. No attempt has been made here to list the numerous sources used for this study since a bibliography on the economics of education is soon to be published under the auspices of O.E.E.C. In addition to works on the economic and financial aspects of education, we have used numerous monographs on national education systems, general statistical reviews, national yearbooks, and expenditure accounts as well as statistical publications from national and international agencies.

2. The Statistical Division of the Social Sciences Department of Unesco gave access to its files containing *inter alia* the returns to the comprehensive Unesco questionnaire ST/Q/37 on education in 1957.

3. The Manpower Division of O.E.E.C. provided data of population in the base year and population forecasts (the base year for the latter being 1956 in most cases).

4. The Economics and Statistics Directorate of O.E.E.C. provided figures of gross national product for the base year and estimates for 1970, at base year prices, as well as price indices and exchange rates for converting national currencies into U.S. dollars.

5. Estimates of the gross national product of the Soviet Union are mainly based on: "Comparisons of the United States and Soviet Economics", Papers Submitted by Panelists Appearing Before the Subcommittee on Economic Statistics, Joint Economic Committee, Congress of the United States. Parts I and II, Washington 1957. The exchange rate chosen as reasonable for the purposes of this study (6 Roubles to 1 U.S. Dollar) is also mainly based on that report.

6. The Office for Scientific and Technical Personnel of O.E.E.C. made available all relevant material in its files and, for the purpose of this study, sent out two questionnaires to selected experts of Member and Associated countries (OSTP/60/S/4630 of 7th October 1960, and OSTP/61/S/3206 of 3rd May 1961) as well as detailed requests for information to selected Member and Associated countries. The returns to these questionnaires and requests received before 30th June 1961 constitute the main source of the statistical tables contained in this study.

II. NOTES ON STATISTICS AND METHODS

7. The use of round figures explains the small inconsistencies in certain totals. As already mentioned, it was not always possible to get figures for the same year, and this may also account for some slight inaccuracies.

a) *Enrolment and Teachers*

8. The figures relate to full-time students in public and private institutions. We accepted the definition given in the Unesco questionnaire (ST/Q/37):

> "A pupil (student) is a person enrolled in a school for systematic instruction at any level of education. A full-time pupil (student) is one who is enrolled for full-time education for a substantial period of time."

9. The interpretation of what is a substantial period has been left to national agencies; it varies considerably from country to country and from one type of school to another. In the questionnaire OSTP/61/S/3206 an attempt was made to define a part-time student as:

"in apprenticeship or gainful employment participating part-time in institutions being a part of the formal education system."

10. But the result was not altogether satisfactory; there is reason to believe that students in some countries who appear in our tables as full-time would be counted as part-time in other countries, and vice versa. Excluding part-time students sometimes meant arbitrary decisions. This may have introduced a certain margin of error in student numbers and enrolment ratios for the base year, but has had much less effect on the forecast. The forecast for expenditure includes all expenditure on formal part-time education, the rate of increase of which has been assumed to be the same as that of full-time education.

11. Similar considerations apply to the exclusion of students over the age of 24. It was known that in certain countries a quarter or a third of the students in higher education were over 24, but they had to be excluded because this information was available for a few countries only. However, the rates of increase forecast for students in the third age group were used to calculate all education expenditure allocated to this group.

12. For about half the countries covered in this study student numbers were available for most age groups by single years; where they were not thus available, the numbers had to be estimated in the light of knowledge of national education systems and of such figures as were available on the number of students in various grades.

13. It was more difficult to calculate the number of teachers for each age group, as all our sources gave them by type of education. Some of these types fitted in with one or other of our age groups, but others did not. To solve the problem we used student/teacher ratios typical for our age groups, applied them to the numbers of students calculated or estimated for each age group as described above, and thus arrived at rough estimates of teacher numbers for each age group.

14. In many cases, our figures were confirmed or corrected by experts or agencies in the twenty-two countries concerned whom we had asked to check them; in other cases the estimates are our exclusive responsibility.

b) *Expenditure*[1]

15. In most cases the expenditure figures available did not cover the whole educational effort, and the portion not covered varies from country to country. In some cases, only the expenditure of the central Ministry of Education was available; in others all public expenditure at all levels of government and by all authorities contributing to formal education was obtainable.

16. In our sources expenditure on pre-school education was sometimes included in that for the first level; higher education often included expenditure on research and on clinics to a varying extent; adult education, expenditure on youth activities outside school and other fringe items were sometimes said to be included in a total of "other current expenditure". As far as possible, expenditure on pre-school education, youth activities, libraries outside educational institutions, education in military establishments, research outside higher education, adult education, theatres, radio, television and other mass media was excluded from our figures.

17. On the other hand, we considered that to exclude transfer expenditure, such as grants to students, pensions, contributions to pension funds and social security

---

1. See also paragraphs 172 and 235 above.

schemes, even interest on debts, would give a false impression of the real weight of educational costs. The same is true of some items of welfare expenditure, such as health services in schools, meals, books, transportation, etc. These were assessed as far as possible net of any revenue they produce. In the forecast, transfer and welfare items were treated separately as far as possible, allowing for different rates of increase. Pensions, for instance, may be expected to increase *pari passu* with GNP per head.

18. Expenditure on private education, where not available, was estimated on the basis of numbers of pupils and teachers in private education and of average cost per pupil and per teacher in public education. In some cases, where the cost of private education was known to be on average higher or lower than that of public education, this was taken into account.

19. Total current expenditure was distributed as between the three age groups on the basis either of information available or of estimates as indicated above. A typical proportion in European countries was found to be 70: 20: 10, whereas in North America and in the Soviet Union it was more like 60: 25: 15. From the results of our forecasts, it can be seen that the proportion tends generally to become 50: 30: 20.

20. To the amounts of current expenditure by age groups (excluding fringe expenditure mentioned above) we applied factors of increase resulting from our forecasts of GNP per head, student numbers and student/teacher ratios. Where current expenditure for 1957 was given, we used for each age group separately the formula:

$$E_{70} = E_{57} \times \frac{St_{70}}{St_{57}} \times \frac{St/T_{57}}{St/T_{70}} \times \frac{GNP_{c\,70}}{GNP_{c\,57}}$$

where E = current expenditure, St = number of students, St/T = student/teacher ratio, and GNP_c = gross national product per head.

21. As there was no valid way of forecasting capital expenditure, except in a very few countries, we estimated it roughly as equal to 20 per cent of the forecast total current expenditure in 1970.

Appendix II

STATISTICAL DATA FOR INDIVIDUAL COUNTRIES

TABLE 1. POPULATION OF SCHOOL AGE AND STUDENTS BY AGE GROUPS
BASE YEAR

Thousands.

COUNTRY	BASE YEAR	5—14 POPU-LATION	5—14 STU-DENTS	15—19 POPU-LATION	15—19 STU-DENTS	20—24 POPU-LATION	20—24 STU-DENTS	5—24 POPU-LATION	5—24 STU-DENTS
Sweden	1960	1,142	943	589	190	462	51	2,193	1,184
Switzerland	1956	827	650	345	79	349	12	1,521	741
Luxembourg	1957	38	29	20	5	22	1.2	80	35.2
Belgium	1957	1,341	1,279	533	168	584	32	2,458	1,479
United Kingdom	1957	8,054	7,956	3,258	572	3,183	123	14,495	8,651
France	1958	7,581	6,827	2,689	827	2,986	113	13,256	7,767
Denmark	1957	813	621	324	60	287	16	1,424	697
Norway	1957	609	471	224	80	199	19	1,032	570
Germany, F.R.	1958	6,968	5,591	4,276	753	4,200	193	15,444	6,537
Netherlands	1958	2,254	1,928	878	288	790	37	3,922	2,253
Iceland	1957	34.7	25.4	11.7	6.8	11.7	0.8	58.1	33
Austria	1957	988	838	595	78	418	16	2,001	931
Ireland	1957	572.7	530.5	232.1	45.5	179.1	7.5	983.9	583.5
Italy	1957	7,359	5,796	4,190	659	4,017	155	15,566	6,610
Yugoslavia	1956	3,278	2,175	1,654	280	1,761	72	6,693	2,527
Spain	1958/59	5,253	3,937	2,965	393	2,947	96	11,165	4,426
Greece	1956/57	1,375	1,024	741	125	764	25	2,880	1,174
Portugal	1957/58	1,657	932	725	64	743	23	3,125	1,019
Turkey	1959/60	6,460	2,890	2,863	94	2,666	30	11,989	3,014
O.E.E.C. area		56,604	44,443	27,113	4,767	26,569	1,022	110,286	50,232
Canada	1958	3,513	3,066	1,266	581	1,186	110	5,965	3,757
United States	1958	33,901	30,477	12,489	8,267	10,920	1,307	57,310	40,051
O.E.C.D. area		94,018	77,986	40,868	13,615	38,675	2,439	173,561	94,040
Soviet Union	1958	37,454	26,769	16,967	8,245	20,343	1,661	74,764	36,675

TABLE 2. ENROLMENT RATIOS BY AGE GROUPS
BASE YEAR[1] AND PROJECTION FOR 1970 (HIGH ALTERNATIVE)

COUNTRY	5—14 BASE YEAR	5—14 1970	15—19 BASE YEAR	15—19 1970	20—24 BASE YEAR	20—24 1970	5—24 BASE YEAR	5—24 1970
United States	89.9	90	66.2	75	12.0	16	69.9	69.4
Canada	87.3	88	45.9	55	9.3	12	63.0	64.1
Sweden	82.6	82	32.3	48	11.0	12	54.0	54.3
Switzerland	78.6	83	22.9	33	3.4	7	48.7	51.6
Luxembourg	76.3	85	25.2	35	5.4	7	44.0	49.4
Belgium	95.4	96	31.5	45	5.5	8	60.2	61.4
United Kingdom	98.8	99	17.6	31	3.9	6.6	59.6	58.9
France	90.1	92	30.8	47	3.8	7	58.6	58.6
Denmark	76.4	82	18.5	35	5.6	7.6	48.9	51.0
Norway	77.3	82	35.7	60	9.5	13.1	55.2	59.2
Germany, F.R.	80.2	85	17.6	30	4.6	7.5	42.3	54.8
Netherlands	85.5	88	32.8	45	4.7	7.0	57.4	55.8
Iceland	73.2	82	57.9	65	6.8	8	56.7	64.3
Austria	84.8	86	13.1	25	3.7	5	46.5	51.9
Ireland	92.6	93	19.6	25	4.2	5	59.3	59.7
Italy	78.8	84	15.7	40	3.9	6	42.5	53.6
Yugoslavia	66.3	85	16.9	30	4.1	7	37.8	52.7
Spain	74.9	85	13.3	22	3.3	5.5	39.6	47.3
Greece	74.5	77	16.9	24	3.3	3.5	40.8	44.8
Portugal	56.2	70	8.8	18	3.1	4	32.6	41.1
Turkey	44.7	55	3.3	6	1.1	2	25.1	31.9
Soviet Union[2]	71.5	80	48.6	60	8.2	12	49.1	60.1

1. For the year to which the data refer, see Appendix II, Table 1.
2. See footnote 1 on page 61.

TABLE 3. POPULATION OF SCHOOL AGE AND STUDENTS BY AGE GROUPS
PROJECTIONS FOR 1970

Thousands.

COUNTRY	5—14 POPU-LATION	5—14 STUDENT LOW	5—14 STUDENT HIGH	15—19 POPU-LATION	15—19 STUDENT LOW	15—19 STUDENT HIGH	20—24 POPU-LATION	20—24 STUDENT LOW	20—24 STUDENT HIGH	5—24 POPU-LATION	5—24 STUDENT LOW	5—24 STUDENT HIGH
Sweden	1,064	873	873	532	213	255	618	68	74	2,214	1,154	1,202
Switzerland	823	658	683	402	113	133	414	21	29	1,639	792	845
Luxembourg	40	32	34	25	7	8.8	25	1.5	1.7	90	40.5	44.5
Belgium	1,414	1,357	1,357	702	281	316	699	42	56	2,815	1,680	1,729
United Kingdom	8,308	8,225	8,225	3,992	1,130	1,250	4,262	256	281	16,562	9,611	9,756
France	7,903	7,192	7,271	3,996	1,598	1,878	4,210	210	295	16,109	8,999	9,444
Denmark	743	594	609	364	102	127	396	26	30	1,503	722	766
Norway	626	488	513	302	136	181	313	31	41	1,241	656	735
Germany, F.R.	8,270	6,864	7,030	3,770	943	1,131	3,320	216	249	15,360	8,019	8,410
Netherlands	2,142	1,842	1,885	1,078	377	485	1,170	58	82	4,390	2,277	2,452
Iceland	41	30.7	33.6	14	8.4	9.1	13	0.9	1.0	68	40	43.7
Austria	1,030	875	886	460	69	115	484	19	24	1,974	963	1,025
Ireland	546	508	508	219	44	55	195	8.8	9.7	960	560.8	572.7
Italy	8,470	6,437	7,115	3,974	1,391	1,590	4,276	171	257	16,720	7,999	8,962
Yugoslavia	3,828	2,680	3,254	1,990	398	597	1,718	86	120	7,536	3,164	3,971
Spain	5,659	4,524	4,810	3,194	479	703	3,175	127	175	12,028	5,133	5,688
Greece	1,463	1,097	1,127	671	134	161	802	28	28	2,936	1,259	1,316
Portugal	1,628	977	1,139	813	89	146	764	27	31	3,205	1,093	1,316
Turkey	8,413	4,200	4,630	3,492	140	209	3,471	49	69	15,376	4,389	4,908
O.E.E.C. area	62,411	49,457	51,983	29,990	7,653	9,350	30,325	1,447	1,853	122,726	58,551	63,186
Canada	4,700	4,136	4,136	2,000	1,000	1,100	1,800	180	216	8,500	5,316	5,452
United States	40,940	38,846	36,846	19,454	13,618	14,590	17,800	2,314	2,848	78,194	52,778	54,284
O.E.C.D. area	108,051	90,438	92,965	51,444	22,271	25,040	49,925	3,941	4,917	209,420	116,645	122,922
Soviet Union	48,000	36,000	38,400	22,518	11,260	13,510	19,744	1,974	2,369	90,262	49,234	54,279

TABLE 4. TEACHERS BY AGE GROUPS OF STUDENTS
BASE YEAR[1] AND PROJECTIONS FOR 1970

Thousands.

COUNTRY	5—14 BASE YEAR	5—14 1970 LOW	5—14 1970 HIGH	15—19 BASE YEAR	15—19 1970 LOW	15—19 1970 HIGH	20—24 BASE YEAR	20—24 1970 LOW	20—24 1970 HIGH	5—24 BASE YEAR	5—24 1970 LOW	5—24 1970 HIGH
Sweden	43.0	39.7	44.0	9.0	10.1	15.0	3.0	4.0	6.5	55.0	53.8	65.5
Switzerland	24.1	24.4	29.7	3.6	5.2	7.4	1.2	2.1	2.4	28.9	31.7	39.5
Luxembourg	1.21	1.33	1.7	0.3	0.42	0.68	0.1	0.13	0.18	1.61	1.9	2.56
Belgium	63.9	67.8	75.4	10.5	17.6	22.6	2.6	3.5	5.6	77.0	88.9	103.6
United Kingdom	311.1	321.3	348.5	45.5	89.7	102.4	15.8	32.8	34.3	372.4	443.8	485.2
France	243.8	256.8	290.8	33.1	63.9	75.2	7.1	13.1	18.6	284.0	333.8	384.6
Denmark	20.0	19.2	23.4	5.4	9.3	11.5	1.6	2.6	3.0	27.0	31.1	37.9
Norway	18.8	19.5	22.3	4.7	8.0	10.7	1.9	3.1	3.4	25.4	30.6	36.4
Germany, F.R.	164.0	201.8	251.0	32.8	42.9	56.5	12.8	14.4	16.6	209.6	259.1	324.1
Netherlands	58.4	55.8	67.3	14.4	18.8	26.9	3.7	5.8	6.8	76.5	80.4	101.0
Iceland	1.0	1.2	1.68	0.4	0.5	0.6	0.1	0.1	0.12	1.5	1.8	2.4
Austria	30.3	31.3	36.9	7.0	6.3	10.5	1.4	1.8	2.2	38.7	39.4	49.6
Ireland	16.5	15.9	18.1	3.3	3.1	3.9	0.6	0.7	0.8	20.4	19.7	22.8
Italy	263.1	292.6	338.8	54.4	115.0	135.9	9.7	10.7	16.0	327.2	418.3	490.7
Yugoslavia	67.8	83.7	108.5	14.0	19.9	29.9	4.8	5.7	8.0	86.6	109.3	146.3
Spain	98.4	113.2	141.5	19.7	23.9	35.2	5.3	7.0	10.9	123.4	144.1	187.5
Greece	25.2	27.0	32.2	6.1	6.5	8.1	1.0	1.1	1.4	32.3	34.6	41.7
Portugal	26.5	27.8	33.5	4.0	5.6	9.1	1.7	2.0	2.4	32.2	35.4	45.0
Turkey	60.2	87.5	102.9	4.1	6.1	9.1	1.9	3.1	4.3	66.2	96.7	116.3
O.E.E.C. area	1,537.3	1,716.5	1,968.2	272.3	452.8	571.2	76.3	113.7	143.5	1,885.9	2,283.1	2,682.9
Canada	105.2	142.6	165.4	35.1	58.8	64.7	7.8	12.9	15.4	148.1	214.3	245.5
United States	1,088.5	1,315.9	1,535.2	486.3	801.1	858.2	108.9	192.8	237.3	1,683.7	2,309.8	2,630.7
O.E.C.D. area	2,731.0	3,175.0	3,668.8	793.7	1,312.7	1,494.1	193.0	319.4	396.2	3,717.7	4,807.2	5,559.1
Soviet Union	1,275.0	1,714.0	1,920.0	550.0	751.0	965.0	119.0	141.0	197.0	1,944.0	2,606.0	3,082.0

1. For the year to which the data refer, see Appendix II, Table 1.

TABLE 5. CURRENT, CAPITAL AND TOTAL EXPENDITURE ON EDUCATION
BASE YEAR

COUNTRY	BASE YEAR	EXPENDITURE (Millions of U.S. dollars)			TOTAL EXPENDITURE = 100	
		CURRENT	CAPITAL	TOTAL	CURRENT	CAPITAL
Sweden	1960	379.0	88.9	467.9	81.0	19.0
Switzerland	1956	179.2	30.7	209.9	85.37	14.63
Luxembourg	1957	5.6	0.2	5.8	96.55	3.45
Belgium..............	1957	299.0	18.7	317.7	94.11	5.89
United Kingdom[2].....	1957	1,941.5	413.0	2,354.5	82.46	17.54
France	1959	1,418.5	403.0	1,821.5	77.88	22.12
Denmark	1957	126.0	27.8	153.8	81.92	18.08
Norway	1957	111.0	35.0	146.0	76.03	23.97
Germany, F.R.	1958	1,137.0	366.9	1,503.9	75.60	24.40
Netherlands	1957	333.0	71.8	404.8	82.26	17.74
Iceland...............	1957	2.8	0.8	3.6	77.78	22.22
Austria...............	1957	131.8	5.2	137.0	96.20	3.8
Ireland	1957	42.5	4.5	47.0	90.43	9.57
Italy	1957/58	823.8	54.1	877.9	93.84	6.16
Yugoslavia	1957	133.6	40.3	173.9	76.83	23.17
Spain................	1960/61	148.9	17.6	166.5	89.43	10.57
Greece	1957	36.2	3.9	40.1	90.27	9.73
Portugal.............	1957	33.1	9.0	42.1	78.62	21.38
Turkey	1959/60	89.8	16.4	106.2	84.56	15.44
O.E.E.C. area		7,372.3	1,607.8	8,980.1	82.1	17.9
Canada	1958	1,170.3	113.4	1,283.7	91.17	8.83
United States	1958	16,580.0	4,203.0	20,783.0	79.78	20.22
O.E.C.D. area........		25,122.6	5,924.2	31,046.8	80.92	19.08
Soviet Union.........	1958	8,350.0	1,494.0	9,884.0	84.82	15.18

1. Percentages below 10 do not seem to be likely. It must be assumed that in the cases of Luxembourg, Belgium, Austria, Ireland, Italy, Greece and Canada, capital expenditure of certain levels of Government or Ministries other than the Ministry of Education had not been included in the information available.
2. Including current expenditure on loans.

TABLE 6. CURRENT EXPENDITURE ON EDUCATION FROM ALL SOURCES BY AGE GROUPS OF STUDENTS

BASE YEAR[1] AND PROJECTIONS FOR 1970

Millions of U.S. dollars.

COUNTRY	AGE GROUP												
	5—14			15—19			20—24			5—24		
	BASE YEAR	1970 LOW	1970 HIGH	BASE YEAR	1970 LOW	1970 HIGH	BASE YEAR	1970 LOW	1970 HIGH	BASE YEAR	1970 LOW	1970 HIGH
Sweden	246.0	290.3	319.8	95.0	134.9	189.1	38.0	64.2	97.7	379.0	489.4	606.6
Switzerland	116.4	156.0	190.9	44.8	85.1	122.3	18.0	41.9	48.0	179.2	283.0	361.2
Luxembourg	3.9	5.7	7.3	1.4	2.6	4.2	0.3	0.5	0.6	5.6	8.8	12.0
Belgium	194.0	257.0	282.0	75.0	156.0	209.0	30.0	49.0	77.0	299.0	462.0	568.0
United Kingdom	1,359.1	1,692.0	1,794.0	388.3	924.0	1,050.0	194.1	488.0	512.0	1,941.5	3,104.0	3,356.0
France	993.0	1,453.3	1,633.7	283.7	732.2	855.9	141.8	353.1	488.3	1,418.5	2,538.6	2,977.9
Denmark	88.2	116.4	141.1	25.2	58.7	73.1	12.6	28.1	32.5	126.0	203.2	246.7
Norway	77.7	104.9	120.4	27.8	61.4	82.0	5.5	11.9	12.7	111.0	178.2	215.1
Germany, F.R.	795.9	1,452.1	1,737.9	227.4	423.6	564.3	113.7	189.0	212.4	1,137.0	2,064.7	2,514.6
Netherlands	233.0	315.0	377.0	67.0	124.0	176.0	33.0	73.0	85.0	333.0	512.0	638.0
Iceland	1.7	2.5	3.5	0.8	1.3	1.6	0.3	0.4	0.5	2.8	4.2	5.6
Austria	92.2	135.5	155.7	26.4	36.2	56.6	13.2	20.4	24.6	131.8	192.1	236.9
Ireland	31.1	38.3	43.0	9.5	11.8	14.5	2.0	2.9	3.2	42.5	53.0	60.7
Italy	576.7	1,026.5	1,188.0	164.5	557.0	654.2	82.3	144.8	218.9	823.8	1,728.3	2,061.1
Yugoslavia	86.9	225.5	291.4	26.7	80.1	120.1	20.0	50.6	72.3	133.6	356.2	483.8
Spain	96.8	168.4	210.1	29.8	54.8	80.4	22.3	44.5	69.5	148.9	267.7	360.0
Greece	23.5	39.1	46.1	9.1	14.9	18.6	3.6	6.3	7.8	36.2	60.4	72.5
Portugal	21.5	30.1	36.3	6.6	12.3	20.2	5.0	7.8	9.3	33.1	50.2	65.8
Turkey	56.4	109.2	127.6	22.4	54.3	66.5	11.0	24.2	34.2	89.8	187.7	228.3
O.E.E.C. area	5,094.0	7,617.8	8,705.8	1,531.7	3,525.2	4,358.6	746.7	1,600.6	2,006.5	7,372.4	12,743.6	15,070.9
Canada	702.1	1,235.7	1,432.3	292.6	658.3	719.8	175.6	374.0	447.8	1,170.3	2,268.0	2,599.9
United States	9,416.0	13,535.0	15,188.0	3,966.0	7,781.0	8,295.0	3,198.0	6,722.0	8,283.0	16,580.0	28,038.0	31,766.0
O.E.C.D. area	15,212.1	22,388.5	25,326.1	5,790.3	11,964.5	13,373.4	4,120.3	8,696.6	10,737.3	25,122.7	43,049.6	49,436.8
Soviet Union	5,010.0	13,577.0	15,180.0	2,087.0	5,781.0	7,388.0	1,253.0	3,007.0	4,198.0	8,350.0	22,365.0	26,766.0

1. See Appendix II, Table 5.

DISCUSSION

DISCUSSION

Chairman: Mr. COOMBS (U.S.A.)

The *Chairman* suggested some of the main issues around which the discussion could usefully revolve. First was the proposition that spending on education was an essential part of economic development in that it enabled countries to avoid the shortage of qualified manpower which was often the principal bottle-neck to expansion. Secondly, there was the question of the usefulness of targets and plans for the orderly but rapid expansion of education. Thirdly, and linked to this question, there was the problem of measuring a country's educational effort; expenditure on education in relation to the gross national product was one important measure of this effort, but by no means the only one. Was it essential for the O.E.C.D. countries to increase the proportion of the gross national product flowing into the educational enterprise? In considering how education could best be developed it was useful to look at all the different aims, cultural, social and political as well as economic, which education must satisfy.

Turning to the more practical issues raised by the study of Professors Svennilson, Edding and Elvin, the *Chairman* proposed that the meeting should focus its attention on two major and related points: what were the possibilities of effecting a better utilisation of resources within the educational system? how could the supply of teachers be improved?

TARGETS FOR EDUCATION AND NEEDS FOR QUALIFIED MANPOWER

Professor SVENNILSON said that an objective assessment of the difficulties in achieving a well-balanced expansion made it desirable to make longer-term provision for the necessary flow of resources into education. This was particularly so in the case of teachers. It was because of the teacher shortage that the authors, in formulating their projections, could not envisage as rapid an expansion of education by 1970 as seemed desirable from an economic and social point of view. Such considerations had led them to the conclusion that there was a strong need systematically to establish long-term targets and to organize the logistics of educational expansion. Such logistics should be based on forecasting the flow of young people through the various age groups and also the demand for the various types of education and skill brought about by economic growth.

Professor SVENNILSON felt that the organization of educational logistics must become the responsibility of qualified research units which should work on a permanent basis in close contact with the Ministries and other bodies concerned with educational development. The method of *ad hoc* Committees and investigations did not seem to be sufficient if bottle-necks of highly qualified manpower within the educational system itself, the economy or society as a whole were to be avoided. A major reason for these bottle-necks could be found in the fact that targets for the expansion of education were inadequate and that their implementation did not take place in as rapid and well co-ordinated way as necessary.

Mr. PART (United Kingdom) emphasized the unwisdom of relying too closely on estimates of future manpower needs as the basis for educational planning. Several years ago the United Kingdom, convinced that it was necessary to place greater emphasis on the quality of its manpower, particularly scientific and technical personnel, had planned to double the annual output of scientists and technologists between 1956 and 1970. In point of fact, the annual output would be doubled by 1964 and would thereafter continue to rise. The United Kingdom authorities had developed a technique of "forward looking" for five years; this was fairly definite for the earlier years and less definite for the fourth and fifth years; it covered the whole field of expenditure. But longer-term "forward looking" was not possible except for selected problems, such as the fifteen to eighteen age group, university expansion, expansion of technical education; and a major review of the whole provision for higher education was now taking place. All these exercises related to 1970 or later. But the speaker expressed the view that a comprehensive plan for education was impracticable because there was no agreement in the country on what the rate of economic growth should be or on the steps by which full-time education should be increased.

Professor ELVIN referred to the doubts expressed by Mr. Part as to the value of projections of manpower needs in formulating targets for education. In his view educational policies turned on long-term estimates of many factors of which teacher supply was perhaps the most important. The timing of new developments in policy required the most careful longer term consideration of all the relevant demographic, economic and other factors.

MEASURING THE EDUCATIONAL EFFORT

Mr. DYMOND (Canada) said that it was necessary to approach the question of targets of expenditure on education viewed as a proportion of the gross national product in a very criticial state of mind. The Report under discussion was a good starting point for analysing what each country is getting from its educational system. Full examination should cover the complete educational structure, including adult education and training in industry. It should be aimed at finding out whether education is serving needs, both economic and cultural, in the most efficient way possible. Education should be judged in part as an industry is: it is on the basis of economic criteria that one should judge whether it is doing an efficient job in terms of expenditures made.

To illustrate his point Mr. DYMOND mentioned Canada, which has one of the highest ratios of GNP devoted to education of any of the countries represented. He thought that one reason for this was that the Canadian system was not as efficient in economic terms as that of many other countries. Administrative costs were high because there were ten separate provincial administrations. There was perhaps overspending on structures and on elaborate educational plant such as gymnasia and swimming pools. There was also considerable wastage in the system due to "drop out" during higher education. All these factors should be carefully appraised.

Mr. LYONS (O.E.C.D. Secretariat) made a strong plea for improved and regularly issued statistical data which would enable Governments to know what they were getting for their money and adjust their programmes accordingly. At the present time few countries possessed sound statistics on education by firms, and statistics on pupils, teachers and graduations in secondary and higher technical education were far from satisfactory. In many countries data on the professional qualifications of the labour force needed to be improved. How could Governments judge what policy to follow with regard to teachers, for example, if they had not adequate information on the qualifications, or in some cases even the numbers, of the existing teaching force?

Mr. LYONS agreed with the previous speaker that there was not necessarily any virtue in the fact that one country spent a higher proportion of its gross national product on education than another unless it could be shown that it was deriving more real benefit from it. While, in general, no-one disputed the proposition that more money was needed to improve educational systems in many countries, it was necessary to examine specific cases of how resources were being used. Federal Germany, for example, had achieved one of the highest rates of economic growth in the western world, but its expenditure on education was lower relative to GNP than in many advanced countries. Was Germany living on its intellectual capital (including the refugees), or was the "output" of the existing educational system better adapted to economic needs, and educated people better utilized, than in other countries?

Mr. PART said that education was in some respects a very intangible thing even if proper allowance is made for the length of teacher training, the number of hours per year that each student studies and each teacher teaches, the different standards aimed at and attained in different countries at different ages; as has been said, education is what is left after one has forgotten all that one has learned.

Mr. PART mentioned four indicators which, in his view, were useful in measuring educational effort. They were:

a) Enrolment ratios of pupils in the combined age groups of the population, i.e., 5 to 14, 15 to 19, and 20 to 24. It was essential to include part-time education.

b) The ratio of pupils to teachers in each of the three age groups.

c) Indicators of the quality of teachers in terms of the length of their education and training.

d) The percentage of expenditure on education in the gross national product. This required very careful and precise definition on both sides.

On techniques of planning Mr. PART said that British experience suggested that political and economic uncertainties made it impracticable to formulate a precise comprehensive plan for as long as ten years ahead, but it was both necessary and desirable to undertake detailed studies on this time-scale for selected sectors and this had recently been done in the United Kingdom for the 15-18 age group, university expansion, the demand for and the supply of teachers and the expansion of technical education. A wide-ranging survey of higher education over the next twenty-five years was at present in progress. For comprehensive detailed planning the United Kingdom now favoured a three year plan combined with a "forward look" for the following two years; the intention was to review these plans annually.

M. FOURASTIÉ (France) criticised the results of presenting expenditure on education, in the "Targets" study, in dollar terms. This method might tend to misleading estimations of educational effort in some countries because the official exchange rate did not reflect the internal purchasing power of the currency. Thus the United States had seven times as many teachers as Italy, whereas its expenditure on education, in dollars, was twelve times as large; this difference seemed hard to explain. M. FOURASTIÉ also stressed the importance of taking due account of part-time education in making comparisons of educational effort. When preparing targets of expenditure, it should be remembered that the number of hours worked by teachers will tend to decline in the future.

Professor SVENNILSON accepted the criticism of M. Fourastié on the point of exchange rates. The authors had been very conscious of it and had tried as far as possible to use other measures than currency values, such as enrolment ratios, teacher/student ratios and similar quantitative measurements; but they had thought that it would be useful to sum up the order of magnitude of the financial problem if only imperfectly. The authors considered the possibility of using exchange rates other than the official ones, but they found that they would be faced with very complex problems; they had therefore used the official rates and provided all the elements of projection, so that the reader could, if he wished, work out and apply other exchange rates.

The speaker agreed with M. Fourastié that educational outlays per head of population or per student could not be satisfactorily compared in dollars owing to the misleading effect of applying prevailing exchange rates. At those rates a thousand dollars represented a smaller volume of teachers' services in the United States than in Italy or France. The percentage of educational expenditures in the gross national product used in the study could, however, be regarded as a useful measure for comparison.

Professor EDDING said that the authors had excluded part-time education for all countries, except for the Soviet Union where it leads to the same diplomas as full-time education. Nevertheless, even if part-time students were excluded, the Soviet Union would still be at a higher level in terms of enrolment ratios than most European countries.

Summing up this part of the discussion, Professor SVENNILSON said that this study was an essay in an international survey of trends in this field. The difficulties arising out of lack of national statistics were such that the authors had often despaired of being able to complete the study. Clearly, this type of survey could be no substitute for national planning. The authors had proceeded from the broad question, "how large a part of each generation should go how far in education in order to meet the needs of economic growth?" National planning would be in a better position to answer such questions in a realistic way.

THE AIMS OF EDUCATION

Many speakers felt that it was vitally necessary to examine the use to which education was being put before deciding how much to spend on it. Dr. TENA ARTIGAS (Spain) observed that it was not possible to separate the study of the quantity of education from the study of the nature of education. The amount of expenditure could change considerably according to the alternatives adopted. M. FOURASTIÉ urged that the fundamental aims of human culture should be paramount in working out long-term plans for education; the training of manpower was not the only consideration. We should always have in mind the dramatic difficulties with which humanity will be faced in the years to come when it tries to create a real mass culture.

Professor VITO (Italy) supported the view that the culture and education of men was the main aim, and expenditure the means to this end. This approach had implications for the return on education expenditure which differed from those arising when growth was the main aim.

Dr. WOHLGEMUTH (Austria) felt that a bridge could, and should, be built between the technological and the literary type of education. The gap between the two was a great danger. This might be avoided by establishing the right balance in curricula as between scientific, technical and humanistic subjects.

Dom. RAEBER (Switzerland) saw a very close connection between education and economic development, because at the root of education was the need for life and work. Manpower was at the beginning of every culture, and work with the hands is really the essence of culture and of economic development.

Mr. ERDER (Turkey) considered that, methodologically, this dichotomy could best be resolved by putting the main emphasis on the manpower aspect of projections of needs for education. This projection method provides one with a picture of what should be the minimum targets; these could then be increased by applying other social standards.

Professor SVENNILSON saw no essential difficulty in reconciling the cultural and the economic sides of the problem. The authors had tried to express the cultural aspects of education within the simple economic terminology of consumption. But when speaking of education as consumption, they had not only considered the value of this consumption as measured by its cost, but had also looked at education in relation to welfare. Some formulation of a general welfare theory as applied to education, covering all aspects of the problem, cultural values as well as investment, was clearly necessary. The situation was that we can invest while we consume; we can become more cultured while becoming more productive for the future. There is within education a choice between the more technological direction of education and the more general type of education for the common citizen. Professor Vito, who belongs to the Italian school of economists, would be able to develop in a very elegant way the special situation which arises when it is not a question of choice between consumption and investment, but where the two take place at the same time. Mr. Erder's plea for priority for manpower assessments represented emphasis on the investment aspects of education.

Mr. GASS (O.E.C.D. Secretariat) said that it would be difficult, following this discussion, to use the slogan "education is an investment" without being aware that there were many subtleties and relationships which ought to be taken into account. The fact that education could, at the same time, be viewed as consumption and investment represented an important argument in its favour. The question of a possible conflict between education for cultural and manpower needs should be solved at the level of practical planning. Mr. GASS mentioned part of the summary of the findings of the conference on "Ability and Educational Opportunity in a Modern Economy", organized by O.E.C.D. at Kungälv, Sweden, in June 1961. This read: "The impulse of States towards the development of scientific manpower doesn't run counter to the demand of individuals for the opportunity to develop a full human stature. Yet no delegate could have gone away with the comfortable assurance that this is an immutable relation. On the contrary, because of the very aim towards economic efficiency and betterment which the O.E.C.D. countries pursue, it is realistic to anticipate a future society in which the two themes could clash."

The Improvement of the Educational Process

Professor SVENNILSON said that, from comparisons of the proportion of educational spending in GNP or in government budgets, he drew the conclusion that the expansion of education was not mainly a problem of finance, but of efficient organization. This was not to deny the need for more financial resources—Professor Elvin and Dr. Wohlgemuth had both stressed that money was essential for educational expansion—but was intended to draw attention to the need for improving the efficiency of education as an industry.

Dr. TENA ARTIGAS supported this argument. Increasing expenditure was not the only way to obtain results in education; it was also essential to increase the yield. It was only recently that people had begun to question why, after eight or ten years at school, students seem to have learned so little. Some excellent educationalists thought that the yield of the educational enterprise was not adequate. Countries should, therefore, make arrangements to improve the yield of education as part of their longer-term plans for developing it. The educational system of 1970 must not just be to-day's system on a larger scale. What is required is to examine all the complex elements of to-day's educational system, including those parts of it which are outside the formal system, and decide how to reshape it rationally so that it works better before making plans to enlarge it.

Mr. SCHMIDT (Denmark), mentioned that politicians and the public in his country well understood that more money should be spent and more should be done to improve education. But there was resistance to change in other quarters. Changes in the educational system would meet with opposition from local organizations, parents' organizations and the teachers' organization. It was not, for example, the main task of the teachers' organization to improve the educational system, but to improve the conditions of teachers and their living standards.

The Supply of Teachers

The *Chairman* introduced the discussion by endorsing the view that the major barrier to the expansion and improvement of education was the shortage of teachers. To solve this problem, the first essential was to know future needs well in advance. In establishing plans to meet these needs, the drop-out factor should be fully taken into account. In some countries, such as the United States, the drop-out rate was very high indeed.

Another problem to be tackled was that of the financial rewards for teaching. Since teachers' salaries fell largely within the public sector, the possibilities of competing with industrial salaries were limited. Nevertheless the premise of the authors of the report that over the next ten years teachers' salaries will keep pace with the rise of the gross national product *per capita* might have to be revised because of the increased demand for teachers; the relationship between teachers' salaries and salaries in general might have to be altered to the advantage of teachers.

It was important to examine the possibilities of bringing back to the teaching profession some of the people who had left it, particularly women whose children had grown up, and to increase the opportunities for women to enter the teaching profession.

Looking at the demand side, the *Chairman* asked why the teaching profession had not developed the division of labour between the highly-trained professional person and the less skilled assistants as had been done in architecture, medicine and elsewhere. The highly-trained teacher should not have to waste his time helping children off with their snow suits or erasing blackboards. The possibilities of greater teamwork and specialization among teachers should also be studied. New devices such as teaching machines or learning machines should be examined, as should also the use of television, but the best self-instructional device was still the book, and books could and should be improved.

All these methods served to raise the productivity of the teacher. They would tend to reduce the required number of teachers to more manageable proportions without impairing the quality of education. They would also make possible a higher salary scale.

Mr. HERMSEN (Netherlands) said that the Netherlands authorities had raised teachers' salaries, and introduced a liberal system of scholarships for teacher training as well as tax benefits for parents of students. There had been considerable publicity, by radio and other means, to attract people into teaching. As a result, it was hoped to improve the teacher/pupil ratio in primary schools by 1963. The situation in secondary schools was slowly improving, and it seemed certain that by 1970 the scientific staff at universities would be adequate. A very difficult problem still to be solved was that of differentials in salaries as between science teachers and teachers in the humanities.

Professor VITO said that the problems of teacher supply at the different levels in Italy were broadly analogous to those mentioned by Mr. Hermsen.

Professor SCHULTZ (United States) urged that the cost to the economy of opportunities foregone, i.e., human resources withdrawn from other productive efforts, should not be omitted when assessing the real cost of education. In the case of college and university students this accounted perhaps for sixty per cent of the real cost to the economy, and in the case of mature pupils at secondary schools also for something like sixty per cent.

Then, too, if the value of the students' time were taken into consideration, there would be a greater incentive to make education more efficient.

The *Chairman* remarked that in an economic system where the productivity of manpower was rising due to technological improvements and application of capital, industries which had remained manpower-intensive encountered increasing problems. The educational industry was unique in that it was both a producer and consumer of manpower; it was pressed to expand its output, but was at a competitive disadvantage to secure enough manpower to enable it to do so.

Dr. WOHLGEMUTH said that in Austria there was a shortage of teachers in rural and technical schools. Among measures being adopted he mentioned the granting of tenure with pension rights to teachers coming from industry, measures to encourage the return of married women to teaching, scholarships, higher salaries especially in rural areas, and special allowances for teachers in senior classes or in isolated areas.

Dom. RAEBER said that in Switzerland there were shortages of all types of teachers. Differences in salaries between teaching and industry were very large. Measures taken to overcome this shortage included moderate increases in salaries, publicity, re-training of existing teachers for promotion to a higher level of education, and incentives to attract people back into teaching. The fact that the religious convictions of the teachers are no longer a consideration had also added to the supply of teachers.

A United States delegate submitted that there was no shortage of teachers; there was a shortage of teaching. By this he meant that not enough attention had been given to the problem of making a more effective use of teachers. The argument was widely accepted that teachers were dedicated individuals and should be paid, somewhat like ministers of religion, a low salary, because raising the salary might mean lowering the quality. This kind of thinking was an impediment to greater efficiency in the educational enterprise.

Mr. SCHMIDT said that the severe shortage of primary and secondary school teachers in Denmark had necessitated a reduction in the number of school hours. To meet this shortage it had been necessary, among other things, to recruit non-professional teachers; engineers from private undertakings had been enrolled as part-time teachers. The speaker emphasized the importance of taking a long-term view of the teacher shortage. If it were known that this shortage would be eliminated automatically by the existing rate of supply, temporary expedients might be all that was necessary. But if the shortage were to continue or grow worse there would be need for more fundamental measures. In Denmark the teachers' organization had set up a working group to study this problem, and their findings were that the teacher shortage would disappear in a few years, giving way to a surplus. Therefore, they warned against measures for increasing the number of teachers. They had obvious reasons and interests for taking that attitude. But the Government had made a new investigation into the question and had come to the conclusion that at the present rate of supply of teachers the shortage would become more severe in the next 10 or 20 years. This shows the importance of having a sound basis for planning.

Professor ELVIN agreed that the crucial problem in education was the supply of teachers, but he suggested that the first question was to examine how far this problem was of a short-term nature and how far it was due to profound underlying social and economic changes. A short-term problem is inevitable in any period of expansion, because of the length of time it takes to train a teacher. But there is the question of knowing how far the difficulty lies in recruiting competent people for teaching and how far it lies in a shortage of facilities for teacher training. Only recently the difficulty in the United Kingdom had been much more one of shortage of places in teacher training colleges than of willingness to enter the profession. Then there is the problem of wastage. In the United Kingdom there has been a sensational increase in drop-out due to the high marriage rate of women teachers. We know that by 1990, these young women will have finished raising their families and be ready to go back to teaching. But meanwhile emergency measures have to be taken to attract back to teaching those who have left it and also to bring into teaching those who, while not possessing the usual professional training, do have the skill, ability and vocation to teach children.

Discussing the demand for education, Professor ELVIN considered that much could be done to speed up the opening of new universities. In his view the mechanics of the process of expansion should be studied. The question of machines to assist teaching should be approached with great care. There was a profound feeling that education was different from mere instruction, and that the learning machine and its analogues were perhaps of greatest use in matters of instruction.

It must not be forgotten that education is not just the teaching of subjects but the formation of persons, and this consideration justified even highly-skilled teachers in carrying out minor tasks which brought them into contact with the individuals they were teaching. A balance should be struck between conservatism and innovation. It would be dangerous to forget the value of books in the teaching process.

Referring to the long-term social factors influencing the supply of teachers, Professor ELVIN commented that the teaching profession had been traditionally the way of social advancement for the bright children of working class parentage, and the social and financial attractions of teaching should be increased now that there were other more attractive openings for them, particularly in industry.

Mr. VAIZEY (panel of experts) observed that, while great care should be taken before it was said that a particular shortage was a long-term problem, this was the case in teaching. The supply and demand of teachers in general—and science and mathematics teachers in particular—was a problem in practically every country and one which seemed likely to become more acute over the years. The reasons for this had been stated by the O.E.C.D. Secretariat in a study with which the speaker had been associated. They were, first, the population bulge in practically every country; second, the steady lengthening of school life; and third, the switching of interest in modern societies towards science and mathematics and other subjects which required highly skilled teachers and rather intensive teaching.

Now, was this long-term problem a structural one or one which could be solved by paying higher salaries? In almost every country teachers' salaries had risen quite substantially in recent years, perhaps even more than was generally realized because, at the same time, the quality of teachers had declined seriously in many cases. The conclusion seemed to be that salaries were not the main answer. In practically every country investigated, the demand for teachers formed such a high proportion of the total demand for qualified manpower that only marginal adjustments could be made by raising salaries. The basic question was how to increase the total supply of qualified people fairly rapidly. It was quite clear that doubling or trebling the supply of qualified manpower in general over a period of 10 years would be a real pre-condition for solving the teacher shortage, whereas doubling or trebling teachers' salaries—even if this were possible—would certainly not do anything but threaten to bleed other sectors of the economy of qualified personnel. Moreover, there is a limit to the amount that can be paid in teachers' salaries, and in a number of countries this limit has been almost reached. There is a danger that the demand for teachers will decrease if they become so expensive that governments cannot afford to pay them.

Another point which emerged from the O.E.C.D. study was the extraordinarily wasteful use of teachers in many countries. Perhaps the biggest source of waste was the teaching of pupils who, partly for financial reasons, leave school before their courses are completed. Also, there were universities in the United Kingdom in which the wastage rate was 20 % and other universities with wastage rates of only 2-3 per cent between the time of entry and of graduation. In principle, there is no reason why the performance of the worst universities in this respect should not be raised to that of the best.

It was also necessary to look very critically at such things as the age of attendance at school. The United Kingdom was completely out of line with other countries in this respect. It would be very interesting to know whether, after 10 years of compulsory education from 5-15, English children were better or worse educated than those in countries with 9 years of education from 7-16 years. It would also be interesting to examine the length of school holidays and the length of the school day throughout Europe and North America. In principle, it should be possible to find out fairly easily the right answers to these questions, and more research should be carried out on these topics, instead of research in expensive and unrewarding areas.

In conclusion the *Chairman* pointed to the great danger that the expansion of education might lead to an erosion of quality so subtle and imperceptible that it would be almost too late before it became apparent. If the normal logistics for staffing schools were followed, we might indeed get a deterioration of quality, although we might get the requisite numbers of students.

A distinguished educator in the United States, President Charles Johnson of Fisk University, had observed that if we try to solve teacher shortage simply by getting enough bodies to keep the teacher/pupil ratio at the level we desire, all that might be accomplished would be to fill the schools with mediocre people as teachers who will communicate their mediocrity in an intimate environment.

Governments could take action in various ways. The first was to plan. The second was to inform the public and to overcome the institutional and political resistances which often arise when policies are elaborated from the economist's point of view.

III. THE CHALLENGE OF AID
TO NEWLY DEVELOPING COUNTRIES

Papers by W. Arthur Lewis,
F.H. Harbison, J. Tinbergen
in association with H.C. Bos and John Vaizey

PREFACE

The O.E.C.D. Member countries—a community of more than 500 million people including nearly all industrialized nations with high living standards—feel very strongly their responsibility towards the less developed countries. Two reasons should prompt our activities in this field: first, that these countries need our aid and, second, that we are able to give it. The Convention of O.E.C.D., which came into force in October 1961 when this new Organization replaced the Organization for European Economic Co-operation, states explicitly that one of the three aims of the new Organization will be to contribute to sound economic expansion in the less developed countries, non-member as well as Member countries, not only with financial aid or by providing expanding markets for their products, but also with technical assistance.

This is a new aim which did not figure in the Convention of O.E.E.C. But since O.E.E.C. was created in 1948, the world has altered very much: no fewer than thirty-five new countries have come into being, most of them underdeveloped and struggling to emerge from poverty and ignorance. Now the fact is that, in spite of the valuable activities of the United Nations and its Specialized Agencies, including the World Bank and the Special Fund, about nine-tenths of all development aid is given on a bilateral basis; and over nine-tenths of this comes from O.E.C.D. countries. There are thus very good reasons why O.E.C.D. should have made aid to underdeveloped countries one of its principal aims.

The work of O.E.C.D. on development assistance has been prepared during nearly two years by the Development Assistance Group. The purpose of this Group was to co-ordinate and rationalize the policies of the main donor countries with a view to improving and increasing the flow of aid to less developed countries and to facilitating private capital exports to these countries. The Development Assistance Group has now become a Committee of O.E.C.D. and will pursue these same activities with a new scope and vigour.

However, financial capital is not enough: human capital is equally important. And harmony between the growth of human capital and of financial capital will be one of the main problems of developing countries. There is little point in building steel mills and power stations if there are no engineers or skilled technicians to run them. In fact, human capital, in the form of educated people with skills for jobs, may be even more important than financial capital. And herein lies the crux of the problem for many newly developing countries. It takes no more than a few months to negotiate a loan; it may take two or three years to build a power station or a factory; but it takes something like fifteen to twenty years to transform a bright boy or girl into a competent engineer, an agricultural expert, or a university professor.

But professional skills and qualified manpower are in short supply even in North America and Western Europe. Even more scarce are people who are able to elaborate and apply strategies for human resource development. It is therefore of the utmost importance to rationalize our efforts so as to make the best possible use of these limited human resources for the benefit of the underdeveloped areas.

Many valuable suggestions for the future work of O.E.C.D. and its Member countries in this field are to be found in the Washington Conference papers and proceedings published in this volume. It is made clear that just as important as financial support is the provision of help to newly developing countries in assessing their longer term educational needs, in working out a sound order of priorities for meeting these needs, in providing university and school teachers, in receiving foreign students, and in assisting in the creation of educational institutions. The major difficulty is the shortage of teachers, not only in the underdeveloped areas, but in the advanced countries as well. The latter will have to co-ordinate their efforts carefully if the sacrifices they will be called upon to make from their own scarce resources are to yield the greatest benefit to the newly developing countries.

It is therefore essential that the advanced countries work together in devising practical means for maximizing the effectiveness of their assistance. Speedy, generous and co-ordinated action is required if the growth of material resources in the newly developing countries is not to be impeded by a lack of human capital.

Thorkil KRISTENSEN
Secretary-General

CONTENTS

PREFACE 5

Chapter I

THE STRATEGY OF HUMAN RESOURCE DEVELOPMENT IN MODERNIZING ECONOMIES
by F.H. Harbison

INTRODUCTION	9
THE IMPERATIVES AND CONSTRAINTS OF ACCELERATED DEVELOPMENT	10
Imperatives	10
Constraints...	11
THE MANPOWER PROBLEMS OF MODERNIZING ECONOMIES	14
Manpower Shortages...	14
Labor Surpluses...	17
Manpower Analysis..	18
THE COMPONENTS OF A STRATEGY OF HUMAN RESOURCE DEVELOPMENT	19
The Building of Incentives...	20
The Training of Employed Manpower....................................	22
Formal Education...	24
THE IMPLEMENTATION OF THE STRATEGY.................................	29
The Strategy in Summary..	29
Some Obstacles to be Overcome..	31
Implementing Machinery...	32

Chapter II

PRIORITIES FOR EDUCATIONAL EXPANSION
by W. Arthur Lewis

INTRODUCTION	35
ABSORPTIVE CAPACITY..	36
PRIMARY EDUCATION...	38
SECONDARY EDUCATION..	39
ADULT EDUCATION...	43
UNIVERSITY EDUCATION..	44

Chapter III
SOME OF THE MAIN ISSUES IN THE STRATEGY OF EDUCATIONAL SUPPLY
by John Vaizey

INTRODUCTION	51
THE STRUCTURE OF EDUCATION	55
Rural Education	56
Urban Education	58
Technical Education	58
Choosing the Appropriate Levels of Education	59
Private Education	60
Women's Education	61
OBSTACLES TO EDUCATIONAL EXPANSION	61
The Education Structure	62
Social Factors	63
The Teacher Problem	63
The Financial Cost	65
FOREIGN AID	67
CONCLUSION	69

Chapter IV
THE GLOBAL DEMAND FOR HIGHER AND SECONDARY EDUCATION IN THE UNDERDEVELOPED COUNTRIES IN THE NEXT DECADE
by J. Tinbergen and H. C. Bos

INTRODUCTION	71
THE FUTURE NUMBER OF STUDENTS	73
DEMAND AND SUPPLY OF TEACHERS	76

LIST OF TABLES

1.	Number of Students in Higher Education in 1958-1959	73
2.	Enrolment Ratios for Higher and Secondary Education in 1958	74
3.	Number of Students per 1,000 Inhabitants for Groups of Countries according to per capita Income Level	74
4.	Number of Students in Higher Education - 1958 and 1970	76
5.	Number of Students in Secondary Education - 1958 and 1970	76
6.	Number of Teachers in Higher Education - 1958 and 1970	77
7.	Number of Teachers in Secondary Schools - 1958 and 1970	78

DISCUSSION	81

I

THE STRATEGY OF HUMAN RESOURCE DEVELOPMENT IN MODERNIZING ECONOMIES

by

F. H. HARBISON
Princeton University

INTRODUCTION

The newly developing nations of the world are in a state of revolt. They have rejected the notion that poverty, squalor, and disease are preordained. They want high-speed modernization and are resentful of those who caution that economic growth in the advanced Western countries was a gradual process. Even the forced-draft development of the Soviet Union is for them too slow. As Nehru once remarked, India must learn to run before she learns to walk. The newly developing nations are interested not just in economic growth: they are hoping and planning for *accelerated development;* they think in terms of leaps rather than steps in building a modern social, political and economic order.

Accelerated development is, of course, a goal rather than a firm prospect for the future. All of the newly modernizing nations may not be able to leap forward; some may stand still, and others may even fall backward. But the vast majority of the nations of Asia, Africa, and Latin America are increasingly engaging in deliberate planning to achieve it. They are groping for a *strategy* of accelerated development, and also for a strategy for getting aid from the economically advanced countries.

In this paper, I propose to list briefly some of the imperatives and also some of the constraints in devising a strategy for accelerated development. I then propose to concentrate on the elements of a strategy of human resource development, after first examining the patterns of manpower problems which seem to be emerging in the modernizing countries. Finally, I shall discuss the machinery for implementation of a strategy for human resource development.

The concepts set forth in this paper have grown out of my work with the Inter-University Study of Labor Problems in Economic Development, and I am indebted to my colleagues, Clark Kerr, Charles A. Myers, and John T. Dunlop for many of the thoughts expressed. They, however, will not want to be held responsible for any perversions of their ideas in the pages which follow.

THE IMPERATIVES AND CONSTRAINTS OF ACCELERATED DEVELOPMENT

IMPERATIVES

The country which commits itself to accelerated growth will find that it is imperative to do certain things. It must increase sharply its rate of savings by one means or another. It must place emphasis on industrial development, but at the same time it must modernize and increase the productivity of agriculture. It must invest wisely both in real capital and in people. In so doing, it must develop a sense of priority and timing, so that savings and manpower are directed into the most productive channels. All of this requires integrated planning and co-ordination of effort.

If the newly developing nations are to have accelerated growth —more rapid, more sweeping and more dramatic than the "historical development" of the advanced nations—they must take deliberate, unprecedented and sometimes drastic measures. They must quickly and sharply increase taxes; they must restrict the too rapid expansion of consumption particularly by the wealthier classes; they must compete successfully for available foreign aid; and they must be prepared to think in terms of long-range economic growth rather than short-term political expediency. Most countries have the capacity for rapid growth, but it is questionable whether some of them can develop the will to do the hard things which are necessary to bring it about. On this point, Arhur Lewis has sounded a rather pessimistic note:

> "Politics is exciting to young countries, and politicians in these countries have attracted to themselves all the glamour which was previously reserved for priests and kings, not excluding the military parades, the salutes of guns, the yachts and the country houses. We must resign ourselves to the fact that most of the new countries will be too preoccupied with other matters to give to economic development the priority which it needs."[1]

I do not share completely Lewis' pessimism. Some, though certainly not all, young countries will find the road to accelerated development. In general, the successful countries will be those which are able to accumulate physical and human capital rapidly and to utilize both in high-priority, productive activities.

---

1. W.A. Lewis, "Problems of New States", paper delivered at the Weizman Institute, Rehovoth, Israel. August, 1960.

So much has been written about physical capital formation that no further elaboration is called for here. Let us assume that, on the average, a rapidly modernizing country may need to invest 20 per cent or more of its national income each year in order to achieve something approaching the goal of accelerated growth, and that, through taxation, forced savings, foreign aid or other measures, it must accumulate savings at this rate. My contention then is that it must have a correspondingly high rate of human capital formation in the form of the skilled people and institutions which are indispensable for the modernization process.[1]

In the view of the prominent economists, less than one-third of the increase in national income of countries can be explained by quantitative increases in factor inputs—such as capital and labour.[2] The "residual" is explained by *qualitative* improvements in these inputs, such as more productive capital, more productive human resources, economies of scale and other factors. Though an accurate break-down of the residual has not yet been made, the most important factors appear to be the upgrading of human resources—through education, training, health improvement, etc.—as well as the development of knowledge and technology, which are, of course, closely associated with education. From this, it is reasonable to conclude that the wealth of a nation is at least as dependent upon the development of human resources as upon the accumulation of material capital.

There is, however, little to be gained by argument over which is the more important—physical or human capital. Both must be accumulated at high rates of speed if rapid growth is to be achieved. A country's capacity to utilize effectively physical capital is dependent upon the availability of human capital, and *vice versa*. And it is essential for politicians and planners to understand that any development plan which does not give high priority to human capital formation is simply unrealistic and almost certainly destined to fail, for experience has shown repeatedly that high-level manpower does not appear automatically or magically as dams, roads, factories, hospitals, radio stations, and airports come into existence.

CONSTRAINTS

In planning modernization, the leaders of the newly developing countries operate within a context of pressures which limit the range of realistic policy alternatives. Try as they may, the planners and politicians can neither escape these constraints, nor alter them significantly.

---

1. Some of the 20 per cent investment, of course, may be in institutions contributing to human resource development as discussed later.
2. See Theodore W. Schultz, "Capital Formation by Education", *Journal of Political Economy*, vol. LXVIII, no. 6. For estimates as low as 10 to 25 per cent, see H. M. Phillips, "Education as a Basic Factor in Economic and Social Development", *Final Report* of Conference of African States on the Development of Education in Africa, Addis Ababa, May, 1961.

The first is the rapidly rising population growth. In nearly all of the newly modernizing societies, birth rates tend to remain high, while death rates decline as a result of the spread of public health measures and medical services. Even if there are no religious or cultural resistances to birth control, it is virtually impossible to have a fall in birth rates commensurate with the drop in death rates in these countries. Overpopulation in Asia and parts of the Near East is already a serious problem. The high rates of population increase in Latin America give cause for alarm. And even in the relatively uncrowded areas of Africa, the population explosion is imminent. An increasing population nearly always complicates the achievement of accelerated growth. The problems of feeding and health are magnified; expenditures for education must be augmented. A new nation attempting to achieve accelerated growth is like a man weighing over 250 pounds training for a two-mile run!

Second is the problem of rural-urban migration. With the spread of education, the development of transportation, and the very success of the appeal of modernization, people seek an escape from a "life-sentence" to traditional farming and flock to the cities much faster than employment, houses, water supplies, and other public services can be provided.

Third, as the idea of modernization takes root, so does the desire for immediate improvements in standards of living. The upper classes in particular will increase their consumption of such things as motor scooters, automobiles, refrigerators, radios, hi-fi sets, and television. The poorer classes will want more to eat and more to wear.

Men are told today by their leaders and by international organizations such as Unesco that education is a human right. As a result, the demand for education on the part of all classes becomes particularly strong. In Brazil, families will wait in queues for two or three days at the opening of schools in an attempt to get their children in only to be turned away because of insufficient places. In some countries, children who cannot get *into* schools seek to learn by standing outside at the windows, straining to hear what the teacher is saying *inside*. In the African countries, the building of a school in one village immediately results in pressure from surrounding villages for schools.

Universal primary education is a goal to which all political leaders today must be committed. The increase of primary education creates irresistible pressures for increase in secondary education, and the expansion of secondary education makes expenditures for higher education almost mandatory.

Fourth, practically all of the modernizing nations are dependent upon external aid of one kind or another. They must have financial help from the advanced countries; they must import, temporarily at least, high-level manpower from abroad in order to make use of accumulated knowledge and modern technology; in many cases they must count on foreign countries to maintain and stabilize the prices of raw materials which they sell in the world markets. Distasteful though it may be to the leaders of the modernizing countries, they are in significant respects at the mercy of the more advanced nations. They cannot go it alone.

Fifth, although inextricably dependent upon the services of foreigners, the modernizing countries are always under pressure to get rid of them as speedily as possible. In countries newly emerging from colonial status, the expatriates in the civil service must be replaced wherever possible by nationals. The foreign-owned industrial corporation must open the avenues to higher managerial positions to nationals as soon as they can qualify. The resentment against expatriates who cultivate the art of making themselves indispensable runs high. The newly educated elites are strongly convinced that they have a right to the foreigners' jobs. This is why so much store is placed upon "Nigerianization", "Africanization", or "Indianization" of high-level manpower. The foreigner is needed desperately. He may arrive through technical assistance, or with a new entreprise, or as a consultant. But, except in those countries (i.e., Brazil, Argentina, Chile, Mexico, etc.) where he may remain to become a citizen, he is supposed to expedite his departure. No perceptive political leader rests easily when the top posts in government or industry are occupied by foreigners.

Sixth, the newly modernizing nations must above all maintain political independence while striving for economic independence. The desire to remain neutral in the East-West struggle is becoming ever stronger. Indeed, many nations look at the East competition as an opportunity to increase their demands for foreign aid.

Seventh, the leaders of modernizing nations always encounter some resistance to change. The extensive family system, traditional ethical valuations, and legal concepts often stand in the way of innovation. Vested interests, such as large rural landowners or organized religious powers, and their political allies may be expected to offer resistance to basic reforms which the modernization process demands. Such traditions and powerful groups are not easy to brush aside and, for many years to come, the developing countries will continue to have dual economies consisting of a modernizing sector and a vast traditional society responding very slowly to the need for change.

Finally, the *symbols* of modernization are important to the newly developing countries. To several African nations, an international airline is an imperative. In Egypt, the new steel mill is a tangible symbol of the commitment to industrialization. Brazil has built a fabulous new capital city in the heart of the country. Nigeria and Ghana have lavish new universities, and more are planned. In most modernizing countries, there are likely to be impressive new government buildings, modern apartments, luxury hotels, and broad new boulevards. Television stations are appearing throughout Latin America and Africa. Everywhere there are new shining factories, huge dams and projects, and plans for big jet airports. These are tangible manifestations and concrete reminders of the commitment to modernization and accelerated growth. As such they are, in the minds of the modernizing elites, almost indispensable elements in any program of development.

The constraints listed above lend support to the view that economic development is as much a political as an economic process. At any rate, the politicians cannot be expected to follow the theoretical trails blazed by the economists. So, the planners and their technical supporters, while being fully aware of the imperatives for rapid growth, must help to design a strategy which will be viable under the cross-fire of practical constraints which throw obstacles in the path of development and narrow the range of rational choice.

THE MANPOWER PROBLEMS OF MODERNIZING ECONOMIES

Most modernizing economies are confronted simultaneously with two persistent yet seemingly diverse manpower problems: *the shortage of persons with critical skills* in the modernizing sector and *surplus labor* in both the modernizing and traditional sector. Thus, the strategy of human resource development is concerned with the two-fold objective of building skills and providing productive employment for unutilized or under-utilized manpower. The shortage and surplus of human resources, however, are not separate and distinct problems; they are very intimately related. Both have their roots in the changes which are inherent in the development process. Both are related in part to education. Characteristically, both are aggravated as the tempo of modernization is quickened. And, paradoxically, the shortage of persons with critical skills is one of the contributing causes of the surplus of people without jobs. Although the manpower problems of no two countries are exactly alike, there are some shortages and surpluses which appear to be universal in modernizing societies.

Manpower Shortages

The manpower shortages of modernizing countries are quite easy to identify, and fall into several categories:

    i) In all modernizing countries there is likely to be a shortage of highly educated professional manpower such as scientists, agronomists, veterinarians, engineers, and doctors. Such persons, moreover, usually prefer to live in the major cities rather than in the rural areas where in many cases their services are most urgently needed. Thus their shortage is magnified by their relative immobility. And, ironically, their skills are seldom used effectively. In West Africa and also in many Asian and Latin American countries, for example, graduate engineers may be found managing the routine operation of an electric power sub-station or doing the work of drafsmen. Doctors may spend long hours making the most routine medical tests. The obvious reason is that:

ii) The shortage of technicians, nurses, agricultural assistants, technical supervisors, and other sub-professionnal personel is generally even more critical than that of fully qualified professionals. For this there are several explanations: First, the modernizing countries usually fail to recognize that the requirement for this category of manpower exceed by many times those for senior professional personnel. Second, the few persons who are qualified to enter a technical institute may also be qualified to enter a university, and they prefer the latter because of the higher status and pay which is accorded the holder of a university degree; and finally, there are often fewer places available in institutions providing intermediate training than in universities.

iii) The shortage of top-level managerial and administrative personnel, in both the private and public sectors, is almost universal, as is the dearth of persons with entrepreneurial talents.

iv) Teachers are almost always in short supply, and their turnover is high because they tend to leave the teaching profession if and when more attractive jobs become available in government, politics, or private enterprise. This shortage is generally most serious in secondary education, and particularly acute in the fields of science and mathematics. It is a "master bottleneck" which retards the entire process of human resource development.

v) In most modernizing countries there are also shortages of craftsmen of all kinds, senior clerical personnel such as bookkeepers, secretaries, stenographers, and business machine operators, and of other miscellaneous personnel such as radio and television specialists, airplane pilots, accountants, economists, and statisticians.

I shall use the term "high-level manpower", or alternatively "human capital", as a convenient designation for persons who fall into categories such as those mentioned above. The term "human capital formation", as used in this paper, is the process of acquiring and increasing the numbers of persons who have the skills, education, and experience which are critical for the economic and political development of a country. Human capital formation is thus associated with investment in man and his development as a creative and productive resource. It includes investment by society in education, investment by employers in training, as well as investment by individuals of time and money in their own development. Such investments have both qualitative and quantitative dimensions—i. e., human capital formation includes not only expenditures for education and training, but also the development of attitudes toward productive activity.

As stressed earlier, a central problem of all modernizing countries is to accelerate the process of human capital formation. Now human capital may be accumulated in several ways: it may be *imported from abroad* through a variety of means such as technical assistance, expatriate enterprises, hiring of consultants, or immigration. It may be *developed in employment* through on-the-job training, inservice programs of formal training, management development seminars, part-time adult education classes, better organization of work, creation of appropriate attitudes and incentives, and better management of people. Finally, it is developed through *formal education* in schools, technical training centers, colleges, universities and other institutions of higher learning. The development process is assisted at all levels by improvements in public health and by better nutrition.

The analysis of human capital formation is thus parallel and complementary to the study of the processes of savings and investment (in the material sense). In designing a strategy for development, one needs to consider the total stock of human capital required, its rates of accumulation, and its commitment to (or investment in) high-priority productive activities.

The rate of modernization of a country is associated with both its stock and its rate of accumulation of human capital. High-level manpower is needed to staff new and expanding government services, to introduce new systems of land use and new methods of agriculture, to develop new means of communication, to carry forward industrialization, and to build the educational system. *Innovation*, or the process of change from a static or traditional society, requires very large "doses" of strategic human capital. The countries which are making the most rapid and spectacular innovations are invariably those which are accumulating this kind of human capital at a fast rate. Here we may make two tentative generalizations:

First, the rate of accumulation of strategic human capital must always exceed the rate of increase in the labor force as a whole. In most countries, for example, the rate of increase in scientific and engineering personnel needs to be at least three times that of the labor force. Subprofessional personnel may have to increase six to nine times as fast. Clerical personnel and craftsmen usually should increase at least twice as fast, and top managerial and administrative personnel will normally need to increase at a comparable rate.

Second, in most cases the rate of increase in human capital will exceed the rate of economic growth. In newly developing countries which are already faced with critical shortages of highly skilled persons, the ratio of the annual increase in high-level manpower to the annual increase in national income may need to be as high as three-to-one, or even higher in those cases where expatriates are to be replaced by citizens of the developing countries.

The accumulation of high-level manpower to overcome skill bottlenecks is a never-ending process. Advanced industrial societies as well as underdeveloped countries are normally short of critical skills. Indeed as long as the pace of innovation is rapid, the appetite of any growing country for high-level manpower is almost insatiable.

LABOR SURPLUSES

The overabundance of labor is in most countries as serious a problem as the shortage of skills. Its more common manifestations are the following:

i) In nearly all countries the supply of unskilled and untrained manpower in the urban areas exceeds the available employment opportunities. The reasons are not far to find. First, large urban populations are likely to build up prior to, rather than as a consequence of, the expansion of industrial employment. Then, as industrialization gains momentum, the productivity of factory labor tends to rise sharply, and this limits the expansion of demand for general industrial labor. Indeed, modern industrialization may even displace labor from cottage and handicraft industries faster than it is absorbed in newly created factories. Again, government service is able to provide employment for relatively few people. And finally, unless development is extremely rapid, trade, commerce, and other services simply do not absorb those who cannot find jobs in other activities. But despite relatively limited employment opportunities and overcrowded conditions, the modernization process impels people to migrate from the rural areas to the cities. And, as progress is made toward universal primary education, nearly every modernizing country is faced with the problem of mounting unemployment of primary school leavers.

ii) In overpopulated countries, such as Egypt or India, the rural areas are also overcrowded resulting in widespread underemployment and disguised unemployment of human resources. Indeed, in many countries it is evident that total agricultural output could be increased if fewer people were living on the land and the size of agricultural units was increased. Thus, surplus labor in rural areas in most cases is no asset and in some cases is definitely a liability for increasing agricultural output.

iii) The "unemployed intellectual" constitutes an entirely different kind of surplus. In many countries there would seem to be too many lawyers or too many arts graduates, and there may be instances also of unemployed or underemployed engineers, scientists, economists, and even agronomists. The unused intellectual, however, is unemployed only because he is unwilling to accept work which he considers beneath his status or educational level. In particular, a university education creates very high employment expectations. In some countries, a university degree may be looked upon almost as a guarantee of a soft and secure job in the government service, and in most it is assumed to be a membership card of the elite class. But, even in rapidly modernizing countries, the purely administrative jobs in the government service become filled fairly rapidly;

the demand for lawyers is certainly not as great as, for example, the demand for technically trained personnel. And in some societies where large enterprises are owned and managed by members of family dynasties, even the opportunities for professionally trained engineers and technicians may be limited, at least in the early stages of development. Rather than accept work beneath his status or employment in remote rural areas, the university graduate, and sometimes even the secondary school leaver as well, may prefer to join the ranks of the unemployed. A sizeable quantity of unused human capital of this kind reflects a wasteful investment in human resource development and poses a serious threat to a country's social and political stability.

iv) There are other miscellaneous kinds of surplus labor. For example, the introduction of new processes and automated machinery may throw skilled labor out of work. And, in some countries, immigrants and refugees swell the ranks of the unemployed.

Unfortunately, there is no reason to believe that accelerated growth will by itself solve the problems of labor surplus such as those described above. In part they are the inevitalbe consequence of a too rapid population growth over which planners and politicians may have little or no control. In part, they are diseases inherent in the modernization process itself, and are directly related to rising aspirations. Some are aggravated and others alleviated by rapid growth.

Some labor surpluses, however, can be eliminated and others reduced substantially by a well-conceived and balanced program of economic growth. A strategy of human resource development, therefore, must make an attack on surpluses as well as shortages.

Manpower Analysis

As indicated above, no two countries have exactly the same manpower problems. Some have unusually serious surpluses, and others have special kinds of skill bottlenecks. Politicians and planners, therefore, need to make a systematic assessment of the human resource problems in their particular country. Such assessment may be called "manpower analysis".

The objectives of manpower analysis are:

a) The identification of the principal critical shortages of skilled manpower in each major sector of the economy, and an analysis of the reasons for such shortages;

b) The identification of surpluses, both of trained manpower as well as unskilled labor, and the reasons for such surpluses; and

c) The setting of targets for human resources development based upon reasonable expectations of growth.

Such targets are best determined by a careful examination, sector by sector, of the utilization of manpower in a number of countries which are somewhat more advanced politically, socially, and economically.

Manpower analysis need not be based on an elaborate or exhaustive survey. It involves no precise calculation of the numbers of people needed in every occupation at a future period. Nor is it a projection of past trends. The purpose of manpower analysis is to give a reasonably objective picture of a country's major human resource problems, the interrelationships between these problems, and their causes, together with an informed guess about probable future trends. It is both qualitative and quantitative, but it is based more upon wise judgment than upon precise statistics. In countries where statistics are either unavailable or clearly unreliable, the initial manpower analysis may be frankly informed guesswork. Indeed, detailed manpower surveys and precise projections are likely to be misleading, because they give a false impression of accuracy.[1]

In conclusion, the major shortages and surpluses of manpower in most countries are easy to identify. Many of them are common to all modernizing societies. Manpower analysis, based on relevant comparisons with other countries at different stages of development, is useful in assessing particular problems and probable future trends. To be sure, there is need for research in manpower supply and demand as related to economic growth. But those who are responsible for the planning of accelerated growth cannot and need not wait for the completion of definite studies before designing a realistic strategy for human resource development.

THE COMPONENTS OF A STRATEGY OF HUMAN RESOURCE DEVELOPMENT

A strategy of human resource development then is one of the imperatives of any program for accelerated growth. And to be viable, it must be realistic and take into consideration the constraints which were mentioned earlier. The planners can do little to stem the increase in population; the politicians cannot go back on their promises of rapid achievement of universal primary education; they can rely only temporarily on expatriate manpower as a source of human capital. The resources which they can allocate to education are limited by competing demands for investment in roads, factories, dams, and irrigation systems; and nothing can be done which is inconsistent with the bolstering of economic and political independence.

What then are the feasible policy alternatives? What instruments are available for policy implementation? What obstacles lie in the path

---

1. The Inter-University Study has developed some working papers on manpower assessments and human resource development which treat this matter in greater detail. It is also working on comparisons of manpower utilization in countries at various stages of development.

of development of a sound strategy? These are the central questions posed in this paper.

A strategy of human resource development has three essential components: the building of appropriate incentives, the promotion of effective training of employed manpower, and the rational development of formal education. These three parts are interdependent: the country's leaders cannot concentrate on only one or two of them at a time; they must plan an integrated attack on all three fronts at once.

THE BUILDING OF INCENTIVES

The purpose of building incentives is to encourage men and women to prepare for and engage in the kinds of productive activity which are needed for accelerated growth. To accomplish this, the compensation of an individual should be related to the *importance of his job in the modernizing society*. It should not depend upon his level of formal education, the number of degrees held, family status, or political connections. And the relative importance of jobs should be based not on tradition or heritage from colonial regimes but on an assessment of the manpower needs of the developing economy.

If, for example, agricultural officers or village workers are desperately needed in rural areas to carry out a program of modernizing agriculture, their pay may have to exceed that of professionally trained people who have desk jobs in the cities. If a technician with limited education can perform work normally assigned to an engineer, he should receive the same pay as the engineer on that job. If science and mathematics teachers are urgently needed in secondary schools, their rates of remuneration should be higher than that of other less urgently needed teachers (whether university graduates or not) and perhaps higher also than that of professionally trained people in some other less essential activities. If technicians, nurses, and foremen are in very short supply (as is the case in most modernizing countries), their rates of pay may need to be higher than those of some university graduates holding administrative jobs which many other persons could do. In some cases, the medical technician or the agricultural assistant who is willing to live in the bush deserves to be paid as much as the doctor or the agronomist who insists upon living in the city. And the manager of an enterprise who may have had only a limited secondary education is entitled to higher remuneration than the university graduate who is subordinate.

Large outlays for education are unlikely to produce the kind of high-level manpower needed if the proper incentives are lacking. In many developing countries, any university degree is looked upon almost as a right to employment in the government service. Thus, a university graduate is also strongly motivated to prefer work in the large urban areas. The idea that a university education is a "permanent escape from the bush" is widespread, for example, in Africa. In Nigeria the reason for the critical shortage of agricultural specialists of all kinds is not the lack of places in agricultural schools but rather the reluctance of students to go into them.[1] Obviously, in the minds of young people, the employment opportunities are not as attractive in agriculture as in some other fields which are less vital for the country's development. For the same reasons, technical education, particularly at the intermediate level, has had little appeal in Nigeria. As the Ashby Commission pointed out:

> "... the literary tradition and the university degree have become indelible symbols of prestige in Nigeria; by contrast technology, agriculture and other practical subjects, particularly at the sub-professional level, have not won esteem".[2]

I would argue most strongly that situations of this kind will not be corrected by publicity, exhortations of prime ministers, and the building of more educational institutions. They will be changed only when the system of rewards and status values in a modernizing society are changed and the initiative in making changes must come from the government itself in the form of a complete revision of the entire system of reward of government employees. The failure of politicians and planners to come to grips with this problem will produce in the newer countries, as it has already done in Egypt and India, an army of unemployed intellectuals.

By the same token, the problems of rural-urban migration and the unemployed primary school leavers are not likely to be alleviated substantially by mere changes in the curriculum of primary and secondary schools. In this age of rising aspirations and spreading mass communication, the sons of farmers are not going to sentence themselves to *traditional agriculture* if they can possibly avoid it. The only fundamental solution is the *modernization of rural life.* This calls for sweeping measures such as land reform, agricultural research and extension services, widespread rural community development programs, the effective utilization of rural labor in the building of roads, irrigation systems, houses, and schools, and other programs aimed at making rural life more productive and attractive. If people see a positive reason for remaining in the rural areas and a promise of a better life there, the problem of revision of curricula in the schools is relatively easy to handle.

A detailed discussion of the need to develop agriculture lies beyond the scope of this paper. It is necessary only to point out that none of the modernizing countries are likely to solve many of their most pressing human resource problems unless they find the means of revolutionizing rural life. Industrialization by itself will never solve the problem of surplus labor in most of today's underdeveloped countries; government employment, petty trade, and domestic services will not soak up the teaming masses in overcrowded cities; and the retention of surplus human resources in traditional agriculture, even if it were possible,

---

1. See *Investment in Education*, The Report of the Commission on Post-School Certificate and Higher Education in Nigeria, Federal Ministry of Education, Lagos, 1960, p. 21.
2. *Investment in Education, Ibid.* p. 5.

would simply result in more disguised unemployment. Again, to quote Arthur Lewis, "If agriculture is stagnant, it offers only a stagnant market, and inhibits the growth of the rest of the economy. The core of the doctrine of "balanced growth" is that neglect to develop agriculture makes it more difficult to develop anything else".[1] Similarly, the failure to develop effective measures for productive utilization of human resources in rural areas will make it infinitely more difficult to solve the manpower problems in any other part of the economy.

Thus, a primary condition for the solution of all manpower problems whether they be critical skill bottlenecks in the modernizing sector or mounting labor surpluses throughout the nation, is the building of appropriate incentive. Lacking this, massive expenditures on training and education will contribute little to accelerated development. The notion that there is always a direct relation between the development of education and economic growth can be misleading, and planners should be wary of accepting it without careful scrutiny.

The leaders of the modernizing nations probably have the means to influence the structure of wages and salaries if they have the courage to do so. It most cases, the government is by far the largest employer of manpower, and private employers are strongly influenced by the patterns which it sets. But, being bound by tradition and constrained by established interests bent on preserving the *status quo*, some politicians and planners think that it would be rather arbitrary suddenly to gear remuneration to the relative importance of occupations as determined by development objectives. Yet, it is equaly arbitrary and even politically dangerous to cling to an archaic system of reward which may have been inherited from a past era of colonialism. In committing themselves to planned, accelerated development, the modernizing nations are charting a revolutionary course. And if they are to follow it successfully, they must discard traditional and orthodox ideas, many of which they have borrowed from the advanced nations which never had to face the same kinds of problems.

THE TRAINING OF EMPLOYED MANPOWER

The potentialities of fully utilizing government agencies, private employers, expatriate firms and foreign technical experts as trainers and developers of manpower are enormous, but this is seldom fully realized by the leaders of most modernizing countries. Human resource development is usually equated with investments in formal education, and government, business, and education leaders for some reason cling to the notion that schools and universities can prefabricate the skills needed. They may be quick to see the need for technical training but, unfortunately, just as quick to assume that the system of formal education must be given the responsibility for it.

---

1. W. Arthur Lewis, "Reflections on the Economic Problem", paper delivered to the Oxford Conference on Tensions in Development, New College, Oxford. September, 1961.

At this point, it is important to understand that training and education are two quite different processes, and planners should draw a sharp distinction between them. Training involves the development of specific skills which are needed to perform a particular job or series of jobs. Education involves the acquisition of general knowledge and the development of basic mental ability. Both training and education are involved in human capital formation. Education is, of course, a prerequisite for various kinds of training. But this does not mean that the *responsibility* for training and the *responsibility* for education are inseparable.

The strategy of modernizing nations should be to shift as much responsibility as possible for *training* onto the major employing institutions—government ministries, public or quasi-public entreprises, private industry and commerce, and foreign-owned and managed firms. At the same time, the strategy should aim to exploit more systematically the training possibilities of technical assistance.

The government, as the largest employer, should take the lead in shouldering this responsibility. Most of the arts of public administration can be developed effectively by a well-conceived and organized program of in-service training. It is likewise practical for the appropriate employing ministries to train craftsmen, senior clerical employees, and even certain categories of sub-professional technical personnel. Each major government ministry, therefore, should have an organization responsible for on-the-job training, in-service programs of instruction, supplementary off-the-job programs of training in cooperation with educational institutions, periodic examination of accomplishment, and certification of qualification for promotion and advancement. The techniques of in-service training of this kind are available but the idea that the government-as-employer should assume responsibility for such training is completely strange and unorthodox to most leaders in newly developing countries.

At the same time, pressure should be exerted upon private employers to assume a corresponding responsibility for training. The larger enterprises should be expected to have foreman training and manager development programs. They should also be required to assume major responsibility for training their own craftsmen, clerical workers, and some categories of technicians as well as semi-skilled production workers. In short, the development of human capital through in-service training should be accepted as an integral part of business operations.

The small employer can also carry some of the burden of training, and in practice he often carries more than his share. In Nigeria, for example, most lorries and automobiles are repaired in small shops consisting of an owner and several apprentices, who may even pay him for the opportunity of learning a trade. The handicraft industries in most countries are completely dependent upon an informal apprenticeship system. The planners in the modernizing countries will be well advised not to replace such systems with costly vocational schools, but rather to try to improve them by providing programs of technical assistance in apprenticeship and on-the-job training.

The foreign-owned enterprise can be a powerful instrument of human capital formation if it is handled properly, because its training capacity is usually greater than that of the local entreprises. The host country should allow the foreign firm to bring in as many expatriates as it wishes, *provided* that it guarantees to train local nationals to take over their jobs within a reasonable specified time. In most instances, the foreign firm trains more people than it uses itself. For example, craftsmen and mechanics trained by an expatriate oil company may take jobs in other local industries; or service station attendants may soon become independent dealers. A well-trained foreman in a foreign-owned truck assembly plant may be a future organizer of a locally managed parts factory. Unquestionably, a more deliberate and carefully planned policy of using expatriate firms as training institutions could greatly accelerate the process of human capital formation in many countries, and politicians should be more concerned with exploiting this asset to the maximum than in placing arbitrary restrictions on the employment of expatriate personnel.

Finally, the newly developing countries should fully exploit the potentialities of technical assistance as a training medium. The purpose of technical assistance should be to train one or more nationals to do work which was previously done by a foreigner, or not done at all. It is shortsighted to invite foreign technical experts to a country to handle operations or merely to make studies or surveys. In whatever activity they are engaged, the responsibility of foreign experts should be to train counterparts—to transmit knowledge by training people.

The advantages of utilizing employers and technical assistance as trainers and developers of manpower would appear to be blindingly obvious. But the failure to do so is almost universal in newly developing countries. Outside technical experts are employed in operations, and often no local counterparts are assigned to them for training. Government ministries are too busy to spend time on in-service training, and complain when vocational schools and universities send them poorly trained recruits. The idea that training is a continuous process of human resource development rather than a simple pre-employment indoctrination seems to escape politicians, planners, and public and private employers alike. The solution here is relatively simple. The employing enterprises should be given the *responsibility* for a considerable amount of training and also the incentives to provide it. If they have the incentives, the means of carrying out this training will not be lacking.

FORMAL EDUCATION

No one would argue, of course, that all training activity can or should be undertaken by employers. Teachers, engineers, scientists, agronomists, doctors, and many kinds of sub-professional personnel are not likely to be effectively trained in employment. And some kinds of crafts are learned better in schools than through apprenticeship or on-the-job training.

In the main, however, the essential function of formal education is to prepare people for training rather than to train people for particular occupations. In other words, the principal output of formal education should be "trainable" people. Like a photographic film, the capacities of people are developed after exposure to productive activity. Pre-employment education, as in the coating of the film, determines the future sensitivity of man for understanding and continuous learning.

Nearly all modernizing countries have rejected the idea of *gradual* elimination of illiteracy; they are determined to have universal primary education in record time. This must be accepted as a major objective in any program of accelerated development. But in many countries particularly in Africa and parts of Asia, universal primary education cannot be achieved in the next ten to fifteen years if the educators insist on the same teacher-student ratios and teacher qualifications as those in the advanced countries. More often than not, the developing countries are being forced to sacrifice quality to quantity in their mass attack upon illiteracy.

It is unquestionably true that the cost of primary education must be held down; otherwise it will consume most of the resources which are more urgently needed for secondary and higher education. Most of the developing countries currently spend less than 4 per cent par annum for formal education of all kinds, and, in view of competing demands for funds for development purposes, it is doubtful whether many of them will be able to raise this to 5 or 6 per cent in the next decade or two. And the need for high-level manpower is such that most modernizing countries will have to devote well over two-thirds of total educational expenditure to secondary and post-secondary institutions.

Consequently, developing countries should concentrate their attention on finding new techniques of education which can be utilized effectively by large numbers of teachers who themselves have had little more than primary education and which can maximise the strategic services of a very small group of more highly trained personnel. The application of new teaching techniques—visual aids, programmed learning, instruction by radio and television, revised and simplified curricula and texts—offer a real challenge both to the developing countries and the assisting countries. The discovery of new techniques for primary education will be given much more serious consideration once it is understood by politicians, planners, educators, and outside experts alike that under conditions of accelerated growth it will be impossible to raise substantially either the pay or the qualifications of teachers in the near future.

The main purpose of primary education is to make people literate and to make them more effective citizens in the modernizing society.

It is not and should not be vocational education, and indeed most educators in advanced as well as underdeveloped countries are united in opposing such an orientation. It must, however, provide a means of selecting and preparing those who are to proceed to secondary level education.

One of the consequences of rapid introduction of universal primary education is to raise aspirations of people more rapidly than places in secondary schools and jobs can be provided. This is one of the penalties of rapid modernization. In time, however, the social and political pressure for more secondary education will assist the rapid accumulation of high-level manpower.

If a country demands accelerated development, the proportion of students in secondary education must rise sharply. The secondary school leavers constitute the main reservoir from which "trainable" high-level manpower must be drawn. Its size and quality, therefore, are critical for human capital formation. As in the case of primary education, streamlined methods of instruction and new educational techniques are needed. But, at the secondary level, the main consideration is not to keep costs from rising; it must be to provide high-quality education for an ever-increasing minority of the school-age population.

The proportion of the school-age population in secondary education will depend upon the stage of development. In the least developed countries less than one per cent of the normally eligible age groups (12-18 years) are in secondary schools. Some of the more advanced African countries have been able to raise this proportion to 4 or 5 per cent. Egypt, India and some of the Latin American countries have ratios as high as 15-20 per cent. In most of the industrially advanced countries, it is already in excess of 50 per cent. Thus, in most modernizing countries there is underinvestment in secondary education and need for an immediate and sharp increase. The Conference of African States on the Development of Education recommended that the tropical African countries as a whole increase the proportion of school-age population in secondary schools from an average of 3 per cent in 1961 to 23 per cent in 1981, during which period universal primary education would also be achieved.[1]

The major mission of secondary education is to give students firm grounding in verbal and written communication skills, mathematics, foreign languages, history, social studies and science. In this process, some attention should be given to development of manual skills as well. In most cases, the aim should be breadth of education rather than specialization at an early stage, and especially if a large part of occupational skill development is to be left to later training in employment or to post-secondary educational institutions.

---

1. Conference of African States on the Development of Education in Africa, Addis Ababa, 15-25 May, 1961: *Outline of a Plan for African Educational Development*, Unesco, Paris, 1961.

Vocational training at the secondary level presents particular problems. It is expensive, and competent teachers are very difficult to find. Modernizing countries often waste large sums of money in misplaced emphasis on primary and secondary vocational schools. In some countries, for example, students who prove to be unfit for higher academic training are sent to vocational schools, and as a consequence these become the catch-basins for incompetents. And, in many instances, the training received tends to be of poor quality and not sufficiently relevant to the occupations which the students later enter. As stressed above, the policy of newly developing countries should be to place more responsibility on employers to train workers for specific occupations, and to this end funds might better be channelled into the training of trainers in employing institutions than into the proliferation of poorly equipped and poorly staffed vocational schools.

There is a need, however. for teacher training institutions at the secondary level (primarily to provide elementary school teachers). In addition, a limited number of well-staffed and well-equipped craft training centers are undoubtedly necessary, as are certain kinds of secretarial schools and agricultural training institutions. But plans for these should be carefully made after analysis of expected manpower requirements and the training potentialities of the employing enterprises.

The mission of higher education is two-fold:
    a) to provide liberally educated persons for positions of leadership in the modernizing society; and
    b) to develop high-level technical manpower.

The newly developing countries are keenly aware of the importance of higher education, and except in rare cases, they are not likely to underinvest in it; but, in terms of developement objectives, they are prone to place the wrong emphasis on the investments which they make.

It is probably reasonable to assume that, on the average, the newly developing countries can and will provide higher education for about 20 per cent of those who complete secondary education. The crucial questions then are: what proportion should have university level education and what proportion should take intermediate training? what proportion should concentrate on technical studies and what proportion should devote themselves to academic studies? and, of those who should have university-level education, what proportion should be educated at home and what proportion should be sent to study abroad? in each country these issues are likely to be resolved partly by logical analysis and partly by political expediency.

The logical answers may be found in part by a manpower analysis. Typically, a manpower analysis might suggest that 2-4 students should pursue studies at the intermediate level (two or three years beyond secondary) for every one who takes a full university course (ranging from four to six years). It would probably also suggest that, in a country committed to accelerated growth (with emphasis on industrialization and modernization of agriculture), at least half of the students at both the intermediate and university level should concentrate on subjects such as science, engineering, medicine, agriculture, veterinary medicine, or pharmacy. Another 25 per cent should go to intermediate-level teacher-training colleges, and the remainder should concentrate on law, letters, social sciences, and business administration.[1]

From an economic standpoint, the logical course for the typical country would be to build institutions at home to take care of practically all students at the intermediate level, and to send a substantial portion of those qualified for university level work to foreign institutions, at least until the country is rich enough to afford first-class university level education without cutting into the high-priority need for investment in secondary and intermediate higher education.

The politicians, however, will have difficulty in accepting such a rationalized program for higher education, even if it is based upon a quite reliable manpower assessment and even if it can be demonstrated to be the more rapid and least expensive way of producing trainable high-level manpower. The reasons are obvious.

As the number of secondary school graduates increases, the government will be under pressure from students and irate parents to provide *more places* in universities. And as long as university degrees determine in large measure the starting salaries for the better jobs (irrespective of what subjects have been studied), students will want to by-pass the intermediate institutions. Moreover if *numbers* are important to the politicians the universities will tend to offer more places in the non-scientific areas than are needed. Because the cost of educating an engineer or scientist is 3-4 times that of educating a lawyer or a man of letters and arts.

But this is not all. From the standpoint of national grandeur and prestige, a university is a much more impressive symbol of modernization than a teacher training college, an intermediate technical training institute, or a "junior college of arts and sciences". A university along with an international airline, a steel mill, and television stations, is important in the eyes of the leaders of newly developing nations. Finally, too much reliance on sending university level students abroad for study is often considered to be inconsistent with bolstering economic and political independence.

Modernizing countries will therefore probably commit themselves to spend more money on universities than they should and tend to neglect the development of intermediate education; and they are likely, in the interest of providing the maximum number of places for university students, to understress scientific and engineering education. This leads eventually to the lowering of standards of the university, reliance

---

1. In practice, of course, manpower assessments in individual countries will show a wide variation from this "typical model". The Inter-University Study is engaged in research and hopes to have available shortly more empirical evidence on this subject.

on professors who teach only part time because of poor salaries, and the development of obstacles to innovation in the form of professors who have a vested interest in the *status quo*.[1] In the end, the education and training offered in universities may sink to a level below that of a good teacher training institution or technical or junior college, and the curriculum is likely to be unrelated to the needs of a rapidly modernizing society.

In view of these pressures, how can modernizing countries give the needed emphasis to intermediate-level training and to science and engineering studies in the universities? As already stressed above, it is rationally desirable and politically feasible to gear remuneration of jobs, particularly in the government service, to their relative importance for the country's development rather than to formal degrees or educational levels. If this were done, the artificial value of the traditional academic university degree would soon disappear and students would have an incentive to enter the intermediate technical training institutions, secondary teachers' colleges, and scientific and engineering faculties in the universities. These would become the new avenues to positions of high pay and status; and parents and students would then exert pressure to expand and improve these avenues. In this way, the adaptation of the system of higher education to the needs of a rapidly modernizing society would become politically more feasible. And, this need not conflict with the university's mission of providing liberally educated persons for positions of service and leadership in the nation. The modernizing society will always have important and highly-paid positions for the well-educated lawyer, arts graduate, and social scientist. But, it should not allow large numbers of poorly educated university graduates to use their degrees to claim high-level positions for which they are not well prepared.

THE IMPLEMENTATION OF THE STRATEGY

THE STRATEGY IN SUMMARY

Only the bare skeleton of a strategy of human resource development has been presented above. It is admittedly over-simplified; many important questions have been passed by; and some elements of the strategy have been implied but not mentioned specifically. However, the strategy as a whole has a consistent rationale, and it has been presented primarily to stimulate serious discussion among those who are committed to accelerated development.

It has been argued that investments in formal education alone are not likely to solve either critical skill shortages or persistent labor

---

1. The Inter-University Study is involved in studies in a number of countries aimed at analysis of the university as a stimulating or retarding force in economic development and the factors which make for adaptability of the system of higher education to development needs.

surpluses in modernizing societies. Investments in education are likely to contribute effectively to rapid growth only:
>   a) if there are adequate incentives to encourage men and women to engage in the kinds of productive activity which are needed to accelerate the modernization process and;
>   b) if appropriate measures are taken to shift a large part of the responsibility for training to the principal employing entreprises.

The building of incentives and the training of employed manpower, therefore, are necessary both as a means of economizing on formal education and as a means of making the investment in it productive.

In the building of incentives, a cardinal principle is that the status and remuneration attached to occupations should be related to their importance as measured by the high-priority needs of a developing society, and not to arbitrary levels of education, degrees, family status or political connections. This is essential for the accumulation of human capital and for its most effective utilization. The surpluses of labor, particularly those connected with rural-urban migration and the unemployment of primary school leavers, may be reduced in part by a far-reaching program of modernization of agriculture and rural life as a counterpart to a program of industrialization. Because of rapidly increasing populations and the emphasis on an early universalization of primary education, however, there will still be large numbers of unemployed or underemployed persons in most modernizing societies.

The potentialities of fully utilizing government agencies, private employers, expatriate firms and technical experts as trainers and developers of manpower, though very great indeed, are seldom exploited fully. Thus, a key element in the strategy of human resource development is to shift as much as possible the responsibility for training to the major employing enterprises, and to provide the necessary technical guidance to enable them to develop in-service training programs along modern lines.

The third component of the strategy is wise judgment and prudent investment in building the system of formal education. This calls for giving priority to investment in and development of broad secondary education. It requires that the costs of universal primary education be kept as low as possible by applying new techniques which can make effective use of relatively untrained teachers, the contribution of a very small but strategic group of highly-trained personnel. Finally, in the area of higher education, the strategy stresses the need for giving priority to investment in intermediate-level training institutions and the scientific and engineering faculties of universities. But this does not mean that the production of graduates in other faculties should be neglected.

The three essential components of the strategy are interdependent and call for a well designed and integrated attack on all three fronts at once. And it is imperative that the strategy of building and utilizing human resources be an integral part of a country's national development program.

The strategy assumes that the politicians of the country are firmly committed to the goal of accelerated development, and that they have the will to do the things which are imperative for its attainment. It recognizes, however, that there are certain constraints over which the leaders have little or no control and which narrow their choice of policy alternatives.

Such strategy ought to provide a logical framework for the formulation of policies to govern manpower utilization and development. It should identify the major sectors where foreign technical assistance is required, and provide the criteria for determining priorities. It should be instrumental in integrating fragmented activities into a well coordinated effort.

SOME OBSTACLES TO BE OVERCOME

Quite apart from the constraints listed earlier in this paper, there are other obstacles to the implementation of such a strategy. The most formidable, perhaps, is traditional thinking. Those who are accustomed to traditional methods of elementary education are suspicious of new techniques. Most of the leaders of the underdeveloped countries are unaware of the great strides made recently in the methodology of in-service training in the advanced countries. The thought of overhauling the wage and salary structure of government ministries is frightening. The idea of tampering with higher education to turn out larger proportions of sub-professional personnel is not consistent with the kind of indoctrination one may have had at Oxford, Cambridge or the Sorbonne. And the very thought that there is a strategic relationship between incentive, in-service training and formal education is strange and difficult to grasp. Yet those who preach the revolutionary doctrine of planned, accelerated growth—more rapid and more sweeping than anything before—must be prepared to reject outworn concepts and employ the most modern techniques available. In their approach to development, they must be more modern in many respects than the advanced nations from which they seek aid and advice.

The governmental structure of the developing countries is another obstacle. Thinking and planning tend to be in compartments. The ministries of education deal only with formal education, and some do not even have jurisdiction over technical education. Ministries of labor are concerned with employment standards and some aspects of training skilled and semi-skilled labor. The ministries of industry, commerce and agriculture are likely to be preoccupied with technical and financial questions. The economic development ministries or development boards, if they exist at all, are generally concerned with physical capital formation, the balance of payments, and other urgent economic questions. They are likely to assume that trained manpower will appear magically as soon as factories, dams, roads, and ditches are completed. The traditional economic planners are likely to banish human resource development to that "no-man's-land" of social welfare. Thus, no ministry or board is in a position to see the problem as a whole. Each grasps rather blindly for some program of manpower development, and in justification makes wild claims for its indispensable role in promoting rapid growth.

Until recently, moreover, foreign technical experts have added to the confusion and fragmentation of effort in this field. Each has a particular package to sell; each normally deals with only one ministry; each with tireless zeal tries to "educate the top leadership" on the importance of a particular project. There is "competition among the givers." In the developing country, offers of help may be forthcoming from the United Nations, Unesco, the I.C.A., the West German Government, the Soviet Union, and other governments as well as several private philantropic foundations and a host of church missions and other voluntary organizations. Each essentially offers assistance in a specialized field.

This "competition among givers" is desirable in many respects. It offers the developing countries a range of choice. It puts pressure on the givers to do as good a job as possible. It gives the recipient countries a feeling that many nations and many institutions are concerned with their welfare. And it makes it easier for them to maintain a position of neutrality . But there are obvious drawbacks. Aid is given without regard for broader, underlying problems. The energies of the recipient governments are consumed by a proliferation of scattered and unrelated projects. Often the best qualified local manpower is lured away to foreign countries on fellowships, study tours and other exciting ventures, leaving virtually no one at home to handle the day-to-day work of project development. And, worst of all, in some countries the politicians are tempted to use some of the givers as scapegoats by asking for "a survey by experts" as a convenient means for postponing action on a thorny problem.

IMPLEMENTING MACHINERY

The design of a strategy calls for integrated rather than compartmentalized planning. The implementation of a strategy requires co-ordinated activity. What machinery then is necessary for this implementation?

Since manpower problems are the concern of many ministries, the program of human resource development must be implemented by an inter-ministerial board. In addition to members of the government, this board should normally include representatives from the non-government employers and from organized labor. It is essential, however, that such a board have a secretariat. And this board and its secretariat should be integrated with whatever machinery is established for general economic development planning. Among its key functions are:

    i) Co-ordination and approval at the national level of *all requests* for external and technical assistance involving manpower and human resource development.

ii) The determination of priorities in the strategy of human resource development, and the continuous re-assessment of these priorities as the program progresses.

iii) The assessment of human resource problems through periodic manpower analysis.

iv) The promotion and stimulation of planning activity by the ministries represented on the board, as well as by employer and labor organizations.

v) The co-ordination of the above planning activities.

vi) The integration of human resource development strategy with other components of the country's plans of economic and political development.

vii) The general review of all activity connected with human resource development, and periodic evaluation of the work of the various agencies which assume responsibility for it.

viii) The selection and design of research projects which may be useful for the formulation, implementation, and evaluation of the strategy of human resource development.

Formal machinery such as that suggested above is not difficult to establish. Its effectiveness, however, will depend upon the calibre of its leadership and its secretariat, and also upon the effective use of the right kind of foreign experts as consultants; in short, upon the quality of the people concerned.

A human resource strategy board should be neither a statistical agency, nor a study commission, nor a long-range planning organisation. Though primarily concerned with policy formulation, it may also have executive responsibilities. The top staff, therefore, should be neither statisticians, nor professional educators, nor economists as such. They should be *strategists*—persons who combine political insight with a rational understanding of the processes of modernization, and who are able to comprehend the inter-relationships between the component parts of an intricate program for accelerated development.

So far advanced countries have been unable to send such strategists to the newly developing countries. This has been partly because the need for a coherent strategy has not been recognized; partly because the recipient countries have been wary of foreigners who want to "mastermind" their development; but mainly because the type of strategists needed are in rare supply.

Here then lies the crux of the problem: *the training of strategists in human resource development*. This is a task which calls for joint effort by both givers and recipients of technical assistance. And indeed no other task is more important to the future of developing nations.

II

PRIORITIES FOR EDUCATIONAL EXPANSION[1]

by
W. Arthur Lewis
Principal
University College of the West Indies, Jamaica

INTRODUCTION

Poor countries cannot afford to pay for as much education as richer countries. They have therefore to establish priorities in terms both of quantity and of quality.

The requirements of economic development help in setting priorities, but they are not over-riding. Education was not invented in order to enable men to produce more goods and services. The purpose of education is to enable men to understand better the world in which they live, so that they may more fully express their potential capacities, whether spiritual, intellectual or material. Indeed, through the centuries the traditional attitude of "practical" men towards education has been that it unfits its recipients for useful work. Certainly, most people would agree that education is desirable even if it contributed nothing to material output.

From the standpoint of economic development, one may distinguish between types of education which increase productive capacity and types which do not. Teaching an African cook to read may increase his enjoyment of life, but will not necessarily make him a better cook. Education of the former kind I have called investment education, while the latter kind is called consumption education. From the standpoint of economic development, investment education has a high priority, but consumption education is on a par with other forms of consumption. The money spent on teaching cooks to read might equally be spent on giving them pure water supplies, or radios, or better housing, and must therefore compete in the context of all other possible uses of resources.

---

1. This paper appeared in *Social and Economic Studies* Vol. 10 No. 2 June 1961, under the title "Education and Economic Development".

In this perspective the needs of economic development help to determine the minimum amount which must be spent on education. How much to spend above this minimum depends on how rich the society is, and on competing claims. This article is confined to seeking to discover the nature and limits of investment education.

ABSORPTIVE CAPACITY

It is fundamental to this approach that the amount of education which "pays for itself" in a poor country is limited. Some confusion has been caused by applying to these countries the conclusions of statisticians who try to measure the yield of education in rich countries, and who emerge with such conclusions as that the yield of investment in humans exceeds the yield of investment in physical resources. In the first place, investment in humans is not to be equated with education, as normally conceived in institutional terms. Human capacity is improved by education, public health, research, invention, institutional change, and better organization of human affairs, whether in business or in private or public life. To attribute all improvements in productivity to education would therefore be more than a little naive. Secondly rich countries have a greater capacity to absorb the products of schools than have poor countries, so even if we could isolate the average yield of various types of education in rich countries, this would throw no light on the marginal yield of similar types in poor (or for that matter in rich) countries.

An over-supply of educated persons is a familiar feature in poor countries, e.g., the over-supply of university graduates in India in the 1930's, or the over-supply of primary school graduates in some West African countries today. An education system may very easily produce more educated people than the economic system can currently absorb in the types of jobs or at the rates of pay which the educated expect. This is a short-period phenomenon. In the long run the educated learn to expect different jobs and to accept lower rates of pay. But the long run may be very long, and the jobs accepted may gain very little from the education received.

Part of the difficulty of absorption is due to the education system producing the wrong kinds of education. The balance between primary, secondary and higher education; between general and vocational studies; between humanities and sciences, or between institutional and in-service training—all these need to be blended in the right proportions if education is to be a help rather than a hindrance to economic development. Because the pattern of education was formed many centuries before the modern technological revolution occurred, most education systems give too little weight to the natural sciences and technology, whether at primary, secondary or higher levels, so that a surfeit of persons trained in literary studies, side by side with an acute shortage of persons trained in scientific, biological or mechanical arts, is a feature of several countries.

Careful survey and planning are needed if the education system is to produce the balance of skills which the community exactly needs at its particular stage of development.

Nevertheless, the problem is not wholly or even mainly one of balance. The main limitation on the absorption of the educated in poor countries is their high price, relatively to average national output per head. In a country where most people are illiterate, the primary school graduate, whose only skills are reading and writing, commands a wage much higher than a farmer's income. A university graduate who, in a rich country, commences at a salary about equal to a miner's wage, may, in a poor country, receive five times a miner's wage. In consequence all production or provision of services which depends on using educated people is much more expensive, in relation to national income, in poor than in rich countries. The poor countries may need the educated more than the rich, but they can even less afford to pay for or absorb large numbers.

In the long run the situation adjusts itself because the premium for education diminishes as the number of educated increases. Either the educated have to accept less; or else they are unable to resist the pressures which cause the wages of the less educated to rise faster than their own. The grumbling of the middle and lower middle classes as their privileges diminish is a universal phenomenon, and not infrequently has political consequences. Upper classes based on land or capital have always favoured restricting the supply of education to absorptive capacity, because they know the political dangers of having a surplus of educated persons.

The situation is particularly acute in Africa, where senior administrative salaries have had a considerable premium above similar salaries in Europe, in order to attract European recruits. In consequence, the range of personal incomes is wider than anywhere else in the world; much wider than in Asia, where senior salaries are only about a half of their European equivalents. Now that Africans are taking over the top administrative jobs, they are asking, in the name of the sacred principle of non-discrimination, to be paid the same salaries as Europeans, as it were necessary to spend 50 per cent more on them to attract them away from positions in Europe. Many African politicians have stamped on this ridiculous proposition, which handicaps development by making it unnecessarily expensive, and also merely substitutes the yoke of the African B.A. upon the neck of the African peasant. The ultimate outcome cannot be in doubt, but much passion will be expended on the way.

As the premium for education falls, the market for the educated may widen enormously. Jobs which were previously done by people with less education are now done by people with more education. The educated lower their sights, and employers raise their requirements. Primary school teaching illustrates this admirably. In the poorest countries, the requirement is completion of a primary school education. At the next level, it is education. In most American states it is now completion of a college education; and in one or two American cities one cannot become a primary school teacher without an M.A. degree. Similarly, ten years ago people wondered what the United States would do with its flood of college graduates; but as the premium on college graduates has diminished, business men have decided to hire increasing numbers even for jobs requiring no special skill.

As a result of this process an economy can ultimately absorb any number of educated people. It follows that it is erroneous, when making a survey of the need for skilled manpower, to confine one's calculations to the numbers that could be absorbed at current prices. One ought to produce more educated people than can be absorbed at current prices, because the alteration in current prices which this forces is a necessary part of the process of economic development. On the other hand, this adjustment is painful, and fraught with political dangers. Like all social processes, it requires time for relative smoothness.

PRIMARY EDUCATION

To give eight years of primary education to every child would cost at current prices about 0.8 per cent of national income in the U.S.A., 1.7 per cent in Jamaica, 2.8 per cent in Ghana and 4.0 per cent in Nigeria. The main reason for this wide difference is that, while the average salary of a primary school teacher is less than 1 1/2 times per capita national income in the U.S.A., a primary school teacher gets three times the per capita national income in Jamaica, five times in Ghana, and seven times in Nigeria. If the cost of education is to be kept within taxable capacity, widespread provision of education belongs to a stage of development where the premium for education has already diminished to reasonable proportions.

Apart from its cost, universal primary education, if attained with speed, raises problems of absorption. In a community where only 20 per cent of children enter primary school, and only 10 per cent finish the course, the demand for primary school graduates is such that they command considerable salaries in white collar jobs. If the number entering primary school is pushed up from 20 to 80 per cent of the age group within ten years, as has happened in some West African countries, the result is frustration. The children pouring out of the primary schools look to the town for clerical jobs, and are disappointed when they do not find employment. The towns fill up with discontented youths faster than houses, jobs, water supplies, or other amenities can be provided, and urban slums and delinquents multiply while the countryside is starved of young talent.

The situation is sometimes blamed on the failure of rural schools to adapt their curricula in such a way as to orientate rural children to rural life. This, however, is only part of the problem. The primary school leaver's expectations derive not from the curriculum but from the status which his immediate predecessors have enjoyed. In a developed economy the wage of an unskilled labourer (which is all that primary education produces) is about one-third of the average income per occupied person; but a primary school leaver in Africa expects about twice the average income per occupied person. Obviously, if literacy became universal it would be impossible to pay every literate person twice the average income. If the primary school leaver is to get twice the average income, he can fit only into those parts of the economy which yield twice the average income, and the rate of absorption of primary school leavers then depends on the rate at which these modernised sectors of the economy are expanding. He will fit into a revolutionised agriculture with modern practices and equipment, but it is useless to expect him to fit into the three-acres-and-a-hoe farming of his father. Any good primary school will widen a child's horizons, and create expectations which primitive farming cannot fulfil. So even if rural schools concentrate on rural life, their products are bound to suffer frustration unless the whole social fabric of agriculture is being modernised at the same time.

Cutting the cost of education by reducing the length of the primary course makes absorption still more difficult. Several African countries have now adopted a six-year primary course. This means that hordes of youngsters are turned on to the labour market, aged 12, with high expectations and low skills. In part this is a borrowing from British or French or American systems, where universal six-year primary education is followed by universal schooling of some secondary type for at least a further three years. In the absence of this secondary stage, African countries would do better, from the standpoint of absorption into the economy, if they gave primary education to fewer children for a longer period, of say eight or nine years.

The limited absorptive capacity of most West African economies today—especially the backwardness of agriculture—makes frustration and dislocation inevitable if more than fifty per cent of children enter school. This, coupled with the high cost due to the high ratio of teachers' salaries to average national income, and with the time it takes to train large numbers of teachers properly, has taught some African countries to proceed with caution—to set the goal of universal schooling twenty years ahead or more, rather than the ten years ahead or less which was associated with the first flush of independence movements. This decision is highly controversial to those for whom literacy is a universal human right irrespective of cost, to those who feel that it is better to be taught by untrained teachers than not to be taught at all, and also to those who see in the frustration generated by incapacity of the current social fabric to absorb, the very stuff which will promote needed change rapidly. On the other hand, considering that in most African territories less than 25 per cent of children aged 6 to 14 are in school, a goal of 50 per cent within ten years may be held to constitute revolutionary progress.

SECONDARY EDUCATION

If the poorer countries tend to expand primary education too rapidly, their failure to make adequate provision of secondary education is a major handicap to economic development.

The products of secondary schools are the officers and non-commissioned officers of an economic and social system. A small percentage goes on to university education, but the numbers required from the university are so small that the average country of up to five million inhabitants could manage tolerably well without a university of its own. Absence of secondary schools, however, is an enormous handicap. These schools supply the persons who with one or two more years of training (in institutions or on the job) become technologists, secretaries, nurses, school teachers, bookkeepers, clerks, civil servants, agricultural assistants and supervisory workers of various kinds. The middle and upper ranks of business consist almost entirely of secondary school products, and these products are also the backbone of public administration. To have to import large numbers of people at this level, paying them in salaries and allowances two to three times what they could get in rich countries, is a blow to most development schemes. In industry it makes production costs absurdly high. In public administration it puts many desirable schemes—such as agricultural extension or nursing services—beyond the range of taxable capacity. While, as for democratic social life, the absence of a good sprinkling of educated people, serving voluntarily in public agencies (local government, cooperative societies, etc.) and acting as an informed public opinion, exposes society too easily to deception and corruption. When one compares the countries which have become independent since the second World War, there is a clear difference between those whose business and public affairs are still run mainly by expatriates, under Ministers of the country, and those which are really competent to run their affairs at all levels, because their secondary schools have supplied streams of people for intermediate and higher posts in business and administration.

The proportion of the population needed in secondary schools is a function of the level of development. If we include nurses, secretaries and school teachers, the proportion of the adult population holding jobs for which a secondary grammar school education is now normally considered an appropriate preliminary is about 5 per cent in Jamaica. This is higher than the proportion who have actually completed secondary education. It is the number of jobs for which a secondary education would now be expected. In African countries the current proportion is very much smaller, because the subsistence sector is so much greater. The number who have received secondary education is only a fraction of one per cent, while the number holding jobs for which a secondary education is considered appropriate is probably between 1 and 2 per cent.

One can calculate the percentage of the age cohort who should receive secondary education from the formula:

$$x = \frac{n(a+b+c)}{m}$$

where:
x = proportion of age cohort to be recruited;
n = ratio of number of secondary-type jobs to adult population;

m = ratio of number in age cohort to adult population;
a = normal percentage wastage of nationals of the country;
b = abnormal wastage due to replacement of expatriates;
c = percentage rate of growth of the number of secondary type jobs.

Of these c is the most difficult factor to assess. In a community such as the United States, which is already nearly saturated with secondary school types, the rate of growth of numbers cannot much exceed the rate of growth of population. In a community like Jamaica, where the modernised sector of the economy employs only about a half of the population, and is still making inroads into the numbers engaged in subsistence farming, petty trading and domestic service, secondary school type jobs probably grow slightly faster than the normal rate of growth of national income, since they depend mainly on the growth of the public sector, and of other service industries. The current growth rate in Jamaica is probably about 6 per cent per annum. In West Africa, where the modernised sector is still smaller, its expansion relatively to the whole economy is still faster (especially as public services are growing rapidly) and secondary school type jobs may be growing by as much as 8 per cent per annum. In this area too, the proportion of expatriates in secondary type jobs is abnormally high, and a large wastage figure may be expected; say 15 per cent of that proportion in each year. One may thus guess that the percentage of the age cohort required in secondary grammar schools is:

In Jamaica $\quad x = \dfrac{0.05\,(0.02 + 0 + 0.06)}{0.04}$

$= 10.0$ per cent

In Nigeria[1] $\quad x = \dfrac{0.01\,(0.025 + 0.005 + 0.08)}{0.045}$

$= 2.4$ per cent

These ratios are just about consistent with the demand for secondary education on the part of parents. In most of the poorer countries at present, parents of about 8 to 12 per cent of the children who start primary education want these children to go on to secondary education of the grammar school type; and where government schools are not provided, many private schools of very poor quality, charging low fees, spring into existence to meet the demand. If good grammar schools are provided for 10 per cent of children entering primary school, this will just about meet both parental demand and also absorptive capacity.

The obstacle to providing secondary education in West Africa is not so much recurrent cost as capital cost. Recurrent cost is abnormal, for reasons already given. Cost per teacher is 30 times per capita national income in Nigeria, compared with 12 times in Jamaica, and with only

---

1. This is an average for the whole country. The situation differs widely in the three regions.

twice in the United States. Nevertheless, even in Nigeria, to provide, grammar school education for 5 per cent of the age group costs a little less than 1 per cent of national income. The fantastic burden is the cost of building schools. One can build a good secondary school in England for £ 50,000, but the cost of a school for a similar number in Ghana may be £ 250,000. This is because many West Africans have persuaded themselves that only boarding schools are appropriate to Africa. The argument runs as follows: "To get a fully specialised staff, a school must have 20 teachers. Therefore it must have 500 students. Therefore, assuming 5 per cent schooling, it must draw from a population of 70,000. Since very few African towns have a population exceeding 10,000, it follows that most African towns cannot support a day secondary school. Therefore the solution has to be boarding schools." A boarding school, complete with dormitories and staff houses, costs £ 250,000. The argument can be attacked at either end. Must a secondary school have 20 teachers? If, instead, it started with only six teachers, one could build a series of day schools in 3 times as many small towns. Even when the school has to be large, the British solution is boarding, but the American solution is the school bus, which is hardly known in Africa. Some financial sense is badly needed in planning secondary schools in Africa. It is obviously absurd to take the line that Africa's way to secondary education must be through building Etons for the majority of African children.

Grammar schools are not by any means the only, or in numbers even the chief, form of secondary education. If one follows some authorities in reserving the term "primary" for education up to age 12, and in using the term "secondary" for all education between 12 and 18, then some secondary education should be provided for all children who complete primary education, since such children are not ready for the labour market at 12. Children who do not go on to grammar school pass into secondary schools with a practical bias, known as "middle" or "intermediate" or "central" or "modern secondary" schools, or into the practical streams of "comprehensive schools" or, in the French system, into the "first cycle" of secondary schooling. Except in the United States of America, the great majority of children end their schooling here.

A few of these children are ready, at about age 15, to pass into vocational schools, for full-time technical training. It is hard to judge how large this group should be. People possessing the skills taught in such schools—building, metal working, engineering—comprise from 2 to 8 per cent of the working population in less developed countries, but it does not follow that 8 per cent of children should enter such schools. The traditional training for these trades is a system of apprenticeship. In the United States of America, where nearly 70 per cent of children are kept in school until age 17, vocational schooling has had to substitute for on the job training up to that age. Elsewhere, it is probably cheaper and more effective to rely on apprenticeship; to put not more than 2 per cent of the age cohort through full-time courses, and to arrange part-time courses for the rest.

Actually, in poor countries half the age cohort should enter agriculture. Primary and intermediate schools in rural areas have an agricultural bias, but they see the child through at most to age 15. Governments provide farm schools to train agricultural assistants for government service, but very few provide courses for students who wish to farm. Probably the ideal is for the child to start farming at 15, and then around age 18 to go to a practical farm school for about six months to see modern techniques. It is true that agricultural extension can be done on farms by peripatetic agricultural assistants, but this is not an adequate substitute for an intensive course for bright young farmers, any more than "training-within-industry" is a complete substitute for vocational schools.

When the grammar school children leave school, between 16 and 18, they are ready for specialised training. The great majority will go straight into employment, and receive on the job training as clerks or technical assistants. Other need preliminary training of say from six months upwards, to become secretaries, medical technicians, nurses, agricultural assistants, primary school teachers, junior engineers, or as the case may be.

Very few of the poorer countries make adequate provision for this specialised but sub-professional training. This is because the supply of educational facilities is not properly planned in relation to the needs of economic and social development. The making of "manpower surveys" is spreading as a remedy for this defect. The technique of making such surveys is still rudimentary. Asking employers how many people they intend to employ, or would like to employ in various categories, yields interesting answers, but these answers do not necessarily add up to absorptive capacity. It should be possible, from examining the manpower statistics of different countries in different stages of development, to produce some coefficients which would act as a check on the results yielded by questionnaires, but basic work of this kind is only just starting in the universities. Meanwhile it is clear that even rudimentary manpower surveys help governments to appreciate the need for specialised training facilities for people between ages 16 and 20, so greater use of such surveys is certainly to be commended.

ADULT EDUCATION

The quickest way to increase productivity in the less developed countries is to train the adults who are already on the job. Education for children is fine, but its potential contribution to output over ten years is small compared with the potential contribution of efforts devoted to improving adult skills.

This field is almost wholly neglected. In the government hierarchy it belongs not to the Ministry of Education but to the Ministries of Trade, Agriculture, Mining, Health, Communications, Community Development and others. Most of these Ministries are too busy making new regulations and processing forms to regard adult education as a major part of their functions.

Yet there is ample testimony to what adult education can achieve, whether in the form of training-within-industry, evening classes, or sandwich courses in urban centres; or in the form of agricultural extension, health programmes, or community development in rural areas.

Experience shows that the secret of success is to make adult education into a popular mass movement. There is not much point in offering adult classes if adults do not wish to attend classes. The Danish folk movement, or the Russian literacy campaigns or any other adult education movement has been successful in so far as it has stirred the imaginations of the people, and created a mass desire to learn. Some popular African leaders, like M. Sekou-Toure of Guinea, understand this very well, and are therefore likely to succeed in getting adult education, in one form or another, to contribute substantially to economic and social development. Elsewhere, adult education languishes as much for want of understanding as it does for lack of funds.

UNIVERSITY EDUCATION

The number of university graduates who can be absorbed at low levels of economic development is relatively small. The proportion of jobs in Jamaica for which a university education is now considered normal corresponds only to about 5 per thousand of adult population; and the corresponding figure for Nigeria, according to Professor Harbison's count[1] is only around 1 per thousand of adult population. We can apply to these figures the same formula and the same rates of growth as for secondary education (leaving out the coefficient for expatriate wastage, since the number of expatriate graduates does not decline with independence; there are fewer pensionable civil servants, but more expatriates on contract). We may thus guess that the proportion of the age cohort who should graduate from the university is:

In Jamaica $$x = \frac{0.005\ (0.022 + 0.06)}{0.035}$$
$$= 1.17 \text{ per cent}$$

In Nigeria $$x = \frac{0.001\ (0.028 + 0.08)}{0.04}$$
$$= 0.27 \text{ per cent}$$

The answer we get for Nigeria corresponds to about 2,200 students leaving the university each year, and is not far from Professor Harbison's. The answer for Jamaica, if generalised for the area served by the University College of the West Indies, gives an output of 900 students a year, or a total undergraduate body, allowing for wastage, of about 3,300 stu-

---

1. Cf. Ashby Report, *Investment in Education*, Lagos, 1960.

dents, compared with the current total of 980 students at U.C.W.I.[1] The postulated increase of 6 per cent per annum would bring this figure up to 5,500 students by 1970.

Most of the new African countries do not at present have enough students to justify building a university; it is cheaper for them to send their students abroad. In a country with a population of 2,000,000 putting say 0,5 per cent of the age cohort into university, the total student number comes only to 700. This is quite uneconomic for a university with the broad range of faculties which is usually sought. A liberal arts school of the American type is economic with 500 students, but to be economic a British type combination of Faculties of Arts, Science and Social Science needs about 1,200 students; Medicine needs 300 students, and Agriculture and Engineering need 200 each. This makes about 2,000 students in round figures. All the universities founded in Africa since the war have been costing from 3 to 5 times as much per student as it costs to run a university in Europe.

In so far as these exorbitant costs are due to abnormally high staff/student ratios, ranging upwards to 1 to 3, as against 1 to 8 in Britain, or 1 to 20 in liberal arts colleges, they are temporary, and will pass as student numbers expand. But this is by no means the only cause. In British universities the cost of the average university is about £ 4,000 a year per teacher. In universities in British tropical Africa the cost per teacher exceeds £ 6,500 a year. This is mainly because the teachers, two-thirds of whom are recruited in Britain, have to be paid higher salaries and given greater allowances than they get in Britain, and cost the African universities, including passages, at least £ 1,500 a year more than they would cost in Britain. Even the African teachers are paid about £ 1,000 a year more than African civil servants of equivalent education. On top of this, these universities are not sited in towns, where they could use public facilities (and contribute the maximum amount to public life) but have in every case been sited away from towns, where they have to maintain their own police, telephone exchanges, electric power stations, sewerage disposal, transport and other services, and have therefore to carry a service organisation about five times as large as is carried by an urban university. For the same reason the capital cost, in terms of student hostels and houses for the teaching

---

[1]. The total number of West Indians in universities is about 4,000, of whom 3,000 are in British, American or Canadian universities. Allowing for the longer degree courses in North America, and for the fact that a very large proportion of the students in North America are part-time students, the annual output of West Indians from universities is now probably about 900. The current shortage of graduates is due to the fact that a large proportion of those who qualify in North America do not return to the West Indies; there is also considerable unbalance as between faculties. The West Indian university problem is not to have more students enter university (apart from the postulated increase of 6 per cent per annum) but to provide more university facilities in the West Indies, both to fill the gap of the students who do not return, and also because U.C.W.I. has more to offer to West Indians than they can get in foreign universities, in terms of suitable curricula as well as of emotional balance.

staff, is simply fantastic, especially having regard to the extravagant housing standards which have been traditional for Europeans in the British tropics. As it happens, the capital cost of African universities seems likely to be met mostly by grants from the treasuries of Britain, France and the United States, but the recurrent cost is an immense burden, except to the extent that it is met by France in the former French territories. (Costs in the West Indies are similarly extremely high.) The situation is very different in India, or in Egypt, where university lecturers are recruited locally, and cost no more than other nationals of equivalent education. Just as African educators want to build Etons for every secondary school child, so also they have loaded on to the backs of their taxpayers, who are among the poorest in the world, the most expensive universities in the world outside North America.

However, even if the cost per student were no higher in Africa than in Britain, the cost to Africa of training a student in Africa would still exceed the cost to Africa of sending him to Britain. This is because an African student in Britain pays only a small fraction of the cost of his training; the rest is met by the British taxpayer's grant to the universities. So long as tuition fees in Europe are negligible, it will always cost an African economy more to train students at home than it would cost to send them to similar universities in Europe. (One can send a student for £600 a year, whereas even with utmost economy the tuition and maintenance cost at a British-type African university will not fall below £1,000 a year.) It is not possible for a large country to place all its students overseas, but this is feasible for a small country, especially while the percentage of students for university training is still small. From the economic point of view, therefore, one must ask: why should a small African country (or the West Indies) have its own university, when two or three or four times as many students could be sent abroad for the same money?

The chief reason why it is worthwhile, from the economic point of view, to have a university at home, even though it costs more than sending students abroad, is that the function of a university is not confined to teaching students. If it were merely a question of teaching, there could be no doubt about the answer. For though one can argue on either side in terms of the atmosphere of a home university, or the suitability of its curricula, or the advantages of foreign travel, the net result of such argument fades into insignificance besides the possibility of sending 5 students abroad for every 3 who might be trained at home (assuming the most economical set-up). Only if foreign aid provides all the capital and a third of the running expenditure can a purely teaching university justify itself on economic grounds.

Apart from teaching, a university contributes to its community through the participation of its teachers in the life of the country, and through its research into local problems.

A poor country has very few educated people. To have in its midst a body of one or two hundred first class intellects can make an enormous difference to the quality of its cultural, social, political and business life. This, however, depends on participation. If the university is built in the bush, and isolates itself as a self-contained community, it misses a tremendous opportunity of service. Countries rich in income and talent can afford to bury their universities in the countryside. But the universities of poor countries should be in the heart of urban centres, where they can do most good. (This also incidentally greatly reduces the cost of lodgings and of services.) The opportunities for participation are immense: membership of public boards and committees; contributions to professional societies; guidance of teacher training colleges; availability for consultation by administrators and business people; membership of musical, dramatic, artistic and other groups; journalism and radio work; adult education classes. If the staff of the university is not giving active leadership in all these fields, it would be cheaper to close the place down, unless it is also doing excellent research.

A country needs to have some research institutions whether it has a university or not. If the same people do teaching and research, only a part of the university cost should be charged against teaching. The question therefore arises whether teaching and research should be combined.

The British theory that every university must regard itself as primarily a research institute with students, doubles the cost per student. A research institute type of university has a staff/student ratio of 1 to 10 (excluding medicine) with a maximum teaching load of ten hours a week; whereas a university where the staff are not expected to do research can have a staff student ratio of 1 to 20, with a teaching load of 20 hours a week. Any university which adopts the British ratios must insist that any staff member who does not make significant research contribution must be fired. For a poor country in Africa or elsewhere to load itself up with the expense of a British type university, and accept from its teachers that they should be judged primarily by teaching results, would be folly of a high order.

One can argue persuasively that the first university in any poor country should be of the research institute type, provided that the research test is rigidly applied to its staff. However, as student numbers expand, it becomes progressively harder to justify the multiplication of these expensive structures in poor countries. The great majority of students entering a university are not research types and do not need to be carried to the frontiers of knowledge. What they need is a broad education, to fit them for administration, commerce, or teaching up to fifth form level. For this, the American conception of a liberal arts degree (which combines science, humanities and social studies) is much more relevant than the British Honours degree. There should be at least one university engaging in high quality research, and offering high quality Honours degrees, on the basis of high entrance standards. But, as numbers expand, the majority should be diverted into liberal arts colleges.

Here the teacher student ratio can be halved, and (since one does not need top flight researchers) teacher salaries can be more in line with salaries in the public services;[1] if in addition most of the students live at home, one can get the cost of a student down to perhaps two-thirds of what it would cost to send students abroad. To mitigate the prejudice which exists in British circles against such conceptions, one must add that, as in the United States, any graduate of one of these liberal arts colleges who displayed special talents, could go on to the major university for post-graduate training.

Similar principles could be applied to professional training, but with less justification. In every profession there are at least three layers; top flight researchers, professionals and sub-professionals. In agriculture, there are specialists, general agronomists, and agricultural assistants trained in farm schools. Medicine has specialists, general practitioners, and a third layer of nurses, dispensing chemists and medical technologists. Engineering has its scientists, its professional engineers, and its third layer of technologists.

The proportions in which these layers are combined are different in rich and poor countries. The rich countries can afford to spend much more proportionately on research than the poor countries, so the need for top-flight scientists and specialists is proportionately greater. Such men also need long periods of stimulation working in first class laboratories abroad, so the universities of poor countries should not try to put too much of their resources into superior training of first class men. The bulk of their work must be the training of the second layer.

The ratio of numbers in the second to numbers in the third layer is also smaller than in rich countries. Because of the high cost of engineers, doctors and agronomists, one employs fewer of these and more technologists, nurses and agricultural assistants, who therefore carry greater responsibilities. This is reflected in the ratio of jobs for which a degree is currently considered necessary to jobs for which a grammar school education is considered appropriate, which is more like 1 to 10 in poor countries, compared with 1 to 5 in Europe.

Because of the high cost of training graduates, it is sometimes suggested that the universities in poor countries should lower the standards of professional training, on the ground that it is better to have say 100 three-quarter trained doctors, who can be spread over the countryside, rather than 70 well trained doctors, leaving 30 per cent of the population without a doctor. This has been done in some places. The alternative policy is to mass produce not the second layer, but the third, and in the process even to upgrade the training of the third layer. One then floods the countryside not with low-grade dentists, but with high grade dental assistants; not with poorly trained agronomists, but with well trained agricultural assistants. If this policy is adopted, the corollary is to up-grade the training not only of

---

1. The British practice of paying all university teachers according to a single scale would not be appropriate to a country which has different kinds of universities.

the third layer, but also of the second layer. For the second layer professional now has many more third layer people working under him: he resigns to them more of the routine work, and concentrates to a greater extent on the more difficult tasks. His administrative responsibilities are also greater. From this it follows that he needs an even sounder training than his professional colleague in Europe. It is indeed quite arguable that, what with language difficulties, greater administrative responsibilities, and the need to work in isolation from specialist advice and laboratory analysis, professionals need at least one more year of training in poor countries than in rich countries.

I have written at some length on university education because the economic aspects of this subject are very different in poor countries from what they are in rich countries, and are nevertheless so seldom considered. It tends to be assumed that what is right in Britain must also be right in Nyasaland. Even in Britain, university people are not good at seeing themselves in their social context; most of the best of them are too busy teaching and doing research, to worry about such an abstraction as the social and economic context of a university, and when such people arrive in the tropics, it is easier for them to continue old patterns than to invent new ones. The subject is fraught with difficulty, and merits widespread informed discussion.

III

SOME OF THE MAIN ISSUES IN THE STRATEGY OF EDUCATIONAL SUPPLY

by
John VAIZEY
University of London

INTRODUCTION

Any study of economic development in the less-advanced countries inevitably focuses attention on their human resources. For, unlike capital, labour is the factor of production which is to be found in relative abundance in these countries, and it would seem logical to aim at making more use of it and at raising its quality as a step towards economic progress.

Whether development is based on a more or a less capital intensive technology, it will involve the use of modern and often complex processes in some parts of industry, agriculture, civil engineering and public health. This, in turn, calls not only for highly-trained specialists, but also for skilled and semi-skilled workers. The supply of this specialist and skilled manpower is mainly a question of education. The value of education as a means of raising productivity was clearly demonstrated in U.R.S.S. in the 1920s. In 1924 the Gosplan carried out an investigation of the economic effects of the ten-year plan for the development of the schools. It was estimated that the work of people who had received primary education was almost one and a half times more productive than that of illiterate workers of the same age doing the same work; and that the work of those who had received secondary education was twice as productive, while that of graduates was four times as productive. It was concluded that the entire cost of extending the school network was covered by the increase in productivity thus achieved—and that within the ten-year period of the plan.[1]

---

1. Stanislas Stroumiline, *"La Planification en U.R.S.S."*, Editions Sociales, Paris, 1947.

The evidence for the place of education in economic growth is confused and rudimentary.[1] It can be said that its role is an important one, in two respects. It has a direct effect on economic growth through the supply of skilled manpower and a subtle and pervading influence on such matters as the attitude towards progress adopted by society. In many parts of the underdeveloped world one of the major considerations is how to create and develop the desire for economic progress, in other words, how to induce people to want to change a way of life which has been theirs for centuries or even millenia. Until recently education in many underdeveloped areas has had social and religious purposes which often ran directly counter to some attitudes desirable for economic progress and development. Here perhaps lies the most important task of education reform. This is something imprecise and indefinable but which nevertheless is of basic importance.[2]

It is clear that economic development is closely related to the extent, structure and balance of education. In the pages that follow, emphasis will be laid on those sectors of the educational system which have the biggest part to play in developing the less-advanced territories and on the most economical ways of spreading education in those regions.

Although underdeveloped countries differ considerably from one another, certain features are common to most of them. They all have a low income per head; they are usually overpopulated in relation to employment opportunities; they are predominantly agricultural and their agricultural methods are backward; they all have a shortage of foreign exchange which severely limits their possibility of importing capital equipment; and their political leaders all share an urgent desire for the economic growth of their countries.

Certain broad generalisations may also be made about education. These countries have a large proportion of children in the population; comparatively few of the children are at school and many of them do not stay there for long; the number of teachers is small, and the pupil/teacher ratio is very high, especially in the public sector; many of the teachers have low qualifications; education often follows a traditional pattern ill-adapted to contemporary economic and social needs; as a consequence in many countries a relatively large number of people with some education are unemployed; the rate of withdrawal of pupils before they have completed their course is very high; lastly, education programmes often lack consistent planning and co-ordination and are poorly administered.

In some countries, especially Central, East and West Africa, there is a serious shortage of educated people at all levels. The Ashby Report has shown in Nigeria, for instance, that the gaps can only be made

---

1. See John Vaizey, *The Economics of Education*, London, 1961; also Michael Kaser in *Needs and Resources for Social Investment*. Intern. Social Science Rev., 1960, pages 1-7.
2. This is the aspect of education which Alfred Marshall emphasized in *The Principles of Economics*, 1890; a theory later developed by Schumpeter in *Capitalism, Socialism and Democracy*, 1947.

up by importing trained and skilled people from abroad. Elsewhere, however, where the education system has progressed further, or is based on wide-spread traditional education, there is serious unemployment. In these countries the problem of producing teachers is in part one of transferring the unemployed into useful teachers. In the other countries the problem is one of finding teachers *ab initio*, but even here difficulties will arise unless there is a system which makes adequate use of skilled people.

Education uses people as pupils and teachers. Since, by definition, productivity of labour is low on average, and since in many parts of the world there is heavy unemployment, from an economic point of view the real costs of the development of education are surprisingly low; although as I suggest later, its budgetary cost are high.

The chief merit of education as a means of economic development lies in the fact that it does not make heavy demands on the scarcer resources. The foreign exchange component of education is low, consisting mainly of the import of foreign experts and teachers, textbooks, scientific equipment and other ancillary material which rarely total more than 5 per cent of the total cost of education (except in the higher branches). In fact, education is probably one of the easiest forms of development which can be undertaken by a poor country.

To fulfil this purpose, education must be closely related to the needs of the country for growth. To copy the pattern of the advanced countries has frequently led to a serious maladjustment between the needs of the economy and the output of the education system. The heavy unemployment among intellectuals and educated people in many of the underdeveloped countries may give the impression that there is too much rather than too little education; in fact, such unemployment emphasizes the lack of co-ordination between planning for education and planning for economic development. In any case, the education provided in these countries should be sufficiently flexible to enable people to move from one type of job to another with comparative ease.

It must be emphasized that unless the programmes for economic development include policies to make use of all the skills that are produced, and for producing the right sort of skills, there will be a tendency to develop unemployment among educated people. The labour market functions imperfectly in poor countries, and it is difficult for a man, once trained, to adopt unskilled work; he will remain unemployed. This is a serious economic loss and a social danger.

The contradiction between the needs of underdeveloped areas and the concept of education as it obtains in the highly-developed countries is illustrated by medical training. One of the urgent needs of the underdeveloped world is the eradication of certain major diseases. The technology for undertaking such a programme is available. Medical supplies such as serum and drugs can usually be obtained as part of foreign aid. But there is a grave shortage of doctors which considerably slows down the implementation of the programme, and at the same time considerably raises its cost because of the high salaries which have to be paid.

The length of medical education required for disease eradication programmes is less than that required for general practice, which is in turn less than that required for consultancy work. Yet the formation of all these three categories of doctors is the same up to first-degree level. Professionalism prevents the emergence of medical auxiliaries to perform the limited yet urgent task of disease eradication. Clearly, there is a conflict here between the immediate economic needs of an underdeveloped country and the concept of education in medicine in a developed society. This and similar conflicts are not easy to solve, but must constantly be borne in mind if educational planning is to be practical.

The basic problem of education at the moment, however, is more its scarcity than its quality. This scarcity is made worse by population pressures.

In most underdeveloped areas the growth of population is almost as rapid as that of incomes so that income *per capita* is falling. In India, it is barely keeping pace; in Pakistan it is declining. Nowhere is there a real possibility of rapid capital accumulation as long as this population pressure persists. There is a high proportion of children to the economically active part of the population: 13 or 14 to 10, instead of 6 or 7 to 10 as is common in the advanced parts of the world. For this reason in education the problem is not so much one of developing and spreading education as one of maintaining the present proportions of children at school. Indeed, it seems at times as if the educational facilities are going to be submerged beneath the flood of children during the 1960s. Perhaps education can be used to help to stem the population.

In Europe, the fall in the size of families roughly coincided with the spread of education and the prohibition of child labour. It may be argued that in the underdeveloped areas the same causes would produce the same effects. It is certain that prohibition of child labour in conjunction with compulsory education would make large families much less profitable. It may also be thought that education would dispel some of the ignorance which is often the cause of large families. It would also raise the status of women, which would tend to reduce the size of families. But it would require a complex analysis to draw any firm conclusions as to the possible role of education in stemming the population tide.[1]

It is against this background that an attempt will now be made to examine certain educational problems which appear to be common to most underdeveloped countries and to suggest the broad lines along which an educational strategy for economic growth might be developed.

---

1. See R.M. Titmuss, B. Abel-Smith and A. Lynes, *Education in Mauritius*, London 1961.

THE STRUCTURE OF EDUCATION

A basic question which arises in connection with the structure of education is that of striking a proper balance between the various sectors of education, or between various regions of a country.

In the Declaration of Human Rights the right of all children to free primary education suggests how powerful are non-economic judgements in education; to provide this education expenditure must be greatly increased. An economist, however, may point out that a better use of resources might result from a prior strengthening of other sectors of education. In one respect at least the educator would agree with him: if primary education is to be extended without a worsening of pupil/teacher ratios, there must be a big increase in the output of teachers which in turn calls for a corresponding increase in secondary education. In Portugal, for instance, the present rate of output of teachers would have to be quadrupled in order to achieve within ten years the aim set out in the Portuguese law of providing for every child six years of compulsory education. It can thus be legitimately argued that teacher training and the strengthening of secondary education must inevitably precede any substantial development of primary education.

Problems of the same nature can arise in deciding whether to extend technical or general education.

Somewhat different is the problem of regional imbalance. Most countries have their highly developed areas and their backward areas. In Pakistan there is the contrast between West Pakistan and East Pakistan; in India, between Bombay and Bengal; in Nigeria it is the northern region that lags behind; in Egypt it is upper Egypt; in Italy it is Sicily and the region south of Naples. These contrasts often coincide with racial, linguistic or religious divisions in the country. Consequently there is political pressure from the poorer areas demanding to be brought up to the level of the richer, and any apparent neglect may unleash centrifugal forces which threaten the political stability of a country. Thus, in the second five-year plan Pakistan is directing aid from its west wing to its east wing which is equivalent to the total amount of foreign aid Pakistan hopes to receive during this period. As West Pakistan is near the point where self-sustained development would be possible, the diversion of large resources to the east wing may delay, in the opinion of some experts, the development of the country as a whole, since a self-sustaining west wing might have been in a better position to assist the east wing than it is at present. What is true of the economy in general is true of education in particular. By 1970 West Pakistan could become a region with a comparatively advanced educational system, able to make an important contribution to the development of education in the eastern wing. But what may be economically desirable is not always politically possible.

Similar problems arise in connection with the balance to be struck between rural and urban education. It is clearly easier in almost every way to develop education in the towns than in the country; and it is almost certainly more effective in its results. Yet in the poorer countries there is considerable pressure on the government to spend as much *per capita* on rural education as on education in the towns. The technical feasibility of developing urban education is so much greater than that of developing rural education that the imbalance is nevertheless likely to be permanent—as indeed it is even in the highly developed countries. Moreover, this imbalance corresponds to the needs of the economy, for its fastest growing sectors—industry, commerce and administration—make proportionately far greater demands on skilled manpower than does agriculture.

RURAL EDUCATION

Many of the underdeveloped countries, particularly in Asia, have between three-quarters to four-fifths of their population in rural areas. This population is frequently scattered in isolated homesteads or small villages. It is often intensely conservative and often has no tradition of education, except perhaps of a predominantly religious kind. Families are big, the authority of the elders is unchallengeable, and the children form an essential part of the working force as at present organised. Where schools have already been established, they are small and often have only one teacher who himself has to work as a farmer or labourer to eke out his pay. There is often hostility in the village between the teacher and other members of the community, particularly the priest.

At the outset, a certain distinction must be made between those countries which have decided to give priority to agriculture as the major means of economic growth, and those which have decided to give priority to industry. In the latter, the development of rural education is likely to be slow and to represent to some extent a wasteful use of resources. There will of course be local political pressures for the diversion of funds to rural education, but the amount of effort which should be devoted to it ought to be as low as is politically feasible. The problems of improving education in countries relying on agriculture are almost insuperable, and this is itself an argument against such a policy.

In those rural areas depending almost exclusively on subsistence agriculture, there arises the question of non-monetary economy, in other words of payment in kind. There is no local money available to pay teachers brought from the outside. On the other hand, payment from central government funds to teachers recruited on the spot might not be effective, since there is not a sufficiently developed local market to permit them to spend their incomes. In these areas a large part of the development of education is on a subsistence basis. The teacher's reward will have to be made up largely of payment in kind: housing, food, clothing, furniture (which can all be provided from local sources), perhaps also certain social security benefits.

In any case, the problem of teacher recruitment will always be difficult. People qualified to teach live mainly in the towns and are unwilling to go back to the country, and the country people do not take readily to townsmen as teachers. It might be possible perhaps to make it a requirement that no graduate remain unemployed in the town so long as there are rural teaching posts waiting to be filled. But the imposition of such severe measures would require a sense of national service and purpose which in most cases would have to be created and developed. Alternatively, those who are eager to work in town schools might be required to serve first for a certain period, say three to five years, in rural communities. This, in fact, is the method used in France and some other European countries to recruit teachers for village schools.

It should be recognised, however, that any young man or woman being sent into a village is being presented with a lonely life, frequently in an hostile and discouraging environment . This feeling of isolation might be overcome to a certain extent by concentrating rural education wherever possible, either in one central village, or at a point most convenient for a group of villages. It would also be better to build one school with two teachers rather than two schools with one teacher each.

As can be seen, rural education need not be as expensive as it is often thought to be. Even the question of school building can be solved without any great expenditure; there is no reason why a village school should not be a simple building made from local materials and constructed by village craftsmen on the basis of voluntary or compulsory service. In many countries with a largely non-monetary economy, compulsory labour is a form of taxation frequently used.

It should be borne in mind that in the areas considered here there is no tradition of literacy and, indeed, even those who have become literate have little occasion to read or write. It is worth considering whether rural education programmes should not be carefully correlated with programmes for agricultural extension services, land reform, the adoption of new agricultural techniques and community development. It would then be less important to provide a teacher in the accepted sense than to provide what has come to be called a multi-purpose worker who can give training in agricultural skills and elementary hygiene as well as conventional education.

Lastly, there is the perennial problem of school attendance in rural areas. The rhythm of agriculture dictates that at certain times of the year all hands should be working in the fields, whilst at other times almost all hands are idle. Therefore any attempt to forbid the use of child labour in rural areas would almost inevitably break down at the first harvest or at the first local disaster. Furthermore, the use of child labour in agriculture may in itself be a useful means of developing agriculture—if the children have learnt better techniques than their parents have known, they may themselves become useful educators. Moreover, there is likely to be a considerable scarcity of educational facilities in most rural areas for a long time to come, so that there would be little point in enforcing child labour laws in the interest of school attendance in these areas. It is believed that at least one-fifth of the children enrolled in schools in Pakistan do not in fact attend at all except on the days when inspectors are known to be in the neighbourhood. Any attempt to forbid child labour in these circumstances would be doomed to failure and liable to bring the law into contempt.

URBAN EDUCATION

Urban education is of particular importance to countries in which emphasis is being laid on industrial growth. It can be said in general that in all countries urban education is far in advance of rural education. The geographical concentration of the population makes for bigger schools; it also makes possible the provision of secondary schools. The teachers have better qualifications, and the higher standard of living permits more money to be spent on education. The problem of a non-monetary economy does not arise, and it is much easier to organise the administration of education. And as the towns grow faster than the population as a whole, the concentration of education in the towns becomes more and more accentuated, especially as it is in the towns that the development of higher skills is most urgently needed.

The development of urban education raises several serious difficulties.

First, there is the question of capital expenditure for buying land and building schools. This is mainly a problem of allocating local resources, as the foreign exchange element of this expenditure is negligible. As will be seen later, however, foreign aid can make an indirect contribution here by permitting the diversion of local resources from other projects to school building.

Second, there is the problem of recruiting a sufficient number of adequately qualified teachers, which raises a set of difficulties quite different from those encountered in rural education. It raises in fact the whole question of the status and pay of teachers which, however, will be discussed separately in a later section.

Lastly, there is the problem of school attendance. The more active and intelligent children in towns are likely to be in good jobs. They cannot be easily traced in the rapidly expanding and overcrowded towns which characterise the underdeveloped areas, all the more as they shift their homes continually and are not registered for any governmental purposes. It would need therefore a very strong supervisory force of school-attendance officers and child-labour officers if children are to attend schools in any great number.

TECHNICAL EDUCATION

It is evident that technical education must have a high degree of priority as it is directly connected with the provision of skilled manpower.

The first question which arises in this connections is the degree to which the general curriculum should be given a technical bias. It has been urged that all education should have *some* practical bias, and there are strong pedagogic arguments to support this policy.

Next, it may be asked to what extent special technical institutions should be separate from other schools and colleges. The disadvantages of separation are more obvious than the advantages. Separation may imply lower status for the technical institutions, and also lead to over-specialisation in skills which may become redundant.

Thirdly, how far should technical education be developed in conjunction with actual work in industry, commerce and agriculture? The great advantage of this approach is that it economises in manpower: the worker-student is directly productive while learning, the teacher is directly productive while teaching. On the other hand, this kind of education is often wasteful because the drop-out rate is high; and it may also have severe limitations in developing true skills.

The major problem however is that of providing technical teachers. They have to be recruited from among those who are already technically qualified and mature, and are therefore likely to expect higher rates of pay than other teachers, even though their academic qualifications are lower. A solution to this technical training problem is the "each one, teach one" process, where every skilled worker is also qualified and expected to teach another person. A meeting held under the auspices of Unesco recommended that all technical courses should include some pedagogical preparation, so that skilled workers can transmit their skills effectively.[1]

As can be seen, the difficulties in the way of developing technical education are partly social, partly connected with the educational structure, partly financial, but mainly due to the shortage of qualified teachers.

CHOOSING THE APPROPRIATE LEVELS OF EDUCATION

As has already been observed, the expansion of one sector of education implies corresponding changes in other sectors. But it is not easy to trace the eventual effects of what may seem to be a simple decision to expand any one sector.

Part of the answer will be dictated by the nature of manpower requirements. If there is an acute and persistent shortage of certain kinds of skill, the level of education for those skills will have to be provided. However, the higher the level of education called for to provide these skills, the broader will have to be the expansion of the base because of the drop-out at each level.

But another part of the answer will be dictated by the availability of funds, teachers and other resources. Women may be available as primary teachers but not as secondary teachers; arts graduates may be relatively plentiful, while scientists may be in short supply. In each case, the solution will depend on the particular circumstances.

---

1. Michel Debeauvais, *Tiers Monde*, Janvier-Juin 1960.

PRIVATE EDUCATION

In many countries private education is more extensive than it might appear at first sight. It is estimated that in Portugal, for instance, private education is dominant at the secondary education level both in quality and quantity and because of the high social standing of the classes which use it. This is also true of Turkey and the countries of the sub-continent of India. Unesco points out that in several African countries (especially those formerly under British or Belgian administration) the major part of education is privately organised and financed, although it also benefits from public subsidies.[1]

Furthermore, a surprisingly large proportion of the total expenditure on education comes from private sources. In Portugal this proportion may well be one-third; if account is taken of this private expenditure, the percentage of the national income devoted to education reaches the level which was obtained in the United Kingdom between the two World Wars; whereas if only public expenditure is taken into account, this percentage sinks to the level obtaining in the United Kingdom at the turn of the nineteenth century. It is because the available statistics do not take account of this private sector that the picture of education they project is distorted, particularly in the field of secondary education where the private sector plays such a large part.

Here it may be useful to ask to what extent secondary education should be free and to what extent it should be fee-paying. In some underdeveloped countries secondary education is entirely free, but in most, parents have to make some contribution, so that the public sector is to some extent dependent on revenue other than taxes. On the other hand, the private sector, while benefiting from public subsidies, is mainly dependent on revenues from fees, investments, grants and donations. Clearly any increase in revenue from fees is to be welcomed, because it releases public funds for purposes which private funds would be unwilling to finance. The arguments against privately-financed education are not as strong as they are sometimes thought to be. Social surveys show that it is predominantly the well-to-do who avail themselves of public education at the higher levels. As they are well able to afford to pay for their children's education, it is in a sense paradoxical that they should be provided with it free, in fact at the expense of the less-favoured members of the community. In this instance, the provision of free public education represents a tranfer of income from the poor to the well-to-do. It is much more logical to provide substantial facilities for the education of able children from poor families in private as well as public schools. The provision of such scholarships should be a major element of educational strategy in the less-advanced countries, because it will affect the whole development of private education.

Private education often reflects confessional, racial or social

---

1. Unesco/Ed/Africa/2, Paris, January 1960. *Rapport provisoire sur les besoins de l'Afrique Tropicale.*

divisions. It would be an error, however, to assume that because this is, or is believed to be, the case, the educational planner should ignore the private sector or dismiss its economic value. In particular, vocational teaching in many skills is almost exclusively a private responsibility of firms and employers. Any strategy for educational development which ignored the private sector or sought to eliminate it would be expensive and wasteful, although such a policy might be justified on social and political grounds.

WOMEN'S EDUCATION

Women's education appears at first sight to have a low priority in terms of providing skills for the labour market, though even here certain obvious exceptions—teachers, nurses and textile workers—must be kept in mind. The place of women in less-advanced countries is determined by their low social status, and in almost all societies by the fact that their main role is played in home-making. Nevertheless, this situation is not immutable: in the U.S.S.R. women make a full contribution to the labour force.

But it is precisely in home-making that women's education can have its most far-reaching effects. It is in the home that attitudes are fixed, ways of life established and traditions continued. The profound change in patterns of behaviour and expectations which is necessary if the concept of economic progress is to be introduced into traditional societies must depend in great part upon the attitude of the home-maker. Women's education therefore should have a high priority not only on social and human grounds, but mainly because it is likely to be the way—possibly an indispensable way—of removing social, cultural and psychological barriers to economic growth.

Nor should education for providing skills be ignored. In the Soviet Union 69 per cent of the teacher force is female, and in the United States the percentage is slightly higher. The woman-teacher is less costly because she has less opportunity of lucrative alternative employment and also because women's wage rates generally are lower than those of men. The employment of women-teachers is therefore a means of reducing the cost of education, which is in itself a sufficient justification for the education of women.

OBSTACLES TO EDUCATIONAL EXPANSION

From what has already been said, it is clear that the development of education involves some major choices which have to be made in the light of local conditions. Should emphasis be put on rural or urban education, on the education of men or women, on primary or secondary education? But even when the choices have been made, there remain some formidable obstacles to be overcome in implementing them. These obstacles may be due to a faulty structure of education, or to some social factors, more frequently to the shortage of teachers, and almost invariably to a lack of financial resources.

The Education Structure

As has already been noted, the educational pattern in the underdeveloped countries is often copied from advanced countries and does not correspond either to the needs or the means of the country. It is therefore in itself an obstacle to the expansion of education at almost all levels.

One of the most important aspects of this maladaptation is the high rate of "wastage" due to the drop-out of pupils at all levels of education. Out of a primary class in Pakistan only 2 per cent of qualified people will eventually emerge. In the medical college at Daccan of every hundred students enrolled only two doctors are eventually produced, which makes the average cost of training a doctor extremely high. It follows that, unless the causes of this drop-out can be tackled successfully, it is important that some sort of qualification should be awarded at intermediate stages, so that there is always something to "show" for whatever knowledge or training has been acquired and which can be put to economic use. This emphasizes the value of changes which tend to split long courses with high final qualifications into intermediate stages, each of which is rewarded with some kind of useful qualification. This seems to be well understood in the Soviet Union, where it is common for 90 per cent of the students to succeed in passing examinations. It is relatively rare for any student to fail and withdraw from a course for purely academic reasons. In a poor country anyone who has some training is more useful than someone without any training—provided that certain elementary standards of initial selection are maintained.

It is important to inquire into the causes of drop-out. One of them is undoubtedly inadequate selection of pupils. The problem is often to discourage pupils from beginning an education that they will never be able to complete. This appears to be the case in Indian universities, and careful selection would appear to be especially important for higher levels of education. Another cause of drop-out is that promotion from one grade to another often depends on the achievement of a certain standard. It would seem that automatic promotion, which is practised in some "progressive" systems of education, reduces the drop-out, but it could hardly be applied to any but the lower levels of education. Apart from these factors, due to the structure of education, there are also economic and social causes of drop-out. These will, however, be considered in the next section.

Another aspect of inapposite structure relates to high-level specialisation. A good example is the training of nuclear physicists in India. Sometimes a heavy burden is placed on the whole educational system in order to produce a few highly-trained specialists in a limited field. The cost of these specialists is out of proportion to their possible output, and there is here a strong case for the regional development of higher specialised insitutions in which the number of students must be severely limited. This, of course, runs counter to the traditional view of the functions of a university, but it is a view which does not always conform to the economic necessities and possibilities of a poor country.

SOCIAL FACTORS

As already noted above, the major causes of drop-out are often of a social nature: parental opposition and lack of means. It is in this connection that such things as social expenditure have been introduced into education. It takes the form of free or subsidised meals, free or subsidised medical treatment, maintenance grants, assistance towards boarding costs and scholarships towards fees.

The role of social expenditure in education is much wider than merely reducing the drop-out rates: it may often be the principal means in reducing social inequalities and thus attracting the able but impecunious into education.

In all countries, including the United Kingdom, the United States and the U.S.S.R., access to educational facilities is unequal. Children of poor parents, children who live in the country, children from big families are all handicapped compared with children of rich parents, children from towns and children from small families. Since underdeveloped countries all have a predominance of unskilled workers, country dwellers and big families, the handicap arising from these factors is relatively more severe than in the developed countries. This handicap can only be overcome—and this only in part—by judicious social expenditure.

THE TEACHER PROBLEM

Undoubtedly the central problem in the development of education is the supply and the status of teachers. The expansion of teacher-training is perhaps the most urgent educational need of the underdeveloped countries.

Apart from untrained teachers, there are three main sources of recruitment for teachers: the normal schools, teacher-training colleges, and universities and other institutions of higher learning. University graduates usually provide the teachers for secondary and higher education while the other two categories (together with the untrained) provide teachers for the primary schools. In order to expand the teaching force, there must therefore be either an expansion of teacher-training facilities, or an increase in the length of service of teachers, or an import of teachers.

Obviously in the case of underdeveloped countries, the biggest quantitative need is for education at lower levels, and consequently the major sources of teachers-training must be the normal schools (where the pupils act as part-time apprentice teachers) and the teacher-training colleges. As the latter take their students from secondary schools, any expansion of the teacher-training colleges entails an expansion of secondary schools, which in turn requires an increase in the number of teachers qualified for teaching in secondary schools. This increase can be achieved either by the expansion of university-training or by redirecting existing graduates into teaching. As for the normal schools, they take their students in most cases directly from the primary schools and have little difficulty in attracting recruits, first because they usually offer the only opportunity for the students to acquire a secondary education, and also because the students can join the teaching force at a very early stage.

In addition, there is urgent need for the in-service training of teachers. The establishment of colleges to give short residential course or, in larger towns, part-time training should have high priority, and incentives should be provided, in the form of promotion prospects, to encourage teachers to follow this form of further education. The Ford Foundation has begun a programme which makes available such in-service refresher courses in India and Pakistan, and programmes are being widely used elsewhere.

An important consideration in providing an adequate teaching force is the economic and social status of the teacher. The structure of salaries generally in the underdeveloped countries does not reflect the conditions of the labour market for skilled people; salaries reflect, more often than not, local social status rather than scarcities of skills, and in many countries the status of many teachers is low.

It has already been remarked that the result of this is unemployment among people with skills. The market price of a teacher, for example, may well be below what is conventionally acceptable. In general it is quite impractical to suggest that teachers should be paid more; though their low pay is one of the reasons for their low social status. In part, salary differentials in teaching can attract the better graduate, or encourage teachers to work in poor areas; but professional communities may militate against such measures. A campaign to raise the social status of teaching may be a substitute for a hopelessly expensive proposal to raise pay scales; in the long run, a revaluation of all skills by a national wage policy is probably a *sine qua non* of an adequate policy to make use of scarce skills in the interests of economic development.

Salaries are not the only incentive; since social security in these countries is rudimentary, the provision of fringe benefits of all kinds for teachers would constitute an important incentive for entering the profession. The first inducement which might perhaps be offered is a guarantee of permanent employment, and the second a retirement pension. It is important to realise that retirement pensions offered now on a non-contributory basis to teachers in their twenties will only fall due for payment around the year 2000, by which time these countries may hope to have much larger national incomes than they have at present. Consequently even quite generous pension schemes would not put any immediate burden on the exchequer. Housing and medical services are other incentives which governments can generally provide at a lower cost than that a private individual would have to pay.

A vital role in the teaching profession must be played by women.

In the case of primary education, they are the major source of the supply of teachers in most countries (at least outside the Muslim world). It is therefore necessary to strengthen considerably the secondary education of girls which, in most countries, has fallen considerably behind that of boys. However, most women teachers will have a predominantly literary bent or at least an anti-scientific and anti-technical bent. It becomes therefore important to consider how boys and girls in primary schools staffed predominantly by women can be taught at least elementary mathematics, technical subjects and possibly some science. It might be possible to counteract this anti-scientific bent of women teachers by adopting co-education in secondary schools. It should be remembered that in underdeveloped countries secondary education structure reflects one of three major models, those of France, of the United Kingdom and of the United States, and that copying the British and French models has meant the separation of boys and girls at secondary school level.

As has already been pointed out earlier, women teachers cost less than men teachers, so that their extensive employment makes for a reduction in the cost of education per pupil which must be a major aim in these poor countries.

There is laslty another potential source of teachers which should not be neglected; the unemployed graduate and the unemployed educated person who is not a graduate. This group poses a serious social problem in the underdeveloped countries. In India there are three-quarters of a million unemployed graduates, and in Pakistan there may well be 70,000 (they are the equivalent of high-school graduates). Burma, Ceylon, the Philippines and the Middle East countries also have considerable numbers. To draw these people into teaching, it would be necessary to give to the teaching profession a social prestige and status which owed little to financial reward. Indeed, it is difficult to see how any economically viable educational development can take place at all rapidly without first arousing an intense spirit of public service.

FINANCIAL COST

But however great the obstacles which lack of teachers, social conditions or maladapted educational structure can put in the way of educational expansion, they could to a very large extent be overcome if sufficient financial resources were available. It is the financial cost which is far and away the greatest obstacle to educational growth in the under-developed countries.

In most of these countries, a very big effort is being made in education, and the proportion of the national budget devoted to it is very high. In Ghana it represents 20 per cent and in Nyasaland 13 per cent of the national budget. This effort has been particularly marked in newly independent countries, which may be an indication of the political importance attached to education. In view of this high proportion of the budget devoted to education, any substantial expansion must clearly put a considerable strain on budgetary resources and run into conflict with the many other competing claims. Hence the great importance of measures designed to avoid waste and to raise the "productivity" of the educational system, measures which have been discussed in previous sections of this paper.

Here it may be added that there is considerable scope for economies in this field. Anderson has calculated that, in terms of school days, four years of Soviet education are equivalent to five years in the United States.[1] The Pakistan Education Commission drew attention to the considerable "under-production" in Pakistan, due mainly to a too light teaching load for the staff and a too light work load for the pupils at all levels of education.[2] On a very conservative estimate, it might be possible to raise educational productivity by at least a fifth just by a more rational use of existing resources. Unesco has suggested the use of teams made up of economists, educationists, architects, engineers, and others to evolve the most economical means of using buildings, manpower, books and other facilities.[3] Thus it is important that educational administrators should not be drawn exclusively from amongst ex-schoolteachers, as is usually the case; and that other specialists should be given full executive functions and not act in an advisory capacity only.

Attention has also been drawn to the ways in which education can be provided at little money cost (see in particular the section on rural education). The economist should also consider ways in which education can be financed without drawing directly upon the national budget. It has been suggested, for example, that every major enterprise using skilled manpower should be required to provide educational facilities for the children of its workers, and also to pay a special tax or contribution towards the education system in return for the "education" of the skilled workers it employs.[4] Thus a direct link could be established between the education system and the economic life of the country.

Other supplementary sources of finance might be provided by fees charged to parents who can afford them, and also by charitable gifts and endowments to education encouraged by tax exemptions.

It is true that many of the methods suggested appear to discriminate, either between town and country, or between social classes, or against the teaching profession, or against large enterprise. But if educational growth is not to place an intolerable burden upon the national budget, certain choices must be made, and it is not altogether unfair to place part of the burden on those who make the greatest use of education and who can afford to contribute towards it.

---

1. C. Arnold Anderson, "Russian Education", *School Review*, Chicago, Spring, 1959.
2. *Report of the Commission on National Education*, Karachi, 1960, paragraphs 81 and 89.
3. *Rapport provisoire sur les besoins des pays de langue arabe*, Unesco, ED/Arab Sit/2, rectricted, December 1959, paragraphs 49-52.
4. This proposal is also made by J.K. Galbraith, *Saturday Evening Post*, 5th March, 1960.

FOREIGN AID

It is in principle almost impossible to transfer educational resources from one country to another except in the form of students, teachers, books and ancillary aids; and in primary education the use of foreign teachers is exceedingly difficult if not impossible because of the language barrier. At the same time, it is clear that in the next twenty years the advanced countries of Europe and America will be putting considerable demands on their own educational systems and will themselves probably be suffering from an acute shortage of teachers, so that not many would be available for use in the underdeveloped world. A more indirect form of educational assistance would be foreign supply of goods which permitted the diversion of internal resources to the expansion of education.

The role foreign aid can play is threefold. First, it can provide experts for the planning of educational strategy. Secondly, it can provide for short terms skilled teachers in subjects which are particularly necessary in the underdeveloped areas and for which no local staff is yet available; but this can be only a comparatively small development in certain sections of secondary and higher education. Thirdly, the advanced countries can take a certain number of students into their own institutions of secondary and higher education. Unesco has calculated that there are at present approximately 300,000 students being educated abroad. The greater part of these students represent interchange between the advanced countries themselves. However, with the expansion of higher educational facilities now taking place throughout the developed world, there will clearly be a substantial increase in the number of places available to students from the less-advanced countries.

The financial cost per student educated abroad is high and there should therefore be careful selection to ensure, first, that they are not likely to fail in their studies and, second, that they will take up posts corresponding to their qualifications on their return to their own country. None of these requirements is being fulfilled at present. In many universities the failure rate amongst students from underdeveloped countries is higher than that of the nationals. And there is also sometimes considerable opposition to the employment of foreign-trained students when they return home. This is an obvious waste of resources. Students should only be accepted if they have a good command of the language of the country in which they will be trained and if they are guaranteed suitable employment on their return. There also seems to be a class of "professional" students whose contribution to his own country is unreasonably delayed and whose existence is facilitated by the competition between host institutions for the abler students from the underdeveloped countries. There is a strong case for careful examination of this problem.

This form of aid, where all or part of the cost is borne by the host government, can make a substantial contribution to education in the underdeveloped countries, provided it is carefully administered. It can be especially valuable in the case of highly specialised education which could not in any case be acquired in the home country. As against this, the effects of foreign education may be unsettling for the student and, on his return, he may form a caste or class apart which would reduce his usefulness to his community.

Another form of aid, the sending of isolated foreign teachers for short periods, has been found to be usually ineffective. What is essential, is the creation of teaching cadres and one method which has proved successful in doing this is the process of "institution-building". A host institution in an advanced country accepts students and staff from a university, school or research institute in an underdeveloped country, and in return sends its own students and staff in considerable numbers to the "guest" institution. In this way permanent and solid links are established; the staff of the institution in process of being developed have a body from which to seek advice, while both sides can continue with their normal career pattern; moreover the difficulties with regard to housing, superannuation, salaries, etc.. which hinder considerably service abroad on an individual or *ad hoc* basis, are easily overcome.

A basic problem raised by foreign aid in education is that of language. Outside Latin America, higher education in many underdeveloped countries is conducted in a major foreign language.[1] This is often a necessity as in most of these countries there are several local languages, and usually the language of the ex-colonial power which is spoken by the educated classes constitutes one of the main unifying forces of the country.

The use of a major foreign language makes access to international scholarship easier and also makes possible the direct use of foreign teachers and experts. On the other hand, the disadvantages are substantial. It divides the culture; it restricts education at higher levels to those who have a good command of the foreign language, which generally means to certain social groups; it puts great emphasis on learning by rote, so that the great majority of students will have only an imperfect understanding of what they are learning; lastly the use of a foreign language often offends national sensibilities, and there is a political trend towards developing local languages.

From the economist's point of view, the question is whether the cost of translation and printing of books and articles in the vernacular is greater or less than the cost of teaching in a foreign language, bearing in mind the cost which would be involved in the change-over; teachers accustomed to the use of a major foreign tongue would find it difficult to teach in a native tongue. Translation and local printing are comparatively cheap as they make use of local resources; and they also permit a saving in foreign exchange. Moreover, for much advanced work the foreign language would still be used as a major second language (as

---

[1]. Exceptions are a few local religious universities in some countries; Egypt; the West Indies (where the native language is English); Siam; Japan; China; but even in these countries there is a tendency for some institutions to teach in a major foreign tongue.

English is in Scandinavia and Russian in Poland); which would reduce the number of books and articles that need to be translated to the less recondite ones. It may be pointed out that what is really important in the learning of a major foreign language is the acquisition of *reading* skill. In this way the vernacular could be used as a teaching language, thus making possible a more rapid expansion of the education system thanks to the removal of the language barrier; whilst the use of the major foreign language for advanced work would be limited to *reading*.

A last point which should be emphasized is that books should—and could—be made available in abundance to students at schools and universities. As the marginal cost of producing additional copies is low, the advanced countries could supply them at little expense to themselves. Alternatively, type settings could be sent for local printing, thus helping the local employment situation.

CONCLUSION

In this brief study the main emphasis has been on ways and means of expanding education in the underdeveloped countries. An attempt has been made to outline very broadly a strategy for educational growth. If the poor countries are to be educated it cannot be done by traditional methods; a radical re-examination of school organisation and teaching techniques is essential to the fulfilment of the task of education.

IV

THE GLOBAL DEMAND FOR HIGHER AND SECONDARY EDUCATION IN THE UNDERDEVELOPED COUNTRIES IN THE NEXT DECADE[1]

by
J. TINBERGEN and H. C. BOS
Netherlands Economic Institute, Rotterdam

INTRODUCTION

This paper is an attempt to estimate the need for qualified manpower in the newly developing countries during the next decade, and to assess the order of magnitude of the effort required, both in terms of students to be trained and of teachers to be provided. Such assessments help to give a concrete meaning to the concept of aiding the underdeveloped countries of the world; they may also be useful in discussions of international aid programmes in the field of education and help to avoid grossly overestimating or underestimating the magnitude of the effort called for.

The estimates presented here are not projections or forecasts based on past trends, but target figures expressing desirable future levels of educational activity. Particular emphasis has been laid on highly qualified manpower in the fields of natural sciences, technology, and agricultural sciences at university or similar level. The importance of scientists and technologists for the economic development of a country is obvious and is far greater than that of university graduates in other fields. In fact, it is often the shortage of scientists and technologists that constitutes the greatest obstacle to economic expansion.

The target year to which the estimates apply is 1970. This would seem to allow sufficient time for implementing the plans. The estimates

---

1. We acknowledge gratefully the statistical assistance which Madame M.S. Solliliage of O.E.C.D. has given us in the preparation of this paper.

refer to low-income countries outside Europe and are given as totals for regions.

A rational way of estimating future manpower needs would be to calculate them on the basis of economic output as planned for the future. For example, if we know the relationship between the number of scientists and technologists and the level of production in the most important industries, and if we know the future level and composition of the total national product, we can estimate roughly the number of scientists and technologists that will be needed in the future. On the basis of this estimate, we can calculate the number of students to be educated in science and technology, and by comparing this number with the existing capacity of educational institutions we know what additional capacity will be required and can calculate the amount of investment necessary to achieve it (university buildings, laboratories, equipment, etc.). If enrolment in these fields of higher education is to increase substantially, it may also be necessary to expand secondary education to ensure an adequate supply of students for universities and technological institutions.

This method consists then in calculating manpower requirements on the basis of a national production plan which has been established independently of manpower requirements. A more refined method would consist in trying to determine production and manpower requirements simultaneously, taking into account the investments necessary in both industry and education.

Unfortunately, there are several reasons why neither of these methods can be applied for estimating manpower requirements of underdeveloped countries. First, for most of the countries concerned there are no long-term economic plans giving the level and composition of the national output for our target year. Further, our knowledge of the relationship between input of skilled labour and output of goods is almost non-existent. Even the much more modest aim of relating the number of scientists and technologists to total output encounters a number of difficulties which cannot be overcome without much more elaborate study.

For these reasons, a very rough way of estimating the future demand for qualified manpower had to be followed, and the results should only be considered as an indication of the orders of magnitude involved. In short, we have tried to assess the expansion of higher and secondary education on the basis of the *desirable* increase in per capita income of the newly developing countries during the period ending 1970. Estimates have been made of the increase in the number of students and teachers at the different levels, both for general and science education, and special consideration has been given to the question of how far the underdeveloped regions can be expected to supply the required number of teachers themselves, and how far they will be dependent in this respect on assistance from the advanced countries. In spite of the tentative character of the estimates made here, it would appear that some firm conclusions can be based on them.

THE FUTURE NUMBER OF STUDENTS

The target figures for the number of students in higher and secondary education in the underdeveloped areas in 1970 have been assessed on the basis of three factors:
1. the number of students in the base year 1958—the most recent year for which more or less complete statistical information is available;
2. the population growth in the period 1958-70;
3. the desired increase in enrolment ratios in the period 1958-70.

Tables 1 and 2, which show the present situation with regard to numbers and enrolment ratios, reflect the low educational levels of the underdeveloped countries, particularly in the field of scientific, technological and vocational education.

TABLE 1. NUMBER OF STUDENTS IN HIGHER EDUCATION IN 1958/59

In thousands.

	TOTAL NUMBER OF STUDENTS (ALL FACULTIES) 1	NATURAL SCIENCES 2	AGRICULTURAL SCIENCES 3	TECHNOLOGY 4	TOTAL SCIENCE AND TECHNOLOGY = (2) + (3) + (4) 5	NUMBER OF SCIENCE AND TECHNOLOGY STUDENTS PER M. OF POPULATION
Africa[1]	129.9	9.1	7.1	9.5	25.7	180
Latin America[2]	490.1	18.0	9.8	51.6	79.4	445
Asia, excl. India[3]	632.6	54.1	25.2	69.7	149.0	410
India	833.4	218.4	9.6	28.3	256.3	645
Europe[4]	706.1	130.6	14.7	92.5	237.8	1,170

1. Algeria, Basutoland, Chad, Ghana, Kenya, Liberia, Libya, Madagascar, Mali, Senegal, Sudan Rep., Morocco, Nigeria, Rhodesia and Nyasaland, Sierra Leone, Tunisia, Uganda, United Arab Republic, Mauritius.
2. Costa Rica, Dom. Republic, Guatemala, Haiti, Honduras, Mexico, Nicaragua, Panama, Barbados, Jamaica, Trinidad, Tobago, Argentina, Brazil, Chile, Columbia, Ecuador, Paraguay, Peru, Uruguay, Venezuela.
3. Afghanistan, Burma, Cambodia, Ceylon, Rep. of China, Hongkong, Indonesia, Iran, Iraq, Jordan, Rep. of Korea, Lebanon, Malaya and Singapore, Pakistan, Philippines, Ryukyu Islands, Thailand, Turkey.
4. Austria, Belgium Denmark, Finland, France, Fed. Rep. of Germany, Netherlands, Norway Sweden, Switzerland, United Kingdom.

Source: Basic Facts and Figures, Unesco 1960.

TABLE 2. ENROLMENT RATIOS FOR HIGHER AND SECONDARY EDUCATION IN 1958

	NUMBER OF STUDENTS IN HIGHER EDUCATION PER MILLION INHABITANTS		NUMBER OF PUPILS IN SECONDARY AND HIGHER EDUCATION PER 1,000 INHABITANTS		
	ALL FACULTIES	SCIENCE AND TECHNOLOGY	GENERAL	VOCATIONAL	TOTAL
Africa	920	180	4.4	1.2	5.6
Asia	2,740	445	16.5	1.0	17.5
Latin America	1,990	550	9.3	4.5	13.8
W. Europe	3,500	1,170	24.0	13.0	37.0

The next factor to be considered is population growth. According to Professor P. N. Rosenstein-Rodan's estimates, the total population of Africa will rise by 24 per cent, that of Asia by 28 per cent, and that of Latin America by 36 per cent between 1958 and 1970. In order to maintain the present ratio between the number of students and total population, enrolment will have to increase by the same percentages.

However, it is not a question of maintaining the present ratios, but of raising them, and this requires closer consideration.

The present enrolment ratios for individual countries show a wide disparity—which however is narrowed down when we consider larger and more homogeneous aggregates of countries. In Table 3 a certain number of countries for which the relevant data were available were grouped together within each of the three regions according to their per capita G.N.P., and the number of students per 1,000 inhabitants of the age groups in question was calculated for each income group.

TABLE 3. NUMBER OF STUDENTS PER 1,000 INHABITANTS FOR GROUPS OF COUNTRIES ACCORDING TO PER CAPITA INCOME LEVEL

PER CAPITA INCOME LEVEL	IN HIGHER EDUCATION PER 1,000 INHABITANTS IN THE AGE GROUP 20-24	IN SECONDARY EDUCATION PER 1,000 INHABITANTS IN THE AGE GROUP 12-19		
		GENERAL	VOCATIONAL	GENERAL AND VOCATIONAL
Africa :				
less than $ 100	1	28	1	29
$ 100—less than $ 250	29	83	21	104
Asia :				
less than $ 100	22	123	3	126
$ 100—less than $ 250	50	144	21	165
$ 500—less than $ 750	58	125	61	186
Latin America :				
less than $ 100	3	17	8	25
$ 100—less than $ 250	17	58	24	82
$ 250—less than $ 500	14	74	27	101
$ 500—less than $ 750	68	50	79	129

Source: Various Unesco and United Nations publications.

Although the value of this table should not be exaggerated—the number of countries included in some groups being fairly small—the figures seem to confirm the relationship one would expect to find between income level and enrolment ratio. In both higher and secondary education the enrolment ratios tend to increase with per capita income, and this tendency can be explained—in the light of the literature on the economics of education—both by the increased demand for, and the stronger ability to supply, education at higher per capita income levels.

Further, the experience of the developed countries shows that enrolment ratios grow at a faster rate than per capita income; but it also shows that, like many other social and economic phenomena, they grow faster in the initial phases of development than in more mature phases.

On the basis of the above considerations, we have made the following assumptions with regard to the target figures for enrolment ratios in higher and secondary education.

1. The overall effort in the underdeveloped world will be aimed at an average increase in per capita income of two per cent per annum during the next decade, and educational levels will have to be adapted to this rate of growth.
2. Enrolment ratios for higher education (excluding third-level teacher training) will increase as follows:
   a) in countries with a per capita income below $250, by 6 per cent per annum, or by 100 per cent between 1958 and 1970;
   b) in countries with a per capita income between $250 and $500, by 4 per cent per annum, i.e. by 60 per cent between 1958 and 1970;
   c) in countries with a per capita income above $500, by 2 per cent per annum, i.e. by 27 per cent between 1958 and 1970
3. For students in science and technology, the enrolment ratios will be trebled in Africa and doubled in Asia and Latin America between 1958 and 1970; they will thus grow faster than those in other sectors of higher education.
4. For secondary education, separate estimates have been made for general and vocational education. No differentiation has been made with respect to income levels, but a uniform growth rate has been assumed for each region as follows:
   a) for Africa the enrolment ratio for both general and vocational education will increase by 6 per cent per annum, i.e. by 100 per cent between 1958 and 1970;
   b) for Asia the enrolment ratio for general education will increase by 2 per cent per annum, i.e. by 27 per cent, between 1958 and 1970, and for vocational education by 6 per cent per annum, i.e. by 100 per cent between 1958 and 1970;
   c) for Latin America the enrolment ratio for general education will increase by 4 per cent per annum, i.e. by 60 per cent between 1958 and 1970, and for vocational education by 2 per cent per annum, i.e. by 27 per cent between 1958 and 1970.

These assumptions, together with the data for 1958 and the anticipated growth in populations, enable us to calculate the number of students in higher and secondary education in 1970. The results of these calculations are summarized in Tables 4 and 5.

TABLE 4. NUMBER OF STUDENTS IN HIGHER EDUCATION 1958 AND 1970

In thousands.

	TOTAL NUMBER OF STUDENTS IN HIGHER EDUCATION		OF WHICH STUDENTS IN SCIENCE AND TECHNOLOGY	
	1958	1970	1958	1970
Africa	170	380	36	130
Asia	1,500	3,070	410	1,050
Latin America	520	1,070	85	230
Total Underdeveloped Regions	2,190	4,250	531	1,410

1. Excluding teacher training institutions.

TABLE 5. NUMBER OF STUDENTS IN SECONDARY EDUCATION 1958 AND 1970

In thousands.

	GENERAL		VOCATIONAL		GENERAL AND VOCATIONAL	
	1958	1970	1958	1970	1958	1970
Africa	960	2,400	260	630	1,220	3,030
Asia	12,340	20,110	740	1,890	13,080	22,000
Latin America	1,710	3,730	880	1,520	2,590	5,250
Total Underdeveloped Regions	15,010	26,240	1,880	4,040	16,890	30,280

DEMAND AND SUPPLY OF TEACHERS

How many teachers, then, will be needed in the underdeveloped regions in 1970, to what extent will these regions be able to supply the teachers by their own efforts, and to what extent will the advanced countries have to assist in the supply of teachers?

It is not simple or easy to answer these questions, mainly because the supply of teachers is not a constant which can be estimated by extrapolation. The newly developing countries may, for instance, make special efforts to increase this supply by developing teacher training institutes and orientating, directly or indirectly, a larger share of university graduates or secondary school leavers towards teaching. However, an expansion along these lines must be seen in the light of what past experience has shown about the interest and ability of university graduates and secondary school leavers to become teachers. But the main reason why the supply of teachers cannot be increased at will is the length of training required. The output of (third-level) teacher training institutes in the next four or five years cannot be influenced by any decisions taken now. This puts limits on expansion of higher and secondary education in the near future, unless one is willing to accept an increase in the student/teacher ratio or the employment of unqualified teachers.

UNIVERSITY TEACHERS

The net increase in the number of university teachers between 1958 and 1970 can be calculated from the increase in the number of university students during that period and an estimate of the (marginal) student/teacher ratio. In this calculation we have neglected the possibility of study abroad, the impact of which is negligible, as will be shown later. To this net increase must be added the replacement needs in order to arrive at the total *gross* demand for teachers. These replacement needs for the period 1958-70 have been assumed to be equal to half the sumber of teachers in 1958, which implies an active service life of about 25 years for the university teacher.

The results of this calculation are shown in Table 6.

TABLE 6. NUMBER OF TEACHERS IN HIGHER EDUCATION (EXCL. TEACHER TRAINING INSTITUTIONS) 1958 AND 1970

In thousands.

	1958	1970	GROSS INCREASE 1958-1970
Africa	7	18	15
Asia	32	84	68
Latin America	45	63	41
Total Underdeveloped Regions	84	165	124

Most, if not all, of these teachers will have to be recruited from those graduating from the universities in the period 1958-70. The number of university graduates produced during this period can be roughly estimated from the number of students in that period and from the average graduate/student ratio, i.e. the number of graduates as a percentage of the number of students enrolled. This ratio amounts to about 10 per cent.

If all university teachers had to come from the body of university graduates in the period 1958-70, the percentage of graduates which would have to go into university teaching would then be 4.5 in Africa, 2.5 in Asia, and 5.5 in Latin America.

The significance of these figures becomes apparent when we consider that:
1. In the developed countries less than one per cent of university graduates find employment as university teachers;
2. The figures given above refer only to teachers and ignore the demand for non-teaching assistants, whose inclusion would at least double or treble the universities' demand for graduates;
3. The university graduates produced during the period 1958-70 will be young people who could probably only fill junior teaching positions, and the incumbents for the senior posts requiring practical experience or specialization will have to be recruited from elsewhere.

The conclusion is inescapable that the underdeveloped countries will be unable to increase from their own resources the number of university teachers by 120,000 during the next decade. It is not possible —nor necessary— to make a reliable estimate of the teacher gap: even if the advanced countries had to supply as little as 5 per cent of the increase, this would mean sending 6,000 more university teachers to the underdeveloped countries. This purely quantitative aspect is one that will need the most urgent attention on the part of the governments and international organization concerned.

SECONDARY SCHOOL TEACHERS

The demand for secondary school teachers can be estimated in the same way as that for university teachers. The teacher student ratio has been put at 1:30, and the replacement demand has been estimated at one-third of the number of teachers in 1958, which seems a conservative estimate. The results are given in Table 7.

TABLE 7. NUMBER OF TEACHERS IN SECONDARY SCHOOLS IN 1958 AND 1970

In thousands.

	1958	1970	GROSS INCREASE 1958-1970
Africa	82	140	90
Asia	553	850	480
Latin America	205	290	160
Total Underdeveloped Regions	840	1,280	730

The supply of secondary school teachers originates from several sources: universities, (third-level) teacher training institutes and colleges, and some types of general secondary schools. Little is known about the relative importance of each of these sources of supply, but it seems logical to assume that teacher training institutes and colleges will be the main supplier. If they were to supply half of the required gross increase in secondary school teachers, the number of pupils at these teacher training institutes would have to increase:

from 8,000 in 1958 to 64,000 in 1970 in Africa,
from 89,000 in 1958 to 310,000 in 1970 in Asia, and,
from 32,000 in 1958 to 100,000 in 1970 in Latin America,

or from about 130,000 to 470,000 for the whole underdeveloped world.

In other words, in order to raise the number of students in secondary education by about 80 per cent between 1958 and 1970, the facilities for teacher training would have to increase by well over 250 per cent. Assuming that it will be possible to attract so many pupils to the teacher training institutes, the crucial point will be the availability of teachers to train them. Moreover, the time aspect of the problem demands a particularly rapid increase in the number of teacher-pupils in the earlier part of the period so that they will be available for teaching in secondary schools in the latter part of the period. These two factors obviously limit the possibilities for expansion.

In the circumstances, the most effective way of expanding secondary education would be to increase the number of teachers in the teacher training institutes. According to our estimates, this number would have to increase from about 7,000 in 1958 to 16,000 in 1965 and to 23,000 in 1970 for the three underdeveloped regions. It is unlikely that the underdeveloped countries themselves could provide more than a few thousand additional teachers before 1965. As the gross increase during this period will exceed the net increase of 9,000, it follows that the advanced countries will have to provide some 8,000 to 10,000 "teachers'teachers" before 1965—a figure which clearly shows the impact the development of secondary education in the underdeveloped world must have on the advanced countries.

These figures assume that only half of the increase in secondary school teachers will come from teacher training institutes, the other half coming from universities and higher secondary schools. If it came entirely from the universities, it would absorb, according to our calculations, 9 to 13 per cent of university graduates during the period 1958-70, a figure which would be reduced to the extent to which teachers could be provided by higher secondary schools. Unfortunately, no information is available on this last point. It should be remembered that this claim on university graduates would come on top of demand for university teachers and would therefore further aggravate the shortage of university teachers or of highly qualified manpower in industry.

STUDY ABROAD

As for the question of relieving the shortage of university teachers by sending students abroad, this possibility is very limited in quantitative terms. In 1958-59 some 50,000 students, or only about 2 per cent of the total number of students in higher education in the underdeveloped countries, were studying in the European countries of the O.E.C.D. area. The proportion was about 3 per cent for students in science and technology.

Generally speaking, it is more expensive to send students abroad than to employ foreign university teachers in the underdeveloped countries. However, the reverse is true when it comes to training a relatively small number of students in specialized subjects requiring expensive equipment, laboratories, etc. It would be useful to study this question more closely and circumscribe the fields in which these conditions apply.

It must also be remembered that, even if the percentage of students from the underdeveloped countries studying abroad remained the same as in 1958, their absolute number in the European countries of the O.E.C.D. area would be doubled by 1970. And as the number of national students in the European countries will have increased at a much slower rate, the proportion of students from underdeveloped countries in the student body of these countries will have increased correspondingly. This is yet another aspect of the problem which requires further study.

DISCUSSION

Chairman: M. COOMBS (U.S.A.)

The *Chairman* asked the authors—Professors HARBISON, LEWIS, TINBERGEN, and Mr. VAIZEY—to introduce their papers, and also invited Mr. PANT (Panel of experts) to add his comments.

Professor LEWIS focussed his remarks on three particular points: the high cost of education in Africa, the widespread confusion which prevails in education almost everywhere, and the problem of suitable curricula for the underdeveloped countries.

FINANCING THE COST OF EDUCATION

With regard to cost and the contribution which the richer countries could make towards it, there is a school of thought which maintains that this contribution must necessarily be small because financial aid is limited to the foreign exchange costs. This is a fallacy to which neither the French nor the British Governments have ever subscribed, always being willing to meet local costs as well as foreign exchange costs. It is the United Nations and the United States which have advocated this doctrine, and a great deal of useful assistance has thereby been prevented. This doctrine might make sense in fields other than education. A foreign aid agency may be justified in insisting that its aid should be limited to, say, 50 per cent of the cost of any project, on the ground that if the recipients had to provide the other 50 per cent, they would do so only if the project was really important to them and if they were prepared to consider it as their own and put all their energy into it. But as far as education is concerned, the underdeveloped countries will in any case be putting a great deal of money and energy into it, and there is no need to fear that they will be halfhearted about it. It is therefore time to abandon this piece of mythology which has been a major stumbling block to educational development.

TECHNICAL SCHOOLS VERSUS UNIVERSITIES

Another stumbling block has been the confusion introduced into education in the underdeveloped countries by the confused state of education in the advanced countries themselves. Ghana was sold the British idea—or what used to be the British idea— that there are two different kinds of engineers: those trained in technical schools, and those trained in universities; and that these are two quite different sets of people. So Ghana established a school of technology in Kumasi and a university in Accra, and then the two institutions engaged in ten years of bickering as to whether a new faculty of engineering should be started in Accra at a cost of an extra million pounds, on top of the million already spent in Kumasi.

WESTERN "CONFUSION" EXPORTED TO AFRICA

Then there is the argument about secondary education in which a number of these countries are now becoming involved; an argument about comprehensive schools, grammar schools, boarding schools etc., all introduced from outside with no obvious meaning in the local context, but creating as much passion and confusion in Africa as they do in Europe or North America.

The same kind of confusion is introduced into university education. African States have followed the educational systems of the countries that formerly governed them; former French territories have the French system, and former British territories the British system. Then along comes the United States willing to make some contribution to education in Africa—and naturally wanting to export to Africa something of its own system. So Nigeria or Tanganyika is suddenly offered large sums of money if it will have a liberal arts college. Now what is a liberal arts college, and how does it fit into the pattern of university education already built up in Nigeria?

In fact, education is being introduced into Africa in much the same way as religion was—by missionaries of various kinds who are just as much interested in fighting each other as in converting the people, and who only succeed in confusing the minds of the natives. Is it not possible to have some kind of œcumenical movement in education? Is not a group such as the one meeting here today best fitted to start such a movement—by preparing some studies and manuals which explain to African educationalists what these various systems are, why they differ from each other, and what are the different purposes each of them suits best? We might thus reduce the confusion caused by the mass of different views pressed upon African governments and educationalists.

ADAPTING EDUCATION TO LOCAL NEEDS

As to the third point—the adaptation of educational content to the needs of underdeveloped countries—it is perhaps best illustrated by an example from the training of doctors. London trains men to be general practitioners, and any doctor who wants to go into public health administration or psychiatry takes a separate post-graduate public health or psychiatry qualification. Therefore, the London medical examinations do not include public health or psychiatry. But in the West Indies or Nigeria the bulk of the doctors produced are destined for public health services and become district medical officers; a large part of their work consists in public health work with a fair amount of psychiatry. And for this they have no training because the medical training system in the West Indies or Nigeria is based on the London system.

Again, in the British system one cannot become a registered doctor before the age of 25. In West Africa the age is 28, because language difficulties add three years to the course. But after this long training, the West African doctor is sent out into the districts where the bulk of his work consists in treating about half a dozen common diseases such as malaria, dysentery, influenza, arthritis, venereal diseases; anything more complicated he has to send to a hospital. So perhaps it would be better to take a youngster of twenty, give him two years medical training of the kind necessary to cope with these relatively simple tasks of recognizing and treating a few common diseases, and thus be able to send medical men instead of one fully-qualified doctor into the districts.

This raises a matter to which really serious thought should be given; what kind of professional training is necessary in those countries where there is an urgent need to multiply the number of professional people of all kinds as rapidly as possible?

A DIFFICULT ART

Underdeveloped countries are always told that they must adapt what comes to them from the West to their own particular needs. But adaptation is a process of invention, a difficult and complicated art, much practised and studied in the advanced countries, but hardly to be expected from the underdeveloped countries. So it is really the advanced countries which are best equipped to study the educational needs and problems of the underdeveloped countries and to tell them how best they can adapt Western systems to their own needs. Therefore, a major contribution which the advanced countries could make would be to provide finance for research into the problems of education in the underdeveloped countries.

The speaker concluded by saying that, if the illustrations chosen by him had been drawn from British or ex-British territories, this was due to his limited personal experience. But he had no doubt that similar illustrations could be drawn from other areas, since these problems were inherent in the meeting of different cultures and were not due to any one particular culture.

NEEDED: STRATEGISTS IN EDUCATIONAL DEVELOPMENT...

Professor HARBISON, in introducing his paper, stressed the fact that the underdeveloped countries are committed not to gradual growth, but to accelerated or even forced growth, committed in fact to attempting the almost impossible, and that our thinking about foreign aid must take account of these aspirations. An illustration which is characteristic of these aspirations was given at the Conference on Education of African States at Addis Ababa last May. The Soviet delegate had told the fantastic story of the accelerated development of education in the Soviet Union, showing how the educational system had been developed within the short space of twenty-five to thirty years. Then the Nigerian delegate rose to his feet and said that he was very much impressed by this account, but the delegate from the Soviet Union should understand that Nigerians and other Africans cannot wait nearly so long as the Soviet Union to develop their educational systems.

The speaker then briefly summed up the main points of his paper, and concluded with the statement that the most important need of all was for strategists in educational development, and that one of the important subjects with which the Conference might concern itself was that of finding and training such strategists, because as yet this species does not exist.

...AND A NEW KIND OF EDUCATIONALIST

Mr. VAIZEY, in echoing the pleas of the two previous speakers for a re-examination of the whole question of what kind of education is consistent with the needs of underdeveloped countries, thought that it was important to face frankly and openly one of the major reasons why the Soviet Union, and to some extent Peoples' China, have been able to develop so quickly. The reason was that every single person who could read and write had a job; and they all had jobs because there was no argument about what sort of job they wanted; they were told which jobs society needed them to do, were sent to do them—and they did them. But he doubted very much whether there were many governments prepared to take the fairly ruthless action which was implicit in many of Professor Harbison's ideas: if his national manpower planning board was to be anything other than another advisory committee, it would have to be prepared at some stage to say to the unemployed intellectuals of the capital cities of Asia, "Tomorrow you ride out on your bicycles to a village and you teach". And this moral and political problem arises just as strongly in relation to the whole question of altering and adapting the education systems in the ways outlined by Professors Harbison and Lewis.

There is certainly great need for educational research. Anyone who has seen home economics experts teaching people in remote villages without electricity how to do refrigerator cooking; or experts teaching people to use equipment which only the top one per cent of American families can afford to buy; or the English Public School Headmaster advising poor countries how to set up public schools which would develop character and initiative while the great majority of their people are walking around with hardly any clothes to wear and very little food to eat; anyone who has seen that is in no doubt that we have to create a new kind of educationalist who is prepared to go and analyze the educational problems of these countries from first principles. These first principles are that educational resources are very scarce; that they have to be spread very widely; and that the most effective use must be made of them.

We have to get away from academic research in psychology and other disciplines, and stop calling this educational research. We must get away from the kind of research worker who goes and sits down for seven years, and after a great deal of academic research comes out with a perfect result to be published in the Journal of Analytical Psychology. What is needed, are workers capable of applying the techniques of operational research to educational problems in underdeveloped countries and drawing the appropriate practical conclusions from them, and not people who arrive with ready-made solutions; workers who can go to Africa and say, "The situation here is that you have one man who can read and write and a thousand people who want to learn to read and write", and who would then produce, on the basis of his operational research, techniques which would enable this to be done within a year. But the speaker was not optimistic about the chances of getting these educational systems adapted to the real needs of the underdeveloped countries.

A Key Point: Teacher Training

Professor TINBERGEN introduced his paper by drawing a comparison between the role of machine tools in industry and that of teachers in education. He illustrated his point by the example of the United States during the Second World War when production had to be stepped up enormously. But this process, to be possible at all, had to be preceded by a huge production of machine tools. Now the striking feature which emerges from a perusal of the figures for that period is that the production of machine tools in 1942 was twice as high as it was before—and also twice as high as it was afterwards. In other words, there had to be first an introductory process, in the shape of an enormous peak in the production of machine tools, but after one year this peak could be allowed to dwindle down again. In the same way, the expansion of education must be preceded by an intensive programme of teacher training reaching a peak in a comparatively short time, and which may be allowed to fall off again later. We do not yet know what shape this graph will take, but we should keep in mind the reality it represents. Nor should we underrate the financial aspect of the problem, although it may not be as difficult as the human aspect. Material investment remains just as necessary as investment in human beings. If we succeed in making a number of people more productive, we thereby throw other people out of employment, and there has to be additional material investment to re-employ them.

The speaker was fully conscious of the very tentative character of the estimates presented by Mr. Bos and himself, and he hoped to be able soon to initiate at the Netherlands Economic Institute some further research into the problem. He would like to see models of economic growth with the education process incorporated in them, and to deal with them along the same lines as an input-output specialist would. Such an analysis would be very useful, but we could not afford to waste time waiting for the results. He differed somewhat from the other speakers when they said that we had to do research first. By all means, let us start research at once, but let us not forget that we have not time to wait, that we must act at once and learn on the job.

As for the figures arrived at in the paper, they are terrifying in that they show what a tremendous—and unprecedented—effort would have to be made in education by the advanced and the underdeveloped countries alike. These figures were of course based on the assumption that average income per head will increase by at least two per cent per annum, a rate considered as desirable for underdeveloped countries. But whatever else they show, the figures point to one main conclusion—that war on poverty requires just as much effort from us as any real war.

Goals for Education: Politics versus Economics

The *Chairman*, referring to the value of projections made by Mr. Bos and Professor Tinbergen, said that one of the great functions of projections is to show us what is impossible and, therefore, to lead us imaginatively to seek out alternative ways of doing things. At the recent conference on African educational development in Addis Ababa an exercise somewhat comparable to Professor Tinbergen's was carried out to determine what finance would be required to meet certain arbitrary goals in education twenty years ahead. The goal was six-year elementary education for 100 per cent of the children, some form of secondary education for about 25 per cent of the relevant age group and some form of higher education for only 2 per cent of the relevant age group. This was a rather modest goal, and there was even some question as to whether politically it would be possible for African leaders to talk about only 2 per cent getting higher education a generation hence. But when the calculations were made, it became evident that even this goal was unattainable economically. Even after the economists had strained hard and made some uneasy assumptions, such as a growth rate of 4 per cent for the next five years and 6 per cent thereafter and an immediate doubling of the percentage of G.N.P. allocated to education, there was still a deficit of 1,000 million dollars a year for five years for Africa south of the Sahara, a deficit which would have to be met by external assistance, but which is far above the present level of external assistance.

The Call for a Technological Revolution in Education

This was a sobering thought. People began to explore premises, and it soon became evident that the most important premise on which the analysis had been based was the technology of education, the conventional methods of teaching and learning, and its corresponding cost factor. It was at this point that a wave of sentiment went through the African leaders in favour of a technological revolution in education which might make it possible to achieve this goal quantitatively and qualitatively by some different means. They knew not which means, but they were eager to explore. For this great industry is basically one of our most conservative industries, not with respect to the affairs of the rest of society, but with respect to its own affairs— its curricula, its salary structures, its folklore. Projections such as Professor Tinbergen's have the effect of shocking us all into a recognition that perhaps we need as radical an approach in education as we have been willing to take in other fields.

Mr. PANT said that the most jarring aspect of the current world was the yawning gap between the living standards in the advanced countries and those in the underdeveloped countries. In real terms, the per capita income in India may be only about one-twentieth of that in the United States. If this gap is to be narrowed, and if the U.S. income per capita expands at a rate of $3\frac{1}{2}$ per cent a year as is hoped, then per capita income in India must expand at a much higher rate, say 7 to 9 per cent per annum. This is a colossal task. To assume a rate of growth of say, 2 per cent means that we are not seriously applying our minds to the problem.

Apart from this gap between countries, there is also a gap within countries, especially within the underdeveloped countries. And it is here that education can play a crucial role; for if it is the main instrument for training qualified manpower, its most fundamental role is in giving equality of opportunity to the vast mass of the people and removing social disparities.

The speaker then gave some indications about long-term planning in India and about the place of education in India's economic, social and cultural life. He pointed out that five years ago the engineering colleges admitted 5,000 students, but now they admit 14,000, and in five years time they will admit about 20,000. But to sustain a rate of growth of 6 to 7 per cent per annum, it would be necessary to admit 60,000 by 1975—more than are at present admitted in all the O.E.C.D. countries put together, excluding the U.S.A.

He thought a major contribution which the advanced countries could make to the expansion of education in the underdeveloped countries would be to evolve, through educational research, new techniques of imparting education, and to help to develop teacher training on a really large scale.

The *Chairman* said he had hoped to derive from the discussion a series of guidelines that might be of help to the assisting countries in adjusting their behaviour and actions so as to provide maximum help. He wanted to end up with the equivalent of the ten commandments, but he wanted them to be couched in positive and not negative terms. He then stated briefly the "ten commandments" which he had extracted and proposed a debate on them. (These "commandments" later formed the subject of a debate, as a result of which they were revised and rearranged. In their final form they are to be found at the end of this summary).

LIFE EXPECTANCY? A FUNDAMENTAL FACTOR

Dr. SINGER (United Nations), after having drawn attention to some UNO publications which had a bearing on the subject of the Conference, said that one fundamental factor which had not so far been mentioned was the high death rate in underdeveloped countries. In the advanced countries, practically 100 per cent of the people educated and trained can be expected to have a full working life of forty to fifty years to repay the investment made in them. In the underdeveloped countries, it must be assumed that the majority of people who receive education and training will die well before the end of their productive period. On the other hand, if the death rate is brought down and the birth rate remains the same, the increase in population would be so explosive that it would absorb all available resources, leaving nothing for education.

Another factor which must be taken into account in connection with one of Professor Harbison's points is the great instability of employment in the underdeveloped countries. It is very difficult to conceive that employers in Africa would find it worthwhile to give education and on-the-job training to people the bulk of whom are likely to leave their employment within a year or two. This instability of employment also greatly adds to the cost of education and training per unit of return.

The speaker felt strongly that investment in education was one of the primary instruments of economic growth. The point made by Professor Lewis that the provision of universal primary education in Nigeria would absorb 4 per cent of the national income was far from being an argument against investment in education. One of the vicious circles at the beginning of development is that everything is too expensive in relation to national income, education investment as well as any other investment. There is no reason why governments in underdeveloped countries should not be able to collect through taxation something like 20 per cent of national income. Educational expenditure could then find its place within the framework of a very much larger government revenue than is the case now. A closer analysis shows that where governments spend little on education, they also spend little on other forms of development. It is a case of spending too little on development in general, rather than a case of education having to compete with other forms of investment.

A PRACTICAL CASE OF EDUCATIONAL DEVELOPMENT: ALGERIA

M. CAPDECOMME (France) gave an account of the working of a plan for educational development in an underdeveloped country—Algeria. In his view it was not possible to develop education in such a country without a plan, and experience had taught him that there should first be a framework, in the form of a general twenty-year plan, and within that framework there should be a more precise five-year plan so as to make planning manageable from a financial angle.

The aim of achieving 100 per cent enrolment in primary education in Algeria was impossible to realize within a short period, if only because of lack of teachers. What was possible was to raise the enrolment in primary schools from 425,000 in 1956 to one million 1961 and to an anticipated 1,200,000 in 1964-65. But that was not enough; something had to be done for those who could not get into primary schools. So another system was added on to the European system—basic education given in specially set up education centres. In those centres children, and also adults, are taught to read and write. Even if their education stops there, they will have learned something which will be useful to them. But these centres are under the same authority as primary schools, sometimes under the direct authority of the same school director; and this means that the more gifted children in the educational centres can be sorted out and sent to the primary school which thus gets the most apt pupils. In 1965 Algeria will have 700 of these centres, mostly in rural areas, but sometimes also in backward urban districts. In the latter they will receive practical education of a technical nature which will enable them to find better jobs.

The great advantage of these centres is, of course, that they do not require qualified teachers, but rather high school graduates or even people just below that level who can be quickly trained and sent to teach for a certain period of time.

Dr. WOHLGEMUTH (Austria) pointed out that of some 10,000 foreign students in Austrian universities nearly a quarter came from African or Asian countries, and described some of the welfare arrangements which have been made to cope with special problems of environment, language, etc. Another movement which is just beginning in Austria aims at providing technical and vocational education for people from the underdeveloped countries.

Dom. RAEBER (Switzerland) said the Swiss Government regarded aid as a humanitarian task and was keeping a flexible attitude as to the form this aid should take. But he thought it should at first be concentrated on essentials.

UNIVERSITY—BEACON OF CULTURE

Dr. TENA ARTIGAS (Spain) thought that in countries where people have not had the benefits of any schooling, it was necessary to educate adults as well as children. This might be done through community education on a village basis by travelling education units. This was done in Turkey in the 1930's, and more recently in the Philippines. The speaker also thought that it was better to set up universities in the underdeveloped countries rather than to send students abroad, first because the best minds could be kept in the country, and also because a university is a beacon of culture which has an important role to play in an underdeveloped country.

Mr. PART (United Kingdom) pointed out that the United Kingdom does not limit its aid to the payment of foreign exchange costs. For many years now its aid for all purposes to underdeveloped countries has amounted to one and a quarter per cent of the national income, excluding aid from private sources. Referring to Mr. Capdecomme's advocacy of a plan covering twenty years, he recalled that this was the period adopted in the Ashby Report and also in the Addis Ababa Report.

As for training other than that received in institutions of higher education, some 9,000 people came each year from overseas to Britain in order to get experience and training in industry.

He agreed with Professor Harbison that training of strategists was most important and had been asked by his government to say that they would welcome discussion of any proposals for this purpose. He also mentioned that the Universities of Cambridge and Bristol were showing an interest in this subject. He then pointed out that there had recently been created in Britain the Department of Technical Co-operation which concentrates in one government department all work dealing with overseas aid, thus reducing overlapping and misunderstandings between different government departments.

In connection with the proposal made at Addis Ababa for regional development groups for buildings, he quoted the United Kingdom experience in the field of school building which resulted in the saving of some £ 200 million in the course of ten years.

Finally, the speaker suggested that it was quite important to take care how views were presented, because the governments of the underdeveloped countries should not be given the impression that the Conference was trying to settle their affairs for them in their absence.

Mrs. HAAS (Yugoslavia) said that, although the final aim of education in her country was to have a more cultivated society, at the present stage it had been found necessary to close a number of general schools and gymnasiums in order to favour secondary technical and economic schools which were more important to the country's immediate needs.

Mr. ERDER (Turkey) insisted strongly on the necessity of planning in underdeveloped countries and also on the need for research. There is above all need for co-ordination of assistance and co-ordination of research, so as to make the best possible use of limited resources and of the very scarce manpower really capable of planning and carrying out educational strategy. He was against the haphazard sending out of teams, but he thought useful work could be done by centralizing information on all aspects of educational development and making it available to those who need it.

Professor VITO (Italy), referring to the question of whether it was preferable to send students from underdeveloped countries abroad or to build universities in the underdeveloped countries, thought that it was not a question of choosing between the two methods, but rather of striking the right balance between these two ways of action. Clearly a distinction should be made in this respect between undergraduate students ans post-graduate students.

Guidance of Foreign Students

The *Chairman* pointed out that what mattered was not so much the number of foreign students as the subjects they studied. He had recently been visited by four political leaders from an East African country who were visiting their students in the U.S.A. Asked what benefits they thought their students were deriving, the four leaders said that the students were doing well academically and were quite happy, but they, the older leaders, were less happy, because a high proportion of the students had chosen social sciences with a view to becoming politicians; and while their country had a severe shortage of agriculturalists, engineers and administrators, the one thing it had no shortage of was politicians. So the sending countries, the Chairman thought, must somehow take more action to guide their students into the disciplines which are most beneficial to their national interest.

Dr. FERRIER (Netherlands) said that the people in the underdeveloped countries wanted better housing, better household utensils, etc., and to them education was the way to get these things. Those who thought that school buildings were sometimes too impressive and too costly should remember that in these countries a school building is a symbol of the priority given to education by the government. He had yet to see a politician in one of these countries who dared tell the people that he was not going to give *all* the money available to primary education. It was undoubtedly necessary to have planning and research, but in the meantime it was urgent to get on with the job of developing education now.

Mr. Mac GEARAILT (Ireland), speaking as a national of a country which had sent thousands of teachers to Africa and Asia, was of the opinion that the results of sending people from underdeveloped countries to study abroad were often unsatisfactory, mainly because the instruction they received was not related to conditions in their own countries. Also, many of them had a tendency to avoid going back. He pointed out that the Council of Europe set up a Working Party last December to study the question of the education of Africans in Africa and in Europe, and suggested that O.E.C.D. acquaint itself with the findings of that Working Party so as to avoid duplication of effort. Lastly, he stressed the need to avoid offending national pride and sensibility in these young countries which often did not consider themselves as underdeveloped at all.

Canadian Education Assistance

Mr. DYMOND (Canada) said that his country's experience and circumstances indicated that, in the field of training foreign students, Canada should concentrate on post-graduates rather than undergraduates. As for providing teachers, Canada had tried to concentrate its effort on sending teacher trainers rather than teachers to the underdeveloped countries. The University of British Columbia will in the next five years establish training facilities for business administration and accounting in Malaya and Singapore, supplying both the research and teaching staff, while senior instructors from Malaya and Singapore will receive instruction at the University of British Columbia. Canada was also developing regional engineering colleges in India of which seven were already in existence.

The speaker thought it was very important to work through an organizational framework which ensured close contact with the underdeveloped countries themselves, such as the Colombo Plan, or the West Indies Programme, or the Commonwealth Aid to Africa Programme. The fact that Canada was in part French-speaking made possible the Canadian Programme of Educational Assistance for the French-speaking States of Africa. Referring to what Mr. Part had said with regard to co-ordination of effort in Britain, the speaker pointed out that Canada had now established in its External Affairs Department an External Aid Office to combine the functions previously carried out by several departments. Lastly, he agreed that there was a very urgent need for the general strategists called for by Professor Harbison and said that Canada would be prepared to consider very seriously co-operative programmes for training and developing such people.

M. FOURASTIÉ (France) first suggested that the Secretariat make a complete inventory of the work done by International Organizations and by national governments in the field of educational development so as to avoid duplication of effort. He then stressed the importance of environment as a social milieu for education. Museums and monuments as well as television were important instruments of self-education. But perhaps the most important thing in economic and educational development was the ability to control impatience—our impatience as well as that of the underdeveloped countries. Development takes time and impatience will only generate dissatisfaction and gnaw away all our work.

TEACHING THROUGH TELEVISION IN THE UNITED STATES

The *Chairman*, in response to the previous speaker's inquiry about education by television in the U.S.A., gave some details about two programmes. One, from Washington, D.C., provided a university level course in two subjects, biology, and the nature of the American government system. The other programme, in the Midwestern States, was aimed primarily at rural schools that had difficulty in getting good teachers in certain subjects; it was broadcast from an airborne station using television tapes produced by some of the best teachers in the United States brought together for this purpose, and it reached some seven million school children.

With regard to the last speaker's suggestion that information be available on what others were doing, the Chairman pointed out that the

National Science Foundation in the U.S.A. had asked Professor De Witt of Harvard to undertake a systematic study of educational progress in the Soviet Union. His 900-page report entitled "Education and Professional Employment in the U.S.S.R." will be published early in December. He hoped that this report would be translated into French, Spanish and other European languages.

EDUCATIONAL RESEARCH

Opening the discussion on educational research, the *Chairman* suggested that it should be considered in the context of both the advanced countries and the underdeveloped countries. Throughout the discussions at the Conference the need had been shown to exist for changes in all educational systems in order to adapt them to the requirements and conditions of the day, changes in curricula, teacher training, architecture of school and university buildings, technology of teaching and learning, etc. If education was to be expanded quantitatively and improved qualitatively, there was an urgent need to improve the utilization of all the resources involved in the educational enterprise.

There seemed to have been general recognition that it would be a long time before we could have all the answers we would like from "fundamental research". We must, therefore, concentrate in the meantime on what has been called "operational research" and which is likely to yield quicker results. It should be focussed on particular activities in education and linked with the development of these activities in countries where resources are most scarce.

Mr. GRANT (United States) stated the conviction of the United States Government that, unless improved techniques could be found for carrying out the development task, the prospects for success were not encouraging. Resources available both from indigenous sources and from outside were very limited and slender in comparison with the enormous needs of the underdeveloped countries. And these improved techniques could only be devised as a result of more knowledge. Following an extensive study made by the President's Science Advisory Council in the Spring of 1961, the United States Government has come to the conclusion that it should sponsor a major research programme in the field of development aid. In the opinion of the Science Advisory Council the bulk of this research (which within a few years would absorb approximately $100 million) should be in what is called the social sciences; and the present concept was that it should be undertaken not directly by the Government, but by private educational institutions and research organizations which would receive government grants for this purpose.

But it would also be necessary to build in the underdeveloped countries themselves a capacity for such research, and major financial provisions would have to be made for this purpose, though no definite conclusion had yet been reached by the United States Government on this point.

The speaker thought that two related problems which will arise in connection with research will be, first, how to communicate this knowledge to those who have to use it without wasting the six to fifteen year period which normally elapses between development of new knowledge and its practical application; and, second, how to ensure a smooth interchange of this knowledge between the advanced countries themselves, especially between the United States and the European countries which will devote or are devoting a great deal of effort to research on these problems. One of the main questions which has yet to be fully investigated is the *kind* of high-level manpower which is needed in the underdeveloped countries as distinct from its size.

Professor ELVIN (panel of experts), drawing on his experience at the Institute of Education in the University of London, made several practical points. The first was a plea for the financing of studies even further removed from research than operational research. As an example, he quoted the practice of the Institute of Education of inviting mature people from overseas to spend a year at the Institute to write a dissertation. This consists, first, of a study of their own work at home seen from a distance—on school inspection, or school administration, or teaching, etc.; second, a study of a similar activity in Great Britain; and lastly, and this is the important point, a discussion on the relevance of the second part to the first part. Comparative studies of this kind have proved very illuminating.

Another point raised by the speaker related to the extent to which a university allowed research work connected with higher degrees and doctorates to be done outside the university. It was absurd that someone doing a doctorate on African education, for instance, should have to spend most of his time in the University of London. There should be liberal provision for absence.

The speaker also advocated more multi-disciplinary research carried out by economists, sociologists and educationists working together. A question, for instance, like "What is the effect on schools of a transition to a cash economy in an African country" could only be answered by collaboration between students of society, of economics and of education.

Another kind of collaboration which is needed is that between staff members of universities in the advanced and underdeveloped countries because, however good the technique, it will serve little purpose if there is no feeling for the society under study.

There is also a great deal of investigation to be done into the wastefulness of some educational administrations. For example, a British Commission looking into the economic affairs of East African countries found that, out of every 1,000 children entering primary school in Uganda, only one completed the first cycle of secondary education, a discovery which produced a very rapid modification of educational policy in Uganda. The task, of course, should have been completed by an inquiry into the reasons for this heavy drop-out.

But there is above all need for fundamental educational research.

Our students from overseas, for instance, are exposed to educational theories which have grown out of Western ways of life. What happens if they try to apply these theories in societies which are very different? How is it possible to talk about democracy in schools which are operating in a culture where the family itself is a microcosm of hierarchical authoritarianism? And how does one teach arithmetic to children of seven who have never played at keeping shop, or handled money, or never counted above ten? And this situation can still be true of rural if not of urban Africa. Can one introduce those children to arithmetic in the same way as one would in New York or Paris or London? And what is the educational problem facing a young person in an African country where his mother tongue or the prevailing local tongue is useless for secondary education and where he may be expected to learn two world languages in higher education? These are some of the problems for which new techniques have to be devised.

Mr. VAIZEY thought that though education, being a service industry, was generally regarded as one which could not raise its productivity rapidly, there was no reason why the technology of education could not undergo the same kind of revolution as the technology of medicine had undergone in the last generation; but for this to happen there must be as big an effort in education as there had been in medicine. A search for such new technology is being made by Greece and Turkey in cooperation with O.E.C.D. in the context of the Mediterranean Regional Project.

He agreed with the previous speaker that sociology and economics are highly relevant to educational research, and referred to the work of Dr. Malleson on student wastage at university level where, by comparatively simple statistical techniques, a large number of causes of student failure had been identified, and as a result very practical advice could be given to universities. Some very good work of the same kind had been done in Belgium, and some remarkable work had been done in France on regional access to educational opportunity, whereby certain areas handicapped by remoteness from urban centres had been identified, thus enabling the French Government to make a really serious effort in those areas. Sweden had carried out some equally remarkable work on the effectiveness of two types of school systems and reached conclusions which seem to be entirely valid.

All these are examples of relatively simple work which can be very useful to administrators and which could be carried out with advantage in the underdeveloped areas. But here the main problem is one of communication: how the knowledge produced could be communicated to those who need to use it, and how those who need it could communicate this need to those who could produce this knowledge.

The *Chairman* said that here was an opportunity for O.E.C.D. and other organizations to parallel the common market in commerce by a common market in knowledge, ideas and research results. But that was not enough: a piece of research once done at Columbia University Teachers College showed that it took between 25 to 50 years for a new, demonstrably good, educational practice to be put into general effect. Clearly, this time lag would have to be cut very substantially.

M. DYMOND (Canada), speaking as the administrator of a governmental research institution, said that the inter-disciplinary problem in research was of great importance, particularly with respect to the research now being undertaken in Canada on the transition from school to work. Young people in certain age groups are asked for details of their educational history, on the one hand, and details of their experience in the labour market and the world of work, on the other. This gives an insight into both the educational system and the labour market, and suggests what possible changes should be made in education and training.

The *Chairman*, concluding the discussion, said that the "theory of divine guidance of research subjects" was no longer appropriate at a time when good research manpower was so limited. We must create a link between the users of research results and the producers of research. And the users—administrators and policy makers—must indicate more clearly what kind of information they require to carry out their respective tasks more wisely and efficiently.

THE "TEN COMMANDMENTS" OF EDUCATIONAL ASSISTANCE

The discussion then turned to the consideration of the "commandments" enunciated earlier in the proceedings by the Chairman. It was made clear that these were neither formal resolutions, nor recommendations, but simply guidelines for assisting the O.E.C.D. countries in their decision-making. The discussion bore on the precise wording of these guidelines, and as a result the Conference reached broad agreement on the following propositions:—

A. Bearing in mind the wide gap between needs and resources in the underdeveloped countries, set the sights high, thinking boldly and without preconceived solutions.

B. Bring reason and clarity to the design of educational programmes and structures, making available objective evaluation of the educational experience of the advanced countries rather than ready-made systems.

Encourage, support and particpate in efforts to develop curricula, programmes, teaching methods, and educational certificates and degrees inherently suitable to the underdeveloped countries, and to their need for creative social change.

Likewise, develop or adapt physical facilities or educational architecture appropriate to the environment and resources of the particular underdeveloped country.

C. Contribute finance toward the development and operation of educational institutions and structures, and not merely the foreign exchange components thereof.

D. Assist underdeveloped countries to assess their present and long-term needs for educational activities in relation to their other economic development objectives, and to develop appropriate strategies and priorities for the balanced expansion of education.

Urgently seek to multiply the number of persons competent in the preparation and application of human resource strategy, both in the advanced and in the underdeveloped areas.

In view of the above emphasis on human resource development, keep in mind the need for phased equilibrium in the development of physical and human capital.

E. Review arrangements and the extent of facilities for receiving students and other trainees from the underdeveloped countries in Western institutions.

F. Provide qualified university teachers and support teacher training so as to help to close the wide gap between the needs and local possibilities of the underdeveloped countries until such time as they can provide sufficient personnel of their own.

G. Encourage and support exchange of information and research, especially of an operational character, in formulating the problems in quantitative assessment of needs and resources and the problems in educational technology.

H. Within national plans of educational development, adjust targets so as to take account of qualified personnel of all types needed to assist development in the underdeveloped areas.

IV. THE PLANNING OF EDUCATION IN RELATION TO ECONOMIC GROWTH

Papers by Raymond Poignant,
Sven Moberg and Moric Elazar

PREFACE

When the Emperor Augustus heard of the decimation of the legions under Varus in the Teutoburger forest, he is reputed to have crashed his noble head against the nearest marble pillar, shouting "Varus, Varus, General Varus, bring my legions back". So it is in the more peaceful, but nonetheless vital, sphere of the development of educational resources for science and technology. Many governments regret to-day the lost years when decisions might have been taken, which by now would have produced the teachers of science, mathematics and technical subjects, of which both the advanced and the under-developed countries are in such great need. But the lost years cannot be brought back.

In the course of the work of the Committee for Scientific and Technical Personnel it has become clear that many of the problems facing national authorities in education are due to lack of foresight years, or even decades, ago. And it would seem that changes in the underlying factors which influence educational policy will be as great in the future as in the past and that the educational structure will tend to grow more complex. If proper account is to be taken of demographic factors, and the demand for education by the economy and by parents, it is essential that governments should have all the necessary information to enable them to draw up long-term targets for education, and balanced programmes to achieve those objectives.

It is, therefore, the view of the Committee that strong emphasis should be put, on both the national and international level, on adequate educational planning, in order to give due regard to the future needs for scientific and technical personnel. In accordance with this view, the work of the former O.E.E.C. was directed towards the stimulation of national activities in respect of measures to increase the numbers of scientific and technical personnel, and in particular the collection of the necessary basic data. Undertakings supported by all Member countries, such as surveys of the supply of, and demand for, engineers, scientists and teachers, formed an important part of the work of the Committee.

At present, the new O.E.C.D. is directly participating, through the Mediterranean Regional Project, in national planning teams in 6 Member countries, who are undertaking major surveys of needs for education over the longer term and are preparing programmes to meet these needs. It is intended to support similar joint activities with national authorities in some of the economically more developed Member countries, where the problems of the collection of data and of long-term educational planning will be studied. Such activities, at national level, will, it is hoped, help countries to formulate targets for education, giving due regard to the needs for scientific and technical personnel.

The papers and summary report of the discussion which follow, include three examples of educational planning under widely different political and administrative conditions, as well as the views of the participants on the general problems related to educational planning. It is my hope that this book will prove to be of some practical interest to Member countries in connection with the assessment of their longer term objectives for education, and particularly scientific and technical education.

Henning FRIIS
Chairman, O.E.C.D. Committee for
Scientific and Technical Personnel

CONTENTS

PREFACE... 5

I
FRANCE
by
Raymond POIGNANT
*Maître des Requêtes au Conseil d'État
Rapporteur général de la Commission de l'Equipement Scolaire, Universitaire et Sportif
au Commissariat Général du Plan, France*

INTRODUCTION... 9

I. TERMS OF REFERENCE, MEMBERSHIP AND WORKING METHODS OF THE COMMITTEE... 11
Terms of Reference... 11
Membership and Internal Organisation............................... 12
Working Methods.. 13

II. FORECASTING SCHOOL POPULATION TRENDS IN THE LIGHT OF DEMOGRAPHIC, SOCIAL AND ECONOMIC TRENDS.. 14

The Demographic Factor... 14
Legal and Structural Factors....................................... 15
Social and Economic Factors.. 16
Conclusions.. 22

III. THE PROBLEM OF CHOICE BETWEEN THE CLAIMS OF THE DIFFERENT COMMITTEES OF THE PLAN. PROBLEMS OF IMPLEMENTING THE EDUCATION PLAN.. 22

The Choice Between the Investment Claims of the Different Committees........ 23
Problems of Implementing the Plan.................................. 24

PROVISIONAL CONCLUSIONS.. 26
Need to Speed up the Expansion of Secondary and Higher Education... 26
Importance of Plans for Educational Development.................... 27
Difficulties in Forecasting Educational Development................ 27
Need to Consider Overall Educational Aims 28

FINANCIAL AND STATISTICAL DATA ON THE PAST AND FUTURE DEVELOPMENT OF EDUCATION IN FRANCE 28

Educational Investment Under the Last Plan and Forecasts for 1962-65......... 28
Increase in Full-Time Attendance at Educational Institutions over the Last Ten Years... 29
Forecast of Enrolments in France up to 1970-71..................... 29

II
SWEDEN
by
Sven MOBERG
*Head of Department
Swedish Ministry of Education and Ecclesiastical Affairs*

I.	INTRODUCTION...	33
II.	BASIC FACTORS OF EDUCATIONAL PLANNING IN SWEDEN...............	34
III.	THE CONTENT OF EDUCATIONAL PLANNING IN SWEDEN..................	36
IV.	THE ORGANISATION OF EDUCATIONAL PLANNING IN SWEDEN.............	38
V.	RELATING EDUCATIONAL TO ECONOMIC PLANNING.....................	40

TABLES

1.	Expenditure on Education in Relation to Total Government Expenditure...	33
2.	Enrolment Ratios (by Age Groups for the Years 1940, 1950 and 1960)......	34
3.	Distribution of "Studentexamen" Passes according to Profession of Father..	35

III
YUGOSLAVIA
by
Moric ELAZAR
*Head of Department
of Education Investment and Planning, Yugoslav Federal Secretariat*

I.	INTRODUCTION...	41
II.	EDUCATIONAL PLANNING IN RELATION TO ECONOMIC GROWTH...........	41
III.	THE FINANCING OF EDUCATION.......................................	45
IV.	CONCLUSIONS...	48

DISCUSSION.. 53

TABLES

1.	Numbers of Schools..	49
2.	Numbers of Students...	49
3.	Percentage of Age Groups Attending Schools...........................	49
4.	Number of Graduates According to Type of School	50
5.	Number of Graduates From Higher Education..........................	50
6.	Budgetary Allocations for Regular School Maintenance..................	50
7.	Sources of Funds for Regular School Maintenance......................	51
8.	Sources of Investments in Education...................................	51
9.	Estimated Increases in Numbers Attending Schools for the Period 1961-1965	51
10.	Present and Projected Manpower Requirements According to Qualifications	52
11.	Estimated Needs and Inflow of Qualified Manpower for the Period 1960-1965	52

I
FRANCE
by
RAYMOND POIGNANT

*Maître des Requêtes au Conseil d'Etat ;
Rapporteur général de la Commission
de l'Équipement Scolaire, Universitaire et Sportif
au Commissariat Général du Plan, France*

INTRODUCTION

Since 1946, France has endeavoured to accelerate rationally its economic development by preparing four-or-five-year "Modernisation and Equipment Plans" showing what the volume and distribution of public and private investment ought to be during the period in order to achieve the selected objective. Each Plan is accompanied by a study on the corresponding development in manpower requirements and the means of satisfying them.

At the outset, in 1946, the preliminary work of the Planning Commission (Commissariat Général du Plan) was confined to six basic industrial sectors, which were given priority at the time because of the disruption of the French economy at the end of the second world war.

As from 1951, however, the preparatory work on the Second Plan (1953-1957) covered the whole of the country's activities. All public and private investment, including that of a social and administrative nature, was then included in a general scheme of economic development.

Special Committees in the main social sectors—housing, health and sanitation equipment, and school and university equipment—will henceforth work parallel with the "vertical" committees on modernisation corresponding to the different sectors of economic activity. In particular, a Committee was set up in November 1951, the "Commission du Plan d'Équipement scolaire, universitaire, scientifique et artistique"[1] for the purpose of establishing an investment programme in this field.

The creation of this Committee marks the beginning of systematic planning on the foreseeable and desirable development of education at all levels; the Committee's mandate was renewed in 1956 (Third Plan 1958-61) and again in 1960 (preparation of the Fourth Plan 1962-65).

---

1. Enumeration corresponding to the work of the Ministry of National Education.

Why does the development of education find a place in the work of the Commissariat du Plan?

In the beginning, the reason was very simple: State education is one of the most important public services and one of the most costly; it is therefore essential for the economists of the Plan, in their study on fixed capital formation and consumption by government services, to take into account the changing needs of the education services. It was primarily for this purpose that the Committee was first set up in 1951 and this was the chief consideration underlying its first report.

But the work of the Committee soon brought to light another important consideration: the work of the Commissariat du Plan being to determine the volume of investment in the various sectors and the volume and distribution of manpower, there naturally tends to be a direct relationship between the demand for skilled or highly qualified manpower revealed by the Plan and the problems of educating the country's youth; it is increasingly evident that investment in education, especially technical, vocational and higher education, must be guided by the foreseeable development of employment.

Seen in this light, the development of education becomes a dynamic factor acting directly on economic growth; expenditure on schools and universities is no longer seen as "administrative expenditure" but as "intellectual investment", the level of which can determine in the long term the rate of economic development.

It is on the basis of these two considerations that the Committee is continuing its work.

This Report does not set out to discuss the whole field of economic planning in France; it will be assumed that the object of this "flexible planning" and the methods of drawing up and implementing the Plan are known. We shall confine ourselves to describing the work of the Commission de l'Équipement Scolaire, Universitaire et Sportif, the methods employed, the difficulties encountered, the results obtained and the uncertainties revealed. The methods of work of the Committee, like those of the Commissariat du Plan as a whole, have developed with each successive Plan; they are here described in their latest stage of development.

In view of the growing importance of education in the modern world, the experience acquired in France can be of great value to countries which feel the need to plan or to accelerate the development of their educational system.

But it is important to note the particular context of the Committee's work:
- as already mentioned, the education development plan fits into an overall national plan;
- the French education system, like the whole of French administration, is highly centralised under the control of the State (finance, programmes, methods, etc.).

These two conditions obviously make it much easier to draw up and implement an education development plan, and they are not to be found in all countries.

However, such differences can only affect the methods for the preparation and execution of an education development plan; the problems to be solved are basically much the same in all industrialised countries; the French experience is thus of definite interest.

***

I. TERMS OF REFERENCE, MEMBERSHIP AND WORKING METHODS OF THE COMMITTEE

TERMS OF REFERENCE

The Committee's terms of reference are:

a) *to determine the overall volume of public investment* (public works and equipment) needed during the period of the Plan *to meet the requirements of the various levels of education*, and distribution of the financing of that investment between the State and local authorities (départements and communes);

b) *to estimate the additional teaching staff required* to keep pace with the increase in school populations and make good the existing backlog, and study measures needed to recruit such staff.

As a secondary activity, the Committee also:

c) *determines the geographical allocation of certain education investments;* this is done in co-operation with the "Regional Plans Committee" and forms part of the efforts made by the Commissariat du Plan to remodel the economic regions of France rationally by a judicious allocation of economic investment. The Committee's work in this field is, however, practically confined to institutions of higher education (including higher technical education). For the other levels of education, the Committee simply determines the overall volume of investment corresponding to the trend of school attendance, while the location of establishments is decided by the Ministry with the help of Regional Educational Committees (Commissions académiques) and the Commission Nationale de la Carte Scolaire;

d) *considers administrative and technical measures* to expedite investment in education.

It should be noted that these functions relate only to *public educational establishments*[1] *controlled by the Ministry of Education* (95 per cent of public investment in education); the terms of reference of the

---

1. The Ministry of Education does not finance investment in private education.

Committee do not extend to the development of certain categories of vocational education, chiefly secondary and higher agricultural education which is controlled by the Ministry of Agriculture and comes within the scope of the Agriculture Committee. Co-operation between the two Committees, in estimating the school population, for example, helps to avoid the worst drawbacks which might result from this division of responsibilities. But this arrangement is not satisfactory; it would be better if all matters pertaining to education were considered jointly.

MEMBERSHIP AND INTERNAL ORGANISATION

Membership

The Committee has the same general structure as the other Committees of the Commissariat du Plan:

Representatives of the public authorities concerned:
— Ministry of Education:
   a) the Heads of all the Departments of the Ministry[1]
   b) one Rector, two Deans, one Principal of a College of Technology (Directeur d'École d'Ingénieurs)
— Ministry of Finance (Budget, Treasury, Economic and Financial Surveys Departments);
— Ministry of the Interior;
— Ministry of Construction (« aménagement du territoire » Department, responsible for regional development);
— Municipalities (represented by three mayors).

Employers' representatives (two members, including the Chairman of the Vocational Training Committee of the C.N.P.F., the French Employers' Federation).

Trade union and teaching staff representatives (4 members).

Representatives of the Conseil Économique (2 members, both chosen from among the representatives of « Associations familiales »).

Other members appointed in a personal capacity from the public or private sectors, including in particular the Chairman of the Manpower Committee of the Commissariat du Plan.

The Committee consists of about 40 members in all. Its Chairman is a Conseiller d'État and its Rapporteur-Général a Maître des Requêtes au Conseil d'État, both appointed by the Commissariat Général du Plan.

Internal organisation

The main work of the Committee is done by six specialised working parties:

---

[1]. The Ministry of Education is thus strongly represented on the Committee and also on the Working Parties. The Committee's Report is therefore the fruit of co-operation between the Ministry of Education on the one hand and, on the other, the Plan officials, other Ministries and representatives of trade unions and employer's federations.

Group 1. Estimating the future size of school populations.
Group 2. Estimating teaching staff requirements.
Group 3. Investment needs for primary and secondary education.
Group 4. Investment needs for higher and higher technical education.
Group 5. *Implementation of the Plan.* Improvement of administrative and financial procedures.
Group 6. *Implementation of the Plan.* Improvement of school and university building techniques.

Each working party consists of:
— members of the Committee chosen for their qualifications in a particular field;
— public and private experts in various fields.[1]

The Committee's Chairman and Rapporteur-General attend all working party meetings, which involves considerable work throughout the year.[2] The Rapporteur-General draws up an overall report on the proceedings of the working parties, each part being submitted to the Committee for discussion in plenary session. Bearing in mind the conclusions reached by the Committee, he also draws up the general report for the Commissariat du Plan.

WORKING METHODS

The Committee employs two main methods:

Enquiries among regional education administrators (Rectors, Deans academy inspectors, etc.)

These enquiries are carried out by the Ministry of Education. They are designed to give, for all categories of education, an inventory of the equipment required in each district according to local demographic, social and economic trends and the replacement needs of existing schools. These inventories are prepared in co-operation with the local official in charge of regional development plans and indicate precisely the location of each item of education investment requested.

These enquiries are processed and summarised by Ministry of Education officials; they provide a *first source of information* on:
— school population trends;
— needs for the replacement of old and unsuitable premises;

---

1. For example, Group 1 includes members of the Committee and experts from various institutes of statistics and economic and social studies, such as the:
— Institut National d'Études démographiques (I.N.E.D.)
— Institut National de la Statistique et des Études Économiques (I.N.S.E.E.).
— Service d'Études Économiques et Financières du Ministère des Finances (S.E.E.F.)
— Bureau Universitaire de Statistique (B.U.S.)
— Service Statistique du Ministère de l'Éducation Nationale, etc.
2. Some of the working parties hold as many as fifteen or twenty meetings.

— needs resulting from population shifts;
— location of future establishments.

It should be noted that the enquiry for the Fourth Plan (1962-65) has been conducted in the light of the educational reform and extension of the school-leaving age to 16, which should come into force in 1967. It has resulted in a preliminary outline of the *network of educational establishments which should cover France in* 1970.

The Investment Plan for 1962-65 will thus be only one instalment of a longer-term education programme.

Surveys conducted at national level by working parties of the Committee

The work of Group 1 is especially important in the evaluation of new requirements.

It consists of forecasting the trend of the total student populations at the various education levels in the light of *demographic, social and economic factors assessed at national level.* The resultant synthesis is compared with the findings of the enquiries among the education authorities.

Studying future trends in the school population at the various levels is the most important and most delicate task of the Committee; it raises the whole problem of relating the development of education to economic and social progress.

This vital aspect of the Committee's work is discussed more fully in Part *II.*

* * *

II. FORECASTING SCHOOL POPULATION TRENDS IN THE LIGHT OF DEMOGRAPHIC SOCIAL AND ECONOMIC TRENDS

Such forecasting is a highly complex process involving numerous factors, each of which will be examined in turn.

THE DEMOGRAPHIC FACTOR

This has been of considerable importance in France since 1951, with yearly age groups of less than 600,000 children giving place progressively to groups of more than 800,000 born from 1946 onwards. The "demographic wave" reached the nursery schools in 1949, the primary classes in 1952 and the secondary classes in 1957; it will burst upon higher education from 1964 onwards.

The combination of this trend with the increasing enrolment ratio in secondary and higher education leads to a forecast of exceptionally rapid growth.

The effects are relatively easy to assess with the help of a good statistical service. The only difficulty is *to assess regional variations:* although the overall birth-rate is stabilized in 1961, in certain regions the school population is increasing or decreasing either because of a *birth-rate different from the average* or, even more, because of *population shifts* due to town planning, large new housing estates, etc.[1]

LEGAL AND STRUCTURAL FACTORS

Trends in school population are closely related to decisions of Parliament and Government regarding:
— the organisation of education;
— the age-limits for compulsory education.

Application of the education reform as from the beginning of the academic year 1960-61

The Ordinance and Decree of 1959 are designed to give a new structure to secondary education. Hitherto, children have been separated at about the age of 11 into those who are to continue in primary education until the age of 14 and those who are to *start on secondary education* (classic and modern); the reform is designed to organise progressively a common two-year course (11 to 13 years of age in principle) for all children at the beginning of secondary education (« cycle d'observation ») and in general tends to replace selection at 11 + for lycées secondaires by a more rational continuous "guidance" based on the real aptitudes and tastes of the children concerned.

It has been decided that the minimum school leaving age shall be extended to 16 *as from* 1967: this means that all French children will be educated to the age of 16. The effect of this change on school populations will in fact be limited by the increase in the number of children *voluntarily* staying on until the age of 16 (up to 1967).

This reform implies regrouping[2] all the pupils of small rural schools after the first five years of elementary education; it will *further increase the enrolment ratio in the various types of secondary education* which follow the « cycle d'observation » and substantially swell investment at this level during the 1962-65 Plan.

It may be noted that the Committee has no voice in shaping the reform, being solely concerned with planning the means necessary to apply it.

---

1. The Committee has estimated that 21,000 new classrooms will need to be built for elementary schools between 1962 and 1965 to meet requirements due to population shifts alone.
2. Usually by organising school transport.

SOCIAL AND ECONOMIC FACTORS

The social factor: the increasing tendency towards prolonged education

It is traditional in France that "long secondary education" (lycées) and higher education (universities) are open to all those who possess the basic knowledge, the only exceptions being the « Écoles d'Ingénieurs » (institutes of higher technology), which have only a limited number of places and generally recruit by way of competitive entrance examinations (concours).[1] There is, indeed a whole system of incentives to encourage the use of these forms of education (the reform of education, the increase in scholarships, etc.).

This liberal approach underlies all the forecasting work of the Committee, which aims at providing places in lycées and universities for all the young people who wish to enter them.

Since the end of the second world war there has been, in France as elsewhere, *a marked tendency towards the voluntary continuation of secondary and higher education:* the proportion of children continuing in education beyond the compulsory limit is steadily increasing as a result of higher standards of living and, more especially,[2] of *a realisation by parents of the importance of continued education for the future of their children.*

In consequence, enrolment ratios above the elementary level are increasing steadily and rapidly; the percentage of the yearly age-group entering secondary education rose from 35 in 1953 to roughly 50 in 1960, while the number of pupils passing the second part of the baccalauréat rose from 43,000 in 1956 to 59,000 in 1960, although at that time the "demographic wave" had not yet reached the top classes of the lycées.

From an analysis of the rising trend of enrolment ratios since 1950 the Committee can make a fairly reliable estimate of the "spontaneous" development of those ratios in the future. However, as already mentioned, these rising ratios now *apply and will in the coming years continue to apply to larger yearly age-groups*, which will mean tremendous increases in school populations between 1957 and 1968:

— doubling of lycée populations between 1956 and 1964;
— doubling of university populations between 1963 and 1969.

The rate of growth will then slacken, reflecting only the "spontaneous" increase in enrolment ratios beyond the age of 16.

Such an expansion is certainly quite unusual in the cultural history of an advanced country; it is causing, and will doubtless continue to cause, a good many difficulties: the premises and especially the teachers

---

1. Even this restriction is tending to be weakened by the creation of Instituts Nationaux des Sciences Appliquées and the provision of applied science facilities for students in the university faculties.
2. The regions with the lowest enrolment ratios are not those with the lowest standard of living; as a general rule and apart from the Paris region, the percentages of children continuing in education after fourteen years of age are highest in the départements of Southern France, where there is little industry.

often cannot be found. But the work of the Committee is governed by the French concept of the function of education, which means that no effort must be spared to fit the facilities to the demand for education rather than restricting access to the limited means available.[1]

It will be seen from what has been said that the Committee's estimates of the trend of the overall school population in secondary and higher education are primarily *based on demographic data and on one vital social fact,* namely the spontaneous increase in the proportion of children staying on after the compulsory school-leaving age.

It is within the context of these overall forecasts of school population trends that the Committee considers the economic factor.

Influence of the economic factor on the Committee's estimates

    a) Existence of a necessary link between educational development plans and trends in active population

There is no need to stress here the prevailing trend in the structure of active population in *the expanding economies* of our Western countries: rapid decline of total employment in the primary sector, slow growth[2] in the secondary sector, and rapid growth in the tertiary sector, with a steadily increasing proportion of middle and top management and skilled personnel *in each sector.*

There is, of course, *a direct connection between these changes in active population and the development of vocational and technical schools as well as institutions of higher education,* since the additional skilled and highly-qualified manpower required will largely[3] be obtainable only from these sources. And this will of course include not only the scientists and technicians about whom so much has been heard in recent years but graduates of all the other disciplines as well—arts, law, economics, etc.

Consequently, the *real* problem for the French planning authorities is to determine the *desirable* distribution of the estimated total numbers as between:

    — general, technical and vocational education at secondary level;
    — arts, science, law, medicine, engineering, etc., at university level.

In the light of this desirable distribution, the Committee determines *the amount of investment to be devoted to each type of secondary school and each branch of higher education.*[4]

---

    1. This social policy is, moreover, certainly the one best calculated to promote long-term economic growth.
    2. Or even stabilization, to be expected shortly.
    3. Apart from transfers from one sector to another and promotion and transfers within the same enterprise.
    4. Although, as will be seen below, this does not entail any regimentation of students.

But to answer such a question means having a *clear idea of future demands for manpower in the different occupations and at each level of qualification.* This is one of the most intricate tasks of the Committee.

b) *Need for long-term forecasting of active population trends*

The Committee's work in this field is normally based on the estimates drawn up by the Manpower Committee of the Commissariat du Plan.

This latter Committee is responsible for estimating manpower demand in terms of numbers and skills in the different occupational branches during the period of the Plan, that is to say four or five years ahead. This constitutes a kind of synthesis of the work done by the various vertical committees.

The report drawn up in this traditional manner by the Manpower Committee contains some useful information, but experience has shown that *a five-year forecast is insufficient to guide adequately the major choices of the Commission de l'Equipement scolaire.*

For instance, during the four-year term of the next Plan (1962-1965), the French economy will be reaping the harvest of investment in education under earlier Plans, while the 1962-1965 Education Plan will not bear fruit until about 1967 at the earliest for those whose training is the shortest (skilled workers), and after 1970 for higher education.

The economic planner thus finds that the results of intellectual investment lag well behind those of conventional physical investment.

There can therefore be *no quick remedy for shortages of highly qualified personnel and it would be dangerous for any country to neglect to forecast its long-term future needs.*

Since education investment in 1962-1965 will at best prepare for the 1969-1973 economic Plan as regards highly qualified personnel, nothing like a reasonable estimate of the distribution of some 450,000 students expected in French universities in 1969-1970 can be made *unless the probable structure of the French active population is estimated at least as far ahead as* 1975.

The Manpower Committee of the Commissariat du Plan has been asked to *try* to fill this obvious gap by extending its forecasts up to 1975.

We need not discuss here the methodology of the work which the Manpower Committee agreed to undertake in Autumn 1960. It is a first attempt[1] and will certainly suffer from the absence of preliminary background studies, but equally certainly it will open the way for capital research in this new field of long-term social-economic forecasting.

The report which the Manpower Committee was asked to prepare is now practically complete, but it has been found that some additional forecasts will be needed before it can be used for the purpose of education planning, so that it will be some time before the Commission

---

1. Though a study of the same kind was made in Italy by SVIMEZ in 1960.

de l'Équipement scolaire can draw from it any conclusions for its own work.

All that will be given here, therefore, is some provisional indication of the method we intend to employ.

c) *How long-term forecasts of active population can be used for the purpose of education planning*

As already stated, the planning of education development by the Commission de l'Équipement scolaire is not dictated by the forecasts of employment trends: education serves humanistic and democratic ends which are largely distinct from strictly economic needs[1] and must be the primary consideration. The Committee's task is simply to try in the general interest to achieve the best possible allocation of educational investment as between the *various branches of specialised education* in the light of employment prospects.

The problem of correlation between diploma and employment

This implies finding a fixed relationship between a person's education and the work he will do in later life.

It is certain, and fortunate, that there is no rigid link between diploma and employment[2] and that any correlations which might be found are rather tenuous.

On the other hand, there is no escaping the fact that certain levels of education do lead to fairly well-defined levels in the hierarchy of employment (though the acquisition of further qualifications may lead to subsequent promotion). The Commission de l'Équipement scolaire and the Manpower Committee thought it might be possible to determine *very broad relationships* between training and future employment, not to be regarded as fixed rules[3] but as giving a reasonable picture of the average situation. On this basis, the following relationships have been assumed.

Presentation of the Manpower Committee's conclusions

For each occupational branch,[4] the Manpower Committee has therefore divided the 1975 active population between the six levels indicated overleaf; this naturally involves a good many difficulties of classification that will not be gone into here. For levels 1, 2, 3 and 4,

---

1. Though anything but contrary to such needs.
2. Not all technologists are graduates, nor are all technology graduates working as technologists; neither have all managers been to a university, nor all skilled workers to an apprentice training school. Moreover, while people with certain diplomas do tend to enter certain professions, there is always the possibility that they may later change to another profession.
3. Except for professions requiring statutory qualifications.
4. Classification by " branches professionnelles " adopted by the Plan and National Accounts authorities.

AVERAGE RELATIONSHIPS BETWEEN EMPLOYMENT AND EDUCATION

LEVEL	EMPLOYMENT	EDUCATION (HUMANITIES AND SCIENCE)	NUMBER OF YEARS OF EDUCATION AFTER THE END OF THE "CYCLE D'OBSERVATION [1]"
1	Highly responsible and complex management functions, heads of departments, technologists and teachers requiring very thorough knowledge of vast and difficult fields	At least one year after the "licence d'enseignement complète"	At least 10
2	Functions requiring a sound knowledge of difficult fields	University degree or diploma in technology	At least 9
3	Technicians and administrators performing functions requiring good knowledge in relatively limited fields	Two years, or at least one year after baccalauréat or diplôme de technicien	6, or more generally 7
4	Supervisors (foremen) and assimilated	Baccalauréat or diplôme de technicien level	On average 5
5	Skilled workers (manual and clerical)	"Certificat professionnel" level	3 to 4
6	Unskilled workers	—	1 year (or 3 years)[2]

1. After age 13 on average, i.e. after the 7th year of school.
2. 3 years when the school-leaving age is raised to 16.

the Committee has endeavoured to specify the proportion with a "humanities" type and the proportion with a "science" type of education. Addition of the figures for the various occupational branches gives the total active population in 1975 at each level of qualification, with a break-down for the higher levels by predominant type of education.

In addition, starting with the present active population and taking into account retirements up to 1975, the Manpower Committee's tables show the numbers who will be entering at the different levels of qualification between 1961 and 1975.

Provisional assumptions of the Commission de l'Équipement scolaire

The work requested of the Manpower Committee cannot be completed until after the various vertical committees have finished the preparatory work for the Plan. If the Commission de l'Équipement scolaire were to wait until then, it would be very late in making its estimates of school populations and investments. The procedure for drawing up the National Plan does not permit of such delay, so that the Committee has no choice but to allocate the additional numbers provisionally as between the different types of secondary and higher education without waiting for the Manpower Committee to supply the information requested.

This preliminary allocation naturally takes into account the known trends of the modern economy; *it postulates a virtually maximum increase in the scientific and technical branches.*

The present assumptions for the year 1970 are as follows:

a) *Secondary education*

"*Long*":[1] 40 per cent of an age-group after 16 [i.e. 17 per cent in technical and vocational education—diplôme de technicien or diplôme d'aide technique level—and 23 per cent in general education, baccalauréat level].

   This gives three times the present percentages in technical and vocational education.

"*Short*"[2] (vocational and general): 35 per cent of a 15-year age-group [i.e. 15 per cent in general education and 20 per cent in vocational education—skilled worker level].

"*Terminal*"[3] *and special:* 25 per cent of a 15-year age-group.

b) *Higher education (allocation of French students)*

In percentage.

	1949	1959	1970
Science andtechnology[4]	19	37	43
Arts, law, social sciences	55	43	41
Medecine and pharmacy	26	20	16
	100	100	100

It will be noted that scientific and technical education is expected to grow very considerably; this growth implies a prior expansion of science teaching in the lycées, and it is not certain that such a rate of expansion can actually be achieved in 1970.

The progressive rate of growth of the various branches of education and the investments essential for each of them have therefore been calculated in the light of these estimates of the allocation of students in 1970.

---

1. 5 years of study after the "cycle d'observation", i.e. to age 18 on average.
2. 4 years of study after the "cycle d'observation", i.e. to age 17 or 18.
3. Not going beyond the compulsory school-leaving age, extended to 16.
4. Including all Ministry of Education "Ecoles d'Ingénieurs".

Can these assumptions be affected by the Manpower Committee's study?

In order to answer this question, it is important to know what kind of conclusions one may hope to draw from the Manpower Committee's forecasts.

Two kinds of approach seem possible:

The first would be to compare the percentages of the active population in the different levels of qualification in 1975 with the percentages of an age-group at the different levels of education.

This method[1] has the disadvantage of taking the 1975 structures as the basis of reference although they are only one moment in a continuous evolution.

The second would be to estimate the number of young people entering *employment* between 1961 and 1975, by level and type of education, and to compare the total for each level with the intake requirements for 1961-1975 as shown by the Manpower Committee's study.

We would be rather inclined to choose the second method.

CONCLUSIONS

It is possible that the findings of the study on future trends in the active population may cause the Commission de l'Équipement scolaire to adjust its original assumptions and modify its investment forecasts accordingly; the changes are not likely to be very considerable. *In any event, the total school and university populations remaining the same, the overall volume of investment needed and its financial cost cannot be substantially altered.*

* * *

III. THE PROBLEM OF CHOICE BETWEEN THE CLAIMS OF THE DIFFERENT COMMITTEES OF THE PLAN—PROBLEMS OF IMPLEMENTING THE EDUCATION PLAN

At this stage of its work, the Committee has carried out its main task and is now pursuing the subsidiary assignments mentioned in paragraphs (*b*), (*c*) and (*d*) of Part I, page 11.

Two problems now arise:

How is the choice made between the claims of the different vertical committees?

How is the educational plan put into effect?

---

1. Which was used by SVIMEZ in the study mentioned earlier.

THE CHOICE BETWEEN THE INVESTMENT CLAIMS OF THE DIFFERENT COMMITTEES

a) The volume of investments which can be put into effect under a particular plan is necessarily limited. But when each plan is prepared, the total investment claims by the vertical committee for public investments (hospitals, transport, housing, schools, etc.) are generally well in excess of available funds. It is therefore necessary to make a choice between the different claims so as to reduce their total to practical limits and give the Plan its fundamental shape and direction.

This choice is made by the Commissariat Général du Plan, in close consultation with the appropriate Committee and the Ministers concerned. Any difficulties that arise[1] are settled by the Prime Minister at a Cabinet meeting.

Some reductions in the proposed programmes may merely mean a certain inconvenience to the public (for example, delay in the development of motor highways), whereas cuts which may be made in the proposals of the Commission de l'Équipement scolaire can have very unfortunate consequences. This was the case as regards the Second and Third Plans.[2]

Priority is generally given to the needs of primary education (compulsory) and cuts can only affect secondary and higher education. But as has already been pointed out, the estimates of the Committee at this level are largely the *reflection of a well-nigh inescapable social problem*. Even if the schools shown to be necessary in the estimates are not all built, the *number of pupils* will be approximately the same. Hitherto, the result has been:

— the overcrowding of existing schools;
— a slowing down in the expansion of vocational and technical schools, which is very serious at a period when *skilled workers and technicians are in short supply*.

To avoid a recurrence of such conditions, the Commissaire Général was instructed by the Government to *give priority to education* in the 1962-65 Plan, and it is therefore possible that practically all of the Committee's programme will be adopted for the period 1962-65.

b) When the different investments have been finally decided, the Commissariat du Plan draws up a general report on the Plan which is submitted to Parliament for discussion.

The figures in the document submitted to Parliament are for guidance only and do not commit the Ministry of Finance; *in fact, they constitute the guiding pattern of public investment*[3] *as decided:*

---

1. i.e. in the event of persistent disagreement with the Minister responsible.
2. 65 per cent of the Committee's requirements were granted under the Second Plan and 80 per cent under the Third.
3. And also private investment.

— either when the annual budget is voted;
— or when special programmes are voted by Parliament.

Thus, in the case of education, the allocations listed in the report submitted to Parliament are not a mere forecast, *but a complete plan for educational development at all levels.*

PROBLEMS OF IMPLEMENTING THE PLAN

Apart from the questions of financing which were dealt with above, a large number of subsidiary problems listed in the Committee's Report must be settled before the educational development programmes in the main Plan can be put into force.

It is the Ministry of Education which takes over responsibility for this stage of the Plan in consultation with the other Ministries and the Commissariat du Plan.

Administrative and technical problems

The Report of the Commission de l'Équipement scolaire contains definite suggestions for improving the procedure for building schools and universities and adopting more efficient building techniques.[1] Although we cannot enlarge upon the actual nature of these suggestions, they are designed to speed up building and reduce costs by:
— simplifying administrative and financial procedure;
— amending the regulations for the award of contracts;
— standardizing building techniques.

After discussion in the Committee's working parties by the various departments concerned, the suggestions are generally put into effect.

Recruiting of teaching staffs

The Committee's Report gives a rough idea of the number of teachers required for each type of education in the light of trends in the school and university population; possibilities of recruiting are considered and in the event of a shortage[2] suggestions are made to promote recruiting. We will not enlarge here on this very important aspect of the Committee's Report.

Ultimately, it is for the Ministry of Education to persuade the Ministry of Finance to provide for the requisite posts in each annual budget, and for the Government to take all steps to recruit teachers.

In this field, French experience has shown that long-term estimates are the only means of forecasting requirements and enabling the requisite recruiting policy to be put into effect.

---

1. This is a continuous process, which was initiated in 1951 and improved in the light of the experience gained from each new Plan.
2. This is the usual situation, owing to the exceptionally rapid growth in the school and university population.

Adapting the execution of the Plan to economic needs

a) Location of schools

The Committee's Report is particularly concerned with apportioning investment to meet the growing enrolment at the different levels of education and, as has already been stated, it fixes the *desirable* location of the establishments which are most important from the economic standpoint: technical colleges, higher institutions, and higher technical establishments. The creation or the development of other types of establishment is studied by the Ministry of Education itself in connection with the school distribution commissions.

b) *Determination of educational syllabuses*[1]

The estimated volume of investment is worked out by calculating *the main categories* of the additional numbers of young people at the various levels and in the different types of education, on the basis of trends in the structure of the active population.

But, as the implementation of the Plan proceeds, a far more detailed analysis *has to be conducted by the authorities, in consultation with the industrial organisations,*[2] to work out detailed syllabuses for the schools to be built or extended. For example, at this stage, it is no longer sufficient to have a total figure for industrial apprentices: the total figure calculated by the Committee must now be apportioned among the various industrial sectors (electricians, plumbers, fitters, etc.), and similarly the number of candidates for *the various types of training* in institutes of technology must be calculated in detail.

For this purpose, the educational authorities generally obtain short-term estimates from the Manpower Committee which give an accurate picture of the number of skilled workers required in each sector. Moreover, when each new school is created, the Directorate of Technical Education can obtain the views of its national consultative committees.

There is in fact continuous development and a succession of limited decisions taken throughout the period of the Plan.

c) *Orientation of students*

There is nothing compulsory in the "distribution" of young people by the Committee in the light of estimated trends in the active population. Experience shows that:

— the establishment of new schools, and
— adequate information to families

are sufficient to ensure that young people are channelled in a direction consistent with trends in employment (as far as they can be ascertained).

---

1. i.e. the organisation of the specialised subjects taught in the school.
2. For technical and vocational schools.

This point certainly holds good in practice as regards vocational, technical and higher technological schools, whose syllabuses are laid down by the authorities; but it is much less applicable to the universities.

Evidently, the expansion of the various university faculties as part of the Plan may in itself enable students to be satisfactorily distributed between the various types of faculties, but within each faculty there may be a serious failure to meet the real needs of the economic system when students are free to choose their special branch (for example, between chemistry, physics, biology, geology, etc., in the Faculty of Science).[1] On this point, *it is essential that students should be more effectively orientated, in view of the progress now being made in surveying structural trends in the active population.*

In conclusion, we must note, although we cannot enlarge upon this point here, that the direction taken by students at university level often depends on the specialisation they adopted in their final years at the classical or modern lycées (baccalauréat in mathematics, sciences or philosophy). In consequence, any expansion in scientific teaching in universities depends on a corresponding expansion in general science teaching in the classical, modern and technical lycées.

PROVISIONAL CONCLUSIONS

As already stated, we do not yet know the general conclusions which are likely to emerge from the Committee's survey on the adaptation of forecasts of the expansion of secondary and higher education to the probable structure of the active population in 1975. It is likely that valuable results will be achieved by this first *practical* survey of an important problem which has hitherto never been discussed except theoretically.

Subject to this reservation, it is possible at this juncture to draw a number of general conclusions from the work done by the Commissariat du Plan since 1951.

Need to Speed up the Expansion of Secondary and Higher Education

The expansion of education has now become the most important driving force in social and political development. Self-fulfilment, true democracy and economic progress all depend on the *same essential requirement*, i.e. that the abilities of every individual should be devel-

---

1. This is at present the case in French science faculties, where the number of geology and natural science students seems to be in excess of requirements. There is no limitation on the number of students in the various specialist branches.

oped to the full by making secondary and higher education widely available to all sections of the community.

So vital is the problem of education that "plans" or "programmes" for material investment must be accompanied by plans for educational development.

IMPORTANCE OF PLANS FOR EDUCATIONAL DEVELOPMENT

Experience has shown that it is *difficult to improvise* in the field of educational expansion; any hasty development is bound to encounter the well known difficulties—shortage of premises and above all shortage of teachers.

It is therefore essential to study this long-term problem and draw conclusions regarding:

— the most desirable rate of supplementary allocations to schools and universities,
— the right policy to facilitate the recruiting of teachers (training, remuneration, etc.).

DIFFICULTIES IN FORECASTING EDUCATIONAL DEVELOPMENT

French experience as briefly outlined above reveals the increasing complexity of the problems which must be solved if successful forecasting is to be achieved in this field. All work of this kind calls for:

a) *Excellent statistics* for the most recent years (the social trends reflected in school and university enrolment change very quickly and an effort must be made to obtain the latest information). In this respect, the work done in France since 1951 has led to considerable progress.[1]

b) *Well-equipped survey departments* able to keep under constant review the trends in the internal and external factors which affect school and university attendance; there is no doubt that here a whole field of research is still open to educationists, sociologists and economists, and special attention might well be devoted to research on long-term trends in the active population, although the real importance of such research is not yet fully established.

c) *The active participation of the various services responsible;* the preparation of an educational development plan must lead to *concrete decisions at government level.* It is therefore essential that all ministerial departments directly or indirectly concerned should be closely associated in this work; in other terms, although certain work relating to the basic facts of the problem has to be carried out by the appropriate services or research institutes, the practical conclusions to be drawn from it must be studied by the responsible authorities (particularly the senior ministerial officials) who alone are competent to advise the Government in making its choice. Any estimates prepared without the participation of those responsible may well be ineffective and even

---

1. Although the statistical services still lack facilities to make the fullest use of the results of their surveys.

useless. From this point of view, the Commission de l'Équipement scolaire et universitaire represents a comparatively satisfactory formula.

NEED TO CONSIDER OVERALL EDUCATIONAL AIMS

Certain members of the teaching profession might feel concerned at seeing the educational development plans integrated into the country's general development plans, which are considered (erroneously) to be largely economic in character.

French experience shows that the work done under the auspices of the Commissariat du Plan in no sense subordinates school and university development to economic exigencies.

It is reasonable that vocational education should be influenced by the demands of the economic system, but, as has already been said, *this training is only one factor in the general task of the educational system.* In the performance of this task all the social and democratic factors we have briefly referred to must be taken into account; nor are these factors in any way conflicting.

All things considered, we will not say that all is well in the field of French education thanks to the work of the Commission de l'Équipement scolaire, universitaire et sportif of the Commissariat du Plan; indeed, we have ourselves drawn attention to the serious difficulties still encountered by the French educational authorities. But it is fair to note that the forecasts compiled by the Committee have greatly helped to bring the whole range of the problem of educational development home to the public and the authorities. The fact that the claims of "intellectual investment" have been laid before the public authorities at the same time as those of other investments has greatly helped to gain gradual acceptance for the idea that the former should have priority.

*
* *

FINANCIAL AND STATISTICAL DATA ON THE PAST AND FUTURE DEVELOPMENT OF EDUCATION IN FRANCE

EDUCATIONAL INVESTMENT UNDER THE LAST PLAN AND FORECASTS FOR 1962-65

For the period 1957-61, investments in school and university facilities (in millions of new francs)—with 85 % State participation and 15 % local participation—amounted to:

1957	1958	1959	1960	1961
1,234	1,494	1,769	1,642	2,108 (estimates)

TOTAL : N.F. 8,247 millions in 5 years.

This important sum did not suffice to cover all needs; nonetheless it constituted a considerable effort.

This effort will be increased during the Fourth Plan covering the years 1962-65. According to the Plan recently adopted by the Government, which will shortly be submitted to Parliament, the new programmes provided for in the Fourth Plan will involve expenditure amounting to N.F. 14,200 millions, (of which the State will provide 12,000 million and the local communities 2,200 million).

The actual payments arising out of these programmes amount to N.F. 12,100 million for 4 years (State: 10,300, local communities: 1,800); the total volume of actual expenditure under the Fourth Plan (1962-65) thus corresponds to an *average increase in expenditure of 72% in comparison with the four preceding years.*

Furthermore, yearly current expenditure (State budget—national education) which rose from N.F. 3,290 million in 1957 to N.F. 6,300 million in 1961 (+ 90 % in 4 years) will continue to increase proportionately.

INCREASE IN FULL-TIME ATTENDANCE AT EDUCATIONAL INSTITUTIONS OVER THE LAST TEN YEARS

The trend in full-time attendance at educational institutions over the last ten years shows the importance of the work of the Commission de l'Équipement scolaire et universitaire.

Total number of pupils or students registered at public or private educational institutions

1950-1951	6,250,000
1951-1952	6,700,000
1959-1960	9,500,000
1961-1962	10,003,000

FORECAST OF ENROLMENTS IN FRANCE UP TO 1970-71

The forecasts on public investments to be made under the 1962-65 Plan were established on the basis of the forecast trend in school population which showed:
— steady expansion of secondary general education;
— an accelerated expansion of technical and vocational education;
— a remarkably rapid expansion of higher education.

DISTRIBUTION OF SCHOOL POPULATION

In thousands of students.

	1951-52			1957-58			1961-62		
	PUBLIC	PRIVATE	TOTAL	PUBLIC	PRIVATE	TOTAL	PUBLIC	PRIVATE	TOTAL
Nursery Schools and Kindergartens	1,000	221	1,221	1,097	210	1,307	1,200	176	1,376
Elementary Schools[1]	3,336	801	4,137	4,655	976	5,631	4,882	946	5,828
Colleges: General Education[2][3]	218	60	278	351	93	444	630	146	776
Colleges: Technical Education[2]	143	70	213	159	90	249	222	130	355
Lycées[2]: Classical and Modern Languages	353	186	539	569	242	811	822	320	1,142
Lycées[2]: Technical[4]	124	35	159	142	44	186	205	59	264
Teacher Training Colleges	15	—	15	18.7	—	18.7	25	—	25
Universities[5][6]	136.9	2[7]	138.9	175.5	2[7]	177.5	235	2	237
Total	5,325.9	1,375	6,700.9	7,167.2	1,657	8,824.2	8,221	1,779	10,003

1. Including special classes and the elementary classes of the lycées.
2. Secondary schools.
3. Including specialised sections.
4. Including the technical sections of the classical and modern language lycées.
5. Including foreigners.
6. To these figures should be added students registered at the Grandes Ecoles. Their number has risen little over the last ten years. There were 31,000 students in 1961-62 who were not registered at a university faculty.
7. Number of students registered at private faculties only.

These forecasts are illustrated in the following tables:

I. FORECASTS OF EXPANSION OF SECONDARY PUBLIC EDUCATION

In thousands of students.

ESTABLISHMENTS	1961-2	1962-3	1963-4	1966-7	1967-8	1970-1	PUBLIC AND PRIVATE 1970-1[1]
General Education Colleges: 6th & 5th forms[2]	325	355	383	452	464	486	
Other forms[3]	305	329	346	372	375	380	
Total	630	684	729	824	839	866	1,057
Classical & modern language lycées: 6th & 5th forms[2]	311	332	350	392	398	403	
Other forms	489	529	568	647	662	701	
Preparatory classes for admission to the Grandes Ecoles	22	24	26	36	39	50	
Total	822	885	944	1,075	1,099	1,154	1,559
Technical Colleges. (full-time courses)	222	244	268	341	363	406	606
Technical Lycées: 6th & 5th forms[2]	24	25	26	27	27	27	
Other forms[4]	205	240	275	377	404	454	
Sections for technicians	6	7	9	16	20	35[5]	
Total	235	272	311	420	451	516	632
GRAND TOTAL	1,909	2,085	2,252	2,660	2,752	2,942	3,845

1. This forecast was established on the assumption that the rate of expansion of public and private education would remain the same as in the last few years. For the forecast concerning private education, the reader is also referred to the table on page 32.
2. The first two years at a lycée or college.
3. Including specialised sections whether recognized or not, and where attendance is assumed to be constant.
4. Including the technical sections of the classical and modern language lycées.
5. Very rough estimate.

This trend in school population corresponds to the following trend in enrolments (secondary schools only):

In percentage.

	1954-5	1960-1	1966-7	1967-8	1968-9	1970-1
14 year-olds	56	69	89	100	100	100
15 year-olds	45	55	79	83	100	100
16 year-olds	37	45	60	64	67	73
17 year-olds	23	28	35	36,5	38	42

II. FORECASTS OF EXPANSION OF HIGHER EDUCATION
(public universities)

FACULTIES	1959-60	1960-1	1963-4	1967-8	1970-1
Law, Economics and Institutes of Political Science	32,500	34,000	45,600	71,000	83,000
Humanistic Studies	57,100	59,500	78,600	115,600	130,300
Sciences & Engineering	65,500	77,200	107,300	177,000	210,800
Pharmacy	8,100	8,500	11,300	17,600	20,600
Medicine	31,300	31,800	43,000	58,600	61,200
Total	194,500	211,000[1]	285,800	439,800	505,900[2]

1. Including 22,400 foreign students and nationals from the countries of the French Communauté.
2. Including 50,000 foreign students and nationals from the countries of the French Communauté.

II

SWEDEN

by

Sven MOBERG
Head of Department
Swedish Ministry of Education and Ecclesiastical Affairs

I. INTRODUCTION

Expenditure on education in Sweden has been increasing in the course of the last twenty-five years, not only in absolute terms, but also in relation to the national product. It rose from less than 3 per cent of the national product in the middle thirties to over 4 per cent of a greatly increased national product in 1960. The bulk of this expenditure is covered by the government, and in the course of the last 15 years government expenditure on education has increased proportionately slightly more than total government expenditure. During the same period, however, expenditure on higher education and research has increased more rapidly than that on lower-level education. This trend is shown in Table 1 (which takes no account of capital expenditure).

TABLE 1. EXPENDITURE ON EDUCATION IN RELATION TO TOTAL GOVERNMENT EXPENDITURE

TYPE OF EXPENDITURE	FISCAL YEAR 1948/49 MILL. KR.	%	FISCAL YEAR 1961/62 MILL. KR.	%
Total Government Expenditure	3,999	100	14,663	100
Expenditure for Higher Education & Research	55	1.4	304	2.1
Expenditure for Lower-level Education	419	10.5	1,571	10.7
Social Welfare Expenditure for Students at all Levels	33	0.8	170	1.2

As the bulk of this expenditure consists of salaries of teaching staff there is little likelihood that it could ever be reduced; on the contrary, there is every indication that it will tend to rise.

The spread of education is bound to have an increasing influence on economic development. In fact, the structure of the labour market is changing slowly but steadily as a result of the increasing number of persons who have benefited from education above the compulsory level. The proportion of people with higher education in the labour force amounts at present to about 1.7 per cent, but is expected to rise to 2.6 per cent within the next ten years and to over 3 per cent within the next fifteen years. However, in a country like Sweden, with full employment and rapid development in most branches of the economy, the supply of highly-qualified personnel tends to lag behind the demand, and it is therefore essential that the education system be adjusted accordingly. In fact, educational policy is regarded as an important tool for the achievement of basic social aims such as equality, security and general welfare. Educational planning, therefore, is likely to become an increasingly important and integral part of national economic planning.

II. BASIC FACTORS OF EDUCATIONAL PLANNING IN SWEDEN

The two basic considerations which underlie educational planning in Sweden are the demand for education on the part of parents and students, and the demand, both present and future, for trained manpower and highly qualified personnel.

The demand for education is assessed on the basis of population statistics for the relevant age groups. Statistical data for each year group for the country as a whole are given yearly, but the break-down of these figures to show the distribution of these year groups in different parts of the country is available only every five or ten years according to the frequency of the population census. In the case of higher education, account must also be taken of changes in the enrolment ratio of students in the relevant age groups, i.e. those above the level of the comprehensive school. These enrolment ratios have risen rapidly in the course of the past twenty years, as is shown in the table below.

TABLE 2. ENROLMENT RATIOS (BY AGE GROUPS FOR THE YEARS 1940, 1950 AND 1960)

In percentage.

AGE GROUP	1940	1950	1960
16 - 18	10	16	32
19 - 24	5	8	13

These figures do not, of course, give a complete picture of the demand, because they do not show the number of applicants who were refused entrance to this further education.

Another important point which must be taken into consideration is the subject of study chosen by the students; yet another is the social and geographical distribution of students, which has undergone considerable changes in the last decade or so. This is shown in the table below as far as the social distribution of students is concerned.

TABLE 3. DISTRIBUTION OF "STUDENTEXAMEN"[1]
PASSES ACCORDING TO PROFESSION OF FATHER

In percentage.

PROFESSION OF FATHER	MALE 1943	MALE 1952	MALE 1957	FEMALE 1943	FEMALE 1952	FEMALE 1957
Farmers, Fishermen	10	11	10	8	10	10
Businessmen	21	19	17	21	18	20
Academically trained	24	24	24	28	26	25
Other Employees	28	25	21	28	27	23
Skilled and Unskilled Workers	14	17	22	10	14	17
Unknown, Miscellaneous	3	4	6	5	5	5
Total	100	100	100	100	100	100
Absolute Numbers	2,707	2,852	4,023	1,534	2,047	3,284

1. The "Studentexamen" is roughly the equivalent of the French Baccalauréat or the German Abitur.

In view of the obvious importance of reliable and detailed population and education statistics for educational planning, Sweden has made a considerable effort since 1945 in developing suitable statistical services whose work is often supplemented by *ad hoc* studies commissioned from outside research workers.

As long as educational policy is mainly confined to providing compulsory comprehensive education, there is little need to consider the requirements of the labour market for specific skills and qualifications. But when educational policy is concerned with education beyond the comprehensive level, the needs of the labour market must increasingly be taken into account by educational planners. The ideal would be a study which showed the requirements of the labour market for the different skills and qualifications for at least twenty years ahead. But as such a study cannot be made in our present state of knowledge, it is important to try to glean at least some idea of long-term trends of certain major factors which affect economic activity, particularly those which affect the labour market.

For this purpose, a special forecasting unit has been established in Sweden within the Central Labour Market Board. Its task is to provide educational planners with studies of future demand for qualified manpower. These studies are based upon temporary hypotheses (models) regarding long-term trends (up to 1980) of such factors as total population and its distribution by sex, age groups and geographical regions, gross national product and its distribution between public and private consumption and investment, total labour force, etc. These models are complemented by inquiries amongst employers about the present situation with regard to their labour requirements and their estimate of their future requirements (usually five years ahead) for the various types of personnel. Another source of information is provided by historical data drawn from population censuses, economic and social statistics, and special *ad hoc* studies bearing on the subjects under review. As many of the methodological problems connected with long-term studies of future demand for personnel have not yet been solved, the work of the forecasting unit must be largely a question of trial and error.

It is interesting to note that a number of studies have been made in Sweden during the last twenty years to forecast the future demand for specific professional groups with very long training (physicians, dentists, secondary school teachers), and that all these studies have had one thing in common—they all have proved to have underestimated the actual demand.

III. THE CONTENT OF EDUCATIONAL PLANNING IN SWEDEN

Educational planning in Sweden bears mainly on:
i) the quality and quantity of educational institutions for the country as a whole and for the different geographical regions;
ii) investment in buildings and equipment;
iii) the size and type of teaching staff and other educational personnel;
iv) social welfare for students and pupils, particularly financial assistance; and
v) the timetable for the implementation of decisions.

The quality and quantity of educational institutions is obviously the fundamental planning problem. For the comprehensive school the qualitative aspect relates to the curriculum, and the quantitative aspect to the length of compulsory education. Both these aspects have been the subject of planning during the past twenty years and this has now culminated in the definite proposal for the 9-year comprehensive school.

For the higher secondary school the main qualitative consideration has been to determine the nature of the three types of gymnasium education (general, technical and commercial), the main lines of the curriculum and the length of study in each of these three types. The quantitative problem has been concerned mainly with the total number of places and the geographical distribution of gymnasia. In the last few years, however, the quantitative relation between the three gymnasium types has become more and more important. At present about 80 per cent of all students choose the general side of the gymnasium, and 10 per cent each the technical and commercial sides. But the demand for people with technical and commercial secondary education has increased rapidly, while at the same time the growing desire for university education has resulted in a great increase in the number of students choosing the general side of the gymnasia. There thus arises the difficult problem of the quantitative relationship between the general side, on the one hand, and the technical and commercial sides, on the other, a problem which will have to be carefully studied by educational planners.

At the university level the main problem is the quantitative one—the number of places for the country as a whole, and the geographical location of new educational facilities. These quantitative aspects have received special attention in the five-year plan for increasing educational capacity, which has recently been accepted by the Swedish Parliament. The qualitative aspects have been concerned with the curricula and the general effectiveness of university education.

As for investment in buildings and equipment, plans have been drawn up for the country as a whole and for different regions. It should be noted that the building of comprehensive schools and gymnasia is the task of local authorities, but as it is subsidized by the central authority, building plans for even a single school must conform to the general building plan for the whole country as elaborated by the central authority. At university level the planning of investment in buildings and equipment is a much more complicated matter, because there is no such fixed relationship between building and equipment costs, on the one hand, and educational capacity, on the other, as there is in comprehensive and secondary education. As a result, the planning of investment in university building and equipment has become closely integrated with policy decisions at government level.

In the matter of teaching staff and other educational personnel, the main planning problem is matching supply with demand, as the implementation of any educational plan depends to a large extent on the future supply of teaching staff. Obviously, any planning for expansion of secondary education must be closely related to plans for developing university faculties which provide the main source of secondary school teachers. In Sweden these plans for university expansion have resulted in the introduction of a new type of university teacher whose main function is teaching and whose teaching load is in principle 396 hours per academic year, as against a normal teaching load of 116 hours for professors who have to devote much of their time to administration and research.

Social welfare measures for students are an essential part of planning for educational expansion. In fact, the great increase in educational capacity beyond the comprehensive school level could never have been achieved without sacrificing quality if there had not been social welfare measures to enable young people from the lower paid social groups to pursue their education. These measures have led to improved mobilisation of the intellectual reserves of Sweden. The main problem in this field now is the appropriate distribution of welfare benefits between the various educational levels.

Lastly, a realistic timetable for the implementation of decisions is of great importance, especially in the field of higher education, where the building problems are often very complex, and for the recruitment of teaching staff and other educational personnel.

IV. THE ORGANISATION OF EDUCATIONAL PLANNING IN SWEDEN

The Swedish administrative system is in some ways unique. Ministries do not as in other countries deal with routine administrative work and the supervision of subordinate offices; this is the function of administrative Central Boards. But some of these Boards also have a planning function. Another special feature of the Swedish system is the great importance of *ad hoc* Royal Commissions; most reforms in the economic, social and educational fields are in fact based on the work of these Royal Commissions. They are appointed and given their terms of reference by the Government. However, the terms of reference are often very general and give the Commissions much freedom in their approach to the problems and in devising solutions. The Commissions often make use of outside experts and research workers for obtaining specific information.

In the field of educational planning the Central Boards concerned are the Board of Education, the Board of Vocational Training, the Office of the Chancellor of the Universities, and the Directorate for the Institutes of Technology; the Board of Building and Town Planning deals with the question of school and university buildings, and there is also a special Equipment Board for universities and similar institutions; the Labour Market Board and the Central Bureau of Statistics provide the educational planners with their main statistical material, particularly that relating to the demand for education and to the needs of the labour market. In 1960 a forecasting unit was set up within the Labour Market Board, and an advisory committee was appointed to guide the working methods of this unit; in addition, in view of the complexity of the methodological problems involved in the work of the forecasting unit, an expert group on methodological problems has been appointed.

Educational planning proper has for decades been carried out within the Royal Commissions. During the last six years four important Royal Commissions on education have been appointed: in 1955 the Royal Commission on Higher Education; in 1957 the Royal Commission on Comprehensive Schools; in 1959 the Royal Commission on Student Social Welfare; and in 1960 the Royal Commission on Higher Secondary Education.

The 1957 Royal Commission on Comprehensive Schools was the successor to the 1940 Royal School Committee and the 1946 Royal School Commission whose reports and recommendations provided the basis for the 1950 Education Act. This aimed at extending compulsory education in principle from 7 to 9 years, at replacing the various types of schools then existing by the comprehensive school, and determining the framework and character of this comprehensive school by experimenta :means over a prolonged period starting in 1949/50. The terms of reference of the 1957 Royal Commission were to evaluate the present school situation and the results of the experience gained since 1949/50 in order to formulate recommendations for a more definite school system and to set out its goals, its curricula and its organisation. The Commission has recently completed its report and it is expected that a new Education Bill providing for a 9-year compulsory comprehensive school will soon be submitted to Parliament.

The 1960 Royal Commission on Higher Secondary Education was appointed to work out a programme for the expansion of gymnasium education in the course of the 1960's. As already mentioned, there had been a rapid expansion of the general side of gymnasium education, and the 1955 Royal Commission on Higher Education had pointed out that there was a risk of not meeting the needs of the labour market if this tendency continued at the expense of the technical and commercial sides. The task of the 1960 Commission was to study this problem and work out a balanced programme for the 1960's. The Commission is now making investigations into the demand for people with higher secondary education, into the recruitment of gymnasium teachers, into the appropriateness of the curricula, etc.

The 1955 Royal Commission on Higher Education was assigned the task of studying the aims and needs of universities and other institutions of higher education and to work out long-term plans for their expansion. The Commission presented six reports on the basis of which a number of decisions were taken by Government and Parliament in the years 1958 to 1960. Among these is a 5-year plan for the expansion of institutions of higher education which is to be implemented gradually, mainly on the basis of work undertaken by a number of organisational committees. One such committee has been set up to plan the expansion of the Institute of Technology at Lund. Another—the Science Co-ordination Committee for Gothenburg—is drafting proposals for the establishment of a science-mathematics faculty at Gothenburg University and the expansion of the Chalmers Institute of Technology. The Committee on New Curricula in the Liberal Arts Faculties is investigating the future employment prospects for the greatly increased number of graduates in liberal arts. The Social Work Education Committee has to examine the question of increased training facilities for social workers. There is also a committee working on plans for increasing the capacity of faculties of medicine, and another doing similar work on dentistry institutes. All these organisational committees work closely with the Ministry of Education and on the most important ones the Ministry of Finance is also represented.

The 1955 Royal Commission has almost completed its work and is now engaged on its last task—the reorganisation of the administration of universities.

Lastly, the 1959 Royal Commission on Student Social Welfare is the successor to an earlier commission whose programme, presented in 1949, was fulfilled by 1959.

Most of these Royal Commissions are composed of members of Parliament representing the major political parties, representatives of employers' and labour organisations and, where necessary, representatives of educational bodies and of the national students' organisation.

Henceforward educational planning by Royal Commissions will be facilitated by the establishment in 1960 of a Planning Division within the Ministry of Education and Ecclesiastical Affairs. Its task consists primarily of analysing the material provided by the forecasting unit of the Central Labour Market Board, of co-ordinating the work of the organisational committees in the field of higher education, and of dealing with the proposals of the Board of Building and Town Planning relating to school and university buildings.

V. RELATING EDUCATIONAL TO ECONOMIC PLANNING

The question now arises of how far educational planning in Sweden can be related to economic planning.

In trying to answer this question, it should be borne in mind that the Swedish economy is highly dependent on international economic trends, and this means that economic planning in Sweden must necessarily be short-term planning. In fact, it is one-year planning based upon the yearly national budget. But the desirability of longer-term economic planning has become more apparent as government expenditure has increased more rapidly than the gross national product in the last decade (it has increased on an average by 4.9 per cent per annum, against an average increase of 3.2 per cent for the gross national product). Indeed, since 1948 a series of long-term economic forecasts and programmes have been worked out by *ad hoc* Royal Commissions, and the results of this work have been used by government, political parties and planners for their longer-term projects.

This tendency towards longer-term economic planning is of great importance to educational planning. Clearly, as long as economic planning remains short-term planning, educational planning, which by its very nature must be long-term, cannot be integrated into it to any significant extent. But as the tendency towards longer-term economic planning develops, it will become easier to co-ordinate educational with economic planning. But the special dilemma of educational planners is and will remain one of timing: economic planning cannot be sufficiently long-term to give the ideal basis for educational planning. The obvious corollary is that educational planning in Sweden must aim at making the educational system as flexible and adaptable as possible.

III

YUGOSLAVIA

by

Moric ELAZAR

*Head of Department
of Education Investment and Planning
Yugoslav Federal Secretariat for Education*

I. INTRODUCTION

Since the end of the war, Yugoslavia has been making enormous efforts to overcome her heritage of economic and cultural backwardness. In spite of many difficulties, her efforts are now beginning to bear fruit, and her rate of economic development is among the highest in the world. The increase that has been achieved in output has made it possible to devote more resources to the development of social services which, in turn, is helping economic expansion. In this context, education has made enormous progress since the end of the war. Thus the population is acquiring not only a higher cultural level, but also a better educational standard which is an important factor in increasing productivity and, therefore, in developing the country as a whole.

Educational expansion since the war has been continuously adapted to economic growth, particularly in the industrial sector and the public services. Very far-reaching changes have been introduced into the educational system in recent years affecting curricula and syllabuses, educational aims, school network and structure, as well as methods of financing. The measures taken are intended not only to enable the schools to adapt themselves to conditions in their immediate surroundings and to the demand for qualified personnel, but also to encourage the schools to become independent, self-managed units in the economy.

II. EDUCATIONAL PLANNING IN RELATION TO ECONOMIC GROWTH

The harmonizing of educational development with the growing needs for qualified manpower due to economic expansion is achieved by means of education planning within the framework of the overall plans for economic development. There have been three five-year economic plans in post-war Yugoslavia (1947-1951, 1957-1961, and

1961-1965), education playing a particularly important part in the one for 1961-1965.

Since an educational plan forms part of an economic plan, it is prepared, adopted and carried out by each of the political-territorial units [Federation, People's Republic or Autonomous Province, District, and Municipality (or Commune)] within the framework of existing laws concerning the founding and maintaining of schools. The plans are adopted by the same procedure as any other legislative act. They are not regarded as binding, however, in the strict legal sense, nor is there any law to punish their non-observance, although the authorities concerned may take specific measures to help put the plans into effect.

The educational plans of the political-territorial units at the different levels must be co-ordinated. Owing to the wide decentralization of educational authority, however, the plans set up by the Federation (and to some extent by the People's Republics) are general in character, showing the direction educational development should take, and the main goals to be achieved. Those at Federal level are drawn up in the light of the planned requirements and general development of the country as a whole; they are concerned mainly with seeing that educational institutions are set up where needed as far as financial possibilities permit, with expanding the material facilities of education, and with co-ordinating educational with industrial expansion.

The plans of the Municipalities and Districts, and to some extent those of the People's Republics, are more concrete since these political-territorial units have more direct powers and responsibilities in the educational field and also draw up plans with their own particular problems in mind. Those problems which concern two or more levels of administration are subject to negotiation on the basis of mutual understanding, assistance and economic interests. The Federation's part is very important in this respect, for, when initiating its plan, it lays down basic instructions and the main goals to be achieved.

The Departments of Economic Planning of the People's Republics, the Districts and the Municipalities are responsible for drawing up their respective Economic Development Plans, including the plan for educational development. These planning departments co-operate very closely with their educational authorities, who make sure that the status and needs of education are thoroughly understood, and that the basic guiding principles for its further development are included in the plan.

Educational plans generally deal with the following matters:

a) *The Training of Highly-qualified Personnel*

An estimate is made of the number of students at the different levels, i.e. (*i*) primary school, eight-year compulsory education, from 7 to 15 years of age, based on demographic factor; (*ii*) secondary school, for 16 to 19 year-olds, and (*iii*) higher education, for 20 to 24 year-olds. These two latter estimates are based on the country's requirements for specialised manpower and its financial possibilities.

b) *The Development of the School Networks*

The location and capacity of school buildings, which are dealt with mainly by the People's Republics, Districts and Communes.

c) *The Financial Investment Required*

The cost of the planned construction is estimated on the basis of the building and equipment standards laid down for the various types of schools, the anticipated number of pupils, and current building costs. A two-shift—morning and afternoon—system operates in most cities, following the sudden increase in the number of scholars.

d) *Maintenance and Running Costs*

These are estimated on the basis of the average cost per pupil according to the type of school. Consideration is also given to the possibility of improving school standards where means permit.

e) *The Number of Students Expected to Graduate*

f) *The Number of Teachers Required*

The plans are formulated to satisfy the economy's needs for skilled and qualified manpower. At the same time, the network of schools is so arranged that it encourages students to undertake the type of training for which need is greatest. We do not attempt, of course, to lay down hard and fast plans for the training and distribution of specific types and numbers of specialised personnel, since this would be contrary to the principle of free movement of labour; students are free to choose the type of vocational school for which they feel they are best fitted. On the other hand, the municipalities and industrial or trade associations meet their needs by offering scholarships or other facilities to suitable persons on a contractual basis.

The People's Republics also make available scholarships to ensure the training of a sufficient number of highly-specialised personnel. Up to now, these methods have effectively provided the numbers and types of scientific and technical personnel required, and there has been no danger of too many of one type being produced at the expense of another.

The education development plans are prepared on the basis of data from, and consultation with, those most directly affected: professional and trade associations, schools, educational workers' associations, etc. The work is done by the educational authorities in close co-operation with the Economic Planning Departments.

Official statistical data or other available information is generally used as a basis for this planning, but special surveys may be made on specific aspects. Scientific or economic institutes may be asked to undertake the examination of certain problems, particularly those concerned with demographic or economic trends.

A careful analysis is made of the statistical data, and, on the basis of this data and of various consultations, the first drafts of the different educational plans are drawn up. These are then co-ordinated and discussed with the Economic Planning Department of the political-territorial unit concerned to make sure they fit in with general economic policy. At the same time they are also examined by the political-territorial units at other levels, and, if necessary, amended to coincide with their development plans.

The Economic Planning Department then sets up the final draft for the economic development plans of its political-territorial unit, and sends it back to the different authorities concerned for their opinion. The educational authorities then reach their final decision on the plan for educational development, which is subsequently submitted to the representative body of the political-territorial unit for adoption.

Whilst the plan is being drawn up, the methods used to assess requirements for highly-qualified personnel in relation to the numbers leaving the various types of school are very carefully counter-checked. In the 1961-65 Development Plan, the Federal Planning Bureau assessed the country's need for highly-qualified personnel according to the multi-sector method, and included both industrial and other sectors. The results obtained were compared to needs as established by the respective branches of the Federal Institute of Economic Planning, and also to generally-accepted averages in respect of numerical ratios between the different skills. Alternatively, the numerical ratio of personnel with specific qualifications to the number of population might be taken, e.g. number of inhabitants per doctor, or any other criteria. It should be borne in mind, however, that our need for qualified personnel is still greater than our possibilities of providing them.

Economic development plans and, consequently, educational development plans, are made for a period of five years, but in practice are carried out on the basis of annual plans which are adopted in the same way as the five-year plans. Since neither economic nor educational plans can be established without consideration being given to long-term trends, we have also drawn up an economic plan showing probable development up to 1980, including labour and qualified personnel requirements. These long-term considerations were borne in mind when setting up the 1961-65 Plan.

The responsibility for carrying out the educational plan falls on the educational authorities in the execution of their routine tasks. They may propose, either independently or in conjunction with the planning services, any measures which immediate circumstances may seem to warrant, and also any improvements to the Five-Year Plan in course.

Industrial units, firms, political organisations, trade unions, etc., are also concerned in carrying out the plans. Since these plans represent a synthesis of widely-varying objectives and interests, they act as a powerful motivation for all concerned in seeing the tasks set are carried out.

The educational development plans we have thus set up have proved reasonably satisfactory, although they are not yet so effective as our economic plans—probably because of a lack of well-defined and tested methodology. However, we hope that international cooperation in the planning of education will prove to be very helpful, particularly concerning the elaboration of a relatively simple methodology which would make possible a comparison of data and the exchange of experience.

III. THE FINANCING OF EDUCATION

As from 1952, almost without exception, education was financed from the budgets of the particular political-territorial unit concerned —Republic, District or Municipality. As a result of the rapid expansion of educational facilities, however, these and other conventional means of finance proved insufficient. In any case, such a system meant that no connection existed between the school and the firm or industrial unit to which the student went on graduating, with the result that the schools were not adapted to supply industry's practical needs.

In view of this, on 1st January, 1961 a new system was adopted, considerably widening possibilities for financing education. As a general principle schools are financed by the territorial-political unit (Republic, District or Municipality) or by the industrial units which are either legally responsible for, or actively interested in, providing specific types of qualified manpower. The Municipalities, being the essential unit in our political system, finance more than 95 per cent of our schools, including all compulsory elementary schools for the 7 to 15 year-old age group, as well as the majority of the secondary vocational, technical and grammar schools. The Municipalities are thus responsible for ensuring the supply of qualified manpower at ordinary level to meet local requirements.

Some secondary vocational and technical schools, as well as some grammar schools, are financed by Districts, which recently have also accepted financial responsibility for advanced and university-level institutes of education to help meet the local need for highly-qualified personnel.

The majority of the institutions of higher education are financed by the People's Republics. The Federation does not finance education directly, but uses the means at its disposal to influence the direction of its development, to speed up the expansion of schools providing the personnel most urgently needed, to encourage the wider use of modern equipment, etc.

The new system provides for a more active participation of industrial units and individual firms in the founding and financing of schools. Since a rise in productivity and more efficient administration depend on the availability of adequate means of vocational training and general education, industrial units will have to devote increasing resources towards providing the type of education they need, and may now become the founders or co-founders of schools in their territorial-political unit.

Apart from elementary schools, therefore, which without exception are financed by the Municipality, there is no hard and fast rule concerning the type of school for which a particular level of authority is responsible. Responsibility may vary according to local conditions, requirements and possibilities. Since the interests of the industrial unit, Municipality or District obviously coincide so far as the training of locally-required types of qualified manpower is concerned, the new system will make it easier to overcome specific shortages. In view of the economy's ever-growing interest in the provision of institutes of higher education, a District's participation in their financing makes it easier for the People's Republic to carry out its desired programme and to set up larger educational units—thus achieving a more even and balanced expansion and making facilities available to a larger number of people. These institutes of higher education easily adapt themselves to local surroundings and are able to arrange their curricula, if necessary, to meet specific needs, thus producing more highly-specialised personnel at lower cost.

Schools founded by Municipalities, Autonomous Regions or People's Republics, are financed by means of special, legally-constituted funds. These funds consist of budgetary allocations (as a rule for the same amount as was previously allocated), and of "educational fund" contributions made by firms and industrial units on the basis of a fixed percentage of each wage-earner's salary. These latter contributions represent a new, important source of school financing, and are to be used for investment purposes. The proceeds are divided between the Municipality, which must receive at least 60% of the amount collected in its territory, and the People's Republic. Other contributions may also be made by the representative bodies of the political-territorial unit.

Schools founded by Districts continue to be financed by District budgets.

Investments in school buildings, as well as running and maintenance expenses, are paid for from the educational funds of the Municipalities, Autonomous Regions, and Republics founding them. A programme is set up covering income and expenditure for several years, the projects within this programme being shown on the annual balance sheet. Schools in underdeveloped areas receive help from the educational funds of the People's Republics and the Federation.

The annual budgetary allocations made by the representative bodies of the political-territorial units to education may be in the form of either a lump sum or a percentage of the budget, but must in any case be sufficient to cover the normal running expenses of the schools that they have either singly or jointly founded.

These allocations to education are estimated on the basis of a fixed percentage of the taxpayers' income, the costs of running and maintaining existing schools, and expenditure on building, equipment, and maintenance of new schools. A reserve is set aside for unforeseen expenditure.

Education committees are responsible, in line with directions received from the representative body of the political-territorial unit, for deciding how the funds shall be allocated to provide the most efficient network of schools in their area. The composition of these committees, and their close contacts with all interested, ensure that consideration is given to every aspect of educational need.

Under the new system, the school itself is responsible for its own expenditure. It receives from its founder a fixed amount per pupil, determined by the representative body of the political-territorial unit or, if the founder is an industrial unit, by its top-level, self-management body. This amount is calculated according to a standardised procedure, taking into consideration the type of school, equipment standards in other schools of the same type, working conditions, etc. The amount allocated should be sufficient to cover all personnel and material costs, including teaching aids and equipment.

The funds received by the school correspond to the activities for which it is legally responsible. It may, however, undertake other activities, i.e. the holding of courses for adults at the request of an industrial unit, and thus increase its revenue. This possibility provides a means for the school to improve its own material standard, increase its teachers' salaries and contribute at the same time to the expansion of education in general.

All monies received by the school constitute a single fund which may be allocated with no other control than that of the auditors. Any surplus funds may be disposed of at the end of the year, or the school may set up its own investment or other fund.

A new economic relationship has thus been established not only between the school and its teachers, but also between them and the community in which the school is situated.

At the same time, the school has acquired increased importance as an independent economic unit, and the responsibilities of the teachers' collective for ensuring satisfactory school and teaching standards have been increased. New wage incentives have been introduced to bring teachers' salaries into line with their qualifications, results obtained, etc.

The new system of financing education is expected to provide not only the necessary funds required for immediate use, but also greater stability in educational finance in general. The new contribution, in the form of a fixed percentage of the wage earner's income, means that funds will be automatically available. This will not only facilitate the setting up of long-term development programmes on a wider and more independent basis, but also ensure the greater independence of the schools by making available an adequate and regular source of revenue. At the same time, contributions from the Federation and the People's Republics will enable the underdeveloped areas to extend their school network.

Finally, the fact that firms and industrial units may now found and maintain any particular school it is in their interest to create, means that not only will students have better opportunities for practical work, but that industry will be better able to influence curricula to see that it effectively links theory with practice. Firms or industrial units who found and maintain schools pay for them directly (not through an educational fund), any such amounts being entirely independent of the funds mentioned above.

IV. CONCLUSIONS

I have tried to give a description of what I consider to be the essential elements in the planning and financing of education in Yugoslavia. The real significance of the measures taken, however, cannot be appreciated without a knowledge of the circumstances leading up to them.

Without going into a mass of detailed explanations, I should, however, like to draw attention to the fact that, before the war, Yugoslavia was an agricultural country, under-developed industrially, and with very limited educational facilities. Illiteracy was very widespread. To-day, she is faced with the task of providing a dynamic economy with a vast number and variety of highly-qualified personnel. Obviously, the period since the liberation has not been sufficient for the whole of this task to be successfully completed. It will require several decades of strenuous effort.

Our first efforts had to be directed mainly towards industrial investments, although the importance of education was never underestimated. The enormous increase in the numbers of students necessary meant that it was impossible to provide facilities for all of them immediately, even though we have considerably increased our contributions to education, both absolutely and relatively.

The system was, therefore, aimed at getting the maximum benefit from the means available. At the same time, we accord great importance to the building up of a new social relationship in which education will take over its own management and will accept greater responsibility within the framework of socialist democracy. Such a relationship will grant those who are directly interested in, and who provide or take part in the training of, qualified manpower, the right to take decisions on all-important problems concerning such training. This does not prevent the authorities at a higher level from having the right to exert an influence over such activities with a view to co-ordinating and directing educational development as a whole. Such a right, however, is not given specifically by law, but is implied in the task of co-ordinating effort and developing mutual assistance in the educational field.

The tables given in the annex to this report show more clearly the basic quantitative relationships in the expansion of education in Yugoslavia.

TABLE 1. NUMBERS OF SCHOOLS

TYPE OF SCHOOL	ACADEMIC YEAR 1938/39	ACADEMIC YEAR 1959/60	INDEX 1959/60 (1938/39 = 100)
Total...	*10,353*	*17,300*	*167.1*
Elementary schools.............................	9,190	14,417	156.8
High, technical and other secondary schools........	300	638	212.7
Schools for skilled workers........................	770	767	99.6
Schools for highly-skilled workers................	—	111	—
Higher and graduate schools and universities.......	27	149	551.9
Other schools[1]....................................	66	938	1,421.2
Centres for vocational training...................	—	280	—

1. These include schools for adults (except those for highly skilled workers which are shown separately), special schools and schools for complementary education.

TABLE 2. NUMBERS OF STUDENTS

TYPE OF SCHOOL	ACADEMIC YEAR 1938/39	ACADEMIC YEAR 1959/60	INDEX 1959/60 (1938/39 = 100)
Elementary schools...........................	1,560,460	2,589,576	165.9
High schools, tech. and other secondary schools.	51,171	198,663	388.2
Schools for skilled workers....................	69,672	134,928	193.7
Schools for highly-skilled workers.............	—	11,237	—
Higher and graduate schools and universities.....	16,978	104,786	617.2
Other schools.................................	9,753	72,159	739.9

TABLE 3. PERCENTAGE OF AGE GROUPS ATTENDING SCHOOLS

TYPE OF SCHOOLS AND AGE GROUP	1938/39	1952/53	1957/58	1959/60	1964/65 FORECASTS
Elementary schools (age 7 to 15 years)...	—	69.0	82.7	84.0[1]	92.5
High schools, technical and equivalent schools (age 16 to 19 years)[2].........	—	13.8	23.1	26.3[1]	35.6
Higher and graduate schools and universities (age 20 to 24 years)[3]................	—	1.6	3.0	3.6[1]	6.4
(All students in relation to total population)	0.11	0.32	0.46	0.56[1]	0.78

1. Estimate.
2. Including schools for skilled workers.
3. Many of the students, particularly those studying on part-time basis, are outside the 20 to 24 age group.

TABLE 4. NUMBER OF GRADUATES ACCORDING TO TYPE OF SCHOOL

TYPE OF SCHOOL	1955-56 (1956)	1959/60 (1960)	WHOLE PERIOD 1955/56-1959/60 (1956-1960) TOTAL	ANNUAL AVERAGE
High schools, technical and other secondary schools	22,631	36,390	148,160	29,632
Schools for skilled workers	29,363	37,350	170,105	34,021
Schools for highly-skilled workers	1,120	3,705	12,670	2,534
Universities, graduate and higher schools	8,286	14,928	54,032	10,806
Universities only	6,328	9,974	35,452	7,090
Technological	1,435	1,959	7,161	1,432
Arts	1,031	1,937	6,427	1,285
Sciences	512	920	3,545	709

TABLE 5. NUMBER OF GRADUATES FROM HIGHER EDUCATION

TYPE OF SCHOOL	1956	1957	1958	1959	1960
Total number of graduates	8,286	8,386	10,206	12,220	14,928
Index (1956 = 100)	100.0	101.0	123.2	147.5	180.2
Of these:					
In all technological faculties	1,435	1,288	1,338	1,511	1,959
Individual faculties:					
Architecture	185	155	208	287	377
Civil engineering	346	314	308	305	324
Mechanical engineering	363	321	272	270	445
Electronics	221	238	235	268	336
Geology	27	36	34	41	30
Industrial chemistry	207	141	209	247	325
Mining	86	83	72	93	122

TABLE 6. BUDGETARY ALLOCATIONS FOR REGULAR SCHOOL MAINTENANCE

Funds in million dinars at current prices.

Fiscal year	1955	1956	1957	1958	1959
Academic year	1954/55	1955/56	1956/57	1957/58	1958/59
Total	27,601	31,888	38,062	48,347	57,638
Index (1955 = 100)	100	111.5	137.9	175.2	208.8

TABLE 7. SOURCES OF FUNDS FOR REGULAR SCHOOL MAINTENANCE

Funds un million dinars at current prices.

BUDGETS	1957 FUNDS	1957 %	1958 FUNDS	1958 %	1959 FUNDS	1959 %
Total	38,062	100.0	48,347	100.0	57,638	100.0
Municipality	25,645	67.4	34,613	71.6	42,582	73.9
District	5,959	15.6	6,501	13.4	6,203	10.7
Republic	6,458	17.0	7,233	15.0	8,853	15.4

TABLE 8. SOURCES OF INVESTMENTS IN EDUCATION

Funds in million dinars at current prices.

SOURCES	1957 TOTAL	1957 %	1958 TOTAL	1958 %	1959 TOTAL	1959 %
Total	12,436	100.0	15,503	100.0	24,320	100.0
Index 1957 = 100	100.0	—	124.7	—	195.6	—
Total budgetary allocations	5,255	42.3	3,611	23.3	7,346	30,2
Contributions from personnel in industrial units	5,948	47.8	7,389	47,7	9,351	38,5
Contributions from housing funds	1,233	9,9	2,677	17.3	4,211	17.3
Contributions from the economic reserves of the Federation	—	—	611	3.9	406	1.7
Contributions from the Gen. Investment Fund	—	—	1,217	7.8	1,614	6.6
Other contributions	—	—	—	—	1,392	5.7

TABLE 9. ESTIMATED INCREASES IN NUMBERS ATTENDING SCHOOLS FOR THE PERIOD 1961-1965

TYPE OF SCHOOL	1959/60	1964/65	INDEX 1964/65 (1959/60 = 100)
Total	3,111,349	3,805,900	120.9
Elementary schools	2,589,576	2,994,500	115.6
Secondary education:			
High schools, technical and other secondary schools	198,663	273,300	137.6
Schools for skilled workers	134,928	206,200	152.8
Schools for highly-skilled workers	11,237	30,000	267.0
Higher education	104,786	154,800	147.7
Other schools	72,157	147,100	203.9

TABLE 10. PRESENT AND PROJECTED
MANPOWER REQUIREMENTS ACCORDING TO QUALIFICATIONS

In thousands.

CATEGORIES OF STAFF	1960 TOTAL	%	1965 TOTAL	%
Total employed in industrial and other activities...	2,967,0	100.0	3,972,0	100.0
Administrative and technical staff with higher and advanced education.....................	103.8	3.5	188.8	4.8
Administrative and technical staff with secondary education...............................	312.5	10.5	480.0	12.1
Highly-skilled workers........................	176.0	5.9	258.2	6.5
Skilled workers..............................	771.5	26.0	1,096.0	27.6
Others (semi-skilled and unskilled)...	1,063.5	54.1	1,949.0	49.0

TABLE 11. ESTIMATED NEEDS AND INFLOW OF
QUALIFIED MANPOWER FOR THE PERIOD 1960-1965

CATEGORY OF STAFF	NEEDS	INFLOW	APPROX. % OF NEEDS COVERED	SHORTAGE
With higher education...............	113,800	110,000	97	— 3,800
With secondary education............	225,000	167,500	74	—57,500
Highly-skilled workers...............	116,500	93,500	80	—23,000
Skilled workers.....................	465,000	420,000	90	—45,000

DISCUSSION

Chairman : Mr. COOMBS (U.S.A.)

Professor ELVIN (panel of experts) introduced the discussion by pointing to the long-term nature of the educational process and the consequent need for reasonably long-term educational planning. But how could educational planning be integrated with economic forecasting which seemed to be most effective over the short or medium term? The speaker also asked what basic factors should be taken into account when formulating long-term plans for education, in particular, how the needs of the economy for highly qualified manpower could be taken account of? Which authority should draw up these plans, how should they be carried out and by whom? It was necessary to bear in mind that the role of central government in carrying out educational programmes and in the administration of education varied very much from country to country. Finally, the speaker suggested that the Conference should address itself to the problem of information and to the research necessary to obtain it, which was a vital prerequisite for educational planning.

EDUCATIONAL AND ECONOMIC PLANNING

M. POIGNANT (panel of experts) said that the development and planning of education was a response not only to economic needs, but also to demographic factors and social aims, such as the desire of governments and parents to lengthen the period of study as part of general cultural development. Education, insofar as it takes these factors into consideration, is dependent on economic growth only in that it presents society with a long-term bill which must be met.

The speaker emphasised that the planning of higher education in France was based on the concept that all those who are able and wish to enter universities should be encouraged to do so. It was for this reason that university expansion in France up to 1970 would be the fastest in the Western world. The French authorities had not taken account of long-term forecasts of the manpower structure in deciding the main lines in planning their higher educational facilities, but hoped to do so in the future. They had accepted the major hypothesis, on the basis of economic projections over the next twenty years, that the development of higher scientific education and secondary technical education should be expanded to the maximum possible extent. The speaker hoped that the results of the long-term projections now being made would provide further data on the needs for various types of education. He felt that all countries—or perhaps international organisations—should undertake major studies on the relationship between needs for highly qualified manpower and educational planning.

M. FOURASTIE (France) said that the projections made by the Manpower Committee, of which he was president, made it clear that in 1975 the French economy would need not only increasing numbers of scientists and engineers but also of people trained in the human sciences, such as psychology, human relations, philosophy and literature. We are moving rapidly towards a society in which the working week will be much shorter, and education must therefore take more account of the cultural needs of man's leisure hours.

Mr. ELAZAR (panel of experts) said that rigid long-term forecasts of manpower needs might be undesirable because of the rapid changes which were taking place in technology. Nevertheless, the global manpower requirements indicated by the Yugoslav long-term economic projections up to 1980 are very large. The fact that shortages of high-level personnel would probably prove a bottleneck to rapid economic growth had already produced a sharp swing towards technical education in the plan for 1961-65.

EDUCATIONAL PLANNING IN THE MEDITERRANEAN COUNTRIES

Mr. GASS (O.E.C.D. Secretariat) told the Conference about the Mediterranean Regional Project which had been adopted, in co-operation with O.E.C.D., by the Governments of Greece, Italy, Portugal, Spain, Turkey and Yugoslavia in order to work out proposals for the long-term programming of resources into education. National research teams had been established in each country, and the first stage of the work—surveys of the present situation of, and needs for, education—was nearing completion in several countries. The second stage—establishing targets for education at the different levels and types—was of particular interest in that national teams were trying to take account of needs for highly qualified manpower. The third stage of the work would be to prepare programmes for directing the flow of the necessary resources into education so as to pass from the existing situation to that projected; these proposals would serve as a guide to decisions on education in future years. Finally it was hoped that O.E.C.D., in conjunction with the six national directors, would produce an analytical report bringing out the main results of the national studies.

Mr. DOUSSIS (Greece) emphasised the interest felt by his Government in the O.E.C.D. Mediterranean Project and the contribution which Greece had made to the methodology of the project in tackling problems of long-term educational development. Investment in education as an integral part of rapid economic growth has to be planned a long time ahead. The Greek team was paying great attention to the development of the economy, branch by branch, and to manpower needs as a guide to distributing educational effort between technical and non-technical disciplines.

Professor ALVES MARTINS (Portugal) stressed the value of international co-operation in the planning of education in the six participating countries and the great importance of timely measures to improve the supply of scientific and technical manpower. The Portuguese Institute for Higher Economic and Statistical Studies, of which he was the Director, had been a pioneer in studying the link between economic and educational planning and the means of satisfying the needs for scientific and technical personnel. The Mediterranean Regional Project had grown out of the initial interest of the Portuguese Government in 1960.

Dr. NOVACCO (Italy) said that the participation of Italy in the Mediterranean Regional Project had arisen out of the Government's interest in long-term forecasts of manpower needs and targets for education. The Association for the Industrial Development of Southern Italy (of which Dr. Novacco is Executive Secretary) had produced for the Government a first report on the needs for highly qualified personnel in Italy in 1975 and the consequential demands on the educational system. This first approach would be deepened, within the framework of the Mediterranean Project, as regards the programming and costing aspects, the link between educational qualification and occupational situation, and the regional development of education.

EDUCATIONAL AND ECONOMIC PLANNING IN OTHER COUNTRIES

Mr. KLEPPE (Norway) thought that there would be no difficulty in combining a ten-year or even longer-term plan for the development of education in Norway with the shorter-term programmes in the different economic sectors. Judging from his experience in the Norwegian Ministry of Finance, the speaker saw the great difficulty governments experienced in accepting certain formal economic commitments many years ahead. But long-term educational planning was justified in its own right, and it seemed desirable that the present short-term educational planning in Norway should be supplemented by some long-term planning. To do this, there must be research to clarify the nature of long-term targets and the means of implementing them.

Mr. MOBERG (panel of experts) was also of the opinion that long-term comprehensive planning was vital because of the nature of the educational process, and that it could be a useful framework within which to take shorter-term decisions on priorities. Sweden was entering a period when high-level manpower would be more essential than previously to ensure a high rate of economic growth. The labour force would grow more slowly; indeed, the raising of the school leaving age would have this effect. Thus an increase in expenditure on education would have to be taken into consideration when preparing plans for economic development in Sweden.

M. DARIMONT (Belgium) said that co-ordination of educational and economic planning was not always an easy matter. There was the case, for instance, when increases in educational budgets were motivated by purely political considerations without direct relation to economic planning. Belgium was an example of a country where there existed no systematic educational planning in relation to economic planning. Allocation of funds to respective educational media were subject to a political "Inter-scholastic covenant". At a time when such funds were being increased at a very rapid rate, the need was felt for a rationalisation of their employment by the organising authorities. How to achieve co-ordination of the activities of the state, local authorities and private school bodies, within the framework of national educational planning closely integrated in the general economic context, was indeed a complex problem.

THE RELATIONSHIP BETWEEN PLANNING AND THE IMPLEMENTATION OF EDUCATIONAL PROGRAMMES

Professor ELVIN, referring to the question raised by M. DARIMONT, stressed the importance of considering how the system of consultation, committees, activities of central and local government could enable planning to function sensibly and permit the successful carrying through of educational programmes.

Mr. SCHMIDT (Denmark) said that his country should be considered underdeveloped as far as planning and organisation of education were concerned. Firstly, decisions about educational policy were not the responsibility of a single authority or ministry; primary and secondary education was mainly decided on and financed by local authorities, while responsibility for higher education was spread among various ministries. Secondly, there was a general lack of information. Recently some study had been done on the supply of teachers and buildings; it was not possible to know how many class rooms or teachers there were in secondary and primary schools. Nor was it known how many students were enrolled at Copenhagen university; the only exact figure known was for the number of students passing examinations.

The first prerequisite to educational planning in Denmark would be to collect full information in order to have a basis for forecasting trends. The second task was to co-ordinate the decisions of the different authorities at local, regional or national level. The reform of the administration of education in Denmark had begun; control of vocational education had been moved to the Ministry of Education; the Government had decided that a National Advisory Council on Education was to be set up; the structure of the Ministry of Education was to be reviewed. But Denmark was only at the beginning.

Dr. FREY (Federal Republic of Germany) said that, with its decentralized administration of education and its liberal economy, Germany might also be considered somewhat underdeveloped as far as the planning of education was concerned. Nevertheless, between 1950 and 1960 no less than 14,000 million marks ($ 3500 million) were invested in new schools and universities without any centralised planning at all. But this was basically reconstruction work, so that the need for an overall plan had not been so important. At present, 7,000 million marks ($ 1750 million) were being spent each year on schools and universities in Germany by the eleven autonomous members of the Federal Republic, which had their own budgets and financial resources and took their own decisions.

The speaker felt that, the reconstruction period having come to an end, it was now time to set up a general planning function co-ordinating the direction, equalizing the burden and supplementing the planning of the different Länder. It is essential that the responsible regional and municipal authorities should, from the outset, co-operate in this centralized planning and participate in the necessary measures for its implementation.

Mr. McMurrin (United States) said that in the United States education was decentralised; institutions of public higher education being largely under the control of individual states, and schools being controlled by states and local communities. Private education was also important. The problem was how to achieve certain clear-cut national goals in education, including committing educational resources to foreign obligations, while respecting state and local control.

The speaker pointed to examples of the fruitful action of the Federal Government in education. The advanced state of American agriculture was due to the fact that for the past hundred years the Federal Government had supported agricultural research and vocational training. The Government is examining the desirability of extending its support for all types of vocational training. But the large issue remains of effective overall planning to improve education and satisfy manpower needs without destroying local school control and initiative.

Dr. Ferrier (Netherlands) said that in his country the Central Plan Bureau undertook overall economic planning and that there was a special educational planning section within the Bureau which worked under the direction of the Minister of Education. There was a special department for educational statistics within the Central Bureau of Statistics and it might reasonably be said that, as a result of its work, the Netherlands authorities had a clear and complete view of the educational situation. The authorities were undertaking a large expansion of education with the help of the appropriate specialised planning Commissions, and it was planned that by 1970 six per cent of the gross national product would be devoted to education.

Mr. Moberg thought it important that the purely planning functions should be kept separate from the decision-making functions. In Sweden, the central planning machinery was organised within the Ministry of Education, its main function being to co-ordinate the activities of the several large Government commissions which have been planning the development of different types of education. It also analysed the work being done in a special unit concerned with manpower needs (the Labour Market Board) from the standpoint of educational development. The speaker felt that this machinery in the Ministry of Education should become a fully operative central planning division for education, and policy was moving in that direction. There was no doubt that the appropriate place for the operation of the central planning function was at the heart of the Government.

Mr. LÖWBEER (Sweden) urged that more attention be given to the decision function. How could long-term plans for education win the support of politicians who are often reluctant to plan for a longer period than that covered by their mandate? How was it that French politicians had become so receptive to such proposals for education?

M. POIGNANT stressed that during the past fifteen years French parliamentarians had approved three Plans for economic development and that these had included sections for the expansion of education. On each occasion, they had asked the Government to increase the credits for education in accordance with the conclusions reached by the School Committee of the Plan. In fact the principle of the planned development of educational activities no longer met significant opposition in France.

In the speaker's opinion, planning for educational development was an absolute necessity; and though several systems were possible, the French system had the merit of simplicity and of working well in practice within a highly centralized State. If the Government were to work on a day-to-day basis, no rational solution could be found to such problems as the supply of teachers or investment in school buildings; demographic trends and the educational implications of social change would be overlooked. The new plan concerning educational investment up to 1965 had been based on projections extending to 1975. During the period of the plan, educational investment would increase by seventy-two per cent, compared with a rise in total civil investment of forty per cent and in national income of twenty-six per cent.

Professor EDDING (panel of experts) pointed out that planning activities were hampered not only by lack of the relevant data, but also by lack of clarity in basic definitions and classifications. This was true in most countries, and even more so as far as international comparability was concerned. Much work and research remained to be done.

V. INTERNATIONAL FLOWS OF STUDENTS

Paper by J.R. Gass and R.F. Lyons of the O.E.C.D.
Directorate for Scientific Affairs

PREFACE

How can study abroad best be used so as to contribute most to economic development? What is the proper balance between increasing higher educational facilities at home and sending students to other countries? The Committee for Scientific and Technical Personnel, whose work it is to promote the necessary expansion of the numbers of highly qualified scientific and technical personnel needed for economic progress, has taken up these questions as a result of its examination of existing strategies for developing these resources in some of the Mediterranean countries.

It is necessary that study abroad should be used as an integral part of the strategy of the advanced countries in extending help to the newly developing countries for the growth of their human resources. It has become clear in the course of the Committee's work over recent years that the magnitude of this task in the Mediterranean countries, and *a fortiori* in the much less developed countries outside Europe, requires special measures and policies to produce the teachers and resources necessary for a rapid expansion of education. Many forms of international assistance have been studied including assistance in long-term assessments of needs and priorities for education, financial grants, the establishment of institutions abroad, help in improving curricula and the supply of foreign teachers. It is essential that all these elements of assistance and the judicious use of study abroad should be linked in a well-planned effort by the advanced countries to fit into the long-term strategies for human resource development which have to be worked out by the newly advancing countries themselves.

The attached study was submitted in June, 1961 to the then Governing Committee for Scientific and Technical Personnel which, taking note of the limitations of the statistical data referred to in the introductory pages to the paper, found that it was of such interest as to justify wide diffusion and further study of the whole subject. It is the hope of the Committee that this further study, particularly with regard to the disciplines followed by foreign students, special courses for potential teachers, and the optimal use of facilities for study abroad, will enable Member countries to take the appropriate decisions.

Henning FRIIS

TABLE OF CONTENTS

PREFACE.. 5
Notes on Sources and Definitions........................... 8
  I. INTRODUCTION.. 9
  II. THE FLOW OF FOREIGN STUDENTS....................... 11
  III. THE FLOW OF FOREIGN SCIENCE STUDENTS............... 17
  IV. GEOGRAPHICAL ORIGIN OF FOREIGN STUDENTS............. 19
  V. POLICY PROBLEMS..................................... 23

ANNEXES

  I. Foreign Students in 1958-59........................ 26
  II. Foreign Science Students in 1958-59................ 27
  III. Foreign Students by Area of Origin in 1958-59...... 28
  IV*a*. Foreign Students by Area of Origin in Natural Sciences, 1958-59......... 30
  IV*b*. Foreign Students by Area of Origin in Engineering, 1958-59............. 32
  IV*c*. Foreign Students by Area of Origin in Agriculture, 1958-59............. 34

DISCUSSION... 37

LIST OF TABLES

1. Foreign Students in the main O.E.C.D. Receiving Countries in 1958-59..... 11
2. Countries with High Proportion of Foreign Students but Low Enrolment of Nationals in Relation to Wealth - 1958-59......................... 13
3. Countries with Balanced Proportion of Foreign Students and National Enrolment in Relation to Wealth - 1958-59......................... 14
4. Countries with Low Proportion of Foreign Students in Relation to National Enrolment and Wealth - 1958-59................................ 15
5. Science Students in Five Selected Countries - 1958-59.................... 17
6. Total African Students and African Science Students in France and Germany (F.R.)... 21

NOTE ON SOURCES AND DEFINITIONS

SOURCE OF DATA

The data used in this note were obtained through the courtesy of the statistical services of UNESCO. Most of the material has been published in UNESCO "FOREIGN STUDENT SURVEYS" as part of successive issues of "STUDY ABROAD", but some of the more detailed data are unpublished.

DEFINITIONS

Higher education has been defined by UNESCO as covering "institutions" which normally require as a condition of admission the completion of secondary school or its equivalent (e.g. in the form of an entrance examination). Such institutions may be universities, higher technical schools, teacher training colleges, theological colleges, etc.[1] Schools and classes of pre-primary, primary and secondary levels attached to institutions of higher education are not included, nor are adult education activities or university extension work.

A *foreign student* is generally defined as a person enrolled for study at an institute of higher education in a country or territory of which he is not a permanent resident. A foreign student and his country of origin are generally defined according to the permanent place of residence of the student. Many countries, however, employed the nationality or citizenship concept, and this is noted in the tables.

The *number of students* excludes persons attending short summer courses and those who are not full-time students but who are enrolled for correspondence courses or evening courses. The term "national student" as used in this note refers to national students enrolled in their own country.

---

1. With the exception of the United Kingdom for which data on the number of foreign students, as given in this paper, refer to *universities only*.

I

INTRODUCTION

The part which the educational infrastructure of a country plays in long-term economic growth is gaining wider and wider recognition. In economic theory this is reflected in the growing importance attributed to the "fourth factor" — a compound of organization, education, scientific research and all the services which bring together the other three factors. In economic practice it is reflected by the growing awareness of the need to plan expenditure on education as an integral part of the process of national economic development.

It is, therefore, to be expected that international movements of finance capital will be accompanied by international movements of human capital in the furtherance of economic growth. This human capital may take the form of highly-qualified manpower which participates directly in the economic process, such as engineers; or it may consist of highly-qualified people who participate indirectly, such as teachers who help to produce human capital; or it may be in the form of students who go abroad to acquire qualification and skills. The movements of these three forms of human capital are linked together, and in a sense offer alternatives between which an optimum balance must be struck, bearing in mind the political and sociological limitations in each particular situation.

As a result of cultural and economic forces which have operated over a long period, there has developed something in the nature of an international market for higher education facilities between the O.E.C.D. countries themselves. The Annual Review of Member Countries carried out by the Office for Scientific and Technical Personnel has shown how important the influx of foreign students has become to the educational systems of some receiving countries, and how vital access to foreign educational facilities has become to some sending countries. Moreover, movements of highly-qualified personnel between Europe and North America, as well as North American investment to harness unused brainpower resources in Europe, have played a significant role in scientific and technical development since World War II.

But now the predominant task which devolves upon the O.E.C.D. countries is to assist the underdeveloped countries in building up or forming their own educational infrastructure, to offer increased facilities for higher education to students from the underdeveloped world, and to ensure that the flow of human capital is in balance with the flow of finance capital — and *vice versa*. It is in the context of this policy that this paper has been prepared, with the modest objective of analysing international movements in the field of higher education in 1958-59, particularly science education, in order to throw some light on the problems involved in educational assistance to underdeveloped countries both by the individual Member countries and by the O.E.C.D. community as a wole.

II

THE FLOW OF FOREIGN STUDENTS

The flow of foreign students through universities and institutions of higher education of the O.E.C.D. area as a whole has been rather modest: in 1958-59 it represented 2.5 per cent of the total student population of this area. But this overall figure gives little idea of the importance which this flow of foreign students has for the educational structure of some receiving countries and for the educational needs of some sending countries. To countries such as Greece and Turkey, for instance, facilities for higher education abroad are of great importance. They are even more so for the underdeveloped regions outside the O.E.C.D. area; in 1958-59 this area had some 50,000 students from Latin America, the Middle East, Africa, and Asia,[1] compared with some 7,000 students from these regions in U.S.S.R. and 3,500 in Japan.

TABLE 1. FOREIGN STUDENTS IN THE MAIN O.E.C.D. RECEIVING COUNTRIES IN 1958-59

COUNTRIES	FOREIGN STUDENTS TO TOTAL FOREIGN STUDENTS IN 19 O.E.C.D. COUNTRIES[1] %	Ranking order 19 countries	TOTAL FOREIGN STUDENTS TO TOTAL STUDENTS %	Ranking order 19 countries
United States	38	1	1.45	16
France	14	2	7.71	6
Germany (F.R.)	12	3	9.21	5
United Kingdom	9	4	10.68	4
Austria	8	5	31.98	1
Switzerland	5	6	31.63	2
Canada	4	7	5.80	7
Spain	2	8	2.60	11

1. Exluding Luxembourg and Sweden.
Source: Annex 1.

---

1. Since countries sending less than 700 students to the U.S.A. were included in the UNESCO statistics under "others", this estimate is tentative.

As can be seen from Table 1, the eight O.E.C.D. countries which played the largest part in receiving foreign students accounted for 92 per cent of the 125,000 odd foreign students in the O.E.C.D. countries in 1958-59. The United States took in by far the largest proportion.

But the picture is radically changed if we consider the number of foreign students in relation to the total number of students in each country. As will be seen from Table 1, the U.S.A., which took in by far the largest number, devoted only 1.45 per cent of its student places to foreign nationals, whereas Austria and Switzerland, which took a much smaller number, devoted some 32 per cent each. Obviously, a country having a high enrolment ratio of its own nationals will suffer from this kind of comparison.

Bearing in mind these considerations, the O.E.C.D. countries appear to fall into three main groups.

Group A. COUNTRIES IN WHICH FOREIGN STUDENTS FORM A HIGH PROPORTION OF TOTAL STUDENTS, BUT IN WHICH THE NUMBER OF NATIONAL STUDENTS IN THE POPULATION IS RELATIVELY LOW, HAVING REGARD TO NATIONAL WEALTH (see Table 2)

It seems likely that the flow of foreign students, particularly from the underdeveloped areas, into these countries will grow. Any policy for expanding higher education capacity in these countries must therefore take into account the need to provide more places for foreign students.

Switzerland

Within this group Switzerland is of special interest because, whereas in terms of national product per head it ranks fourth among the nineteen countries, it ranks fifteenth for the frequency of national students in total population and tenth for the frequency of all students in the population (see Annex I). Since students fees do not cover the cost, higher education has to be financed by the Federal Government or the Cantons; and it may be asked whether this expenditure takes full account of the tacit commitment to provide an appropriate number of places for students from abroad.

United Kingdom

When assessing the effort of the United Kingdom, it must be remembered that in this country there is a *numerus clausus* for entry into institutions of higher education. The use of enrolment figures therefore puts the British effort in a less favourable light than would be the case if graduation figures were used instead. Even so, there can be little doubt that any plans for expanding higher education will need to take account of the explicit commitment to provide increased facilities for foreign students.

TABLE 2. COUNTRIES WITH HIGH PROPORTION OF FOREIGN STUDENTS BUT LOW ENROLMENT OF NATIONALS IN RELATION TO WEALTH — 1958-59

COUNTRY	TOTAL FOREIGN STUDENTS TO TOTAL STUDENTS %	IN RELATION TO O.E.C.D. MEDIAN FOR 19 COUNTRIES 3.68 = 100	Ranking order	TOTAL NATIONAL STUDENTS TO POPULATION AGED 20-24 %	IN RELATION TO O.E.C.D. MEDIAN FOR 19 COUNTRIES 4.28 = 100	Ranking order	G.N.P. PER CAPITA $ 000 AT 1959 PRICES AND EXCHANGE RATES	IN RELATION TO O.E.C.D. MEDIAN FOR 19 COUNTRIES $ 1,070 = 100	Ranking order
Austria	31.98	869	1	4.85	113	9	0.69	64	12
Switzerland	31.63	860	2	3.69	86	13	1.48	138	4
Ireland	19.89	540	3	4.96	87	8	0.62	57	13
United Kingdom	10.68	290	4	2.82	66	18	1.29	121	6
Germany (F.R.)	9.21	250	5	3.47	81	15	1.07	100	10

Source: Annex I.

Ireland

The expansion of student capacity in the United Kingdom could have a considerable effect on higher education policy in Ireland, since at present nearly two-thirds of all foreign students in Ireland come from the United Kingdom. This policy must also take account of an increasing demand for higher education on the part of Irish nationals. The present capacity is larger than that which would be commensurate with national wealth when the number of national students is related to the population aged 20-24 (see Table 2); but it must be remembered that the size of this age group has been reduced by large-scale emigration of young people from Ireland; when the number of national students is related to the total population (see Annex I) Ireland falls to the 16th place amongst 19 O.E.C.D. countries.

Austria

In one important respect Austria differs from the other members of the group: although it has a higher proportion of foreign students than any other Member country, the proportion of national students in the population aged 20-24 is significantly higher than that commensurate with national wealth (see Table 2) and the proportion of national students in total population is commensurate with national wealth (see Annex I). However, in view of the remarkable rate of growth of the Austrian economy (the gross national product increased by 42.7 per cent between 1954 and 1960) and the growing demand by foreign students, particularly from Greece, for higher education facilities, the balance between foreign and national students will need to be reviewed when planning higher education facilities for future years.

Group B. COUNTRIES IN WHICH FOREIGN STUDENTS FORM A MODERATE PROPORTION OF TOTAL STUDENTS, BUT IN WHICH THE PROPORTION OF NATIONAL STUDENTS IN THE POPULATION IS IN BALANCE WITH NATIONAL WEALTH

This balance is clearly shown in Table 3, in contrast with the imbalance for Group A and Group C. The considerable number of foreign students in *France*, for instance, is offset by the considerable number of national students, i.e. by the extensively developed facilities for higher education, having regard to national wealth.

TABLE 3. COUNTRIES WITH BALANCED PROPORTION OF FOREIGN STUDENTS AND NATIONAL ENROLMENT IN RELATION TO WEALTH 1958-59

COUNTRY	TOTAL FOREIGN STUDENTS TO TOTAL STUDENTS %	IN RELATION TO O.E.C.D. MEDIAN FOR 19 COUNTRIES 3.68 = 100	Ranking order	TOTAL NATIONAL STUDENTS TO POPULATION AGED 20-24 %	IN RELATION TO O.E.C.D. MEDIAN FOR 19 COUNTRIES 4.28 = 100	Ranking order	G.N.P. PER CAPITA $ 000 AT 1959 PRICES AND EXCHANGE RATES	IN RELATION TO O.E.C.D. MEDIAN $1,070 = 100	Ranking order
France	7.71	210	6	6.99	163	5	1.14	106	7
Canada	5.80	158	7	7.72	180	2	2.08	194	2
Belgium	4.78	130	8	7.29	170	3	1.27	118	5
Netherlands	3.68	100	10	4.28	100	10	0.87	81	11

Source: Annex I.

As for *Belgium* and *the Netherlands* (data for Luxembourg are not available), it should be borne in mind that these are important international trading nations and that there is a historical connection between trade and the demand for education from abroad. It might therefore be expected that foreign students will make increasing demands on higher education facilities in the Benelux countries.

Group C. COUNTRIES IN WHICH THE PROPORTION OF FOREIGN STUDENTS IS SMALL IN RELATION TO TOTAL CAPACITY AND NATIONAL WEALTH (Table 4)

It is obvious that in the case of the three Scandinavian countries the small proportion of foreign students is largely due to the absence of those factors which favour the flow of foreign students to most of the countries in Groups A and B. The Scandinavian countries have no ex-colonial connections nor traditional political ties with overseas territories; and the linguistic problem is undoubtedly a handicap to a flow of students from abroad.

The United States

In the United States, however, the small proportion of foreign students is due to a variety of reasons relating to the structure and distribution of education.

TABLE 4. COUNTRIES WITH LOW PROPORTION OF FOREIGN STUDENTS IN RELATION TO NATIONAL ENROLMENT AND WEALTH — 1958-59

COUNTRY	TOTAL FOREIGN STUDENTS TO TOTAL STUDENTS %	IN RELATION TO O.E.C.D. MEDIAN 3.68 = 100	Ranking order	TOTAL NATIONAL STUDENTS TO POPULATION AGED 20-24 %	IN RELATION TO O.E.C.D. MEDIAN 4.28 = 100	Ranking order	G.N.P. PER CAPITA $ 000 AT 1959 PRICES AND EXCHANGE RATES	IN RELATION TO O.E.C.D. MEDIAN $ 1,070 = 100	Ranking order
United States	1.45	39	17	29.2	682	1	2.68	250	1
Norway	2.38	65	13	3.70	86	12	1.14	106	8
Denmark	2.33	63	14	4.83	112	4	1.14	106	9
Sweden	3.33[1]	90[1]		4.92[1]	114[1]		1.43	133	

1. Secretariat estimates; UNESCO Data available for 1953-54 only; Sweden was not included in Annex I.
Source: Annex I.

The most important of these is the great difference in traditional attitudes towards higher education between the United States and the other countries of the West: a far larger percentage of American youth continues education beyond secondary school than is the case in Europe. Thus if the number of foreign students is related not to the total number of students but to the total population of age 20-24, the United States has a higher ratio of foreign students than, say, the United Kingdom. The differing conceptions of higher education are reflected in the nature of certain higher education facilities: liberal arts colleges and junior colleges, for instance, are considered as higher education institutions in the U.S.A. but would not be classified as such in most Western countries. This accounts to some extent for the much higher enrolment figures in U.S. higher education.

Another consideration which is of great importance in making comparisons is the distribution of foreign students in the U.S.A. Most of the institutions of higher education have very few foreign students or none at all. On the other hand, the dozen or so institutions which have the largest numbers of foreign students have a ratio of 6 per cent foreign students to total enrolment. More significantly, these same institutions show an average ratio of more than 13 per cent when foreign students at the post-graduate level are compared with total enrolments at post-graduate level. In certain departments of some post-graduate schools

—engineering, for example—the proportion of foreign students has been estimated to be as high as 50 per cent.

Thus the contribution of the U.S.A. in the field of higher education for foreign students is much more significant than would appear from the comparative figures. Nevertheless the United States authorities are fully aware of the desirability of providing facilities for a higher overall proportion of foreign students. But their ability to do so will depend in part on a better dispersion of foreign students. If about 40 per cent of them continue to come for post-graduate study, mainly in scientific and technical fields, better dispersion will not be easy to achieve.

III

THE FLOW OF FOREIGN SCIENCE STUDENTS [1]

Statistical data for foreign science students in 13 O.E.C.D. countries are given in Annex II. They show that science students in these countries make up 37 per cent of the total number of foreign students. For the United Kingdom (which is not included in Annex II) the proportion has been estimated at 39.5 per cent in 1958-59. If the figure of 37 per cent is applied to the total of 125,000 odd foreign students in all O.E.C.D. countries (excluding Sweden and Luxembourg), we arrive at a total of 46,000 odd foreign students in natural sciences, engineering and agriculture.

The United States was receiving something like 40 per cent of this total in 1958-59. Germany, Austria, France and the United Kingdom also received significant numbers (see Table 5).

TABLE 5. SCIENCE STUDENTS IN FIVE SELECTED COUNTRIES — 1958-59

	THOUSANDS	% OF TOTAL
United States	19.05	40.9
Germany (F.R.)	6.70	14.5
United Kingdom	4.30	9.2
Austria	3.70	8.0
France	3.10	6.7
Others (14 countries)	9.65	20.87
Estimated Total 19 O.E.C.D. countries	46.50	100.0

Source: Annex II and Secretariat estimates for U.K.

These figures emphasize the considerable demand for study in scientific subjects on the part of foreign students, though it would be interesting to know how this demand is changing in relation to demand for higher studies in general. If, as seems likely, the demand for science

---

1. Science students here include also students in engineering and agriculture.

studies is increasing, there would have to be not only a considerable increase of fellowships under existing or new schemes, but an orientation of these fellowships towards those scientific disciplines which are most needed and towards those geographic regions that are most in need of them.[1] This presupposes the establishment of clear and specific objectives.

As can be seen from Annex II, there are marked differences from country to country in the proportion of foreign students who study scientific disciplines. Unfortunately data are available only for some Member countries. These show that in Germany some 45 per cent, and in the United States some 40 per cent of foreign students are in science faculties, whereas in France the corresponding figure is 18 per cent. This difference is partly due to the difference in the methods of enrolment as between the United States and Germany, on the one hand, and France on the other.

---

1. The question of regional distribution is considered in the following chapter.

IV

GEOGRAPHICAL ORIGIN OF FOREIGN STUDENTS

While it is true that facilities for study abroad are an important element of the economic aid which the advanced countries should give to the less advanced countries, it must be recognized that a large increase in the flow of foreign students would create problems of absorption and even necessitate the creation of new institutions in the receiving countries. In fact, with existing capacity the limit may already have been reached. Some of the advanced countries are already facing problems of their own educational development, so that even the current flow of students from abroad places a strain on their educational resources. Any significant expansion in that flow may therefore depend largely on special measures and programmes decided at government level. In devising them, it should be borne in mind that enrolment figures convey only one aspect of the problem of educating foreign students; they tell nothing about the performance of these students in examinations, nor about the social and linguistic problems involved, nor about the balance of foreign students as between the sexes.

FLOWS WITHIN THE O.E.C.D. AREA

Annex III shows that approximately half of the foreign students in the O.E.C.D. countries come from the O.E.C.D. countries themselves, the other half coming from the less developed areas. Within the O.E.C.D. area three main currents may be distinguished. First, there is the transatlantic current—4,700 students from the United States and Canada in Europe, and 7,100 students from the European O.E.C.D. countries in the United States and Canada.[1] But this flow, though small in quantity, is immensely important qualitatively, because it includes a high proportion of post-graduates in science on whom technical discovery and innovation must to a large extent depend.

Second, there is the flow of post-graduates within the advanced countries of the European O.E.C.D. area, a flow which is also important

---

1. In 1958-59 there were also 5,439 Canadian students in the U.S.A. and 1,062 U.S. students in Canada.

qualitatively, but on which no data are at present available. It merits further study as a possible basis for policy action.

Third, there is the flow of students from Member countries with restricted entry to higher education to other Member countries where entry is easy. This is a major factor in determining the flow of undergraduates and was responsible, in 1958-59, for a high proportion of the 8,143 Greek and 2,294 Turkish students abroad, of the 5,527 German students in Austria, Switzerland and France, and for a large part of the flow from the United Kingdom to Ireland. These movements are an indication of the need for an expansion of higher education within the O.E.C.D. countries themselves.

Apart from these three currents within the O.E.C.D. area runs the current of the non-O.E.C.D. European students into the O.E.C.D. area. More than 5,000 of these students—a large number of them Hungarian refugees—went to European O.E.C.D. countries, and an unspecified but considerable number to North America. The flow of students between the O.E.C.D. area, on the one hand, and the Soviet Union and Eastern Europe, on the other, was on a small scale.

FLOWS INTO THE O.E.C.D. AREA FROM THE LESS DEVELOPED COUNTRIES

As is shown in Annex III, the flow of students from the underdeveloped areas has been mainly directed towards either countries which have had a colonial system or countries which have had extensive international trading connections. In the first category come the United Kingdom, France and the Netherlands, where foreign students from former or present colonial territories represented 60 per cent, 39 per cent and 32 per cent respectively of all their foreign students. In the second category Germany and the United States are the most important receiving countries. The United States is the major study area for students from Latin America, Asia and Australasia. Though the relevant statistical data are lacking, it seems probable that the United States has also been taking increasing numbers of students from the new African nations; it would seem, however, on the basis of information that is available, that students from Africa still tend to go mainly to European O.E.C.D. countries, particularly the United Kingdom[1] and France.

The other European countries, particularly those which are major receiving countries, such as Austria and Switzerland, take their foreign

---

1. For information concerning United Kingdom education of overseas students see: Cmd. 1308 March 1961, *Technical Assistance from the United Kingdom for Overseas Development*, pp. 20 et seq. Reference is made to a total figure of 47,500 "people from overseas receiving educational training of some sort, the great majority of them coming from less developed countries and following courses of one year or more... They account for about one in ten of the full-time students at United Kingdom universities and technical colleges and form a sizeable element in the teacher-training colleges" (see Annex I)... "Although educational programmes in the dependent territories have greatly expanded, the demand for higher education still far exceeds the supply. Consequently the numbers of students... have grown formidably in recent years."

students mainly from other European countries; but the German-speaking institutions in Austria, Germany and Switzerland also attract large numbers of students from the Middle East.

Outside the O.E.C.D. area Japan and the U.S.S.R. are the only important receiving countries. In Japan 93 per cent of all foreign students came from Asia, and in the U.S.S.R. rather more than half of the 12,500 foreign students came from Asian countries in 1956-57, the remainder coming from Eastern Europe.

FOREIGN SCIENCE STUDENTS

As regards foreign science students, their geographical origin is shown in Annexes IVa, IVb and IVc, which relate to natural sciences, engineering, and agriculture respectively. It would seem that the geographical pattern outlined above for the flow of foreign students as a whole also holds true for these three groups of science students. Thus in Austria, Belgium, Italy, Norway and Switzerland 70 per cent or more of foreign science students come from Europe, whereas in Germany, France, the United Kingdom and the United States[1] a relatively high proportion come from the underdeveloped areas. As already mentioned above, the high proportion of post-graduates among foreign science students in the United States is a feature of particular importance; the more brilliant students, even if they remain to work in the United States, constitute a reserve of talent on which their countries should be able to draw eventually.

Since the relevant data for the United Kingdom and the United States are lacking, it is not possible to say what proportion of students from the underdeveloped areas was studying scientific disciplines in these two countries. However, figures are available for African students in France and Germany, and these are shown in Table 6.

TABLE 6. TOTAL AFRICAN[1] STUDENTS AND AFRICAN SCIENCE STUDENTS IN FRANCE AND GERMANY (F.R.)

	TOTAL	TOTAL SCIENCE	% OF TOTAL	PER CENT OF TOTAL SCIENCE STUDENTS BY BRANCH OF STUDY		
				NATURAL SCIENCE	ENGINEERING	AGRICULTURE
France	3,327	687	20.6	66.6	20.9	12.5
Germany (F.R.)	302	79	26.2	32.9	48.1	19.0

1. Excluding UAR and Algeria.
Source: UNESCO "Study Abroad" and unpublished data in the UNESCO files.

---

1. For the United Kingdom and the U.S.A. the conclusion is based on information drawn from other sources.

The striking fact which emerges from this table is that the proportion of African students studying science in France and Germany was lower than that for other regions and for students in general. Moreover, the proportion studying agriculture was low in view of the importance attached to agriculture and the priority normally given to it in African economic development. Such facts emphasize that scientific and technical education should be given the highest priority.[1]

---

1. In this connection see "Investment in Education", The Report of the Commission on Post-School Certificate and Higher Education in Nigeria, Federal Ministry of Education, Lagos, 1960.

V

POLICY PROBLEMS

POLICY PROBLEMS IN THE RECEIVING COUNTRIES

It is obvious that, with the growing needs of the underdeveloped countries for qualified personnel and the inability of their educational systems to expand sufficiently rapidly, the flow of students to advanced countries will increase. This is likely to lead to serious problems for the receiving countries, for even the present flow of students is imposing a serious strain on the educational capacity of some countries. As the proportion of national capacity devoted to foreign students varies within very wide limits from country to country (from 31.98 per cent in Austria to 0.40 per cent in Yugoslavia), it may become a matter of common interest to examine the extent to which countries which, for historical reasons, have not yet participated significantly in this form of economic aid to underdeveloped countries might play a bigger part than they have done hitherto.

Another important consideration for all the countries involved is a smoother assimilation of the greater numbers of students from underdeveloped areas. Some special arrangements for this purpose are already in force in a number of O.E.C.D. countries and others are under consideration, and it would no doubt be useful to examine the relative success of these measures. In this context, it may be interesting to note that, in 1960-61, the Soviet Union started a special "university for international friendship" in Moscow, in addition to its normal facilities for foreign students. According to reports, some 500 students from South America, Africa and Southern Asia were enrolled in the autumn of 1960, and the enrolment is expected to increase to three or four thousand students as the faculties of engineering, agriculture, medicine, mathematics and science, economics and law, history and languages are progressively built up. Whilst this may not be a model for the O.E.C.D. countries to follow, there is no doubt that special measures based on a clear policy will be necessary.

Given the difficulties of assimilating students from different cultural and linguistic backgrounds, the problem arises of the balance to be struck between providing educational facilities for students from underdeveloped countries in the advanced countries and building up the educational systems of the underdeveloped countries by providing them with necessary finance and teachers. United States policy, for instance, seems more likely to favour the latter course, at least as far as undergraduate study is concerned. But the two courses are related to each other and should be examined together, though a closer examination of this problem would be beyond the scope of this paper.

One particular aspect of this problem arises in connection with students from the underdeveloped countries who do not return home and who, in effect, constitute a drainage of talent and skill from their own countries. This is a matter which is preoccupying a number of underdeveloped countries, particularly India and Iran. But it also raises policy issues for the advanced countries, not only with reference to the balance to be struck between the two courses mentioned above, but also with regard to the appropriateness of the education provided. They may need to consider whether fellowship programmes could not be more closely geared to the actual pattern of growth in the underdeveloped areas, so as to avoid the acquisition by foreign students of qualifications which are marginal or irrelevant to the needs of their countries.

POLICY PROBLEMS IN THE DEVELOPING COUNTRIES

But study abroad also raises policy problems for the sending countries.

It may be argued that any large-scale outflow of students from a country in process of development for the purpose of obtaining first degrees (as opposed to post-graduate studies) is undesirable because the sending country, by failing fully to mobilize home demand for higher education, deprives itself of important resources for building up the infrastructure of its own higher education (professors, assistants, research capacity, buildings and equipment). This argument does not apply, of course, to specific "crash programmes", such as those for providing science teachers for secondary schools and teachers for technical subjects.

Another argument against study abroad at undergraduate level is that already mentioned in connection with students who, after graduation, do not return home. But they may to some extent be considered as a hidden reserve which, by adequate inducements, may be attracted back to the country of origin.

On the other hand, there can hardly be any argument against study abroad when local facilities are fully employed and when their possibilities of expansion are limited.

Clearly, a major effort needs to be made to develop education in Africa, Latin America and Asia. This task will tax the energies of these newly developing countries to the utmost. The advanced countries, by providing special international schemes to train vitally needed teachers and specialists at secondary, technical and higher level, can make an invaluable contribution to the economic development of these underprivileged countries.

ANNEXES

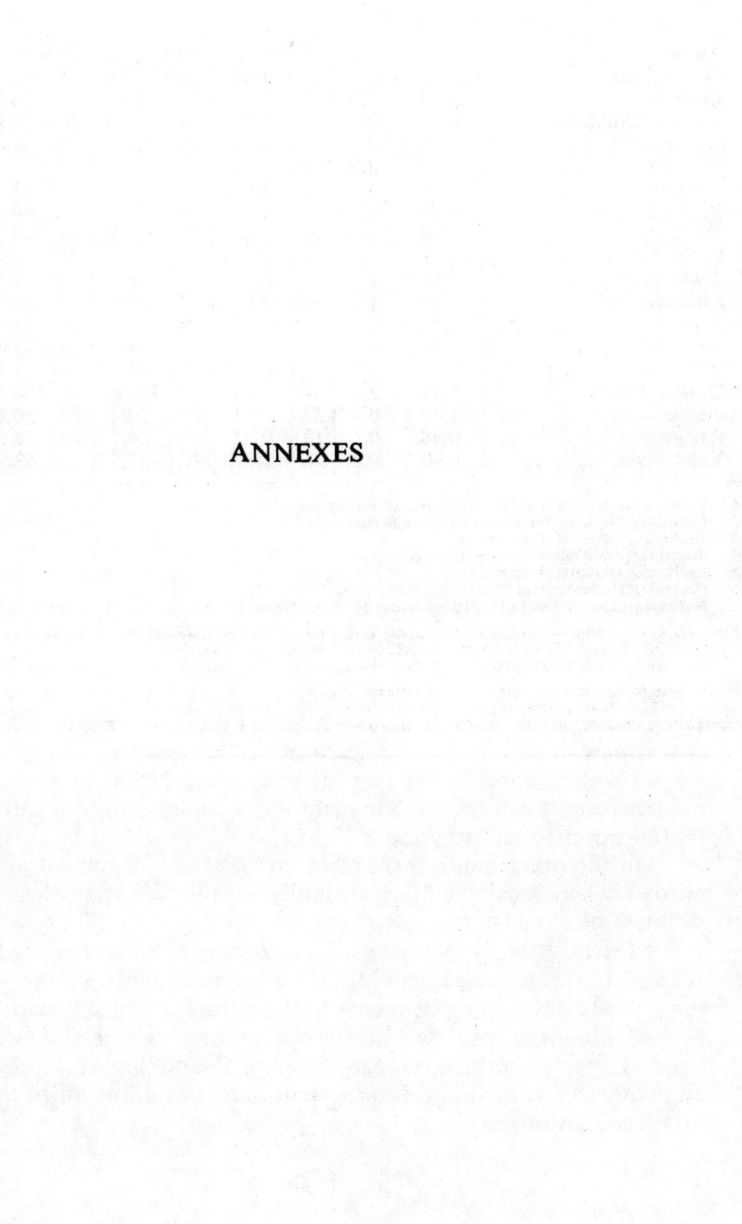

Annex I

FOREIGN STUDENTS IN 1958-59

	COUNTRY OF STUDY	FOREIGN STUDENTS TO TOTAL STUDENTS %	FOREIGN STUDENTS TO TOTAL POPULATION °/₀₀₀	Ranking order	G.N.P. PER CAPITA $ '000 AT 1959 PRICES AND EXCHANGE RATES	Ranking order	NATIONAL STUDENTS TO TOTAL POPULATION °/₀₀₀	Ranking order	TOTAL STUDENTS TO TOTAL POPULATION °/₀₀₀	Ranking order	TOTAL FOREIGN STUDENTS THOUSANDS	Ranking order
1.	Austria[1]	31.98	13.5	*1*	0.69	*12*	28.8	*12*	42.4	*8*	9.5	*5*
2.	Switzerland[1]	31.63	11.5	*2*	1.42	*4*	24.8	*15*	36.3	*10*	6.0	*6*
3.	Ireland	19.89	6.0	*3*	0.60	*13*	24.4	*16*	30.4	*14*	1.7	*12*
4.	United Kingdom	10.68	2.1	*9*	1.25	*6*	17.8	*19*	19.9	*18*	11.0	*4*
5.	Germany[1,2]	9.21	2.9	*6*	1.07	*10*	28.5	*13*	31.4	*12*	15.1	*3*
6.	France[4]	7.71	3.9	*4*	1.14	*7*	46.6	*5*	50.5	*4*	17.5	*2*
7.	Canada	5.80	3.1	*5*	2.08	*2*	50.6	*3*	53.7	*2*	5.4	*7*
8.	Belgium[1]	4.78	2.4	*8*	1.27	*5*	47.0	*4*	49.4	*5*	2.1	*10*
9.	Turkey	4.14	0.8	*13*	0.18	*19*	18.2	*18*	19.0	*19*	2.0	*11*
10.	Netherlands[1]	3.68	1.1	*11*	0.87	*11*	30.0	*11*	31.1	*13*	1.3[5]	*13*
11.	Spain	2.60	1.0	*12*	0.33	*17*	36.5	*8*	37.5	*9*	2.9	*8*
12.	Iceland	2.40	1.1	*10*	2.01	*3*	43.3	*7*	44.4	*7*	0.02	*19*
13.	Norway	2.38	0.5	*15*	1.14	*9*	20.8	*17*	21.3	*17*	0.2	*17*
14.	Denmark	1.61	0.7	*14*	1.14	*8*	44.6	*6*	45.4	*6*	0.3	*16*
15.	Italy	1.52	0.5	*16*	0.53	*14*	33.0[3]	*9*	33.5[3]	*11*	2.5	*9*
16.	United States	1.45	2.7	*7*	2.68	*1*	181.6	*1*	184.3	*1*	47.2[7]	*1*
17.	Greece	1.42	0.4	*17*	0.34	*16*	30.4	*10*	30.8	*16*	0.4	*15*
18.	Portugal[1]	0.48	0.1	*19*	0.23	*18*	26.7	*14*	26.8	*15*	0.1[6]	*18*
19.	Yugoslavia	0.40	0.2	*18*	0.37	*15*	53.3	*2*	53.5	*3*	0.4	*14*

1. Foreign students classified according to nationality.
2. Including the Saar but excluding West Berlin.
3. Excluding "studenti fuori corso".
4. Students from Algeria are not included.
5. Excluding students from Surinam.
6. Excluding students from Portuguese territories.
7. Including 125 students in Puerto Rico and 19 in the Canal Zone.

Sources: On population: O.E.E.C. Statistical Bulletin — General Statistics No. 5, September 1959.
On students: UNESCO "Study Abroad" Vol. XII — 1960-1961.
On gross national product: Data prepared by the National Accounts Division of the O.E.C.D.

NOTE: The Icelandic exchange rate was adjusted in 1960 from 16.3 Icelandic crowns = 1 $ U.S. to 38.0 Icelandic crowns = 1 $ U.S. If this latter rate had been prevailing in 1959, Iceland would have been eleventh out of the nineteen countries instead of third, and the gross national product per capita $ 860 instead of $ 2010.

Annex II

FOREIGN SCIENCE STUDENTS IN 1958-1959

COUNTRY OF STUDY	FOREIGN SCIENCE STUDENTS TO TOTAL SCIENCE STUDENTS %	FOREIGN SCIENCE STUDENTS TO TOTAL FOREIGN STUDENTS %	TOTAL SCIENCE STUDENTS TO TOTAL STUDENTS %	FOREIGN SCIENCE STUDENTS TO TOTAL STUDENTS %	TOTAL FOREIGN SCIENCE STUDENTS (THOUSANDS)
Austria[1]	35.77	38.97	34.87	12.46	3.7
Switzerland[1]	27.40	28.05	32.38	8.87	1.7
Germany[1,2]	11.56	44.03	35.09	4.05	6.7
Turkey	7.08	39.32	22.98	1.62	0.8
Belgium[1]	4.98	30.59	29.39	1.46	0.7
France[3]	3.84	17.56	35.23	1.35	3.1
Netherlands[1]	3.47	34.54	36.64	1.27	0.5[5]
Italy[4]	2.83	46.86	25.16	0.71	1.2
Norway	2.32	38.89	39.89	0.92	0.07
Greece	1.89	32.50	24.45	0.46	0.12
Portugal[1]	0.49	25.64	25.22	0.12	0.03[6]
Yugoslavia	0.43	29.47	27.55	0.12	0.12
U.S.A.	..	40.32	..	0.59	19.05
Japan	0.76	27.84	21.68	0.16	1.05

1. Foreign students classified according to nationality.
2. Including the Saar but excluding West Berlin.
3. Students originating from Algeria are not included.
4. Excluding "studenti fuori corso".
5. Excluding students from Surinam.
6. Excluding students from Portuguese territories.

Source: Country replies to UNESCO Questionnaire ST/Q/42 — "Questionnaire on Enrolment in Higher Education 1958-59". These data have not been published in this form.

NOTE. According to an estimate, made by UNESCO, 39.5 per cent of all foreign students, i.e. 4,300 students, in the United Kingdom in 1958-59 were studying science.

Annex III. FOREIGN STUDENTS

COUNTRY OF STUDY	TOTAL O.E.C.D.[1]	%	OTHER EUROPE	%	NORTH AMERICA	%	LATIN AMERICA[2]	%
Austria[4]	6,113	64.12	1,154[6]	12.10	454	4.76	87	0.91
Belgium[4]	1,017	47.46	274	12.79	291	13.58	56	2.61
Denmark	226	68.28	41	12.39	36	10.88	..	..
France[8]	5,709	32.70	988	5.66	1,612	9.23	664	3.80
Germany[7]	6,421	42.48	1,170[6]	7.74	1,193	7.89	494	3.27
Greece	72	20.00	155	43.06	5	1.39	..	..
Iceland	10	55.56	1	5.55	2	11.11	..	..
Ireland	1,063	61.59	..		..		..	
Italy[8]	1,439	57.58	115	4.60	427	17.09	178	7.12
Luxembourg	—		—		—		—	
Netherlands[4]	282	21.79	146	11.28	167	12.91	—	—
Norway	39	21.67	101	56.11	27	15.00	—	—
Portugal[4]	—		—		—		—	
Spain[10]	593	18.83	—		704	22.36	1,301	41.31
Sweden	..	..	..		..		..	..
Switzerland[4]	3,200	53.59	578	9.68	891	14.92	158	2.65
Turkey	—		—		—		—	
United Kingdom	1,162	10.52	348[5]	3.15	1,373	12.43	135	1.22
Canada	1,028	19.13	94	1.74	1,678	31.22	1,062	19.76
United States	3,714	7.86	—		5,432	11.50	5,018	10.62
Yugoslavia	184	46.35	99	24.94	9	2.27	—	
Total	32,272	26.06	5,264[6]	4.25	14,301	11.55	9,153	7.39
U.S.S.R.[14]	20	0.16	5,966	47.48	—		—	
Japan	—		—		153	4.04	15	0.40

1. Including Yugoslavia.
2. Mexico, Central America and South America.
3. Iran, Iraq, Pakistan, Israel, Jordan, Egypt and Syria.
4. Foreign students classified according to nationality.
5. Students originating from Algeria are not included.
6. Including 1078 Hungarian refugees in Austria, 851 in Germany, 291 in the United Kingdom. Other countries do not specify.
7. Including the Saar and excluding West Berlin.
8. Excluding "studenti fuori corso".
9. Excluding students originating from Portuguese territories (1050 in 1954-55).
10. For 1955-56.

BY AREA OF ORIGIN, 1958-59

MIDDLE EAST[a]	%	AFRICA	%	ASIA	%	AUSTRALASIA	%	OTHERS	%	TOTAL	%
1,373	14.40	34	0.36	76	0.80	11	0.12	232	2.43	9,534	100
152	7.09	103	4.81	103	4.81	23	1.07	124	5.78	2,143	100
..		..		..		..		28	8.45	331	100
1,696	9.72	3,327[5]	19.06	2,121	12.15	392	2.25	947	5.43	17,456	100
4,223	27.94	302	2.00	872	5.77	15	0.10	425	2.81	15,115	100
106	29.44	5	1.39	3	0.83	—		14	3.89	360	100
..		..		1	5.55	1	5.55	3	16.68	18	100
..		..		..		..		663	38.41	1,726	100
149	5.96	102	4.08	63	2.52	7	0.28	19	0.77	2,499	100
—		—		—		—		—		—	
33	2.55	47	3.63	22	1.70	499	38.56	98	7.58	1,294	100
1	0.56	—		—		—		12	6.66	180	100
—		—		—		—		—		[117][9*]	
—		57	1.81	—		47	1.49	447	14.20	3,149	100
n.a.		n.a.		n.a.		n.a.		n.a.		n.a.	
739	12.38	133	2.23	171	2.86	27	0.45	74	1.24	5,971	100
—		—		—		—		—		[2,037]*	
1,371	12.41	3,837[11]	34.73	2,280	20.64	536	4.85	5	0.05	11,047	100
105	1.95	157	2.92	940	17.49	72	1.34	238	4.45	5,374	100
2,836	6.00	see note[12]		12,674	26.83	1,805	3.82	15,766[12]	33.37	47,245[13]	100
—		17	4.28	18	4.53	—		70	17.63	397	100
2,784	10.32	8,121	6.56	19,344	15.62	3,435	2.77	19,165	15.48	123,839*	100
17	0.14	—		6,546	52.10	8	0.06	8	0.06	12,565	100
8	0.21	—		3,514	92.72	35	0.92	65		3,790	100

11. 2959 students originating from United Kingdom territories and not differentiated by country of origin have been included in this table with students from Africa.
12. The United States gave a detailed reply only for countries sending more than 700 students to American universities.
13. Including 125 students in Puerto Rico and 19 in the Canal Zone.
14. For 1956-57.

* Figures in square brackets are not included in the total.

Sources: Country replies to UNESCO Questionnaire ST/Q/42 — "Questionnaire on Enrolment in Higher Education 1958-59".
For United Kingdom, data from Association of Universities of British Commonwealth.

Annex IVa. FOREIGN STUDENTS BY AREA

COUNTRY OF STUDY	TOTAL O.E.C.D.[1]	%	OTHER EUROPE	%	NORTH AMERICA	%	LATIN AMERICA[2]	%
Austria[4]	315	74.29	55[5]	12.97	12	2.83	1	0.24
Belgium[4]	54	41.54	39	30.00	1	0.77	1	0.77
Denmark[6]								
France	477	19.99	225	9.43	25	1.05	60	2.51
Germany[8]	604	37.28	160[5]	9.88	161	9.94	94	5.80
Greece	9	50.00	4	22.22	—		—	
Iceland	—		—		—		—	
Ireland	—		—		—		—	
Italy[9]	337	75.56	21	4.71	10	2.24	46	10.31
Luxembourg	—		—		—		—	
Netherlands[4]	23	28.05	15	18.29	9	10.98		
Norway	4	57.14	3	42.86	—		—	
Portugal[4]	—		—		—		—	
Spain[10]	23	32.39	—		10	14.08	17	23.94
Sweden	—		—		—		—	
Switzerland[4]	499	62.61	110	13.80	10	2.38	39	4.89
Turkey								
United Kingdom								
Canada	—		—		—		—	
United States	542	8.05	—		754	11.19	424	6.29
Yugoslavia	9	50.00	2	11.11				
Total	2,896	22.74	634[5]	4.98	1,001	7.86	682	5.35
U.S.S.R.[13]	—		—		—		—	
Japan	—		—		1	0.17	2	0.34

1. Including Yugoslavia.
2. Mexico, Central America and South America.
3. Iran, Iraq, Pakistan, Israel, Jordan, Egypt and Syria.
4. Students classified according to nationality.
5. Including 54 Hungarian refugees in Austria and 119 in Germany; other countries do not specify.
6. Data given by university and not by field of study.
7. Students originating from Algeria are not included.

* Figures in square brackets are estimates not included in the total.

OF ORIGIN IN NATURAL SCIENCES — 1958-59

MIDDLE EAST[8]	%	AFRICA	%	ASIA	%	AUSTRALASIA	%	OTHERS	%	TOTAL	%
23	5.42	2	0.47	6	1.42	—	—	10	2.36	424	100
8	6.15	3	2.31	5	3.85	2	1.54	17	13.07	130	100
346	14.50	458[7]	19.20	732	30.68	1	0.04	62	2.60	2,386	100
400	24.69	26	1.60	137	8.46	1	0.06	37	2.29	1,620	100
5	27.78	—	—	—	—	—	—	—	—	18	100
—	—	—	—	—	—	—	—	—	—	—	
15	3.36	13	2.91	3	0.67	—	—	1	0.24	446	100
—	—	—	—	—	—	—	—	—	—	—	
2	2.44	4	4.88	2	2.44	16	19.51	11	13.41	82	100
—	—	—	—	—	—	—	—	—	—	7	100
—	—	—	—	—	—	—	—	—	—	[19][11]*	
—	—	3	4.23	—	—	1	1.41	17	23.95	71	100
—	—	—	—	—	—	—	—	—	—	—	
91	11.42	11	1.38	23	2.89	5	0.63	—	—	797	100
										[188]*	
										[1,547]*	
—	—	—	—	—	—	—	—	—	—	—	
357	5.30	—	—	2,533	37.60	159	2.36	1,968[12]	29.21	6,737	100
								7	38.89	18	100
1,247	89.79	520	4.08	3,441	27.02	185	1.45	2,130	16.73	12,736*	100
—	—	—	—	—	—	—	—	—	—	—	
2	0.34	—	—	560	96.22	8	1.37	9	1.56	582	100

8. Including the Saar and excluding West Berlin.
9. Excluding "studenti fuori corso".
10. For 1955-56.
11. Excluding students originating from Portuguese territories.
12. The United States gave a detailed reply only for countries sending more than 700 students to American institutions of higher education.
13. No data for this field of study.

Source: Country replies to UNESCO Questionnaire ST/Q/42 — "Questionnaire on Enrolment in Higher Education 1958-59".

Annex IVb. FOREIGN STUDENTS BY AREA

COUNTRY OF STUDY	TOTAL O.E.C.D.[1]	%	OTHER EUROPE	%	NORTH AMERICA	%	LATIN AMERICA[2]	%
Austria[4]	2,209	72.78	282[5]	9.29	10	0.33	11	0.36
Belgium[4]	281	65.50	59	13.75	2	0.47	6	1.40
Denmark	21	75.00	3	10.71	1	3.57		
France	227	38.41	62	10.49	4	0.68	19	3.21
Germany[7]	2,518	55.22	370[6]	8.11	36	0.79	152	3.33
Greece	16	16.33	41	41.84				
Iceland	—		—		—		—	
Ireland	—		—		—		—	
Italy[8]	338	70.27	19	3.95	9	1.87	34	7.07
Luxembourg	—		—		—		—	
Netherlands[4]	49	15.26	55	17.13	9	2.80	—	
Norway	2	18.18	9	81.82				
Portugal[4]	—		—		—		—	
Spain[10]	5	13.16			1	2.63	13	34.21
Sweden	—		—		—		—	
Switzerland[4]	536	63.80	111	13.21	3	0.36	22	2.62
Turkey	—		—		—		—	
United Kingdom	—		—		—		—	
Canada	—		—		—		—	
United States	853	7.99	—		911	8.53	1,522	14.25
Yugoslavia	39	52.70	15	20.27	3	4.05	—	
Total	7,094	33.48	1,026[6]	4.84	989	4.68	1,779	8.40
U.S.S.R.[12]	—		2,892[1]	39.94[1]	—		—	
Japan	—		—		2	0.62	1	0.31

1. Including Yugoslavia.
2. Mexico, Central America and South America.
3. Iran, Iraq, Pakistan, Israel, Jordan, Egypt and Syria.
4. Foreign students classified according to nationality.
5. Students originating from Algeria are not included.
6. Including 265 Hungarian refugees in Austria and 271 in Germany; other countries do not specify.
7. Including the Saar and excluding West Berlin.
8. Excluding "studenti fuori corso".

OF ORIGIN IN ENGINEERING — 1958-59

MIDDLE EAST[9]		AFRICA		ASIA		AUSTRALASIA		OTHERS		TOTAL	
	%		%		%		%		%		%
436	14.37	6	0.20	18	0.59	2	0.07	61	2.01	3,035	100
46	10.72	6	1.40	5	1.17	1	0.23	23	5.36	429	100
								3	10.72	28	100
90	15.23	144[5]	24.37	29	4.91			16	2.70	591	100
1,166	25.57	38	0.83	224	4.91	1	0.02	55	1.22	4,560	100
28	28.57	—		—		—		13	13.26	98	100
—		—		—		2		—		—	
69	14.35	4	0.83	4	0.83	—	0.41	2	0.42	481	100
11	3.43	1	0.31	7	2.18	161	50.16	28	8.73	321	100
—		—		—		—		—		11	100
—		—		—		—		—		[10][9*]	
—		—		—		—		19	50.00	38	100
82	9.76	35	4.17	32	3.81	4	0.48	15	1.79	840	100
—		—		—		—		—		[336]*	
—		—		—		—		—		[2,508]*	
1,064	9.96	—		2,818	26.38	128	1.20	3,386[11]	31.69	10,682	100
—		2	2.70	8	10.81	—		7	9.47	74	100
2,992	14.12	236	1.11	3,145	14.84	299	1.41	3,628	17.12	21,188*	100
7	0.10	—		4,314	59.58	—		28	0.38	7,241	100
3	0.93	—		303	94.39	2	0.62	10	3.13	321	100

9. Excluding students originating from Portuguese territories.
10. For 1955-56.
11. The United States gave a detailed reply only for countries sending more than 700 students to American Institutions of higher education.
12. For 1956-57.

* Figures in square brackets are not included in the total.

Source: Country replies to UNESCO Questionnaire ST/Q/42 — "Questionnaire on Enrolment in Higher Education 1958-59".

Annex IVc. FOREIGN STUDENTS BY AREA

COUNTRY OF STUDY	TOTAL O.E.C.D.[1]	%	OTHER EUROPE	%	NORTH AMERICA	%	LATIN AMERICA[2]	%
Austria[4]	169	66.02	47[6]	18.36	2	0.78	1	0.39
Belgium[4]	34	35.42	24	25.00	—		1	1.04
Denmark	24	63.16	9	23.68	—		—	
France	14	10.00	14	10.00	1	0.71	7	5.00
Germany[7]	129	27.16	73[6]	15.37	11	2.32	16	3.37
Greece	—		—		—		—	
Iceland	—		—		—		—	
Ireland	—		—		—		—	
Italy[8]	188	89.52	4	1.90	1	0.48	2	0.95
Luxembourg	—		—					
Netherlands[4]	4	9.09	12	27.27	—		—	
Norway	4	7.69	46	88.46	—		—	
Portugal[4]	—		—					
Spain[10]	2	28.57	—		—		4	57.14
Sweden	—		—				—	
Switzerland	8	16.33	31	63.27	—		—	
Turkey	—		—					
United Kingdom	—		—		—			
Canada	—				—		—	
United States	89	5.45	—		76	4.66	217	13.30
Yugoslavia	12	48.00	9	36.00	—		—	
Total	677	22.39	269[6]	8.90	91	3.01	248	8.20
U.S.S.R.[12]	—		654	58.97	—		—	
Japan	—		—		—		1	0.66

1. Including Yugoslavia.
2. Mexico, Central America and South America.
3. Iran, Iraq, Pakistan, Israel, Jordan, Egypt and Syria.
4. Students classified according to nationality.
5. Students originating from Algeria are not included.
6. Including 46 Hungarian refugees in Austria and 63 in Germany; other countries do not specify.
7. Including the Saar and excluding West Berlin.
8. Excluding "studenti fuori corso".

OF ORIGIN IN AGRICULTURE — 1958-59

MIDDLE EAST[a]		AFRICA		ASIA		AUSTRALASIA		OTHERS		TOTAL	
	%		%		%		%		%		%
32	12.50	—		—		—		5	1.95	256	100
5	5.21	6	6.55	21	21.88	1	1.04	4	4.16	96	100
—		—		—				5	13.16	38	100
14	10.00	85[5]	60.71	5	3.58			—		140	100
204	42.95	15	3.16	17	3.58	—		10	2.09	475	100
—		—		—		—		—		[1]*	
—		—		—		—		—		—	
6	2.86	8	3.81	1	0.48	—		—		210	100
—		—		—		—		—		—	
12	27.27	—		4	9.09	7	15.91	5	11.37	44	100
1	1.92	—		—		—		1	1.93	52	100
—		—		—		—		—		[1][9]*	
—		1	14.29	—		—		—		7	100
—		—		—		—		—		—	
9	18.37	—		—		—		1	2.03	49	100
—		—		—		—		—		[279]*	
—		—		—		—		—		[321]*	
196	12.01	—		324	19.85	40	2.45	690[11]	42.28	1,632	100
—		—		1	4.00	—		3	12.00	25	100
479	15.84	115	3.80	373	12.33	48	1.59	724	23.94	3,024*	100
—		—		455	41.03	—		—		1,109	100
		—		140	92.11	7	4.61	4	2.62	152	100

9. Excluding students originating from Portuguese territories.
10. For 1955-56.
11. The United States gave a detailed reply only for countries sending more than 700 students to American institutions of higher education.
12. For 1956-57.

* Figures in square brackets are not included in the total.

Source: Country replies, to UNESCO Questionnaire ST/Q/42 — "Questionnaire on Enrolment in Higher Education 1958-59".

DISCUSSION

Chairman: Mr. COOMBS (U.S.A.)

After a brief introduction by Mr. GASS and Mr. LYONS, the authors of the O.E.C.D. Secretariat report, the *Chairman* opened the discussion by suggesting that it should be broadened so as to include the question of providing university teachers for the underdeveloped countries until such time as they can provide adequate personnel of their own. He thought that in some countries the sending out of teachers was a more disruptive factor in the higher education system than the receiving of foreign students. This was the case in the U.S.A., whose effort could therefore not be measured by any one index such as enrolment figures for foreign students.

FOREIGN STUDENTS IN THE UNITED STATES: TWO-THIRDS FROM THE UNDERDEVELOPED AREAS

He also pointed out that in the U.S.A. in recent years the proportion of foreign students coming from Europe and Canada has been diminishing substantially, while that of students from Asia, Africa and Latin America, but especially from Asia and Africa, has been increasing significantly, so that today students from underdeveloped areas make up two-thirds of all foreign students. But there is something haphazard about the composition of this inflow: certain African countries have, relative to their size, far more students in the U.S.A. than other African countries, and no plan or assessment seems to have been made in this respect by either the sending or the receiving countries. If the sending countries could give a clearer indication of their needs to the receiving countries and at the same time exercise some guiding influence over their own students, a much better job could be done by the receiving countries.

PURPOSE OF TRAINING ABROAD

Mr. PANT (Panel of Experts) said he wished to make some points as one coming from the consuming end. From India's experience it was clear that purposeful planning for higher education abroad was an essential condition for making the best use of these facilities. Students who had gone abroad without any clear idea of what they would do on their return, or those who had not been well guided and acquired qualifications inappropriate to India's current needs, only found themselves idle and frustrated on their return. Apart from these raw students, more partly qualified students should go abroad for further study.

TRAINING ON THE JOB—ATTITUDE OF TRADE UNIONS

Another important problem arises in connection with key personnel for industry and public utilities who need to be trained not in universities and classrooms, but mainly on the job in actual factories or public utilities. There is less willingness to give this kind of practical training than to give formal education, and if trade unions could be prevailed upon to remove obstacles to such training they could make a major contribution to the economic progress of underdeveloped countries.

EXPERTS' VERSUS LOCAL SALARIES

The last point raised by the speaker was the problem posed by the disparity between the salaries of experts from abroad and those of local people doing similar or higher jobs. This creates an undercurrent of dissatisfaction and frustration which could largely be removed if a system were devised whereby foreign experts were paid the normal local salary on the spot, the balance being credited to them in their home country. This would enable the foreign expert to identify himself more closely with the setting in which he works, while helping to keep local salaries and incentives within reasonable bounds. The African system of incentives and salaries has been utterly distorted by being exposed to the high salary levels of neighbouring countries.

Mr. ERDER (Turkey) called attention to two points. The first concerns the setting up of international institutions for whole regions, such as the Middle East Technical University set up in co-operation with the United Nations in Turkey and teaching in English with Turkish and foreign professors. This is a formula worth studying, especially in view of the advantage it presents in that students coming from a similar social environment adjust more easily than they would do in the advanced countries. It would also contribute to easing the problem of the supply of professors.

DRAINAGE OF SKILLS—A REAL DANGER

The second problem mentioned by the speaker was the drainage of skills from the sending countries by the receiving countries. Of Turkey's 9,000 doctors, 2,000 have stayed on in the U.S.A. after training there, notwithstanding immigration regulations, and there are also many engineers in the same case, especially the most competent engineers who constitute a very valuable source of manpower. The problem is a difficult one, because people cannot be forced to live in their own country, but it calls for serious consideration.

Mr. BURCKHARDT (Switzerland), referring to the remark in the O.E.C.D. Secretariat paper "Study Abroad" that Switzerland may not be spending enough for its own students, drew attention to the fact that Switzerland has many high-level professional schools which are not counted as institutes of higher education. As a neutral, Switzerland was fully conscious of its responsibility towards students from underdeveloped countries and recently passed a law creating scholarships for them. But he thought the American Medical Association could help by abolishing or liberalizing the closed shop system in American medical colleges and thus relieve Switzerland of some of the massive influx of beginners in medicine who could just as well study in the U.S.A. The Office for Technical Co-operation in Berne was especially concerned with the welfare of foreign students and there was likely to be some rapid development in this direction.

SCANDINAVIAN ASSISTANCE—A SPECIAL CASE

Mr. LÖWBEER (Sweden) asked whether smaller European countries, particularly the Scandinavian countries where language was a barrier to any large inflow of foreign students, would not do better by contributing experts and finance for the development of educational facilities in the underdeveloped areas rather than trying to take in more foreign students.

Mr. FRIIS (Denmark) hoped that some kind of conclusion on this point would be forthcoming from the experts.

Professor TINBERGEN (Panel of Experts) thought that, for linguistic reasons, these countries could not do as much as the English or French-speaking countries. Yet they could do some useful things for three reasons. The first is that they are less exposed to suspicion and criticism by former colonial territories; the second, that they sometimes have educational "specialities" to offer, such as hydraulics in the Netherlands; and the third, that they are often cheaper than the larger countries, particularly in respect of teachers whom they could send out in larger numbers.

EARNING WHILE YOU LEARN IN AMERICA

Professor Arthur LEWIS (Panel of Experts) thought that the smaller European countries could put more emphasis on taking foreign students, but the main emphasis should be on training people to send out to the underdeveloped countries. In the larger countries the number of foreign students wanting to enter is likely to be greater than is desirable from the points of view of both the receiving and the sending country. Therefore the main contribution of the larger countries should be in helping to expand educational facilities in the underdeveloped countries themselves. But the fact must be faced that one of the reasons why people want to go to study in the developed countries, especially in North America, is the possibility of working and studying at the same time, thereby paying their way through college. And this attraction would remain, however large the expansion of facilities in the underdeveloped countries.

Here the *Chairman* interposed to suggest that, in view of the interest of the discussion as it had developed, the Secretariat might consider publishing a record of it.

Continuing, Professor LEWIS said that one of the reasons why it was not desirable to send so many students to the advanced countries was that mentioned by Mr. Erder, i.e. that so few of them return. He pointed to the great contribution which Jamaica was making to the economy of the United States by sending large numbers of people to study engineering and medecine, and who never return again. Therefore the United States could give more effective assistance by helping Jamaica to expand her own educational facilities, than by taking in Jamaican students though, in answer to a question by the *Chairman*, he said he did not suggest establishing a tariff barrier on the receipt of foreign students.

The *Chairman* pointed out that the U.S. Government exercises very little control over the inflow of foreign students, 90 per cent of whom arrive outside the scope of any government programme.

IMMIGRATION POLICIES—NEED FOR RE-CONSIDERATION

Professor EDDING (Panel of Experts) drew attention, in this connection, to a paper read by Brinley Thomas at the International Population Conference in New-York in September, 1961, the main theme of which was that the richer countries continue to drain off a large part of highly-skilled manpower from the poorer countries merely by maintaining their traditional immigration regulations. There should be a re-consideration of this immigration policy by the richer countries. But in this paper it is also pointed out that the tendency of students to remain in the receiving country is in fact a continuation of a historical trend—the migration from the poorer to the richer countries. The gap between the poor and the rich countries is therefore bound to widen unless we find some way of preventing students from poor countries staying on in the richer countries after terminating their studies. This whole problem certainly needs to be studied more closely.

CROSS-FERTILIZATION AND ADAPTATION TO A NEW ENVIRONMENT

Mr. MCMURRIN (U.S.A.) thought that the question of whether the small European countries should receive more foreign students was not just an economic question, but one which should be seen in the context of cross-fertilization of culture through the exchange of students, teachers and scholars.

M. DARIMONT (Belgium) thought that the contribution of each receiving country should be related to its own special circumstances.

Belgium has made a great effort in helping students from Asia and Africa to adapt themselves to their new environment and has achieved considerable success in this respect, mainly by placing them in families, where they can learn the language and share in the life of the community.

This completed the discussion of the Secretariat's report.

OECD SALES AGENTS
DÉPOSITAIRES DES PUBLICATIONS DE L'OCDE

ARGENTINA - ARGENTINE
Editorial Sudamericana S.A.,
Alsina 500, BUENOS AIRES.

AUSTRALIA - AUSTRALIE
B.C.N. Agencies Pty, Ltd.,
62 Wellington Parade, East MELBOURNE, C.2.

AUSTRIA - AUTRICHE
Gerold & Co., Graben 31, WIEN 1.
Sub-Agent : GRAZ : Buchhandlung Jos. A. Kienreich, Sackstrasse 6.

BELGIUM - BELGIQUE
N.V. Standaard-Boekhandel,
Huidevettersstraat 57, ANVERS.
BRUXELLES : Librairie des Sciences (R. Stoops), 76-78, Coudenberg.

BRAZIL - BRÉSIL
Livraria Agir Editôra,
Rua Mexico 98-B, RIO DE JANEIRO.

CANADA
Queen's Printer - Imprimeur de la Reine,
OTTAWA.
Prepayment of all orders required.
Les commandes sont payables d'avance.

DENMARK - DANEMARK
Munksgaard Boghandel, Ltd., Nörregade 6,
KOBENHAVN K.

FINLAND - FINLANDE
Akateeminen Kirjakauppa, Keskuskatu 2,
HELSINKI.

FORMOSA - FORMOSE
Books and Scientific Supplies Services, Ltd.
P.O.B. 83, TAPEI.
TAIWAN.

FRANCE
Bureau des Publications de l'OCDE,
2, rue André-Pascal, PARIS (16e)
Principaux sous-dépositaires :
PARIS : Presses Universitaires de France,
49, bd Saint-Michel, 5e
Librairie de Médicis, 3, rue de Médicis, 6e
Sciences Politiques (Lib.), 30, rue Saint-Guillaume, 7e
La Documentation Française, 16, rue Lord Byron, 8e
BORDEAUX : Mollat.
GRENOBLE : Arthaud.
LILLE : Le Furet du Nord.
LYON IIe : L. Demortière.
MARSEILLE : Maupetit.
STRASBOURG : Berger-Levrault.

GERMANY - ALLEMAGNE
Deutscher Bundes-Verlag G.m.b.H.
Postfach 9380, 53 BONN.
Sub-Agents : BERLIN 62 : Elwert & Meurer.
MUNCHEN : Hueber, HAMBURG : Reuter-Klöckner; und in den massgebenden Buchhandlungen Deutschlands.

GREECE - GRÈCE
Librairie Kauffmann, 21, rue du Stade, ATHÈNES.

ICELAND - ISLANDE
Snæbjörn Jónsson & Co., h.f., Hafnarstræti 9,
P.O. Box 1131, REYKJAVIK.

INDIA - INDE
International Book House Ltd.,
9 Ash Lane, Mahatma Gandhi Road, BOMBAY 1.
Oxford Book and Stationery Co. :
NEW DELHI, Scindia House.
CALCUTTA, 17 Park Street.

IRAQ - IRAK
Hamid Abdul Karim
Shorja Bldg, Shorja,
P.O.B. 419, BAGHDAD.

IRELAND - IRLANDE
Eason & Son, 40-41 Lower O'Connell Street,
DUBLIN.

ISRAEL
Blumstein's Bookstores Ltd.,
35 Allenby Road, and 48 Nahlath Benjamin St.,
TEL-AVIV.

ITALY - ITALIE
Libreria Commissionaria Sansoni
Via Lamarmora 45, FIRENZE.
Via Paolo Mercuri 19/B, ROMA.

Sous - Dépositaires : GENOVA : Libreria Di Stefano. MILANO : Libreria Hœpli. NAPOLI : Libreria L. Cappelli. PADOVA : Libreria Zannoni. PALERMO : Libreria C. Cicala Inguaggiato. ROMA : Libreria Rizzoli, Libreria Tombolini. TORINO : Libreria Lattes.

JAPAN - JAPON
Maruzen Company Ltd.,
6 Tori-Nichome Nihonbashi, TOKYO.

KENYA
New Era Publications
Ghale House. Government Road,
P.B. 6854.
NAIROBI.

LEBANON-LIBAN
Redico
Immeuble Edison, Rue Bliss, B.P. 5641,
BEYROUTH.

LUXEMBOURG
Librairie Paul Bruck
33, Grand' Rue,
LUXEMBOURG.

MOROCCO - MAROC
Éditions La Porte, *Aux Belles Images*.
281, avenue Mohammed V, RABAT.

THE NETHERLANDS - PAYS-BAS
Wholesale Agent : Meulenhoff & Co., N.V. Importeurs, Beulingstraat, 2, AMSTERDAM C.
Principal Retailer : W.P. Van Stockum & Zoon,
Buitenhof 36, DEN HAAG.

NEW ZEALAND - NOUVELLE ZÉLANDE
Government Printing Office,
20 Molesworth Street (Private Bag), WELLINGTON
and Government Bookshops at
Auckland (P.O.B. 5344)
Christchurch (P.O.B. 1721)
Dunedin (P.O.B. 1104).

NORWAY - NORVÈGE
A/S Bokhjornet, Lille Grensen 7, OSLO.

PAKISTAN
Mirza Book Agency, 65, The Mall, LAHORE 3.

PORTUGAL
Livraria Portugal, Rua do Carmo 70, LISBOA.

SOUTH AFRICA - AFRIQUE DU SUD
Van Schaik's Book Store Ltd.,
Church Street, PRETORIA.

SPAIN - ESPAGNE
Mundi Prensa, Castelló 37, MADRID.
Libreria Bastinos de José Bosch, Pelayo 52,
BARCELONA 1.

SWEDEN - SUÈDE
Fritzes, Kungl. Hovbokhandel,
Fredsgatan 2, STOCKHOLM 16.

SWITZERLAND - SUISSE
Librairie Payot, 6, rue Grenus, 1211 GENÈVE, 11
et à LAUSANNE, NEUCHATEL, VEVEY, MONTREUX, BERNE, BALE et ZURICH.

TURKEY - TURQUIE
Librairie Hachette, 469 Istiklal Caddesi, Beyoglu,
ISTANBUL et 12 Ziya Gökalp Caddesi, ANKARA.

UNITED KINGDOM ROYAUME-UNI
H.M. Stationery Office, P.O. Box 569, LONDON,
S.E.I.
Branches at : EDINBURGH, BIRMINGHAM, BRISTOL, MANCHESTER, CARDIFF, BELFAST.

UNITED STATES OF AMERICA
Mc Graw - Hill Book Company, OECD-Unit,
TMIS Annex, 351 West 41st Street,
NEW YORK 36, N.Y.

YUGOSLAVIA - YOUGOSLAVIE
Jugoslovenska Knjiga, Marsala Tita, 23, P.O.B. 36,
BEOGRAD.

Les commandes provenant de pays où l'OCDE n'a pas encore désigné de dépositaire
peuvent être adressées à :
OCDE, Bureau des Publications, 2, rue André-Pascal, Paris (16e).
Orders and inquiries from countries where sales agents have not yet been appointed may be sent to
OECD, Publications Office, 2, rue André-Pascal, Paris (16e).

O.E.C.D. PUBLICATIONS, 2, rue André-Pascal, Paris-16° - No. 19779/January 1966
PRINTED IN FRANCE